£45

£12-99

N13 NEW

D0323148

THE
LANCASTRIAN
AFFINITY
1361 – 1399

SIMON WALKER

CLARENDON PRESS · OXFORD

Oxford University Press, Walton Street, Oxford OX2 6DP
Oxford New York
Athens Auckland Bangkok Bogota Bombay
Buenos Aires Calcutta Cape Town Dar es Salaam
Delhi Florence Hong Kong Istanbul Karachi
Kuala Lumpur Madras Madrid Melbourne
Mexico City Nairobi Paris Singapore
Taipei Tokyo Toronto
and associated companies in
Berlin Ibadan

Oxford is a trade mark of Oxford University Press

First published by Oxford University Press 1990
Special edition for Sandpiper Books Ltd, 1996

British Library Cataloguing in Publication Data
Walker, Simon
The Lancastrian affinity 1361-1399.
1. England, 1377-1399
I. Title   942.038
ISBN 0-19-820174-5

Library of Congress Cataloging in Publication Data
Walker, Simon.
The Lancastrian affinity 1361-1399 / Simon Walker.
p.   cm.—(Oxford historical monographs)
Includes bibliographical references.
1. John of Gaunt, Duke of Lancaster, 1340-1399. 2. Great Britain—
History—House of Lancaster, 1399-1461. 3. England—Social
conditions—Medieval period, 1066-1485. 4. England—Economic
conditions—Medieval period, 1066-1485. 5. Great Britain—
History—14th century. 6. Lancaster, House of. 7. Feudalism—
England. I. Title. II. Series.
DA247.J6W35 1990
942.03'8—dc20
90-33321 P
ISBN 0-19-820174-5

Printed in Great Britain by
Bookcraft Ltd.,
Midsomer Norton, Avon

For
MY PARENTS

ACKNOWLEDGEMENTS

At an early stage in the research on which this book is based I was sitting in the Round Room of the Public Record Office when a piece of the roof fell to the floor beside me. 'Did that hit you?' the Assistant Keeper kindly asked, though I could not help feeling that, if it had, I would hardly be in a position to reply. Such a sudden and dramatic solution to the diverse problems posed by John of Gaunt and his retainers has seemed, from time to time, the only sensible answer. The list of those I have to thank for ensuring that it was not the *only* answer is a long one. By electing me to a Prize Fellowship, the Warden and Fellows of All Souls College, Oxford, created the conditions that allowed me to write this book. More recently, my colleagues in the Department of History at the University of Sheffield have been accommodating in giving me the time to complete it. Among individuals, George Holmes and Kenneth Fowler made many useful comments on an earlier version of this work while Maurice Keen, who guided my first year of research, has continued to be generous with his time in the intervening years. I have greatly benefited from conversations and correspondence, at various times, with Rowena Archer, Anthony Goodman, Ralph Griffiths, Michael Jones, John Maddicott, John Post, Nigel Saul, Andrew Wathey, and Jenny Wormald. My principal academic debt, however, is to Gerald Harriss, who, ever since I first knocked on the door of New Buildings VI.5, has been a constant source of shrewd advice and deep learning on the subject of later medieval England. What merits this book has are largely due to his help and encouragement.

I must thank the President and Fellows of Magdalen College, Oxford, for allowing me to consult the papers of the late K. B. McFarlane; the Trustees of the History of Parliament Trust for permitting me to inspect the Trust's working files; and the University of Sheffield Research Fund for a grant towards the cost of travel and research. I have been helped in my work by the staff of many libraries and archives, but especially by those of the Public Record Office, Chancery Lane, and the Codrington Library, Oxford. Invaluable practical assistance in the completion of this book was provided by Michael

Dewar, who acted as midwife at the long-distance birth of the thesis on which it is based, and by Humaira Ahmed and Judy Winchester, who typed both book and thesis and were never sparing with their advice, admonition, and coffee. Accuracy should compel me to refrain from thanking Helen, who stubbornly continues to think of 'John of Gaunt' as a recent winner of the Burghley Horse Trials, but I shall do so all the same.

University of Sheffield   S.K.W.
March 1989

CONTENTS

ABBREVIATIONS

The following abbreviations are used throughout this book; full references will be found in the Bibliography. Class names and a brief description of all unpublished sources appear there too. Documents cited in the footnotes by class number alone are to be found in the Public Record Office, London. Crown copyright material is printed by permission of the Controller of Her Majesty's Stationery Office and the Council of the Duchy of Lancaster.

BIHR	*Bulletin of the Institute of Historical Research*
BJRL	*Bulletin of the John Rylands Library*
BL	British Library
CAD	*Descriptive Catalogue of Ancient Deeds*
CChR	*Calendar of Charter Rolls*
CCR	*Calendar of Close Rolls*
CFR	*Calendar of Fine Rolls*
CIM	*Calendar of Inquisitions Miscellaneous*
CIPM	*Calendar of Inquisitions Post Mortem*
Complete Peerage	*The Complete Peerage*, ed. G. E. Cokayne, revised by Vicary Gibbs, H. A. Doubleday, and Lord Howard de Walden (London, 1910–57)
CPR	*Calendar of Patent Rolls*
De Hoghton Deeds	*A Calendar of the Deeds and Papers in the Possession of Sir James de Hoghton, Bart.*, ed. J. H. Lumby (Lancashire and Cheshire Record Soc., 88, 1936
DKR	*Annual Report of the Deputy Keeper of the Public Records*
EcHR	*Economic History Review*
EHR	*English Historical Review*
Foedera	T. Rymer, *Foedera, Conventiones, litterae, etc.*, 2nd edn., 20 vols. (London, 1727–35); ed. A. G. Clarke and F. Holbrooke, i–iii (Record Comm., 1816–30). The latter edition has been used for the period to 1383; the original edition from 1383
Froissart (K. de L.)	*Œuvres de Jean Froissart*, ed. Kervyn de Lettenhove (Brussels, 1867–77)
HMC	Historical Manuscripts Commission
Lewis	'Indentures of Retinue with John of Gaunt, Duke of Lancaster, Enrolled in Chancery, 1367–1399', ed. N. B. Lewis, *Camden Miscellany, 22* (Camden Soc., 4th series, 1, 1964), 77–112
PRO	Public Record Office

Reg. I	*John of Gaunt's Register 1372–76*, ed. S. Armitage-Smith, 2 vols. (Camden Soc., 3rd series, 20–1, 1911)
Reg. II	*John of Gaunt's Register 1379–83*, ed. E. C. Lodge and R. Somerville, 2 vols. (Camden Soc., 3rd series, 56–7, 1937)
Rot. Parl.	*Rotuli Parliamentorum*, 6 vols. (London, 1783)
Rot. Scot.	*Rotuli Scotiae*, 2 vols. (Record Commission, 1814–19)
S. & G.	*The Scrope and Grosvenor controversy: de controversia in curia militari inter Ricardum le Scrope et Robertum Grosvenor, 1385–90*, ed. N. H. Nicolas, 2 vols. (London, 1832)
Somerville	R. Somerville, *History of the Duchy of Lancaster*, i (London, 1953)
Statutes	*Statutes of the Realm*, 11 vols. (Record Commission, 1810–28)
TRHS	*Transactions of the Royal Historical Society*
VCH	*Victoria History of the Counties of England*
Westminster Chronicle	*The Westminster Chronicle 1381–1394*, ed. L. C. Hector and B. F. Harvey (Oxford, 1982)

1

INTRODUCTION

'Too many generalizations have been based upon the quite abnormal retinue of John of Gaunt . . .'.[1] It might fairly be asked whether it requires, or deserves, another lengthy study. The simplest answer is that, with the exception of the Lancastrian estates and their administration,[2] detailed work on John of Gaunt's affinity has hardly progressed beyond the conclusions reached by the pioneers of the modern study of bastard feudalism some forty years ago.[3] One purpose of this book is, therefore, simply to test those conclusions against a more extensive investigation of the available evidence and, if any modifications must be made, to ask what wider implications they possess for the study of English society in the later middle ages.

Valuable analyses of the composition and workings of a number of other affinities are now available, providing a convincing picture of the way a lord viewed his following and it responded to his wishes.[4] Inevitably, the perspective adopted in these analyses is seigneurial, for the most abundant and accessible evidence comes from surviving seigneurial archives. Yet the strength of the bastard feudal tie lay, not in the pre-eminence of the lord, but in an expectation of mutual benefit, a community of aim and outlook between the contracting parties.

[1] J. R. Lander, *Crown and Nobility 1450–1509* (London, 1976), p. 31.
[2] Somerville, pp. 49–70, 90–134, 363–85.
[3] K. B. McFarlane, 'Bastard Feudalism', *BIHR* 20 (1945), 161–80; N. B. Lewis, 'The Organization of Indentured Retinues in Fourteenth-Century England', *TRHS* 4th series, 27 (1945), 29–39.
[4] W. H. Dunham, *Lord Hastings' Indentured Retainers, 1461–83*. Transactions of the Connecticut Academy of Arts and Sciences, 39 (1955); G. A. Holmes, *The Estates of the Higher Nobility in Fourteenth-Century England* (Cambridge, 1957), pp. 58–84; K. Fowler, *The King's Lieutenant* (London, 1969), pp. 175–86; J. R. Maddicott, *Thomas of Lancaster* (Oxford, 1970), pp. 40–66; J. R. S. Phillips, *Aymer de Valence, earl of Pembroke 1307–1324* (Oxford, 1972), pp. 253–68; K. B. McFarlane, *The Nobility of Later Medieval England* (Oxford, 1973), pp. 102–21; C. Rawcliffe, *The Staffords, Earls of Stafford and Dukes of Buckingham* (Cambridge, 1978), pp. 66–86; M. Cherry, 'The Courtenay Earls of Devon', *Southern History*, 1 (1979), 71–99; C. Carpenter, 'The Beauchamp Affinity: A Study of Bastard Feudalism at Work', *EHR* 95 (1980), 514–32; M. A. Hicks, *False, Fleeting, Perjur'd Clarence* (Gloucester, 1980), pp. 182–9.

Fidelity was the foundation of lordship, and the continuance of the institution depended upon the value to both parties of their mutual assistance . . . Just as the lord's aid, support and counsel worked to further the retainer's affairs, so, too, did the retainer repay his lord with counsel, aid, and service, both military and practical.[5]

How the *retainer* viewed the affinity he belonged to; what he put into it, in terms of time, loyalty, and expectation; what he got out of it: these remain largely unexplored questions, because they must be answered from evidence that is scattered, fragmentary, and difficult to interpret. A second purpose of this book is, therefore, to try and view the Lancastrian affinity from within, to see it as the retainer saw it and, by so doing, to 'penetrate into the real world of relationships which lies behind the list of liveries and annuities'.[6] It is becoming clear that this is a task crucial to the understanding of bastard feudalism, for, if the 'affinity represents an attempt by the traditional leaders of society— crown and nobility—to contain the increasingly diversified armigerous class within the old traditions of lordship',[7] then it is only by studying the preoccupations and ambitions of this class that the true nature and purpose of the magnate affinity can be gauged.

In order to do so, the investigation must be pursued at two levels. The Lancastrian affinity will, first of all, be presented as it might have appeared to the duke himself, by drawing upon the archives of his administration to furnish a detailed analysis of the structure, cost, and composition of his following. Then an attempt will be made to set the duke's affinity in a wider context and, by an examination of the careers, wealth, estates, marriages, and wills of his retainers, to suggest how they, in their turn, saw the affinity and discover what they expected from it. To do this, however, means turning the focus of attention away from the duke's court, towards the local communities of shire and hundred, where many Lancastrians spent much of their time and invested most of their prestige. Increasingly, it seems that the crucial ability for a king of later medieval England was to command the loyalty, not only of his magnates, but also of the tight-knit and self-regarding county commonwealths that went to make up the political nation.[8] The

---

[5] Dunham, op. cit. 52.

[6] Holmes, op. cit. 59.

[7] G. L. Harriss, 'Introduction', in K. B. McFarlane, *England in the Fifteenth Century: Collected Essays* (London, 1981), p. xxvii.

[8] C. Given-Wilson, *The Royal Household and the King's Affinity: Service, Politics and Finance in England, 1360–1413* (New Haven, 1986), pp. 264–7.

decisions and actions of central government were mediated and manipulated by the local representatives of a distant authority and for a policy to be accepted it had to conform itself as far as possible to the existing configuration of county society. 'The roots of law, order and administration lay in the localities . . .'[9] and all three must be studied against a local background before a realistic estimate of the position and influence of John of Gaunt's affinity can emerge.

This cannot be done, however, without directly addressing some of the debates currently exercising historians of English society in the later middle ages. How pervasive an influence on that society, for instance, was the network of clientage and patronage represented by the magnate affinity? One view holds that this network 'formed the fabric of contemporary life': a magnate could effectively control a county or counties by using his indentured retainers 'to diffuse the lord's influence through the areas where his estates lay, into the wider affinity, and even among landowners outside the affinity, using above all the power they could wield as local administrators.'[10] The natural corollary of this belief is to emphasize the crucial importance of the nobility in the politics of later medieval England, for 'where the magnates marched, the gentry followed . . . because [they] could hardly ignore the causes of their patrons.'[11] Yet others find it possible to speak of a body of independent county gentry 'who lived outside the embrace of bastard feudalism', more concerned with the preservation of their patrimony and lineage than with any notion of allegiance to a noble household, and capable of responding to the summons-to-arms from their social superiors by a 'masterly inactivity' that left the magnates powerless.[12] Both propositions, naturally enough, have much to commend them. It would be idle to deny, in the face of some well-documented instances of noble dominance, that great magnates could, from time to time, exert a local tyranny. There is no reason to think that, in the Norfolk of the 1440s, Margaret Paston was exaggerating when she advised her husband that he could never live in peace 'but if you have my lord of Suffolks goodlordship while the

---

[9] M. Clanchy, 'Law, Government and Society in Medieval England', *History,* 59 (1974), 77.

[10] J. R. Maddicott, 'Thomas of Lancaster and Sir Robert Holland', *EHR* 86 (1971), 449; C. Carpenter, 'Fifteenth Century Biographies', *Historical Journal,* 25 (1982), 732.

[11] R. A. Griffiths, *The Reign of King Henry VI* (London, 1981), p. 570.

[12] N. Saul, *Knights and Esquires: The Gloucestershire Gentry in the Fourteenth Century* (Oxford, 1981), p. 261; S. M. Wright, *The Derbyshire Gentry in the Fifteenth Century* (Derbyshire Record Soc., 8, 1983), p. 147; I. Rowney, 'Government and Patronage in the Fifteenth Century: Staffordshire 1439–1459', *Midland History,* 8 (1983), 49–69.

world is as it is'.[13] It seems no less certain that, at other times and in other places, such as Sussex in the fourteenth century or Derbyshire in the fifteenth, magnate influence was 'not only diverse but very restricted'.[14] Regional particularities clearly have much to do with these widely divergent conclusions, but behind them lies a fundamental disagreement over the relative social and political importance of magnates and gentry in later medieval England. A study of the Lancastrian affinity under John of Gaunt has an important contribution to make to this debate for, as the greatest lord of his day, particular interest attaches both to the amount of influence wielded by, and on behalf of, his affinity and to any limitations upon that influence that may emerge.

Upon the resolution of this first question turns, to a large extent, the answer to a second: how far was the magnate affinity responsible for the endemic violence and perversion of justice that appears so characteristic of later medieval England? Contemporary complaints about the quality of law and order singled out the great lords and their followers as the chief culprits, and were never more vehement in doing so than during Richard II's reign. In 1381, the speaker of the Commons identified the oppression of the common people by magnate dependants as one of the principal causes of the Peasants' Revolt; in 1384 the Commons demanded a statute against certain local potentates, who were protected from justice by their magnate patrons; in the Merciless Parliament they returned to the attack on the 'second kings' of the shires, identified this time as royal officials and magnate stewards.[15] In the succeeding Parliaments at Cambridge and Westminster, their complaints became more narrowly focused on the lords' livery badges and their wearers, who acted like provincial tyrants in oppressing the common people.[16] If 'the affinity . . . was part of the normal fabric of society'[17] in fourteenth-century England, contemporaries were nevertheless dissatisfied with the state of that society and blamed the magnate affinity for many of its evils.

Recent historians have, however, been sceptical of these petitions,

---

[13] *Paston Letters and Papers of the Fifteenth Century*, ed. N. Davis (Oxford, 1971–6), i. 236.

[14] N. Saul, *Scenes from Provincial Life: Knightly Families in Sussex 1280–1400* (Oxford, 1986), p. 56; Wright, op. cit. 63.

[15] *Rot. Parl.*, iii. 98–103; *Westminster Chronicle*, pp. 80–2; *Chronicon Henrici Knighton*, ed. J. R. Lumby (Rolls Series, 1895), ii. 266–70.

[16] *Westminster Chronicle*, pp. 354–8; *Rot. Parl.*, iii. 265.

[17] G. A. Holmes, *The Later Middle Ages* (Edinburgh, 1962), p. 167.

seeing in them, at the least, a serious over-simplification.[18] Intense competition and pressure for land; the ever-growing complexity of the law relating to landed property; the opportunities for manipulation and collusion this complexity created: all now seem more important causes of disorder than the deliberate lawlessness of the nobility.[19] When it did break out, violence was as much a means of seeking justice as a refusal to accept it, often a last, not a first, resort; its aim was to achieve a settlement acceptable to all parties in dispute, for this was the only way in which a lasting peace could be guaranteed.[20] Far from promoting disorder, the nobility had an important part to play, by acting as extra-legal umpires and arbitrators, in promoting the hoped-for reconcili-ation, and re-establishing the social peace.[21] Yet while admitting all this, it still remains possible to see violence as an essential ingredient of late medieval lordship, a necessary sign of its strength, for it was the permanent threat of physical harm and material destruction which, by making any form of protection that enhanced a man's security perennially attractive, provided a favourable context for the growth of clientage and dependence.

For this reason, neither John of Gaunt nor his retainers could stand aloof from the charges of the parliamentary Commons. The duke himself was, as he remarked to the assembled Commons at Salisbury in 1384, greater than any other lord in temporal matters and worldly power; he was, in addition, a generous giver of the liveries the Commons so disliked. Wearers of his badge, the collar of SS, allegedly thought it would give them the earth and the sky, though they sometimes found that it brought only an unpopularity commensurate with its privileges.[22] As a consistent opponent of the Commons on the

---

[18] C. Carpenter, 'Law, Justice and Landowners in Later Medieval England', *Law and History Review*, 1 (1983), 226–31.

[19] P. R. Coss, *The Langley Family and its Cartulary: A Study in Late Medieval 'Gentry'* (Dugdale Soc., Occasional Papers, 22, 1974), p. 14; J. M. W. Bean, *The Decline of English Feudalism 1215–1540* (Manchester, 1968), pp. 148–97.

[20] A. Smith, 'Litigation and Politics: Sir John Fastolf's Defence of his English Property', *Property and Politics: Essays in Later Medieval English History*, ed. A. J. Pollard (Gloucester, 1984), p. 73; S. J. Payling, 'Inheritance and Local Politics in the Later Middle Ages: The case of Ralph, Lord Cromwell, and the Heriz Inheritance', *Nottingham Medieval Studies*, 30 (1986), 94–5.

[21] E. Powell, 'Arbitration and Law in the Late Middle Ages', *TRHS* 5th series, 33 (1983), 49–67; C. Rawcliffe, 'The Great Lord as Peacekeeper', *Law and Social Change in British History*, ed. J. A. Guy and H. G. Beale (London, 1984), pp. 34–53.

[22] *Westminster Chronicle*, p. 82; *Chronicon Angliae*, ed. E. M. Thompson (Rolls Series, 1874), p. 125; *Historia Vitae et Regni Ricardi Secundi*, ed. G. B. Stow (Philadelphia, 1977), p. 62.

law-and-order issue, who refused their demands for a statute in 1384 and did his best to dissuade the king from any concessions in 1389, the duke made every effort to protect the position of his servants.[23] Any assessment of John of Gaunt's political stature and effectiveness must, therefore, depend in part on his success in doing so. Equally, any examination of the social and political effects of 'bastard feudalism' in later medieval England must attempt some assessment of the Lancastrian affinity's impact on government and justice, both centrally and at the local level. The duke's retinue was so large and his political position so powerful that the investigation may stand as a test-case. If the influence of the Lancastrian affinity on local government and society was baleful, then the Commons—and those historians who continue to follow the Commons in their strictures—still have a strong case to answer. If it was not, then another explanation for the many complaints against violent local crime in Richard II's reign must be sought.

Finally, a study of the Lancastrian affinity may hope to cast some light on the duke of Lancaster himself. Between 1376 and 1399 John of Gaunt was undoubtedly the most powerful of English magnates, yet his character and policies have always proved elusive. Though contemporary eulogies of the duke, as 'the most sufficient person of the realm', even 'the worthiest knight of Christendom',[24] abound, there were others who resented his 'harsh and bitter words' in Council and Parliament and felt his dominance of political life to be excessive, even sinister.[25] The chronicles of the period accurately reflect this division of contemporary opinion. While he was, to some, the 'pious duke', a lover of peace and concord who had been unjustly defamed by his enemies, to others he was a traitor to the realm, who abandoned those he should command in war and led astray those he should lead in peace.[26] As a result, historians have found it unusually difficult, even by their own fractious standards, to arrive at an agreed verdict. On the one hand, John of Gaunt can be described as 'an amiable nonentity of no special attainments', hesitating and tortuous, his policies distinguished by nothing more than their opportunism.[27] On the other, he is

[23] R. L. Storey, 'Liveries and Commissions of the Peace 1388–90', *The Reign of Richard II*, ed. F. R. H. du Boulay and C. M. Barron (London, 1971), pp. 146–9.
[24] *Rot. Parl.*, iii. 286; *Chronicon Henrici Knighton*, ii. 318.
[25] *Rot. Parl.*, iii. 313; *Chronicon Angliae*, 168; *Froissart (K. de L.)*, viii. 460–2.
[26] *Chronicon Henrici Knighton*, ii. 146, 149; *Chronicon Angliae*, 75.
[27] A. B. Steel, *Richard II* (Cambridge, 1941), p. 21; M. V. Clarke, *Fourteenth Century Studies* (Oxford, 1937), p. 39; E. Perroy, *L'Angleterre et le grand schisme d'occident. Étude sur la politique religieuse de l'Angleterre sous Richard II* (Paris, 1933), p. 229 n. 3.

'the most over-mighty subject in English history', 'arguably the most successful politician of the English Middle Ages', imaginative, thrustful, and circumspect in his actions.[28] A study of the Lancastrian affinity may help to clarify some of this confusion, which has arisen, in part, because both chroniclers and historians have sometimes entertained unrealistic notions of the extent of Gaunt's unfettered power and influence. 'However talented and powerful in himself, the ... statesman cannot stand alone, without allies, without a following ...'[29] and a magnate who sought to push the loyalty of his retainers beyond the mutually acceptable might find himself dangerously isolated.[30] Consequently, John of Gaunt was obliged to listen to the advice of his followers and, on occasion, to accept their rebukes.[31] His actions were, to that extent, necessarily constrained by the expectations of his affinity; a careful scrutiny of those expectations is the essential preliminary to a proper understanding of the duke's controversial career.

[28] B. Wolffe, *Henry VI* (London, 1981), p. 99; C. Richmond, *John Hopton, A Fifteenth Century Suffolk Gentleman* (Cambridge, 1981), pp. 3–4; J. S. Roskell, *Parliament and Politics in Late Medieval England* (London, 1981), i. 63.

[29] R. Syme, *The Roman Revolution* (Oxford, 1939), p. 7.

[30] M. A. Hicks, 'Dynastic Change and Northern Society: The Career of the Fourth Earl of Northumberland 1470–1489', *Northern History*, 14 (1978), 97.

[31] *Chronicon Henrici Knighton*, ii. 147; *Chronicon Angliae*, 74–5.

2

THE LANCASTRIAN AFFINITY: STRUCTURE, COST, COMPOSITION

1. Structure

How is the Lancastrian affinity to be defined? Three major categories in its composition may be distinguished: (i) household attendants; (ii) indentured retainers; and (iii) estate officials. The members of each category were united by their shared relationship of dependence towards the duke and were generally, though not invariably, rewarded in the same way—by the grant of an annuity assigned on one of the administrative districts, known as receiverships, into which the Lancastrian inheritance was divided. They were distinguished from each other by the type of service required of them. Household attendants were naturally expected to be around the duke's person for much of the time; their employment was menial, in the strict sense of the term, and comparatively continuous. Indentured retainers, by contrast, were principally required to campaign abroad in the duke's company. In time of peace they were to be ready at his summons but, save in emergencies, this summons was relatively rare. Estate officials were inevitably required to spend the majority of their time on the lands in their charge. Although they were essential to the smooth running of the duke's affairs, their loyalty was as much to the estates they managed as to the person of the duke and their local knowledge was often at the disposal of more than one patron.[1]

Useful for the purposes of analysis, these categories are largely artificial. The duke's household attendants were often, at the upper levels of his administration, his indentured retainers as well; offices on the Lancastrian estates might be treated as purely honorific and be discharged by deputy; one man might combine in his own person all three roles, as retainer, household attendant, and estate official. In the face of this 'sea of varying relationships'[2] created by contemporary

---

[1] See below, pp. 103–4.
[2] G. A. Holmes, *The Estates of the Higher Nobility in Fourteenth-century England* (Cambridge, 1957), p. 79.

custom, the attempt to establish any strict separation of function within the affinity seems fruitless. What matters is less the definition of the parts than of the whole. Should Richard Lilling, who received from the duke a robe of the Lancastrian livery in return for his co-operation over the conveyance of the manor of Chipping Lambourne,[3] be counted a member of the affinity or not? How far must the adjective 'Lancastrian' be stretched if it is to include the whole body of John of Gaunt's followers and supporters?

The practice of the duke's administration provides an answer, although it is scarcely an unequivocal one. When John of Gaunt wished to mobilize his supporters, for a campaign abroad or an important session of Parliament, letters of summons endorsed with the names of individual retainers were sent from the ducal chancery to the honorial receivers, for dispatch to the knights and esquires *de nostre retenue*.[4] At the same time, however, further letters were sent to the receivers, to be dispatched at their discretion to whoever might be suitable for the duke's service.[5] Consequently, on any one occasion the duke's 'affinity' actually consisted of a well-defined core of servants who stood in some permanent relation towards him and a much larger outer circle of 'well-willers'. This outer circle was very fluid indeed, varying in composition on every occasion and, by reason of the method of selection employed, it was as much the creation of the duke's local officials as of John of Gaunt himself.

Exact definition of its limits is, in consequence, misguided, for no precisely defined boundary between loyalty and indifference existed. An indenture of retainer did not introduce a new and alien element into the way men conducted their lives; it merely formalized and recorded, for a specific occasion, the unwritten rules by which they always lived. One good turn deserved another; the principle was explicitly stated and acted upon by Henry IV[6] and it echoes through the correspondence of his father. In the manner a man proves himself deserving by his actions, so will the duke act towards him; serve him well in this matter and, whatever is desired of him, the duke will do to the best of his power; accommodate the duke in his request, as you wish him to help you in time to come.[7] Individuals were called upon to

---

[3] DL 42/2 f. 162.
[4] *Reg. II* 290, 291; *Reg. I* 1731.
[5] DL 29/262/4069 m. 3; *Reg. II* 357, 526, 909.
[6] E.37/28m. 1; cf. *CPR 1399–1401*, 86, 423.
[7] *Calendar of Select Pleas and Memoranda of the City of London, 1381–1412*, ed. A. H. Thomas, pp. 109–11; WAM 57067; C. 115/K2/6684 f. 105.

do the duke and his men a good turn as and when circumstances required and, under normal circumstances, few people would lightly refuse a request from the duke of Lancaster. Thus, when Gaunt began a major programme of building and renovation at his castle of Hertford in the early 1380s, all the surrounding notables—the duchess of Brittany, the bishops of London, Norwich, and Ely, the abbot of Waltham, and the prior of Bermondsey—hastened to make him presents of building-timber. Yet at least one of the donors, the abbot of St Albans, begrudged the gift, saying he would rather have given £30 to let the oaks stand.[8] Such compliance hardly makes them Lancastrians, unless the term is to be emptied of all content. As a description, it is best confined to those who possessed some material incentive for their loyalty, in the form of an office or annuity from the duke. Their devotion was not always above question but, below a certain price, they could be relied upon. Beyond that cynical certainty it is safer not to venture.

'After the deeds and exploits of war', wrote Chastellain of the fifteenth-century dukes of Burgundy, 'the household is the first thing on which the eye alights and, therefore, that which it is most necessary to conduct and arrange well.'[9] Equally, it is the Lancastrian household that provides the best starting-point for an analysis of John of Gaunt's affinity, for, although its military functions, once so important, had largely devolved upon the indentured retinue by the late fourteenth century, in time of peace the household remained the centre of the duke's activities. Financially, it was the more expensive of the two to maintain.[10] Historically, it was from a desire to perpetuate the loyalties forged by service within the household that the characteristic devices of both 'true' and 'bastard' feudalism, the knight's fee and the indenture of retainer, were developed. Accordingly, the indentured retinue is itself best approached by way of the household. Fortunately, the task is rather easier in the case of John of Gaunt than in that of most other magnates, for, besides the incidental information contained in the duke's registers and the accounts of his receiver-general, the survival of seventeen check-rolls of the household and stable, the first five dating from 1381 and the remainder from a period of several years early in the 1390s, furnishes a very precise picture of the Lancastrian household at those times.[11]

[8] DL 29/58/1079 m. 1, 1080 m. 2; *Chronicon Angliae*, p. 164, Walsingham, *Hist. Ang.*, i. 339.

[9] *Œuvres de Georges Chastellain*, ed. K. de Lettenhove (Brussels, 1864), v. 364–5.

[10] See below, pp. 18–20.

[11] East Sussex Record Office, GLY 3469 mm. 1–17. Cf. R. F. Dell, *The Glynde Place*

Its permanent strength in 1381 was about 115, rising to just over 150 by the early 1390s. At its head were the 'bachelors of the duke's chamber'[12] and a few senior officials, numbering about 15 in all and receiving wages at the top rate of 12*d.* a day while *infra curiam*. Below them came the duke's confessor, at the unique rate of 10*d.* a day, and then the next major group, the duke's *escuiers famuliers*, paid at 7*d.* a day. This was a relatively large category, between 21 and 25 strong in 1381, expanding to around 35 men by the 1390s, and most of its members were also retainers of the duke—discounting clerks, only 5 out of the 21 household esquires in 1381 were not members of the indentured retinue as well.[13] Valets, receiving 4*d.* a day, constitute the next major division of the household; they numbered just under 30 in 1381, rising to 35 by the 1390s. Membership of this category characteristically involved possession of some minor household office, such as usher or naperer, which might lead to considerable advancement in Lancastrian service[14] but nevertheless implied a status just below that of gentility. Relatively few of the men in this category became retainers of the duke, for instance, and when Gaunt rewarded one of his valets it was usually by a very modest annuity, perhaps supplemented by a minor post in his estate administration.[15] Below

Archives, A Catalogue (Lewes, 1964), pp. 260–2 for a description of the manuscript. The check-rolls of the household state the name of each member of the household with his daily wage-allowance and tabulate the number of days' attendance each month in order to facilitate the payment of wages *infra curiam*. The stable check-rolls list the use made of all the horses under the control of the office of the stable, giving their name and colour or else the name of the owner and the number of horses assigned to him. By combining the two lists it is possible to reconstruct the hierarchy of the Lancastrian household with some precision; unless otherwise indicated, all information on the household in the following paragraphs comes from this manuscript. Two fragmentary household accounts survive but they contain little of importance: one in Peterhouse MS 42, printed in M. R. James, *A Descriptive Catalogue of Manuscripts in the Library of Peterhouse* (Cambridge, 1899), pp. 60–3, with additions and corrections by M. Sharp, 'A Fragmentary Household Account of John of Gaunt', *BIHR* 13 (1935/6), 154–60; the other in BL Sloane MS 248, f. 1.

[12] *Reg. II* 40; cf. J. M. W. Bean, 'Bachelor and Retainer', *Medievalia et Humanistica*, NS 3 (1972), 121.

[13] Figures obtained by a comparison of East Sussex Record Office, GLY 3469 m. 4*d* (July 1381) with the nearly contemporary *Nomina militum et scutiferum*; for the date of which see below, Appendix V.

[14] e.g. Robert Hatfield became controller of Henry of Derby's household and Peter Melbourne was later chamberlain to Henry, prince of Wales. DL 28/3/4 f. 7v; E. 403/562 m. 7; *CPR 1413–16*, 7.

[15] Among men in this category, John Dowedale was exceptional in receiving an esquire's annuity of 10 marks. Most were less well rewarded: Simon Typet and John Stapleton received 5 marks each, John Skipton 60*s.*, Richard Ilkeston and John Combe

them came the yeomen and grooms of the household, paid at 2*d*. a day, as were the clerks of the duke's chapel and the more important female attendants upon the duchess of Lancaster, and finally a class of menial servants, such as the duke's smith, his messengers, and his band of eight minstrels, each taking 1*d*. a day.

Such, in outline, was the structure of the duke's household. A closer examination will allow some more general conclusions to be drawn from it. Thus, although the Lancastrian household was relatively fixed in its organization, it was, in comparison with the king's, surprisingly fluid in membership. Only two of the fifteen knights (Sir Richard Abberbury and Sir Walter Blount) who staffed Gaunt's chamber in 1381 were still there in 1392. Among the 33 household servants paid, continuously or occasionally, at the esquires' rate of 7*d*. a day in 1381, only 5 still remained in the household ten years later. Equally, only 2 of the duke's household esquires in 1392 had been on his books in the same capacity ten years earlier. These changes in composition faithfully reflected the changing emphases of John of Gaunt's policy. In 1381, his chamber knights fell into three main groups: senior advisers, who had been in his service for many years, such as Sir John de Ipres, Sir William Croyser, and Sir Robert Swillington; a few younger men who had risen rapidly in the duke's service, like Sir Walter Blount and Sir Richard Abberbury; a number of alien knights who had no home in England outside the Lancastrian court, including the Scotsman, Sir John Swynton, the Savoyards, Sir Otes Granson and Sir Jean Grivère, the Poitevin, Sir Jean Manburni, and the leader of the exiled *emperogilados* in England, Sir Joao Fernandes Andeiro.[16] The purpose of this last group was twofold. It imparted to the Lancastrian court a distinctively cosmopolitan glamour that stood witness to the duke's chivalric reputation and, at the same time, announced that his real ambitions were European rather than English in scope. With the passing of those ambitions, the composition of the

50*s*., Henry Cawood and John Burton 40*s*. DL 29/341/5515 m. 2; *CPR 1396–9*, 561; DL 29/212/3247 m. 1, 3248 m. 5; DL 29/58/1081 m. 1. Among the minor estate offices held by men of this rank, John Sprotburgh was the parker of Hay (Yorks., W.R.), Randolph Tynneslowe keeper of the foreign woods at Kenilworth, and Robert Bolthorp the bailiff of the manor of Rodley (Glos.). *Reg. II* 720, 880; DL 29/615/9838 m. 1.

[16] For their careers: G. S. C. Swinton, 'John of Swinton', *Scottish Historical Review*, 16 (1918–19), 261–79; A. Piaget, *Otho de Grandson, sa vie et ses poésies* (Lausanne, 1941); 'Recueil des documents concernant le Poitou contenus dans les registres de la chancellerie de France', ed. P. Guérin, *Archives Historiques du Poitou*, 21 (1890), 181–5; P. E. Russell, 'Joao Fernandes Andeiro at the Court of John of Lancaster', *Revista da universidade de Coimbra*, 14 (1938).

Lancastrian household changed markedly; by the 1390s, the Bohemian knight, Sir Herman Hans, was the only foreigner among the chamber knights.[17]

Equally, the size of Lancaster's household helps to put into perspective some of the more extravagant contemporary claims about his political and dynastic ambitions. Although commensurate with his dignity as a prince of the royal blood, his establishment never remotely rivalled the king's household in numbers and was clearly never intended to do so. Edward III's household was just under 400 strong at the end of his reign and Richard II maintained his own establishment at a very similar figure until 1390, when he embarked upon a programme of expansion which brought his household contingent up to nearly 600 persons by 1396.[18] Although the duke's household also grew in size between 1381 and the early 1390s, the expansion was on nothing like the scale seen in the royal household and was far from uniform. At the top of the hierarchy, the number of chamber-knights fell from 15 to 8 but the number of esquires rose from 25 to 35. As in the royal household, this increase was probably a response to the ordinance on livery and maintenance issued in May 1390, which stipulated that only indentured retainers and those living in the household could legitimately receive a lord's livery.[19] The other area of expansion was among the yeomen and grooms, whose numbers more than doubled between 1381 and 1392. Such an increase had little to do with the duke's political designs and rather more to do with the size of his family. Whereas the ducal stables had made provision in 1381 for a family party consisting of Queen Constance, the duke's daughters Philippa and Blanche (a bastard, who married Sir Thomas Morieux), and his mistress, Katherine Swynford, by 1392 Gaunt's family party had expanded to include Henry of Derby, the four Beaufort children, and Sir Robert Ferrers of Oversley, Joan Beaufort's first husband, and this expansion naturally necessitated a larger body of servants. Even at its largest, though, John of Gaunt's household remained well under half the size of the king's—a smaller establishment, in comparative terms, than Thomas of Lancaster had maintained and, by continental standards, a positively modest one for a peer of his eminence. John, duke of Berry, maintained around 280

---

[17] *Froissart (K. de L.)*, 14. 141–3.

[18] E. 101/398/9, 400/26, 401/2; C. J. Given-Wilson, *The Royal Household and the King's Affinity* (New Haven, 1986), Appendix III.

[19] *Statutes*, ii. 74–5; Given-Wilson, op. cit. 40.

household servants in 1397/8 while, under Philip the Bold, the Burgundian ducal household numbered as many as 350 servants.[20]

The household constituted the inner core of the duke's following. Beyond it, he maintained a larger but less cohesive body of indentured retainers. The two institutions were not, of course, mutually exclusive, for there was considerable overlap between the personnel of the household and the retinue. There are 39 members of the Lancastrian household in 1381 who appear in the nearly contemporary *Nomina militum et scutiferum*, while, by 1392, at least 44 members of an enlarged household were either retained by the duke or drew an annuity of 10 marks from him. What proportion of the duke's whole indentured retinue do these figures represent? The survival of the *Nomina militum et scutiferum*, dating from early 1382,[21] at least allows a precise answer to the question at that date, for John of Gaunt could then call upon 173 indentured retainers—7 bannerets, 70 knights, and 96 esquires. The household contingent thus constituted a substantial minority, just under a quarter, of the duke's whole retinue. Large though this force was, it continued to expand. Between 1382 and 1385, 19 new knights were retained by the duke[22] to replace the 11 who either died or departed from Lancastrian service, while there was a net gain of 20 esquires during the same period. Despite the heavy mortality suffered by the Lancastrian army in Spain, where many of the duke's retainers met their death, it seems likely that his indentured retinue continued to increase in size until the very end of his life. Expenditure on annuities certainly rose on most receiverships during the 1390s[23] and, since the recipients of these annuities were principally esquires,[24] paid a lower fee than knights, the conclusion that the numbers of the duke's retainers continued to rise seems inescapable.

In contrast to the conditions of service in the Lancastrian household, which have to be pieced together from the surviving evidence, the terms on which a retainer took service with the duke were precisely stated in his indenture. These have already been the subject of careful study[25] and, despite considerable variations in the

[20] J. R. Maddicott, *Thomas of Lancaster* (Oxford, 1970), p. 28; F. Lehoux, *Jean de France, Duc de Berri*, ii (Paris, 1966), 390–1; R. Vaughan, *Philip the Bold* (London, 1979), p. 190.

[21] See below, Appendix V.

[22] 25 additional names appear in the *Nomina* but 6 of these were promoted esquires.

[23] See below, pp. 20–1.

[24] 8 indentures of retainer with knights survive from the 1390s and 36 with esquires.

[25] Lewis, pp. 77–85.

details of some contracts, their provisions can be reduced to a basic formula by which the retainer is to serve the duke in peace and war for the term of his life, travelling with the duke wherever he wills, suitably equipped according to his rank, and attending the duke in his household when summoned to do so in time of peace. In return, the retainer receives an annual fee—usually £20 in the case of knights, either £10 or 10 marks in the case of esquires—as well as wages and, sometimes, bouche of court in wartime and when he is in attendance in time of peace. In addition, the duke undertakes to pay the retainer wages during his mobilization for service overseas, provide suitable harness and transport for his men, and, in the earlier contracts, to replace any horses lost on active service. In return, he claims a proportion— usually a third—of all the retainer's gains of war.

Clearly, John of Gaunt's indentures were noticeably less specific on the conditions of peacetime service than about what was required of a retainer in time of war. The principal concern of his contracts was to secure the military services of the men he retained and this was, perhaps, the greatest difference between service in his household and in his retinue; the former was relatively continuous whereas, when he was not on campaign, the duke might require the service of a particular indentured retainer only infrequently. Yet even in peacetime the duke's requirements were not static and from the changing formulas of his contracts something of his changing needs may be deduced.

This is most obviously the case in the early 1380s, when a number of changes in the conditions of service the duke offered were introduced. While 37 out of Gaunt's 157 surviving indentures offer a higher fee in war than peace, for instance, the last of these dates from 1384 and thereafter all his contracts offer the same fee in war and peace. At much the same time, the duke was developing the practice of retaining men without granting them an annual fee—all but one of the 16 contracts of this type were concluded between 1380 and 1385.[26] They constitute an interesting anticipation of those fifteenth-century indentures which offer the retainer no more concrete reward for his service than the promise of 'good lordship'[27] but, if this was all the duke was offering, he had to be certain that his promise would be honoured. It is in this context that the appearance of two otherwise unparalleled

---

[26] *Reg. II* 31, 33–7, 42–4, 50–2, 54; HMC, *Report on the Manuscripts of Lord Middleton* (1911), pp. 99–100; Appendix III, nos. 3, 18.
[27] W. H. Dunham, *Lord Hastings' Indentured Retainers 1461–1483* (New Haven, 1955), pp. 9–10, 51. Only 2 of Hastings's 69 extant indentures offer a cash fee.

indentures, which do *not* insist on the obligation of service overseas, can best be explained. The first of these, drawn up in October 1382, specifically promises that the new retainer, Roger Perewyche, will not be compelled to serve beyond the sea against his will. The second, concluded with William Barewell in April 1383, retained him to work for the duke's honour and profit in England alone.[28] Both men were Midlands esquires of some influence in their respective counties, well entrenched in the administration of the shire, who possessed ample opportunity to do a good turn for their colleagues in the Lancastrian retinue, or a bad one to the duke's enemies. As instruments of Gaunt's good lordship, they were clearly far more use to him at home than abroad.[29]

Taken in conjunction, these three developments in the conditions of John of Gaunt's indentures suggest that during the early 1380s his preoccupations were turning, in the face of concerted political hostility, from military to domestic concerns. Anxious to expand his following as an insurance against his enemies, yet unwilling or unable to burden his estates with additional expense, the duke turned from fees to favour as the instrument of his lordship, with the inevitable result that the pressure of the Lancastrian affinity on the workings of local justice and administration increased. The duke's departure for Spain in 1386 and the improved political conditions on his return in 1389 meant that this policy was not long pursued, but it serves to demonstrate how sensitively the apparently stereotyped formulas of the indenture of retainer could be tuned to serve his need.

Between John of Gaunt's retainers and the rest of his annuitants there was a very definite distinction, sometimes specifically noted by

---

[28] *Reg. II* 52, 54.

[29] Perewyche had been both sheriff of Leicestershire and MP for the county. He was currently a justice of the peace and continued to serve on a variety of commissions in Leicestershire until his death in 1388. *CFR 1377–83* 35; *CCR 1377–81*, 572; *CPR 1381–5*, 252, 255, 347, 496, 590; *CCR 1381–5*, 14. Barewell was a lawyer who had just served as MP for Warwickshire when he was retained by Gaunt and his indenture with the duke marks the beginning of a rapid rise to prominence. In Oct. 1383 he became sheriff of Worcestershire and in Nov. 1384 sheriff of Gloucestershire. Since he held the two posts in illegal plurality he was swiftly removed by royal signet letter, although he managed briefly to have the order countermanded and eventually gained appointment as escheator in Gloucestershire. This rather hectic career was not without its set-backs. He was convicted of extortion while escheator in 1390, and of extortion and false imprisonment while sheriff of Worcestershire. *CAD* i, C. 1579, vi. 4580; *CCR 1381–5*, 290; *List of Sheriffs for England and Wales* (PRO Lists and Indexes, ix, 1898), p. 157; *CFR 1383–91*, 76, 112; C. 81/1343/75, 1344/8; N. Saul, *Knights and Esquires* (Oxford, 1980), p. 136; C. 81/519/6697.

the receiver responsible for the payment of their fees.[30] The retainer's obligation was precisely stated in his indenture but the annuitant's was usually no more specific than the vague but unvarying phrase that accompanied the grant of a fee—good service, done in the past and to be done in the future. Only occasionally was it spelled out what 'good service' actually involved, as in the grant of £100 to Sir Thomas Percy *'pur tant qil sera ovesque nous et de nostre conseill contre tous autres durant sa vie'.*[31] Numerically, the duke's annuitants formed the largest single group within his affinity but most of them were household servants and estate officials in receipt of very small sums, who carried little individual weight and whose principal importance lay in providing a pool of manpower which could be swiftly mobilized in times of crisis. Nevertheless, among them were some more influential figures who received substantial annuities from the duke without ever becoming his retainers. For some of them, such as Sir John Holland, Sir Robert Ferrers, or Sir Thomas Morieux, there was a tie of kinship that made a formal contract superfluous; for others, like Sir John Kentwood or Sir Nicholas Sarnesfield, responsibilities to other lords prevented them from entering into the precisely defined relationship entailed by an indenture of retainer, even though their value to, and reward from, the duke was considerable.

Finally, beyond this outer circle of annuitants, lay a group of noblemen whose relations with Gaunt fluctuated somewhat uneasily between friendship and clientage. In some cases, the Lancastrian connection was, for a brief period, formalized. Ralph, lord Greystoke, agreed to serve in the duke's retinue on the Scottish March for a period of two years, while Gaunt appointed Henry Percy, earl of Northumberland, his deputy on the Border in 1384 and Edward Courtenay, earl of Devon, his lieutenant in Devonshire in 1386.[32] But these were only the most concrete manifestations of a wider network of alliance among the peerage that the duke showed himself anxious, during the early years of his career, to construct. Ties of kinship, wardship, and marriage, such as those the duke deployed to construct the wide-ranging but ultimately evanescent set of alliances by which he sought during the 1370s to unite the interests of the Mowbray,

---

[30] e.g. DL 29/262/4070 m. 2, 402/6448 m. 2.
[31] C. 66/356 m. 14; DL 42/15 f. 50v for Percy's duties as a counsellor.
[32] BL Harleian MS 3988, ff. 41–42; *Rot. Scot.* (Record Commission, 1814–19), ii. 62; BL Add. Cha. 13910.

Hastings, Ufford, and Strange families with his own,[33] rather than the formalized contract and the money fee, were the means most suitable to this end. But such alliances were, nevertheless, maintained in being by the same expectation of mutual benefit that underwrote the promise of an indenture of retainer. In consequence, it was from those families whose estates lay closest to centres of Lancastrian influence, such as the Ferrers of Chartley and the Greys of Codnor,[34] that John of Gaunt received the most loyal and lasting service, for it was they who had most to gain from it. Among his clients, only the Kentish family of Poynings came from an area significantly removed from any concentration of Lancastrian estates.[35]

2. Cost

Such, in outline, was the great affinity over which John of Gaunt presided; a household of 115 men, an indentured retinue 170 strong, and an even larger number of annuitants. How much did it all cost? The most burdensome department to maintain was not the indentured retinue but the ducal household. In 1376/7 it was allocated £10 a day (the annual retaining fee of a substantial esquire) for its expenses but this sum proved insufficient; the actual liveries to the treasurer of the household, including special provision for expenditure in excess of the sum allocated, amounted to £4,767. 11s. 4d. and by 1392/3 the assignment for household expenses had risen to £5,000. Taking into account the additional assignations made to the clerk of the duke's great wardrobe and the treasurer of the duchess's household, this means that the expenses of the whole Lancastrian establishment amounted to £5,767. 11s. 4d. in 1376/7, rising to £7,000 in 1392/3 and falling back slightly to £6,595 in 1394/5.[36] By 1396/7, however, there were signs of retrenchment; the assignation to the duke's wardrobe had been

---

[33] A. Goodman, 'John of Gaunt', *England in the Fourteenth Century*, ed. W. M. Ormrod (Woodbridge, 1986), p. 82.

[34] BL Landsdowne MS 229, f. 21; *Chronica Johannis de Reading et Anonymi Cantuariensis 1346–1367*, ed. J. Tait (Manchester, 1914), p. 183 (Ferrers); see below, p. 211 for the Greys.

[35] Bodl. MS CCC 495, f. 15; *CFR 1369–77*, 6; *Reg. I* 49, 982, 1585; C. 76/52 m. 15, 55 m. 21; C. 61/83 m. 3; *CIPM* XIV, 190 (p. 199), XVI, 610–24.

[36] DL 28/3/1 m. 9, 2 f. 9, 32/21.

reduced from 2,000 marks to £1,000 and only £2,144. 13s. 4d. was actually paid to the treasurer of the household during the financial year.[37] Only a little more than £50 a month[38]—perhaps £625 a year—of this sum went on the wages of the household; the real source of expense was the cost of supplies for the duke's servants and his guests. The only definite figures available for household expenditure on food come principally from an untypical period, 5 July to 1 August 1383, when the duke was away in the North with his retinue and the household establishment at Kenilworth was consequently a small one, consisting of Queen Constance, the permanent domestic officials, and the *familia* of the duke's daughter Katherine.[39] Expenditure was therefore low, averaging around 50s. a day and falling still further when Queen Constance and part of the household left for Tutbury on 25 July. Only on 20 July, when the earl and countess of Warwick, Sir William Beauchamp, and other local notables came to dinner, did it rise significantly above that figure. The contrast with the position in early September, when the duke and his whole retinue were moving southward through Banbury, Oxford, Henley, and Maidenhead to Westminster, is instructive; then the *dieta* of the household averaged over £20 a day, with occasional extraordinary demands pushing the figure up as high as £129. Whereas around 60 people had taken the midday meal at Kenilworth, as many as 148 did so when the household reached Westminster.[40]

How does the duke's expenditure on his indentured retinue compare with these figures? A precise answer can be given only for two consecutive years, 1393/4 and 1394/5, when complete valors of the duke's estates and the charges upon them have survived.[41] In 1393/4, Gaunt's honorial receivers paid £3,047. 5s. 3d. in annuities from estates with a clear annual value of £10,805. 10s. 6d. (i.e. 28 per cent of the total value) while in 1394/5 £3,157. 1s. 3d. was paid in annuities from a clear value of £10,480. 2s. 10d. (i.e. 30 per cent of the total).[42]

---

[37] DL 28/3/5 f. 5. For the purposes of comparison, the costs of the royal household between 1377 and 1395 rose from £19,000 to £27,000 p.a. Given-Wilson, *The Royal Household and the King's Affinity*, p. 94.

[38] e.g. East Sussex Record Office, GLY 3469 m. 11d: wages this month amounted to £52. 16s. 8d.

[39] Ibid. mm. 18–20. These are abbrevement rolls, giving the *dieta* totals of the various departments of the household, with notes of wine and wax consumed.

[40] Ibid. m. 20.

[41] DL 29/728/11980–3 (1393/4), 11984–5 (1394/5).

[42] The latter total includes £110. 11s. 3½d. in annuities marked as due in the parts of the south, but not yet paid.

To these payments must be added the annuities, principally those granted to members of the duke's family and to his alien retainers, which were assigned to the receiver-general's account: these amounted to £379. 3s. 4d. in 1392/3, £189. 3s. 4d. in 1394/5, £159. 3s. 4d. in 1396/7.[43] Thus, although the precise figures fluctuated from year to year, it seems clear that, even before expenditure on the Lancastrian affinity reached its highest levels, annuities paid to his retainers were absorbing nearly £3,500 p.a. of an estate income around £11,000 p.a. This latter figure would, in turn, have been higher but for the manors and lands granted out by the duke to his retainers in lieu of a cash fee, which further diminished the estate liveries available to him and increased the financial burden of the affinity. No comprehensive list of these properties survives and their precise value is consequently difficult to estimate, but it was certainly rather more than the £369. 5s. 6d. worth of land that is readily accounted for from the auditors' certificates and valors.[44] In total, the cost of the duke's indentured retinue must, by 1395, have approached £4,000 p.a.

It is rather more difficult to assess the cost of John of Gaunt's affinity at any earlier stage in his career but an examination of the annuity charges assigned on individual receiverships provides some indication, at least, of the general movement of expenditure.[45] On a number of receiverships, particularly Norfolk, Lincolnshire, the parts of the south and the Welsh lordships of Monmouth and Kidwelly, it is clear that annuity payments reached a high point in the mid-1380s, just before the duke's departure for Spain, which was never attained again during the next decade. In contrast, a handful of honours show a sharp rise in annuity levels over much the same period; payments more than doubled at Tutbury between 1383 and 1393 and at Leicester between 1381 and 1391. Part of this rise, particularly at Tutbury, can be explained by the duke's need to reward those who had served him faithfully in Spain but this will not account for the rapid escalation of annuity charges at Lancaster and Pontefract, which rose by 100 per cent and 150 per cent respectively between 1390 and 1395. The same escalation did not take place on the rest of the Lancastrian estates, for

<hr>

[43] DL 28/3/2 ff. 10–11v; DL 28/32/21; DL 28/3/5 ff. 6–6v.

[44] Total compiled from DL 29/728/11979 m. 2d, 11980 m. 2d; DL 43/15/3, 6. The manors of Bradford and Almondbury (Yorks.), worth £40 p.a., granted to Sir Robert Swillington and the manor of Down Ampney (Glos.), worth £10 p.a., granted to Sir Thomas Hungerford do not appear in the auditors' valors, for instance, C. 136/73/8, 100/2.

[45] Appendix IV.

at Hertford, Pickering, Knaresborough, and in Sussex annuity levels remained remarkably constant during the same period, and so local circumstances, in particular the duke's need to bolster his position in the North after the riots and rebellions of 1392/3, best explain it.

Overall, this analysis would suggest that, although annuity payments rose and fell on an equal number of receiverships in the decade between 1385 and 1395, those showing an increase in payments were financially the more important, with the result that the cost of the Lancastrian affinity was rising, perhaps by as much as a third, within this period. The effects of this increased expenditure were, however, mitigated by the duke's Castilian indemnity of £100,000 and pension of £6,600,[46] which made him less dependent on estate liveries for current income and so enabled him to channel a larger proportion of his resources into his affinity without immediate financial worry. Whereas cash liveries from the ducal estates to his receiver-general totalled £5,683. 7s. 11d. in 1376/7, they were running at a level below £3,000 p.a. by the early 1390s.[47]

These calculations need to be put into perspective for their true significance to emerge, for the payment of fees and annuities rarely absorbed more than 10 per cent of a late medieval magnate's income.[48] Richard, earl of Warwick, spent just under £200 p.a. on fees between 1396 and 1398, for instance, and his son was spending no more than £250, from his gross annual income of £2,500, on his affinity by 1420/1.[49] Edmund, earl of Stafford, was paying out about £325 in fees, wages, and annuities in 1400/1, from estates valued at £2,865. 7s. 2d.; his son, the duke of Buckingham, spent roughly the same proportion of his revenue on the payment of annuities during the 1440s.[50] Even Richard, duke of York, seems to have been only a little more extravagant in his expenditure on retaining fees, although the Neville earls of Warwick and Salisbury may have been spending as much as 20

[46] P. E. Russell, *The English Intervention in Spain and Portugal in the Time of Edward III and Richard II* (Oxford, 1955), pp. 506, 511.

[47] DL 28/3/1 mm. 1–2; DL 29/728/11980–5: £2,915. 2s. 2d. (1393/4); £2,883. 8s. 3½d. (1394/5).

[48] T. B. Pugh, 'The Magnates, Knights and Gentry', in S. B. Chrimes, C. D. Ross, and R. A. Griffiths (eds.), *Fifteenth-century England* (Manchester, 1972), p. 104.

[49] SC 6/1123/5 m. 1; BL Egerton Roll 8769 m. 1d. C. D. Ross, *The Estates and Finances of Richard Beauchamp, Earl of Warwick* (Dugdale Soc., Occasional Papers, 12, 1956), pp. 14–15.

[50] Staffordshire Record Office, D. 641/1/2/6; C. Rawcliffe, *The Stafford Earls of Stafford and Dukes of Buckingham* (Cambridge, 1978), p. 73.

per cent of their income on fees and annuities.[51] Nor had Gaunt's Lancastrian predecessors been any more generous than this; Henry of Grosmont paid no more than £250 p.a. in fees and annuities from estates valued at £3,500 (gross) in 1348 while Henry, third earl of Lancaster, paid out a little under £400 under the same head from estates charged at £5,516 in 1330/1.[52]

By these standards, John of Gaunt was clearly indulging in 'a scale of expenditure to which it would be hard to find a medieval parallel'.[53] His only serious competitor in the fourteenth century was Thomas, second earl of Lancaster, whose retinue appears to have cost between £1,500 and £2,000 p.a., on top of an unspecified sum in the form of estates alienated for life, although just before his exile in 1398 Thomas Mowbray, duke of Norfolk, does appear briefly to have been spending as much as 40 per cent of his current estate revenues on fees for his affinity. Only Henry, third earl of Northumberland, whose grants to his retainers absorbed virtually half his landed income by 1461, ever surpassed Gaunt in the scale of his expenditure on his following.[54] In this respect, the duke owed more to the traditions of munificence he inherited as a cadet of the royal family than to the practice of his fellow magnates. Among his contemporaries, he was matched only by his elder brother, the prince of Wales, who had assigned over £1,500 p.a. in life grants to the chamberlain of Chester's account alone by 1369/70, while his father the king expected to pay out more than a quarter of his ordinary revenue on annuities during the 1360s.[55] The unprecedented size of John of Gaunt's following thus owed less to the political aspirations of a potentially overmighty subject than to a sharp sense of his Plantagenet lineage and the royal obligations that laid upon him.

Did these obligations ever become too burdensome to maintain?

[51] J. R. Lander, *Crown and Nobility 1450–1509* (London, 1976), p. 31; A. J. Pollard, 'The Northern Retainers of Richard Neville, Earl of Salisbury', *Northern History*, 11 (1976), 65–6.

[52] DL 28/32/17; DL 40/1/11 f. 45v. The figure for Henry of Grosmont does not take account of lands and manors demised for life.

[53] K. B. McFarlane, *EHR* 70 (1955), 111.

[54] J. R. Maddicott, *Thomas of Lancaster* (Oxford, 1970), p. 47; R. E. Archer, 'The Mowbrays: Earls of Nottingham and Dukes of Norfolk to 1432' (unpub. Oxford Univ. D. Phil, thesis, 1984), pp. 306–11; J. M. W. Bean, *The Estates of the Percy Family 1416–1537* (Oxford, 1958), pp. 93–6.

[55] P. H. W. Booth, *The Financial Administration of the Lordship and County of Chester 1272–1377* (Chetham Soc., 3rd series, 28, 1981), p. 135; G. L. Harriss, *King, Parliament and Public Finance* (Oxford, 1975), pp. 481, 489. Edward III's annuity bill was estimated at £13,000 from a total annual revenue of around £52,000.

Honorial resources were sometimes strained—in 1384/5 the duke's receiver in Norfolk was unable to meet as much as a third of his annuity bill for lack of ready cash, while when Sir John Fenwick was granted an annuity in 1381 it was assigned either to Dunstanburgh or to Pontefract, if the receipts of Dunstanburgh were too depleted to bear the expense[56]—but such emergency measures were unusual. Most of John of Gaunt's retainers seem to have been promptly paid most of the time; the evidence of their surviving acquittances suggests that, although it was occasionally necessary to wait several months for payment, most Michaelmas fees had been paid by early November.[57] At times, however, more drastic measures were necessary; at Michaelmas 1379, for instance, the duke was compelled to order a stop on the payment of many annuities. Although this lasted, in theory, only a month, the stop was more permanent in some honours, where the receivers did not pay out the Michaelmas 1379 annuities until the following financial year.[58] The reasons for a step so serious are obscure but it seems most likely that the financial burden imposed by the maintenance of the Lancastrian affinity had temporarily proved too great. The situation was certainly serious enough by April 1379 for the duke to make what use he could of his feudal prerogatives by levying a gracious aid for the knighting of his youthful eldest son.[59] This was because, as the receiver-general's account of 1376/7 clearly shows, Gaunt was heavily dependent upon payment from the Exchequer for his services in war to bridge the gap between central household expenditure (£8,742. 16s. 7d.) and the liveries from the ducal estates (£5,683. 7s. 11d.).[60] Hence any appreciable period, such as that between September 1378 and June 1380,[61] when Gaunt was without such payments, may well have left him with a temporary deficit which

---

[56] Norfolk Record Office, NRS 11072 m. 2; Leeds Central Lib., Grantley MS 501; cf. *Reg. I* 1039, 1746.

[57] Surviving acquittances can be found in DL 28/32/22; DL 29/341/5516 (Sir John Seyton); Huntington Lib., HAD 3200 (Sir Ralph Hastings); *Sotheby's Sale Catalogue, 13 Apr. 1981*, no. 98 (Sir John Neville); Northumberland Record Office, ZSW 1/91, 92 (Sir William Swynburn); Nottinghamshire Record Office, Dd Fj 9/7/16 (Sir Gerard Usflete), Dd Sr 28/3/5, 231/54 (Sir John Saville); Leeds Central Lib., Grantley MS 500 (Sir Thomas Metham).

[58] *Reg. II* 72, 77, 111, 114, 136; DL 29/16/201 m. 2, Norfolk Record Office, NRS 3342 m. 2.

[59] Nottingham University Lib., CL D 616.

[60] DL 28/3/1 mm. 3, 9. Exchequer payments amounted to £6,254. 14s. 8d. in the financial year 1376/7, of which £4,060. 3s. 9½d. remained in uncashed tallies at the end of the account.

[61] E. 403/472 m. 14, 478 m. 26.

could only be met by demanding more substantial cash liveries from the honorial receivers, at the inevitable expense of those payments permanently assigned to their charge.

It seems possible that, by the late 1390s, the duke's financial position was again creating the same kind of problems. Deliveries of the Castilian pension, on which the duke had relied to maintain the expenditure necessary for the support of an enlarged retinue, were now more erratic and cash payments from the Exchequer less frequent than they had been. Between 2 March 1395 and his death, Gaunt can be shown to have received only just over £9,000 from these two sources, whereas he was paid nearly £10,000 by the Exchequer alone in the year preceding 2 March 1395. The result was that cash liveries from the duke's honorial receivers to the Lancastrian household, which had been running at under £3,000 a year during the early 1390s, had inevitably to rise; in 1396/7, issues of lands paid to the receiver-general amounted to £4,234.[62] Although no accurate indication of the cost of the duke's affinity survives after Michaelmas 1395, the number of extant indentures dating from the last years of the duke's life makes it seem unlikely that the burden of annuity payments eased appreciably in that period, while, on some receiverships, there is good evidence that he continued to expand his commitments.[63] It is likely, in consequence, that by the end of his life John of Gaunt was again experiencing difficulty in paying for his affinity—a difficulty that was to trouble his son so greatly.

3. Composition

Who were the beneficiaries of this massive expenditure and how did they come to gain its benefits? It is, unfortunately, remarkably difficult to be specific about the motives that prompted John of Gaunt to retain a man. Proficiency in war, it will be argued, was one of the principal attractions a prospective retainer could offer; at home, an assured place in the local administration might, at times, be valuable.[64] In addition, a process of recommendation can often be inferred, by which

[62] DL 28/3/5 ff. 1–2; E. 403/546 m. 14, 551 m. 18, 555 (12 May), 556 m. 28, 559 m. 5, 561 m. 11; E. 401/602 (7 July), 606 (12 May), 609 (22 May), 611 (8 Jan.).

[63] See below, pp. 224–5.

[64] See above, pp. 15–16.

retainers already established in Lancastrian service would put in a good word with the duke for their own followers and dependants. Richard Eton, who had been Sir Richard Burley's esquire, moved swiftly into ducal service after the death of his master in Spain.[65] Thomas Burton came from the service of Sir Frank van Hale; Thomas Whittingham from Sir John Marmion's; William Gaskrigg was an accomplice of Sir Ralph Paynel.[66] The same process was at work among the duke's officials: Thomas Langley entered Lancastrian service by the recommendation of the Radcliffes of Radcliffe, his first patrons; Hugh Wombewell, the duke's attorney in common pleas, had formerly been the personal clerk of Sir William Finchdean, his chief steward.[67] Alternatively, an indenture of retainer might be the reward for conspicuous loyalty under duress or an inducement to compromise in a property dispute; Sir Maurice Berkeley of Uley, who renounced all claim against the Lancastrian foundation of St Mary Newarke over the valuable manor of Wolaston on 31 October 1391, was retained by the duke two days later.[68] Certainly, it was often reward for a considerable period of probationary service: Robert Hatfield's first indenture with the duke dates from 1373, although he subsequently described himself as having been in Lancastrian service since 1361; Thomas Wennesley was already looking to Gaunt for patronage and protection in 1370, although he did not enter the duke's retinue until 1384; Arnold Buada claimed to have served the duke since 1374, although he was not retained until 1391.[69]

Beyond this, the question is obscure and the answer must rely chiefly on inference. There were, however, some clearly defined paths into Lancastrian service and these are worth examining in a little more detail for the light they cast on the process of recruitment. One was the tradition of loyalty and service to the house of Lancaster that John of Gaunt inherited along with the lands of his father-in-law. Individual

---

[65] *Registrum Johannis Gilbert, episcopi Herefordensis, 1375–1389*, ed. J. H. Parry (Canterbury and York Soc., 18, 1915), p. 110; Lewis, no. 11. Burley died on 23 May 1387, Eton was retained by the duke on 26 July.

[66] *CPR 1367–70*, 380 (Burton); *Reg. II* 1235 (Whittingham); *CPR 1381–5* 351 (Gaskrigg).

[67] R. L. Storey, *Thomas Langley and the Bishopric of Durham, 1406–1437* (London, 1961), pp. 2–3; *Select Cases in the Court of King's Bench*, ed. G. O. Sayles (Selden Soc., 82, 1965), vi, p. lxxxv, n. 1, *Reg. I* 353.

[68] *CCR 1389–92*, 500; A. H. Thompson, *The History of the Hospital and the New College of the Annunciation of St Mary in the Newarke, Leicester* (Leicester, 1937), p. 30.

[69] SC 8/221/11019; *Derbyshire Feet of Fines, 1323–1546*, ed. H. J. H. Garratt and C. Rawcliffe (Derbyshire Record Soc., 11, 1985), no. 902; C. 61/108 m. 7.

examples are striking: Sir Thomas Hungerford, the duke's chief
steward, took his name from a manor that was part of earl Edmund's
original endowment and the family connection with the house of
Lancaster was almost as long-standing;[70] Sir Robert Swillington, the
duke's chamberlain, could also trace the Lancastrian allegiance of his
family back to earl Edmund.[71] Feudal geography served to perpetuate
such traditions. The Sulnys of Newton Sulny first witnessed the charters
of the lords of Tutbury when the honour was held by the earls of
Chester; their loyalty, like that of the Okeover family, passed to the
Ferrers, earls of Derby, and, in due course, to successive earls of
Lancaster.[72] The Trumpingtons and the Marmions looked back to the
Lacy earls of Lincoln and Leicester;[73] the Loudhams could trace their
ancestry back to Eustace de Loudham, under-sheriff of Nottingham in
1214, a tenant and client of John de Lacy, and they continued to serve
the lords of Tickhill until 1391, when the last male member of the
family died on active service with his overlord's son.[74]

These were substantial gentry families, who had much of their own
prestige invested in the continued greatness of their patrons, and their
example is enough to make the point that 'bastard' feudal loyalties
were often the legitimate heirs of fully feudal ties. Precisely *how* often
is rather more difficult to say. By the late fourteenth century, territorial
proximity was usually more important than tenurial dependence in
creating links between the magnates and the county gentry. The
deficiencies of feudal tenure in securing service are well known and
need be only briefly rehearsed; knights' fees had become so
fragmented that the actual performance of the service technically
required from the fee-holder was, in many cases, impossible. Indeed,
many of Gaunt's most loyal retainers possessed no direct tenurial
connection with him[75] and even in those cases where the contract

---

[70] *CCR 1318–23*, 47; *CAD* vi. 7449; DL 40/1/11 f. 45v for earlier Hungerfords in
Lancastrian service.

[71] DL 42/2 f. 59v; Canon Beanlands, 'The Swillingtons of Swillington', Thoresby
Society, *Miscellanea*, 15 (1909), 204–5.

[72] I. H. Jeayes, *A Descriptive Catalogue of Derbyshire Charters* (London, 1906), nos.
486, 536; DL 25/2196; *CPR 1317–22*, 232 (Sulny); BL Add. Ch. 27313; Derbyshire
Record Office, 231 M/T 375 (Okeover).

[73] DL 42/12 f. 43 (Marmion); *CAD* iii. B4158, vi. 7447, 7457 (Trumpington).

[74] J. C. Holt, *The Northerners* (Oxford, 1961), p. 50; R. Thoroton, *The Antiquities of
Nottinghamshire* (London, 1677), pp. 289–90; *Expeditions to Prussia and the Holy Land
Made by Henry, earl of Derby*, ed. L. T. Smith (Camden Soc., NS 52, 1894), p. 143: John
de Loudham, *defuncti in partibus de Lettowe*.

[75] e.g. Thomas, lord Roos, held land of 18 different overlords at the time of his death
but none of the duke of Lancaster; *CIPM* XVI. 32–52.

between lord and man *was* secured by land the multiplication of overlords from whom a retainer held his estates meant that it can have done little to assist the stability of the relationship between them. Nevertheless, the influence exercised by the tenurial structure of the duke's estates upon the composition of his following should not be ignored entirely. The 'new feudalism' represented by John of Gaunt's affinity had not lost all its links with the older framework of feudal service. The duke's unchallenged territorial preponderance in Lancashire, the county that produced the largest single number of his retainers, allowed him to preserve a closer correlation between tenure and service than most other magnates could maintain—from a sample of 89 retainers and annuitants, 32 held at least some land from the duke.[76] In particular, the tenurial connection played an important part in the initial formation of the duke's affinity, for a small and homogeneous group among his senior retainers, including Thomas, lord Roos, John, lord Wells, Sir Richard Scrope, and Sir Robert Swillington, had all been tenants of the young earl of Richmond.[77]

This need not cause surprise, for the duke continued to take his feudal resources seriously, pursuing his rights in the royal courts and refusing to recognize enfeoffments to use designed to deprive him of his wardships.[78] Since a man usually chose his patron for the benefits his favour could confer, the duke's rights as overlord, which could be exercised or remitted in a retainer's favour, by ordering the temporary remission of a demand for homage, respite on the payment of a relief, or recognition of an enfeoffment to use,[79] clearly constituted an additional inducement to service. The coincidence of tenure and service in the Lancastrian retinue is, therefore, high enough to suggest that the duke's retainers had not lost all contact with the feudal loyalties of their ancestors but it was the expectation of such additional fiscal benefits, not the mere possession of land, that bound the duke's tenants more closely to his service.

---

[76] S. Walker, 'John of Gaunt and his Retainers, 1361–1399' (unpub. Oxford Univ. D.Phil. thesis, 1986), p. 22 n. 2 for details.

[77] *CIPM* VIII. 546 (Scrope), XI. 217 (Wells), XVI. 32–52 (Roos), 725–50 (Neville); C. 136/73/8 (Swillington).

[78] *Year Books of Richard II, 13 Richard II, 1389–90*, ed. T. F. T. Plucknett (London, 1929), pp. 106–7; DL 28/3/2 f. 16; *Sir Christopher Hatton's Book of Seals*, ed. L. C. Lloyd and D. M. Stenton (Northants Record Soc., xv, 1950), no. 486; *CPR 1381–5*, 507 for an enfeoffment to use by Sir William Frank and Gaunt's reaction to it; DL 42/2 f. 490v for a dispute with Gilbert Umfraville, earl of Angus, over the duke's rights of wardship.

[79] *Reg. I* 1300, 1375; Norfolk Record Office, NRS 3345 m. 1.

In choosing his retainers, John of Gaunt thus had the advantage of drawing upon a group of gentry families who instinctively looked towards the house of Lancaster for patronage and advancement. Within this circle of expectation, however, the duke was free to pick and choose and his choice of servant seems, in fact, to have borne little direct relationship to the choice of his predecessors. A number of his retainers could boast of ancestors who had suffered for their fidelity to Thomas, earl of Lancaster[80] but the relatively full list of earl Thomas's retainers and annuitants, amounting to 90 names in all, provides only 8 men who were the direct progenitors of a retainer of John of Gaunt's.[81] Equally, only two of Gaunt's followers—Sir Edmund Appleby and Sir Walter Blount—could claim close relatives among the men compelled to ransom themselves for participation in earl Henry's rising in 1328[82] and, although some other families, more prudent or less loyal, had begun their long association with the house of Lancaster without being involved in the rising,[83] the list of earl Henry's annuitants for 1330/2 shows very little connection with the followings either of his elder brother or those of his descendants.[84]

The case of Henry of Grosmont's annuitants was rather different, since many continued to enjoy a fee from the Lancastrian estates, granted them by duke Henry, for much of John of Gaunt's lifetime. At least 17 of duke Henry's 107 identifiable annuitants[85] continued to serve Gaunt, some of whom were to become his closest companions—

---

[80] e.g. Sir John Seyton's grandfather was pardoned for his adherence to Thomas of Lancaster in 1318. Thomas de la Mare's father forfeited his property twice for the same cause while both Sir Gilbert Talbot's father and grandfather were taken in arms against the king at Boroughbridge. J. Bridges, *The History and Antiquities of Northamptonshire* (Oxford, 1791), ii. 46–7; C. Moor (ed.), *Knights of Edward I* (Harleian Soc., 83, 1931), iv. 245 (Seyton); *VCH Oxfordshire*, v. 33 (de la Mare); *Complete Peerage*, XII. i. 610, 612 (Talbot).

[81] G. A. Holmes, *The Estates of the Higher Nobility in Fourteenth-Century England* (Cambridge, 1957), pp. 134–42. They are: John Dalton, bailiff of Pickering; William, son of Sir William Fitzwilliam; Sir Nicholas Longford; Sir Ralf de Neville; Sir Adam Swillington; Sir Gilbert Talbot; Sir Giles Trumpington; Sir Gerard Usflete.

[82] *CCR 1327–30*, 528–30.

[83] DL 42/1 ff. 198v (Scargill), 385 (Hastings).

[84] DL 40/1/11 ff. 45v, 51v.

[85] K. A. Fowler, 'Henry of Grosmont, First Duke of Lancaster, 1310–1361' (unpub. Leeds Univ. Ph.D. thesis, 1961), Appendix J conveniently lists them. The names of Sir John Cokayn, Adam de Derby, Thomas de la Mare, Sir Thomas Metham, Sir John Saville, Sir Alured Sulny, and Sir Thomas Ufford may be added. DL 29/368/6152 m. 1 (Cokayn); *CPR 1396–9*, 567 (Derby); DL 42/12 f. 56; *CPR 1364–7*, 328 (de la Mare); DL 29/507/8227 m. 16 (Metham); DL 42/15 f. 414; *CPR 1360–4*, 86 (Saville); SC 6/988/14 m. 4d (Sulny); *CPR 1358–61*, 16 (Ufford).

Sir John de Ipres, Sir Ralph Hastings, and Sir Thomas Metham among them.[86] Yet the continuity of service between the two dukes should not, once again, be overestimated. Continued payment of an annuity is no proof that the annuitant continued to serve, or to come in contact with, his new paymaster and since many of duke Henry's annuitants were his near-contemporaries in age, their active years were often well behind them.[87] A number of duke Henry's annuitants were, in any case, servants of the prince of Wales as well and, on the duke's death, it was to the prince rather than the young earl of Richmond that they turned most readily; Sir Thomas Hereford and Sir Neel Loring are both to be found in Aquitaine with the prince in 1363; Sir Stephen Cosington and Sir William Trussell both served as his bachelors.[88] The less fortunate were unable, or simply unwilling, to find a new magnate patron and John of Gaunt clearly felt under no immediate obligation to employ his father-in-law's former servants. Sir Thomas Lathum, although one of the most important of the Lancashire gentry, received no patronage from the new duke while Sir Norman Swynford, a regular campaigner with Henry of Grosmont, served abroad with Gaunt only once during a military career that stretched into the 1380s.[89]

In addition, the influence of Lancastrian loyalists on the formation of the duke's retinue was counterbalanced by his access to another, quite distinct, tradition of service which existed among the clerks and esquires of the royal household. While Gaunt and his brother, Edmund of Langley, earl of Cambridge, were underage the lands of the royal children were jointly administered by officials appointed by the king. Walter Campeden, Gaunt's first receiver-general, was seconded from Queen Philippa's household[90] while William Nessfield and Godfrey Foljambe both followed suit in moving from her service

[86] The others are: Thomas Burton; John Elmeshale; Thomas de la Mare; John Newmarch; Sir Edmund Pierrepont; Sir John Rocheford; Henry Rose; Sir John Saville; Simon Simeon; Sir Alured Sulny; Sir John Talbot; Sir Nicholas Tamworth; Sir Thomas Ufford; Nicholas Usk.

[87] e.g. although Sir Nicholas Gernoun continued to draw an annuity until 1384, after Henry of Grosmont's death he retired to the pious seclusion of the Minoresses' convent at Bruisyard (Suff.) and remained there, as the constant companion of Maud of Lancaster, until his death. *CPR 1367–70*, 219; *VCH Suffolk*, ii. 131–2.

[88] BL Cotton Julius C IV ff. 288–9; *Register of Edward the Black Prince* (London, 1930–43), iv. 178, 261.

[89] C. 81/952 (53)—1373. Swynford was serving in Brittany in 1368 and 1375, in the Calais garrison in 1377, and in Ireland with Sir William Windsor in 1380. C. 81/915 (36), 967 (14), 988 (1), 996 (65).

[90] *CPR 1350–4*, 333, 459.

to that of her son.[91] This movement from royal to Lancastrian service
was maintained when, on attaining his majority, older and richer than
his younger brother, Gaunt was able to attract a number of the officials
appointed to manage Edmund of Langley's estates to his own
administration. William Nessfield had been steward of the Cambridge
lands before becoming Gaunt's chief steward; Thomas Haselden, later
controller of the Lancastrian household, had acted as Langley's
receiver in Yorkshire, and Robert Morton, the duke's receiver in the
county, was also Edmund of Langley's steward there.[92] The royal and
Lancastrian households had always cross-fertilized each other in this
way[93] and they continued to do so for much of John of Gaunt's career.
Sir William Croyser, his chief steward, had received his training in
royal service, as coroner and clerk of the market;[94] Richard Beverley,
keeper of the royal wardrobe, became treasurer of the Lancastrian
household, as did Thomas Swaby, formerly a clerk in the king's
service;[95] a number of household esquires moved to the duke's service
on the death of Edward III.[96] The movement was generally from royal
to Lancastrian service, presumably because the latter offered comparatively swifter prospects of advancement. Only at the end of Richard
II's reign was the process reversed, when esquires like Richard
Chelmeswyk, Thomas Foljambe, and Hugh Lutterell began gravitating from the duke's service towards the royal household.[97]

John of Gaunt was, therefore, heir to two quite distinct traditions of
service—one royal and one Lancastrian. Both of them played an
important part in the creation of his affinity yet neither of them was
dominant within it and, to this extent, the composition of the duke's
following faithfully reflects a permanent tension, between his duty to
the Crown and his *Hausmachtspolitik*, that was to continue throughout
his life. Within the Lancastrian tradition, a further distinction must be
made, between a generalized desire for patronage, shared by many
gentry families who had done some service to the house of Lancaster

[91] *CPR 1348–50*, 395 (Nessfield); ibid. *1354–7*, 548; ibid. *1358–61*, 282 (Foljambe).

[92] *CPR 1358–61*, 268; ibid. *1361–4*, 149 (Nessfield); ibid. *1374–7*, 398 (Haselden); ibid. *1381–5*, 78 (Morton).

[93] T. F. Tout, *Chapters in the Administrative History of Medieval England* (Manchester, 1920–33), iii. 42, 197–8.

[94] *CPR 1350–4*, 507; ibid. *1354–8*, 161.

[95] Tout, op. cit., iii. 329 n. 3, iv. 192 n. 1 (Beverley); E. 101/396/11 ff. 16*d*, 17 (Swaby).

[96] Geoffrey Chaucer, Nicholas Dabridgecourt, Peter Roos, Robert Urswick, William Wintringham. E. 101/397/5 f. 43v, 398/9 f. 31.

[97] E. 101/402/20 ff. 35–38, 403/10 ff. 43*d*–44*d*.

in the past, and a positive expectation of continued employment and reward, which only the most privileged of Lancastrian servants could command. Gaunt thus inherited many aspirations to serve but few obligations to employ. Whom he chose to retain remained very much his own decision; the Lancastrian affinity very much his own creation.

Some of the needs and aspirations that influenced the duke's choice of servant can be gauged by a brief examination of the regional composition of his affinity. The reasons for the importance of Lancastrian estate geography in the creation of the duke's following are clear enough—the gentry naturally looked to the greatest lord of their neighbourhood because he disposed of valuable local patronage in the form of stewardships, foresterships, and parkerships—but the very size of his estate gave John of Gaunt an unusual degree of discretion in deciding where he should look for support. Changes in the nature and provenance of the service he sought can, therefore, be used to deduce something of the duke's changing ambitions and responsibilities.

Initially, most of the men Gaunt fee'd came from either Yorkshire or Lincolnshire,[98] in strong contrast to Henry of Grosmont's annuitants, many of whom had their grants assigned to the Chaworth lands in Wiltshire and Hampshire or the Warenne lands in Norfolk. Such a distribution of clients faithfully reflected the predominant position of the Richmond and Boston lordships within the honour of Richmond[99] and provided the young earl of Richmond with a close-knit group of northern knightly families to serve as the nucleus of his retinue. In 1359 Gaunt's first company for service overseas already drew on such well-established Yorkshire families as the Scropes, the Fitzwilliams, the Fitzhughs of Ravenswath, and the Constables of Halsham.[100]

---

[98] Yorkshire: Sir William Finchdean of Batley; Thomas Haselden of Wakefield; Sir Hugh Hastings of Norton and Fenwick; Sir Ralph Hastings of Slingsby; Sir Thomas Metham of Metham; Robert Morton of Bawtry; William Nessfield of Scotton; John, lord Neville, of Raby; John Newmarch of Cridling Stubbs; Sir Edmund Pierrepont of North Anston; Thomas, lord Roos, of Helmsley; Sir Michael de la Pole of Kingston, Myton, Cowthorpe, etc.; Sir Richard Scrope of Bolton; Sir Robert Swillington of Swillington; Sir Walter Urswick of Catterick; Sir Gerard Usflete of Usflete and Swanland. Lincolnshire: Sir John Dymoke of Scrivelsby; Sir Andrew Lutterell of Irnham; Sir John Rocheford of South Kelsay; Sir Robert Roos of Gedney; Simon Simeon of Claypole and Kettilby. For full supporting references, Walker, 'John of Gaunt and his Retainers', pp. 27–34.

[99] M. C. E. Jones, *Ducal Brittany, 1364–1399* (Oxford, 1970), pp. 181–2; *CFR 1356–68*, 163–6; ibid. *1377–83*, 274. Richmond and Boston produced nearly two-thirds of the profit of the whole honour.

[100] C. 76/37, 38; C. 81/1737.

As early as 1367, however, Gaunt's following had acquired retainers from Sussex, East Anglia, and the March of Wales[101] and was beginning to develop away from the model of most magnate affinities, in which the lord's influence and the extent of his retainers' support was effective within a single region, sometimes a single county, towards an organization that more accurately represented the full spread of the Lancastrian estates. Under the pressure of war and its demands this process soon accelerated; between 1370 and 1378 the duke recruited his retainers from 22 different counties, from Cornwall to Northumberland,[102] and his retinue became, for the first time, genuinely national in its composition. Yet Gaunt's need for military manpower also led him to shift his principal recruiting-ground from Yorkshire to Lancashire.[103] While his retinue remained an institution designed to provide him with household knights and congenial companions-in-arms, the duke could afford to restrict his recruitment to a relatively high social level,[104] but once the provision of fighting men became the overriding criterion in his selection of retainers then the claims of Lancashire, a poor county with many of whose numerous gentry Gaunt enjoyed direct tenurial links, became impossible to ignore. The higher proportion of esquires among the Lancashire men the duke retained,[105] and the previous careers, often criminal, of men like Nicholas Atherton and William Parr certainly suggest that it was military ability, rather than social position, that John of Gaunt now sought in his indentures.

Changes in the disposition of the Lancastrian estates during the same period served to modify the duke's pattern of recruitment further. Although the surrender of the honour of Richmond to the

---

[101] Sir Ralph Camoys of Trotton and Hawksbourne (Sussex); Sir John Dageney of Cainhoe (Beds.); Sir John Plays of Chelsworth (Suff.) and Great Oakley (Essex); Sir Richard Burley of Burley and Newland (Herefs.).

[102] Sir Walter Penhergerd of Helland (Corn.); Sir Thomas Ilderton of Ilderton and Roseden (Northd.).

[103] 16 retainers from Lancashire: Nicholas Atherton of Bickerstaff; Sir Thomas Banaster of Bretherton and Thorp; Sir John Botiller of Warrington; William Bradshaw of Haigh; Robert Cansfield of Tatham; Ralph de Ipres of Heton; Sir Nicholas Longford of Withinton; Simon Molyneux of Netherton; Adam Newsome of Newsham; William Parr of Parr; Robert Pilkington of Pilkington; Sir Robert Plessington of Great Eccleston; John Sotheron of Mitton; Sir Thomas Southworth of Southworth and Samelsbury; Robert Standish of Ulnes Walton; Sir John Talbot of Warrington. 9 retainers from Yorkshire: Sir John Boseville of Chete; Sir Thomas Colville of Coxwold; Sir Edmund Frithby of Firby and Eddelthorpe; Robert Hatfield of Owston; Sir John Marmion of Tanfield; Sir William Maulevrer of Wothersome; Sir Robert Rockley of Rockley; Sir John Saville of Elland and Tankersley; Sir William Scargill of Ossett and Sandal.

[104] See below, pp. 35–6.

[105] Ten out of 16 at the time of indenture.

Crown in 1372 was rewarded by a compensatory exchange of lands designed, wherever possible, to keep his territorial presence within a specific region intact,[106] it proved impossible to avoid some shift of emphasis in the areas of Gaunt's support. In particular, the loss of the lordship of Richmond itself removed one of the duke's best recruiting-grounds while, by granting his son the honours of Tickhill and Knaresborough in exchange, Edward III effectively moved the concentration of Lancastrian territorial power in Yorkshire to the south of the county, tightening the duke's grip across the northern Midlands but depriving him of the foothold within the 'Northern military zone'[107] provided by Richmond and its adjacent lands. The grant of the lordship of the High Peak to the duke, in exchange for the Richmond lands in Lincolnshire and Hertfordshire—the one exception to the general principle of compatibility—further consolidated the Lancastrian presence in this region, bringing the first recruits from Staffordshire and Derbyshire into the duke's service,[108] while the consequent removal of the Boston lordship from Gaunt's control helps to explain the comparative decline in Lincolnshire's importance as a recruiting-ground in this period.[109]

This pattern of consolidation within already well-established areas of Lancastrian strength, combined with a gradually more intensive exploitation of hitherto neglected counties, continued for much of the 1380s. Lancashire,[110] Yorkshire,[111] and Lincolnshire[112] remained the duke's most prolific recruiting-grounds while Midlands counties like

[106] *The Charters of the Duchy of Lancaster*, ed. W. Hardy (London, 1845), no. viii; *Reg. I* 24–35.

[107] Cf. R. L. Storey, 'The North of England', *Fifteenth-Century England*, ed. S. B. Chrimes, C. D. Ross, and R. A. Griffiths (Manchester, 1972), p. 130.

[108] William Chetwynd of Shavington; Oliver Barton of Williamsthorpe; Sir Walter Blount of Barton; Sir Roger Curzon of Kedleston; Peter Melbourne of Melbourne.

[109] Sir William Cantilupe of Lavington and Kingthorpe; William Spaigne of Boston; John, lord Wells, of Grainsby.

[110] Sir John Ashton of Ashton; Sir Richard Balderston of Balderston; Edward Banaster of Bretherton; William Barton of Middleton; Sir John Dalton of Bispham; Robert Eccleston of Eccleston; Hugh Haywood of Heywood; Sir Richard Hoghton of Lee and Hoghton; Richard Holland of Denton; Sir John de Ipres, le filz, of Aldcliffe; John Parr of Parr; Ralph Radcliffe of Blackburn and Smithills; Richard Rixton of Ditton; Sir Richard Torbock of Tarbock; William Tunstall of Tunstall and Burgh; Sir Geoffrey Workesley of Worsley; Robert Workesley of Booths and Stannistreet.

[111] Sir Thomas Boseville of Chete; William Burgoyne of Calne; Thomas Etton of Gilling; Sir William Fitzwilliam of East Hathelsay; William Kettering of Kirkbyosborne; William Paumes of Naburn; Robert Persay of Levisham; Sir Thomas Routhe of Thorp Pirrow; Sir Richard Rowcliffe of Thornthorpe; Sir David Rowcliffe of Levisham and Wrelton; William Swillington of Barkston; John Wandesford of Kirklington.

[112] Sir Ralph Bracebridge of Wrawby; Sir John Bussy of Hougham; John Deincourt of Blankney; Thomas Driby of Haugham; Sir William Frank of Saltfleetby; Sir Robert

Warwickshire and Leicestershire[113] began, for the first time, to make a substantial contribution to John of Gaunt's following. Further territorial acquisitions again affected this pattern of recruitment, for the build-up of a substantial Lancastrian presence in the March of Wales, through the acquisition of a moiety of the Bohun inheritance followed in June 1384 by a grant of the temporary custody of the Hastings lordships of Pembroke and Abergavenny,[114] saw retainers from Gloucestershire and Herefordshire, as well as the occasional Welshman, assuming more prominence in the duke's service.[115] The contrast with the position on the northern March where, despite Gaunt's frequent journeys to the Border and his responsibilities as lieutenant in the March, there are few signs of Lancastrian recruitment,[116] suggests that estate geography and the concomitant obligations of local patronage, more than the demands of policy, determined where the duke looked for his retainers. In this, 'bastard' feudalism still differed little from any other form of feudalism; lordship over land meant lordship over men.

By contrast, the final decade of the duke's life saw some definite changes in the direction of his own career and, in consequence, the pattern of recruitment among his retainers. Traditional concerns, in particular the need to reward those who had served him faithfully in Spain, continued to bulk large, but the duke's claim to the Castilian throne and the constant state of military preparation it entailed, which had done most to shape John of Gaunt's policies for the last fifteen years, was now finally abandoned. Abroad, his concerns were

Hauley of Mablethorp; Sir William Hauley of Utterby; Sir Thomas Meaux of Billinghay; John Mymott of Carston; Roger Messingham of Lincoln; Sir Ralph Paynel of Broughton and Castlethorp; Sir Thomas Swynford of Kettlethorp and Coleby.

[113] Warwickshire: William Bagot of Baginton; Sir Baldwin Berford of Wishaw and Shotteswell; Sir William Lucy of Charlecote; Sir Baldwin Montfort of Coleshill and Kingshurst; Sir John Pecche of Hampton in Arden; Sir John Peyto of Chesterton and Sowe; John Rous of Ragley.

[114] *CCR 1377–81*, 391; ibid. *1381–5*, 511; *CFR 1388–91*, 42, 80, 312.

[115] Gloucestershire: William Barewell of Alscot; Thomas Berkley of Cobberley; Thomas Bridges of Haresfield; John Giffard of Leckhampton; William Hervey of Southrop. Herefordshire: Sir John Bromwych of Clifford and Credenhull; Sir Thomas Beek of Dilwyn; Roger Burley of Burley and Dorston; Sir Gilbert Talbot of Goodrich Castle. R. R. Davies, *Lordship and Society in the March of Wales 1282–1400* (Oxford, 1978), p. 224 (Henry ap Philip of Kidwelly).

[116] Sir John Fenwick of Fenwick and Matfen and Sir William Swynburn of Chollerton and Capheaton were the duke's only recruits in the area. Sir John Middleton of Jesmond and Bruton (*CPR 1416–22*, 435, *Feudal Aids*, iv. 78, 84) seems unlikely to have joined his retinue so early.

concentrated on vindicating his position in Guyenne; at home, on establishing his bastard children, the Beauforts, in political society and ensuring the peaceful succession of his eldest son, Henry of Derby, to the heritage of Lancaster. The geographical provenance of the duke's retinue shows some signs of this change: regions previously unexploited by the duke, such as East Anglia,[117] began to make a noticeable contribution to his following; while Yorkshire and Lincolnshire, two well-established recruiting-grounds, produced few new retainers in this period,[118] the ever-growing power of the king in his palatinate of Chester caused the duke to concentrate considerable attention on recruiting support within his own palatinate of Lancashire.[119]

The threat to political stability posed by Richard II's heavy programme of retaining in Cheshire helps, in addition, to explain the changing social composition of the duke's following. In the early years of his career, the geographical concentration of John of Gaunt's support in Yorkshire and Lincolnshire was matched by a heavy social predominance of knights over esquires and yeomen; only 17 of the 41 retainers and annuitants who entered his service before 1370 were unknighted when they did so. By the time the *Nomina militum et scutiferum* was compiled in 1382, these proportions had already changed markedly—the duke's indentured retinue then consisted of 77 knights and 96 esquires—and they continued to do so until the very end of the duke's life; 106 of the men he retained between 1387 and

---

[117] William Caston; Thomas Dale of Little Barford (Beds.); Richard Gest of Coston (Norf.); Oliver Groos of Sloley (Norf.); Peter Mildenhall of Brinkley (Cambs.); Thomas Mounteney of Threxton (Norf.); John Payn of Helhoughton (Norf.); William Plumpstead; John Raimes of Overstrand (Norf.); Roger Trumpington of Moggershanger (Beds.); John Reyner of Oakley (Beds.); Ivo de Wyram of Thetford (Norf.).

[118] Reginald Curteys of Wragby (Lincolnshire); Thomas Eland of Raithby (Lincolnshire); William Hoghwyk of Pontefract (Yorks.); Ralph, lord Neville, of Raby (Yorks.); Sir John Rocheford of South Kelsay (Lincolnshire); Sir Ralph Rochefort of Stoke and Scrane by Boston (Lincolnshire); Sir Philip Tilney of Boston and Tydd (Lincolnshire); Nicholas Tournay of Caenby (Lincolnshire); John Wastneys of Todwick (Yorks.); Robert Waterton of Methley (Yorks.).

[119] Nicholas Atherton, le filz, of Bickerstaff; William Balderston of Balderston; John Bispham of Lathum; Robert Bolron of Lancaster; Sir John Botiller of Out Rawcliffe; William Bradshaw of Westleigh; Richard Croke of Whittle; Walter Curwen of Caton; Sir Thomas Fleming of Croston; Sir Thomas Gerard of Ashton and Skelmersdale; Sir Henry Hoghton of Leagram; Sir William Hoghton of Lee and Hoghton; William Hudleston of Copeland; William Hulme of Denton; Robert Laurence of Scotforth and Carleton; Richard Molyneux of Sefton; Robert Radcliffe of Ordsall; Thomas Radcliffe of Heyhouses; John Rixton of Rixton; William Singleton of Fermanholes; John Southworth of Southworth and Samelsbury; Sir Thomas Tunstall of Thurland and Tunstall; Sir Robert Urswick of Upper Rawcliffe; Robert Urswick of Upper Rawcliffe.

1399 were esquires, only 26 of them knights. In part, this was due to the natural wastage of death and retirement and the consequent replacement of the old by the young. The sons of men John of Gaunt had retained earlier in life were now beginning to replace their fathers in his service; at least 13 can be identified entering the Lancastrian affinity between 1387 and 1399.[120] In some cases, this was the direct result of the duke's exercise of his rights of wardship; an upbringing in the Lancastrian household formed a natural preliminary to entry into the Lancastrian retinue.[121] More usually, a process of recommendation must be presumed. Yet while this form of recruitment helped to consolidate the traditions of Lancastrian loyalism current among the duke's retainers, it never constituted an automatic passport to John of Gaunt's service. Sons were sometimes openly hostile to following in their father's footsteps and their fathers were, in turn, usually shrewd enough to hedge their bets by distributing their offspring through several noble households. Sir John de Ipres's eldest son followed him into Lancastrian service; his younger son, Thomas, was left to find his fortune with the earl of Salisbury and the duke of Gloucester.[122] Sir Richard Abberbury sent one son into the ducal household, the other (by the mediation of Sir Nicholas Sarnesfield) to the King's.[123]

Consequently, the changing social composition of the Lancastrian affinity can be best explained as a positive response to a change in the duke's needs and expectations of service, marked by a conscious decision to concentrate on quantity rather than social quality that owed most to Gaunt's desire to lay the foundations of an adequate affinity for his eldest son. The duke had provided Henry of Derby with considerable financial assistance for some years[124] and it was natural that he should seek to buy him support as well. Movement between the

[120] Nicholas, son of Sir Nicholas Atherton; William, son of Sir Richard Balderston; John, son of Sir Roger Curzon; Thomas, son of Sir Thomas Dale; Thomas, son of Sir Godfrey Foljambe; Sir Henry, son of Sir Adam Hoghton; Sir William, son of Sir Richard Hoghton; Thomas, son of Sir William Lucy; Ralph, son of John lord Neville; John, son of Matthew Rixton; Sir John, son of Sir John Rocheford; John, son of Sir Thomas Southworth.

[121] e.g. the cases of Thomas Banaster and Richard Molyneux. *Reg. II* 506; G. F. Beltz, *Memorials of the Most Noble Order of the Garter* (London, 1841), p. 209 n. 1 (Banaster); *Abstracts of Inquisitions Post-Mortem*, ed. W. Langton (Chetham Soc., os 95, 1875) i. 30; DL 28/3/3 m. 3 (Molyneux).

[122] T. Madox, *Formulare Anglicanum* (London, 1702), no. 572; C. 81/1027 (30); BL Add. MS 40859A m. 2 for his service with Gloucester.

[123] E. 403/496 m. 9; E. 101/402/20 f. 38*d*, 403/10 f. 43*d*; *CPR 1396–9*, 109.

[124] DL 43/15/1; DL 28/1/10 f. 1v; *Expeditions to Prussia and the Holy Land Made by Henry, earl of Derby*, pp. lxxxvi–lxxxvii.

households of father and son was common,[125] but during the 1390s the duke began to underwrite Derby's political position in a more systematic fashion by granting additional retaining fees to his son's servants, on condition that they remained with Derby after his own death.[126] By 1399, at least seventeen of Derby's knights and esquires enjoyed the additional benefit of an annuity from John of Gaunt[127] while other members of the Lancastrian household were being seconded to the service of the Beaufort family.[128] The smart companions the duke had sought among his retainers in his youth, the experienced soldiers he had recruited in his middle age were, in his last years, replaced as the predominant group within the Lancastrian retinue by young men prepared to devote a lifetime of service to his children.

Changing political circumstances and the duke's changing ambitions thus left their mark upon the composition of the Lancastrian affinity. Yet the fact that they can be charted so clearly should itself act as a reminder that, important as considerations of estate geography proved to be, the duke's retinue was as much a product of his will as a product of his lands. Just as the long-standing loyalty to the house of Lancaster entertained by some gentry families was balanced, in the formation of John of Gaunt's affinity, by the administrative traditions he brought with him from the royal household, so the duke's search for experienced soldiers of established reputation led him well beyond the boundaries of his estates and helped to spread a thin web of Lancastrian allegiance all over England. Indeed, it was the constant demand for military service imposed upon Gaunt between 1369 and 1375 by his position as his father's principal lieutenant in the war against France that really served to integrate the manpower of the

---

[125] e.g. Richard Chelmeswyk was first retained by Derby, then by Gaunt; after many years' service in the Lancastrian household, Piers Petrewich was eventually granted a corrody as the *serviens* of the earl of Derby. E. 403/533 m. 7; DL 29/615/9839 m. 2 (Chelmswyk); *Reg. 1* 3, 427, 572; E. Sussex Record Office, GLY 3469 mm. 1*d*–5*d*; WAM 2177 (Petrewich).

[126] *CPR 1396–9*, 499.

[127] DL 28/4/1 ff. 6–11; SC 6/1157/4 m. 3; DL 42/16 ff. 142, 144v, 219. John Ashley; Sir Thomas Beaumont; Henry Botquenzelle; William Burgoyne; Sir John Dabridgecourt; Thomas Erpingham; Thomas Gloucester; Robert Hatfield; William Hoghwyk; Peter Melbourne; John Norbury; John Payn; Sir John Robessart; Ralph Staveley; Thomas Totty; Sir Hugh Waterton; Robert Waterton.

[128] Reginald Curteys went into the service of Henry Beaufort; Richard Eton into the service of John Beaufort; John Rixton into the service of Thomas. *CPR 1401–5*, 321; DL 28/3/5 ff. 6, 11, 12; E. 403/562 m. 2.

duke's scattered estates into a single, cohesive affinity. Gaunt could hardly do that by his own presence, for the obligations of government meant that during the last years of Edward III's reign he spent most of his time in or around London. The physical concentration of Lancastrian interests at this time is well indicated by the fact that his senior administrators—Sir John de Ipres, Sir William Croyser, Sir William Finchdean, William Bughbrigg—all found it necessary to buy houses in the capital.[129] When the duke undertook a tour of his Midland estates in the summer of 1374, it was his first trip north of Hertford for five years.[130] For many Lancastrian retainers, therefore, particularly those from his northern estates, the duke's campaigns abroad provided the only available opportunity for personal contact with their lord. Walsingham's report of the duke's piqued 'retirement' from court in the autumn of 1377[131] could, in consequence, be rather better explained as an attempt on Gaunt's part, by extending the range of his itineration, to provide a more effective and personal focus for the loyalty of a following rapidly and recently expanded by his military commitments. That this was not the only effect of the demands of war upon the development of the Lancastrian affinity will emerge from a closer examination of its military duties and rewards.

[129] Corporation of London Record Office, Hustings Roll 100/86, 159; 101/109.

[130] The duke's itinerary, 1369–1377, can be reconstructed in some detail from Bodl. MS CCC 495, f. 15; C. 53/152–4; *Reg. I, passim*; DL 28/3/1.

[131] Walsingham, *Hist. Ang.*, i. 339; *Chronicon Angliae*, p. 169.

3

THE LANCASTRIAN AFFINITY AT WAR

1. Service in War

John of Gaunt's life was dominated by war and the rumours of peace. From 1359, when he accompanied Edward III on his last great expedition to France, until his return from the duchy of Gascony in 1395, he was continually employed in the wars against the French and their allies. Nor was he simply an English war-leader but, by reason of his marriage to Constance of Castile in 1372, a European prince with pretensions to a throne of his own that had to be secured by force of arms. In consequence, Gaunt participated in 12 major military expeditions,[1] besides preparing for several more that failed to materialize,[2] while his responsibility for peace negotiations with the French involved him in 15 separate diplomatic missions.[3]

These facts have an immediate importance for the study of the duke's retinue, historiographical as well as historical. Much of the most distinguished pioneering work on 'bastard feudalism' and the indentured retinue was based principally upon a study of the contracts between John of Gaunt and his retainers.[4] Written at a time when the

[1] Table 1.

[2] Against the French in 1377; against Castile in 1382; to the rescue of bishop Despenser in Flanders in 1383; in Gascony in 1388. DL 28/3/1 m. 7 (1377); *Rot. Parl.*, iii. 114; *Reg. II* 775 (1382); E. 101/39/29; E. 403/499 mm. 13, 17 (1383); E. 159/166, Brevia Baronibus, Trinity, m. 16d, *The Antient Kalendars and Inventories of the Treasury of His Majesty's Exchequer* (London, 1836), ii. 35 (1388). An expedition to Gascony by the duke was still under discussion in 1392, when it was declared in Council that he would soon be in the duchy. J. F. Baldwin, *The King's Council in England During the Middle Ages* (Oxford, 1913), p. 498.

[3] E. 101/314/32; E. 403/421 mm. 9, 12 (Flanders, Nov. 1364), 425 mm. 5, 8, 19 (Calais, Oct. 1365), 456 mm. 15, 20, 457 m. 8 (Bruges, Feb.–June 1375), 459 mm. 2, 21, 24, 28, 31 (Bruges, Oct. 1375–Jan. 1376), 484 m. 3 (March day, May 1381), 496 m. 5 (March day, May 1383), 499 m. 9 (Calais, Nov. 1383), 502 m. 6, 505 m. 19 (Calais, June 1384), 533 m. 6 (Calais, May 1391), 536 mm. 13, 21, 22 (Amiens, Mar. 1392), 541 mm. 17, 22, 543 mm. 5, 14 (Calais, Feb.–June 1393), 546 m. 22, 548 mm. 1, 4, 13 (Calais, April–May 1394), 556 m. 28, 559 m. 5 (March day, Feb. 1398).

[4] N. B. Lewis, 'The Organization of Indentured Retinues in Fourteenth-Century England', *TRHS* 4th series, 27 (1945), 29–39; K. B. McFarlane, 'Bastard Feudalism', *BIHR* 20 (1945), 161–80.

TABLE 1. The Size and Composition of Lancaster's Military Companies

1359	400	France	2 bannerets 35 knights 162 esquires 200 archers[1]
1367		Spain[2]	
1369	1,840	France	6 bannerets 130 knights 364 esquires 1,000 archers 300 Welshmen 40 miners[3]
1370	800	Aquitaine	3 bannerets 80 knights 216 esquires 500 archers[4]
1372	1,000	France	5 bannerets 100 knights 394 esquires 500 archers
	1,200	Spain	6 bannerets 120 knights 473 esquires 600 archers[5]
1373	1,520	France	8 bannerets 150 knights 601 esquires 760 archers[6]
1378	1,000	Sea	5 bannerets 100 knights 394 esquires 500 archers[7]
1380	2,000	Scotland	1 earl 12 bannerets 86 knights 900 esquires 1,000 archers[8]

1384		Scotland[9]	
1385	3,000	Scotland	14 bannerets
			136 knights
			850 esquires
			2,000 archers[10]
1386		Spain[11]	
1394		Aquitaine[12]	

---

[1] E. 101/393/11 ff. 79v, 80.

[2] No exact indication of the size of Lancaster's force for this expedition survives. Froissart, the only source to give a precise figure, is inconsistent, giving 800 men in his first redaction, 1,000 in his second; *Froissart (K. de L.)*, vii. 141. The figure of 1,200 men, given by P. E. Russell, *The English Intervention in Spain and Portugal*, p. 79 seems based on a misreading of C. 61/79 m. 9. 350 archers, not 800, were to be raised from the duke's English lands.

[3] E. 101/68/4 (87).

[4] E. 364/5 m. 5d.

[5] *Reg. I* 51. The duke's indenture envisaged service in either theatre of war. In the end, Edward III changed his plans and required the service of only 800 men from the duke; E. 403/446 m. 31.

[6] *Reg. I* 52. The numbers were subsequently increased to 780 men-at-arms and 800 archers; E. 364/10 m. 1.

[7] E. 101/37/27 (43); E. 403/468 m. 15.

[8] E. 404/12/78 (5 Sept. 1380); E. 403/478 m. 26. The purpose of this expedition is ambiguous. The warrant for issue describes the duke as going to Scotland 'because of the March day' but the Exchequer paid wages of war to the duke and he himself ordered his men to muster at Newcastle, arrayed for war; *Reg. II* 357.

[9] The chroniclers are agreed that the army for this expedition was a very large one, but no precise indication of the size of Lancaster's company survives; cf. Walsingham, *Hist. Ang.*, ii. 111–12; *Chronicon Angliae*, pp. 358–9; *Westminster Chronicle*, p. 67.

[10] E. 403/503 m. 22; N. B. Lewis, 'The Last Medieval Summons of the English Feudal Levy, 13 June 1385', *EHR* 73 (1958), 22 establishes the composition of the duke's men-at-arms. He had originally contracted to bring 800 men-at-arms and 1,200 archers, but this contingent was increased at some time between 13 June and 19 Aug. E. 403/508 m. 12.

[11] After a careful discussion of the evidence, P. E. Russell, *The English Intervention in Spain and Portugal*, p. 418 concludes that the army cannot have been more than 7,000 strong. This can readily be accepted; the figures of the chroniclers point to a smaller force. F. Lopes, *Crónica de Dom Joao I*, p. 201 estimates the Lancastrian army at 5,000 and his figure for the number of men-at-arms (2,000) at least agrees with *Chronicon Henrici Knighton*, ii. 207. *Froissart (K. de L.)*, xi. 326–7 gives the uncharacteristically plausible figure of 4,000 men; this was the size of the force Lancaster had originally proposed taking to Castile in 1382. *Rot. Parl.*, iii. 114.

[12] *Froissart (K. de L.)*, xv. 35 is the only guide available to the size of this force (1,500 men).

wars of Edward I were thought to have brought the indentured retinue
into being and the wars of Edward III to have provided an important
stimulus to the use and preservation of written contracts of service, it
was natural to conclude that, if the indentured retinue had a primarily
military origin, it must fulfil a primarily military function. Subsequently,
the demonstration that 'there was nothing particularly novel or
abnormal in the system of magnate retinues during the reign of
Edward I'[5] has detached the origins of the indentured retinue from the
specific context of his Welsh wars and insisted rather upon its gradual
evolution from a far older system of military organization, based upon
the household, which was already well exemplified in the *familia regis*
of the Anglo-Norman kings.[6] This has directed increasing attention to
the importance of a retainer's peacetime service to his lord, so that it is
now possible to write of 'the . . . widely-held view that purely military
duties were not the most important reason for recruiting a retainer'.[7]
Can this conclusion be applied to the retinue of John of Gaunt as well?
The contention of this chapter is that it cannot. The service the duke
required from his retainers was primarily military; the Lancastrian
retinue remained, as it began, a society organized for war. For a man
with the duke's military and diplomatic commitments, anything else
would have been an expensive luxury.

There are a number of yardsticks by which the importance of war
and war-service in the duke's view of his retinue can be gauged. To
take crude figures first, 253 out of 426 known Lancastrian retainers
and annuitants (60 per cent) can be shown to have served abroad with
Gaunt on at least one campaign.[8] Allowing for the lack of information
concerning the composition of Gaunt's expeditionary forces against
Scotland and the haphazard nature of the evidence yielded by
surviving letters of protection, it is clear that the actual proportion must
have been rather higher, so that the vast majority of the duke's
retainers can be assumed to have fought with him at some stage in
their career. Secondly, the duke's indentures strongly suggest that
warfare was the aspect of a retainer's service in which Gaunt was most
closely interested. Many of his retainers received higher fees in war

    [5] M. Prestwich, *War, Politics and Finance under Edward I* (London, 1972), p. 61.
    [6] J. M. W. Bean, ' "Bachelor" and Retainer', *Medievalia et Humanistica*, NS 3 (1972),
117–31; J. O. Prestwich, 'The Military Household of the Norman Kings', *EHR* 96
(1981), 1–35.
    [7] C. Carpenter, 'The Beauchamp Affinity, A Study of Bastard Feudalism at Work',
EHR 95 (1980), 519.
    [8] Appendix I.

than peace,[9] others were offered no peacetime fee at all,[10] while some of the duke's early indentures are closer in form to agreements with important subcontractors than to a conventional indenture of retainer.[11] Thirdly, a significant proportion of his indentures were granted overseas, at the very end of a campaign, as a reward to the new retainer for his prowess in war.[12] Fourthly, military ability alone was sufficient to command a retaining fee from the duke. Thomas Driffield, a Hampshire esquire retained by the duke in June 1380, never held an office nor served on a commission in England but he had, as he said himself in 1386, been armed for forty years in the old wars and the new,[13] and that was enough to gain him admission to the Lancastrian retinue. Driffield was, moreover, followed in rapid succession into the ducal service by Sir John Thornbury, formerly Hawkwood's lieutenant in the White Company,[14] Sir Geoffrey Workesley, a leader of the English companies in Brittany,[15] and Sir William Frank, another man with extensive military experience.[16] The explanation for this sudden access of military talent is simple. By 1380, it had become clear that the duke's projected invasion of Castile would have to be undertaken with a private army maintained at his own expense and Gaunt was, in consequence, anxious to obtain the best men available. Even between campaigns, he took the opportunity to consolidate the military potential of his retinue.

An indenture of retainer with John of Gaunt was, therefore, an emphatically military commitment. In only two cases was it ever provided that a retainer should not be compelled to serve abroad

---

[9] *Reg. I* 787, 788, 793, 796, 799, 800, 804, 805, 807, 808, 810, 812, 815, 816, 820, 833, 834, 837; *Reg. II* 23, 25, 49; Lewis, nos. 5, 6; Appendix III, no. 2 (24 in total).

[10] *Reg. I 777*, 782, 784, 814, 822, 829, 842, 853, 856, 865; *Reg. II* 27, 28, 30 (13).

[11] Lewis, no. 3; Appendix III, no. 1. (2).

[12] *Reg. I 777*, 778, 779, 783, 784, 864; Lewis, nos. 7–18, 27–30; Appendix II, nos. 8–9 (24).

[13] *The Scrope and Grosvenor Controversy* (London, 1832), i. 59. He had served in Berry and Poitou, been victualler of Bordeaux and captain of La Roche-sur-Yon, and a commander of companies in Brittany and on the sea. E. 403/422 m. 31; E. 101/35/18; *Foedera*, III. ii. 702; SC 1/40/171; C. 81/949 (55).

[14] J. Temple-Leader and G. Marcotti, *Sir John Hawkwood* (London, 1889), p. 148; *Calendar of Papal Registers, Papal Letters, 1362–1404*, 122, 124, 125; Lambeth Palace Lib., Reg. Sudbury, f. 103.

[15] See below, p. 75.

[16] He had served under the prince of Wales, Sir Robert Knolles, the earl of Hereford, Sir Thomas Percy, Sir John Arundel, the earl of Buckingham, and with the duke himself. C. 81/921 (18), 934 (46); E. 101/32/20, 37/28; C. 81/992 (5), 950 (52); E. 404/11/75 (12 May 1380).

against his will[17] and, for the rest, the obligation to fight at the lord's command—'*pur travailler ovesque lui as quelles parties qil plerra*' as the invariable formula has it—was, in its way, as binding as the feudal obligation of knight-service had ever been and enforced by a swift and effective means of distraint. Thus, Thomas Maistreson and Richard Massy had their annuities summarily cut off when, having originally agreed to go to Spain with their lord in 1386, they subsequently withdrew. Although they sent adequate substitutes, payment of their fees was not resumed until 1390.[18] Only if the retainer could prove that the duke had failed to fulfil some part of the agreement between them could he legitimately refuse to serve on a forthcoming expedition.[19]

Consequently, an indenture of retainer provided the duke with a powerful means of compelling military service from his followers. Indeed, the wording of Gaunt's indentures will bear an interpretation giving the duke exclusive rights to a retainer's service, for only the indentures of the most highly favoured contain a clause specifically allowing them to fight wherever they wished when the duke did not require their services.[20] Was this an effective restriction? The example of the Suffolk esquire, Robert Fitzralph, who served both the duke and a number of other commanders with apparent indifference, suggests that it was not,[21] and more extreme instances than Fitzralph can be adduced. Sir Richard Whitfield, a Gloucestershire knight retained by the duke early in 1372, served with seven different commanders in the next ten years but never once with Gaunt.[22]

---

[17] *Reg. II* 52, 54. See above, pp. 15–16 for a discussion of this case.

[18] W. Beamont, *An Account of the Rolls of the Honour of Halton* (Warrington, 1879), p. 22; Lancashire Record Office, Dd X 293/34; DL 29/16/202 m. 2.

[19] Hence the duke's receiver in East Anglia was instructed to pay Sir Roger Beauchamp of Bletsoe his fee for Easter 1373, so that he would have no cause or excuse for refusing to serve on the forthcoming expedition. Sir John Botiller's patent of appointment as sheriff of Lancashire specifically prohibited him from pleading his office as a reason for exemption from service overseas. *Reg. I* 1209, 8.

[20] Lewis, no. 3 (Neville); *Reg. I* 832 (Beauchamp).

[21] Fitzralph already had considerable military experience when retained by the duke in 1372, chiefly in Brittany, and he served under the duke of Brittany (1375) and earl of Buckingham (1380) there, as well as fighting at sea with Sir John Arundel in 1377/8 and Sir John Devereux in 1379. He is best known, however, as one of the captains of bishop Despenser's crusade in 1383. SC 1/40/171; M. C. E. Jones, *Ducal Brittany, 1364–1399* (Oxford, 1971), p. 208; C. 81/965 (33), 996 (61), 976 (32), 991 (47); *Rot. Parl.*, iii. 156–8.

[22] Whitfield served under Knolles in 1370 and during Lancaster's expeditions in 1372 and 1373 he was serving at sea under the command of John Brown. After further service at sea in 1374 with William Neville, admiral of the North, he fought briefly in

Neither was a typical case, however. Whitfield was plainly a professional soldier, in debt at home and dependent for his livelihood on the trade of war, while Fitzralph, too, was a military professional who deliberately avoided public office in England.[23]

For the rest of the duke's retainers, though, service in the Lancastrian company may well have been the only service abroad they saw. The level of military ambition and experience among the English gentry should not be overestimated[24] and many of his retainers may never have wished to campaign under another commander. This suggestion can be given some plausibility by an examination of some of the English armies in the early 1380s—a time when the duke himself made no expeditions abroad. In the earl of Buckingham's expedition to Brittany in 1380, only three Lancastrian retainers can be shown to have served.[25] The earl of Cambridge's Portuguese expedition in 1381 admittedly saw rather greater Lancastrian involvement, but the campaign had been planned in close collaboration with the duke and those of his followers who served were clearly acting on his orders; very few of their colleagues chose to join them.[26] Equally, Robert Fitzralph was almost alone in taking the Cross with bishop Despenser in 1383; only four more Lancastrians can be found among Despenser's

Ireland with Sir William Windsor and then joined the delayed Breton expedition in 1374/5, under the command of John de Montfort. Whitfield served with Montfort again late in 1377 and then joined the earl of Arundel for the St Malo expedition before setting off for Ireland once more with the earl of March in 1380. C. 81/932 (30), 946 (3), 949 (20), 959 (36), 960 (31), 962 (15), 976 (46), 981 (17); *CPR 1377–81*, 485, 488.

[23] *CCR 1377–81*, 126; *CPR 1388–92*, 259 (Whitfield); ibid. *1377–81*, 347 (Fitzralph).

[24] Very few of the Leicestershire gentry saw service on more than 2 campaigns between 1350 and 1400, for instance, while only 4 out of a group of over 40 gentlemen active in Gloucestershire during the same period had served abroad more than twice. G. G. Astill, 'The Medieval Gentry: A Study in Leicestershire Society 1350–1399' (unpub. Birmingham Univ. Ph.D. thesis 1977), fig. 22; N. Saul, *Knights and Esquires* (Oxford, 1981), pp. 285–8; cf. S. M. Wright, *The Derbyshire Gentry in the Fifteenth Century* (Derbyshire Record Soc., 8, 1983), pp. 8–9.

[25] William Barton of Rydale, Robert Fitzralph, and Sir John Dabridgecourt. C. 81/ 995 (54), 996 (61); C. 76/65 m. 28. Protections for this campaign are found in C. 81/ 994–1000; C. 76/64, 65.

[26] Sir Thomas Fichet and Sir Thomas Symond commanded 100 men between them, while Sir Joao Fernandes Andeiro led an 'emperogilado' company. They were acting under a mandate from Lancaster as the guardians of his interests in the Iberian peninsula. Symond, for instance, was charged with carrying the duke's Castilian standard. E. Perroy, *L'Angleterre et le grand schisme d'occident. Étude sur la politique religieuse de l'Angleterre sous Richard II* (Paris, 1933), p. 219 n. 4; P. E. Russell, *The English Intervention in Spain and Portugal in the Time of Edward III and Richard II* (Oxford, 1955), p. 302. Protections in C. 81/1000–1006, C. 76/65, 66. The only other Lancastrian names to appear are Simon Molyneux and Sir Richard Hoo. C. 81/1006 (36, 39).

army of 5,000.[27] Few Lancastrians, then, chose to serve under commanders other than the duke himself once they had entered his retinue. Only in the case of career-soldiers like Whitfield and Fitzralph, dependent upon war for a livelihood, was it plainly impossible for Gaunt to insist upon a monopoly of service. Consequently, the claim to exclusive control over a retainer's military service implicit in the duke's indentures was, in many cases, a realistic one which might be effectively exercised. When he had no military plans of his own, John of Gaunt was generous enough in granting leave of absence to his retainers[28] but the paucity of Lancastrians serving under other commanders shows that the duke was quite able to enforce the conditions of his indentures successfully.

Gaunt's indentured retinue thus served an important military function by allowing him to recruit experienced soldiers for his campaigns and to assure himself of their service. Yet if the retinue's qualitative importance in the composition of the duke's companies is established, what of its quantitative contribution? Is it more accurate to say that 'the duke of Lancaster could . . . put a large army in the field without going outside those already on his books' or that 'only the nucleus of an expeditionary force would be provided from the permanent following of a magnate, even if he was the duke of Lancaster'?[29] Without the retinue rolls lost in the sack of the Savoy it is impossible to give a precise answer, but there is enough evidence to attempt an approximate solution. This can best be achieved by breaking down the Lancastrian companies into their three constituent groups: (i) the contingent provided by the ducal household and retinue; (ii) the contingents provided by the duke's bannerets; (iii) contingents provided by other means—in an attempt to assess their relative importance.

The size of the first of these contingents naturally varied from campaign to campaign but, to judge from the surviving letters of protection, it usually accounted for between 15 per cent and 20 per cent of the duke's whole force. In 1373, 95 of the 540 protections issued (17.5 per cent) were to servants of the duke; in 1378, 33 of the

---

[27] Sir John Ashton, William Fifide, John Wandesford, Nicholas Atherton. C. 81/1013 (63), 1014 (14, 70), 1015 (17).

[28] e.g. a number of the bachelors of his household (Sir Otes Granson, Sir Jean Grivère, Sir Richard Abberbury, Sir Jean Manburni de Linieres) turn up in the Calais garrison early in 1379. C. 81/988 (1).

[29] McFarlane, 'Bastard Feudalism', 165; G. A. Holmes, *The Estates of the Higher Nobility in Fourteenth-Century England* (Cambridge, 1957), p. 80.

159 protections (21 per cent) went to Lancastrians, and in 1386, 80 protections among 558 (15 per cent) were issued to existing Lancastrian servants and a further 14 to those soon to join the ducal retinue. For the Gascony expedition in 1394, organized through the ducal household itself, the proportion of retainers was understandably higher—28 out of the 72 extant letters of protection were for Lancastrians. Whether this proportion of the duke's men seeking letters of protection would hold good if the composition of his whole company were known must remain uncertain but it seems, at the least, a reasonable estimate; a household numbering around 115 men and an indentured retinue 170-strong[30] might well be expected to produce between 15 and 20 per cent of the duke's companies in 1373 (1,520 men) and 1378 (1,000 men). This was not, however, the full extent of the Lancastrian contingent in any of the duke's companies, for most of the duke's indentures with knightly retainers stipulated that the retainer would be accompanied by one,[31] sometimes two,[32] esquires, while during a period of heavy military recruitment a number of indentures envisage that a retainer will bring with him as many men-at-arms and archers as the duke requires of him.[33] Taking these additional forces into account, the proportion of the duke's companies produced directly by the contractual obligations of his servants might reasonably be set at 25 per cent of the whole.

Equally important as a source of military manpower was one particular group among his retainers—the bannerets. This was a small[34] and tightly-knit group of men, nearly all of them from the north of England, nearly all of them from comital or baronial families,[35] who acted as the duke's subordinate commanders on

---

[30] See above, pp. 11, 14.

[31] *Reg. I* 782, 784, 785, 786, 804, 807, 838, 842; Lewis, no. 25.

[32] *Reg. I* 803, 833; Appendix III, no. 2.

[33] *Reg. II* 34, 37, 38, 39–41, 46.

[34] The duke was unable to find his quota of 8 bannerets in 1373. E. 159/153, Brevia Baronibus, Michaelmas, m. 31*d*.

[35] In 1367, Sir Thomas Ufford, brother of the earl of Suffolk, and Sir Hugh Hastings acted as the duke's bannerets but both died soon afterwards. *Life of the Black Prince, by the Herald of Sir John Chandos*, ed. M. K. Pope and E. C. Lodge (Oxford, 1910), ll. 3231–3; Lambeth Palace Lib., Reg. Whittesley, f. 111v; F. Blomefield, *An Essay Towards a Topographical History of the County of Norfolk*, 2nd edn. (1805–10), ix. 513. John, lord Neville, Sir William Beauchamp, who may already have attained this status in 1367, Thomas, lord Roos, and Sir Michael de la Pole acted as the duke's bannerets during the 1370s. *Reg. I* 969, 832, 1107; Lewis, no. 3; *Chandos Herald*, ll. 2247–53. By 1382, the names of John, lord Wells, Hugh, lord Dacre, Sir Richard Scrope, Sir Robert Knolles, and Sir John Marmion can definitely be added. DL 42/14, ff. 8–9. This is the 'Nomina

campaign as well as his major subcontractors. Each banneret was expected to bring with him 20 men-at-arms and 20 archers, although he might bring as many as 100 men in all.[36] Consequently, the recruitment and organization of another sizeable proportion of the duke's company could be swiftly delegated to his most trusted lieutenants. At the March day with the Scots in 1380, for instance, the recruitment of just under a quarter of Gaunt's total force was in the hands of his twelve bannerets. The duke's bannerets could thus be counted upon to provide between 15 per cent (1369, 1370) and 24 per cent (1380) of his military companies, while the service of the rest of his retainers and their own followers might account for a further 20 per cent or more of the whole force. The military resources of the Lancastrian retinue were, therefore, very considerable, constituting less of a nucleus than a backbone for his wartime companies. Yet even on the most optimistic projections, it is clear that the duke still had to find a proportion of his men-at-arms and the vast majority of his archers from outside the resources of his affinity. While preparing for his expedition against Scotland in 1384, for instance, Gaunt ordered his receiver in Lincolnshire to send letters both to his retainers, calling them out, and to other gentlemen of the county, requesting them to serve with him.[37]

Such an approach was largely speculative but there were other, and more reliable, ways of raising the necessary men: by the use of the prerogative machinery of the Crown; by encouraging individual retainers to bring small companies of their own with them; by temporary indentures with important subcontractors. The duke of Lancaster was unusual, though not unique, among the captains of his day in being allowed to use royal commissions of array to fulfil his private contractual obligations, as he did in 1366, 1373 (when commissions of array were used to raise 300 archers for his company in Lancashire and Yorkshire), and 1386.[38] His indentured retinue was, nevertheless, still a useful adjunct to this process, for the duke

---

militum et scutiferum' printed in *Reg. II*, pp. 6–9 but the manuscript has a gap, omitted in the printed text, beneath Marmion's name that is as definite as the gap between the knights and the esquires.

[36] Appendix III, no. 1; *Reg. I* 832; Lewis, no. 3.

[37] DL 29/262/4070 m. 3 '*diversis dominis militis et scutiferis tam de retinentia sua quam alii . . .*'.

[38] M. R. Powicke, *Military Obligation in Medieval England* (Oxford, 1962), p. 209; *Foedera*, III. ii. 799; C. 76/56 m. 31; C. 81/1349 (71).

had the power to nominate his servants to such commissions when they directly affected him,[39] and, since compulsory service under such a commission was understandably unpopular,[40] selected retainers had, in consequence, to be detailed to accompany the arrayed archers from their homes to the sea in order to guard against desertions.[41] At the same time, other retainers might undertake to raise their own companies in order to supplement the personal and prerogative resources at the duke's disposal. The size of such companies varied enormously—an experienced campaigner like Sir John St Lo could bring a force of over 80 in 1373,[42] but such large companies seem the exception rather than the rule. Most retainers contented themselves with a handful of companions.[43]

In consequence, the duke was less reliant upon the small-scale contractors among his own retainers than upon a limited number of independent subcontractors who agreed to provide large companies of their own. Chief among these were Sir Hugh Calveley, who acted as marshal of Lancaster's army and provided him with 120 men in 1370, 200 men in 1372, and a further 175 in 1373,[44] and Sir Thomas Percy, who contracted to bring 240 men with him in 1386 and brought out a further 150 men to reinforce the duke in 1388.[45] Few men could produce forces of this size but, at least for his Castilian campaign, the duke had to make use of many such short-term companies; some raised by those on the outer edges of the Lancastrian affinity, such as Richard, lord Poynings, and Sir Hugh Hastings;[46] others commanded

---

[39] C. 81/1349 (71): Sir Thomas Fichet and Stephen Derneford were among the 4 names transmitted by Gaunt to the Chancellor to be included in a commission to arrest 40 miners to accompany him to Castile in 1386.

[40] e.g. KB 27/454, Rex, m. 13: four Lancashire men, in this case, paid 20 marks to avoid serving as archers with the duke in 1373.

[41] *Reg. I* 1232.

[42] Ibid. 1679.

[43] In 1394/5, for instance, Sir Robert Standish's contingent of 2 men-at-arms and 20 archers was exceptionally large; Roger Molington brought a man-at-arms and 2 valets, Sir Roger Ledes an esquire and 2 archers, Sir Maurice Berkley 2 esquires and 3 archers. DL 29/728/11984 mm. 1, 2, 11986 m. 3d.

[44] *Calendar of Papal Registers, Letters 1362–1404,* 131; *Reg. I* 981, 1000; E. 364/8 m. 6d, 9 m. 1. In fact, when Gaunt's projected Castilian expedition was cancelled, Calveley served on the sea with him with a much smaller force of 35 men.

[45] E. 101/68/10 no. 250; E. 403/519 m. 2; E. 401/571 (14 May).

[46] For Poynings see above, p. 18, Hastings was the son of a Lancastrian retainer and, although never one himself, could look to Gaunt for his good lordship. A. Goodman, 'The Military Subcontracts of Sir Hugh Hastings, 1380', *EHR* 95 (1980), 114–20.

by men like Sir Miles Windsor and Sir Richard Massy, who had no peacetime connection with the duke at all.[47] For his greatest military efforts, therefore, even the duke of Lancaster, who could expect to raise half, perhaps rather more than half, of his military companies through the resources his indentured retinue put at his disposal, had to rely upon short-term indentures, valid only for half a year, and subcontractors upon whose loyalty he had no special call.

2. The Disciplines of War

It is thus possible to establish in approximate terms the contribution of the duke's peacetime affinity, in terms of numbers, to his retinue of war. The affinity's qualitative contribution remains to be considered. Was the continuity of service and stability of personnel, which the indentured retinue has been praised for providing,[48] a reality in the case of Gaunt's companies? In general, the most cohesive companies are likely to be those commanded by a captain of high social standing who receives comparatively regular payment for his troops.[49] Lancaster's companies should, in consequence, exhibit some definite signs of stability. In fact, as Table 2 suggests, the overall rate of re-service under the duke's command, during the period of his heaviest military commitments, was never very high. Some elements of continuity from campaign to campaign can certainly be discerned, yet they appear to have been dependent as much upon the success or failure of individual campaigns as upon the stabilizing influence of the duke's indentured retinue. Thus, almost a third of those who served with Gaunt in Spain in 1367 were still with him in 1373, whereas the re-service rate after the inconclusive campaign of 1369 is, proportionately, a much lower one. Equally, the frequency with which the duke was asked to serve abroad was itself instrumental in creating a certain continuity of service, most marked for the consecutive campaigns of 1372 and 1373, whereas a long gap between campaigns, such as that before the St

----

[47] C. 76/60, 61; C. 81/1031–1040. The other companies mentioned were commanded by Lancastrians: Sir Thomas Morieux; Sir John Holland; Sir Thomas Percy; Sir Walter Blount; Sir William Fifide.

[48] Lewis, *TRHS* (1945), 33.

[49] P. Contamine, *Guerre, état et société à la fin du moyen âge* (Paris, 1972), p. 169 establishes this was the case in France, adding: 'encore en temps de Charles V, c'est l'instabilité qui l'emporte . . .'.

TABLE 2. Re-Service Within Lancaster's Companies

Campaign	Total nos.[1]	Exclusive nos.[2]	Re-service in					
			1367	1369	1370	1372	1373	1378
1359	65	50	4	12	3	0	6	0
1367	100	35	—	49	35	10	32	5
1369	463	397	—	—	66	26	68	19
1370	176	104	—	—	—	30	56	17
1372	175	57	—	—	—	—	—	15
1373	540	361	—	—	—	—	—	11
1378	159	112	—	—	—	—	—	—

[1] The total number of those known to have served with Lancaster on the campaign in question.

[2] The number of those who fought only on the campaign in question.

Malo expedition in 1378, inevitably diminished the continuity of personnel within Lancaster's companies. Nor, to judge from the contingents of Thomas, lord Roos, and Sir Michael de la Pole, were his bannerets able to keep their men together with any greater success.[50] The contribution of the Lancastrian retinue to the stability of the contract army must, therefore, be judged a fairly marginal one.

However, viewing the duke's indentured retinue simply as a means of raising military manpower, without taking into account the type of service he required, misses part of its point. John of Gaunt was as much concerned with *who* served as with how many people served and it was the quality, not the quantity, of his troops that was the more difficult to control. Numbers alone were never the problem, at least for Gaunt. In both 1370 and 1373 his companies were marginally bigger than he was obliged to bring, while in 1385 his contingent was half as large again as his original contract required. Nor was this phenomenon confined to the Lancastrian company; on many campaigns there seem to have been more volunteers for service than the captains could employ, so that part of the army served without pay.[51] Rather, it was

[50] C. 81/947 (40), 952 (40), 985 (38) for Roos's companies; 6 of the 17 who served with him in 1372 reappear in 1373, 4 of the 29 who served in 1373 served in 1378 as well. C. 81/931 (46), 955 (49), 984 (8) for de la Pole's companies; only 2 of those appearing in 1370 appear again in 1373, none in 1378.

[51] *The Black Book of the Admiralty*, ed. Sir T. Twiss (Rolls Series, 1871), i. 456; *Westminster Chronicle*, p. 45. P. Contamine, 'Froissart: Art militaire, pratique et conception de la guerre', *Froissart, Historian*, ed. J. J. N. Palmer (Woodbridge, 1981), p. 141.

finding men of the right quality—both social and military—that presented the problem. The duke's indentured retinue provided him with recruits of an assured military calibre but controlling the social composition of his company was to prove a more difficult task.

As a prince of the blood royal, his companies usually contained a noticeably higher proportion of bannerets and knights than those of his contemporaries, for the social composition of a company was naturally expected to reflect the consequence of its captain.[52] However, knighthood was an increasingly unpopular status, both financially and administratively burdensome to its incumbents, and the duke experienced mounting difficulty in finding sufficient knights to fulfil his contracts. This was implicitly recognized by the diminishing proportion of knights the duke was required to bring with him: in 1369 they had constituted just under a quarter of all his men-at-arms but by 1380 the duke's 1,010 men-at-arms included only 100 knights, while in 1398 there were only 20 among the 200 men-at-arms he took to his last March day with the Scots.[53] Nevertheless, Gaunt still experienced difficulty in meeting this part of his undertaking. In 1369, he was 37 knights short of his quota, in 1370 7 knights short and in 1373 he failed to find the full number of both bannerets and knights required of him.[54] Once again, the duke's use of his indentured retinue was powerless to maintain stability in the composition of his companies.

There were, however, other ways in which the Lancastrian retinue contributed towards the efficiency and cohesion of his military companies. In the first place, it provided a much-needed stability at the *end* of the duke's campaigns when, often chronically short of money, John of Gaunt was unable to halt the gradual disintegration of his army through desertion. This was certainly the case in 1370 when, unable to pay his men for the last six months of their service, he claimed repassage to England for only 342 men, the rump of a contingent originally 800 strong;[55] in 1373, when his captains began threatening

---

[52] e.g. in 1373, Lancaster contracted to provide 158 knights in a force of 760 men-at-arms. Thomas, earl of Warwick, provided 28 knights among 200 men-at-arms and Hugh, earl of Stafford, only 9 knights among 120 men-at-arms. For a knight commander, the number might be smaller still; Sir William Beauchamp brought only one other knight in his company of 500 for Edmund of Cambridge's expedition in 1381. E. 364/9 mm. 11, 13; E. 43/578.

[53] E. 404/14/96 (20 Feb. 1398); E. 403/556 m. 28.

[54] E. 101/396/13 (43); E. 364/5 m. 5*d*; E. 159/153, Brevia Baronibus, Michaelmas, m. 31*d*.

[55] E. 364/5 m. 5*d*. An analogous example may be Edward, lord Despenser's account for the 1373 campaign; by 17 Dec., his original company of 590 was down to 257 men. E. 364/8 m. 10*d*.

to leave him as soon as they reached Bordeaux, unless they received an immediate 'refreshment';[56] in 1386, when many of his company applied to the Castilians for letters of safe conduct to Bayonne.[57] Faced with desertions on this scale, the dependence the duke could put upon a retainer's continued service was clearly of the greatest importance, since his indenture gave a retainer both a motive for staying loyal and an expectation of eventual repayment denied the ordinary man-at-arms.

Similarly, it was to his indentured retinue that John of Gaunt turned for the solution to a second military problem: how to preserve the French outposts of his estates intact. His initial attempt was not a success, for he leased out his Burgundian possessions of Beaufort and Nogent-sur-Marne to a Welsh mercenary captain, John Wyn, at a farm of £100 p.a., only to find that on the renewal of hostilities in 1369 Wyn saw little hope of maintaining his position and promptly changed sides.[58] Consequently, the duke sought more effective ways of maintaining the loyalty of his distant servants. At La Roche-sur-Yon, in the exposed marches of Poitou, he established his new retainer, the dispossessed Poitevin knight Sir Jean Manburni de Linières, as guardian and gave him a strong interest in keeping the lordship safe by assigning his annuity upon it.[59] At Bergerac, strategically vital for its control of communications along the Dordogne, Heliot Buada the castellan was showered with gifts by the duke[60] and, although the Buada family lost much of their livelihood when the castle fell to the French, they continued to be well rewarded for their constancy by compensatory grants of office in Aquitaine and by the admission of Arnold Buada, son of Heliot, to membership of the duke's retinue.[61] In this way, the Lancastrian affinity served as a means of binding distant castellans more closely to the duke's cause.

At home, the possession of a large indentured retinue enabled the duke to respond with speed and flexibility to the changing demands of royal policy. Campaigns were often planned at short notice, the date and venue for the muster altered at even shorter notice, yet it was

---

[56] BL Cotton Caligula D III f. 118.

[57] F. Lopes, *Crónica de Dom Joao I: segunda parte*, ed, M. Lopes de Almeda and A. de Magalhaes Basto (Porto, 1949), 247; Walsingham, *Hist. Ang.*, ii. 193–4.

[58] DL 25/962; Bodl. MS CCC 495, f. 16; *Froissart (K. de. L.)*, vii. 324–5.

[59] 'Recueil des documents concernant le Poitou contenus dans les registres de la chancellerie de France', ed., P. Guérin, *Archives Historiques du Poitou*, 21 (1891), 181–5; *Reg. I* 786.

[60] C. 61/90 m. 2; DL 28/3/1 m. 4.

[61] SC 8/209/10419; C. 61/101 m. 9, 108 m. 7; *CPR 1396–9*, 522; DL 28/3/5 f. 12.

essential that a man in John of Gaunt's position should set an example of efficiency and reliability and this, in turn, necessitated the possession of large resources of reliable manpower. If it was usually easy to find sufficient subcontractors for any campaign, it was equally easy for the subcontractors to default. Thus, when the Gascon knight Sir William Mountendre engaged Egyn de Nille and twelve archers for the duke's *chevauchée* in 1373, he insisted that de Nille should find two pledges willing to bind themselves and all their goods for the full performance of the contract.[62] Such stringent precautions were quite customary, and indicate the relative likelihood of default on the subcontractor's part, whereas an indentured retainer fulfilling the same role was both less likely to default in the first place and more easily subject to an immediate and effective form of distress, in the termination of his annuity, if he did.

In consequence, the duke could place considerable demands upon his men and expect them to be met. In 1377 so little time was allowed to raise troops for the projected naval expedition of that year that reinforcements from the royal chancery had to be drafted in to help the Lancastrian clerks send out letters of summons to the duke's retainers; hardly had this flurry of abortive activity died down than the duke was ordered to array his retinue again and proceed to the March in order to resist a rumoured Scottish invasion.[63] In 1384, the Lancastrian receivers began sending out letters to the duke's men on 26 February, summoning them for a campaign against the Scots scheduled to be in enemy territory before 10 April. The muster was to be at Newcastle on 24 March but the sheriff of Lancaster received an order to dispatch the archers he had arrayed to the muster as late as 17 March. Despite this short notice, the Lancastrian administration responded with great efficiency, for Gaunt had entered Scotland with his army by 4 April, within six weeks of the original decision to mount an expedition.[64] In this aspect of military organization, at least, the possession of a large indentured retinue gave the duke a definite advantage over other captains. In 1373, for instance, he was required to have his company at the sea by 11 June and, although the port of embarkation was changed at a late stage from Plymouth to Dover, he was there by 17 June

---

[62] E. 101/68/6 (30).
[63] DL 28/3/1 m. 7; E. 403/463 m. 4.
[64] DL 29/262/4070 m. 3; PL 3/1/77; *Westminster Chronicle*, p. 66.

whereas some of the lesser captains were unable to make their muster until early July.[65]

It is only possible to catch an occasional glimpse of what this rapid mobilization could mean for a retainer; to see Sir William Cantilupe unable to complete the enfeoffment of his lands because he had to follow the duke of Lancaster to France in the morning; to find Richard, lord Poynings, hurriedly writing his own will at Plymouth, as the Lancastrian army made ready to sail for Spain.[66] Such scraps of evidence suggest that Gaunt's retainers made every effort to respond promptly to his commands. They did so as a matter of obligation, but not of obligation alone, for the honour of both the duke and his retainers was engaged in the faithful performance of the service he had promised.[67] To the contractual obligation of a man-at-arms to his captain an indenture of retainer added the older and more potent bond between lord and man implicit in the compact of brotherhood-in-arms or the act of feudal homage, demanding the same duties of aid, service, and counsel.[68] Hence a retainer's honour was as much engaged in fulfilling his lord's command to serve with him as it was on the field of battle itself. The public duties of service in the national army were expressed by the indenture in the easily apprehensible terms of private honour. The duke's indentured retinue can be shown to have brought him many practical advantages in the recruitment and deployment of his companies but none were more important, or less tangible, than the effect of the contract between lord and man embodied in a life-indenture in providing the essential means by which the individualistic, even anarchic, ethic of chivalry that every man-at-arms professed could be rendered compatible with the constraints of the military discipline necessary for victory.[69]

This was fortunate, for it was in the conventional terms of chivalric excellence that the duke and his retainers pictured themselves and

---

[65] *Reg. I* 310; E. 364/10 m. 1. John Humbleton and Sir Richard Green, for example, did not arrive until 8 July. E. 364/9 m. 9d, 11 m. 8d.

[66] W. T. Lancaster, *The Early History of Ripley and the Ingleby Family* (Leeds, 1918), pp. 44–5; Lambeth Palace Lib., Reg. Sudbury, f. 223v: '*Escript de ma maine en haste le xvi iour de June a Plimouth . . .*'.

[67] *Reg. I*: 63: '*gardez que vous y soiez alors en toutes maneres, si cher come vous desirez nostre honour et le vostre sauver et garder . . .*'.

[68] M. Keen, 'Brotherhood in Arms', *History*, 47 (1962), 14–15.

[69] e.g. Simon Raly, esquire, undertook to observe his contract with Sir Matthew Gournay '*de son corps et gentilesse d'armes*'. Somerset Record Office, DD Wo 25/1. Prof. R. A. Griffiths kindly brought this document to my attention.

wished to see themselves portrayed. An unimpressed Italian observer described how the English ambassadors entered Bruges in 1375 like a company of men-at-arms, the duke at their head with a hawk on his wrist followed by a small, heavily armed group of knights. The same combative air still hung around the Lancastrian delegation at Amiens in 1392, where the duke's men were simply dressed in habits of dark green—as if, thought the chronicler, deliberately disdaining the pomp of the French.[70] In such an overtly military atmosphere, it was the ideals of knighthood and knightly conduct drawn from the chivalric code that governed the conduct of the Lancastrian affinity: the *hautesse* of the duke himself; the *hardiesse* of Sir Ralph Hastings; the courtesy of Sir Ralph Camoys.[71] These were the virtues held up for imitation and they found some answering echoes in the thoughts and actions of the duke's retainers: the *loyautee* shown by Sir Walter Urswick and Sir John Marmion during the Peasants' Revolt, in staying with their lord *'pur prendre bone ou male quel fyne qe purroit avenir'*;[72] the specific bequests of their arms and harness of war in their wills, the testamentary commemoration of former companions-in-arms.[73] More prosaic transactions were animated by the same spirit; Sir Robert Neville swore to observe the terms of his lease of the castle of Hornby *par ma feoie sicome ieo sui leale chivaler.*[74]

For men who thought like this, honour was only to be obtained by prowess in deeds of arms.[75] Those who could say, as Sir Richard Rowcliffe said of the Scropes, that it would take too long to name all the battles they had been in since their first arming,[76] were assured prestige and honour among their contemporaries. It was an assurance that the duke of Lancaster could afford his retainers in abundance and, for the small, socially various élite of the nobly born and the professional warriors from whom the duke hoped to draw the nucleus

---

[70] G. A. Holmes, *The Good Parliament* (Oxford, 1975), p. 60; *Chronique du Religieux de Saint Denys*, ed. M. Bellaguet (Paris, 1839), i. 739.

[71] *Chandos Herald*, ll. 2243–4, 3295, 2729–30, 2615–16; cf. G. Matthew, 'Ideals of Knighthood in Late Fourteenth-Century England', *Studies in Medieval History Presented to F. M. Powicke* (Oxford, 1948), pp. 354–62.

[72] *The Anonimalle Chronicle 1333 to 1381*, ed. V. H. Galbraith (Manchester, 1927), p. 153.

[73] Guildhall Library, MS 9531/3 f. 395 (Sir John Plays); Borthwick Institute, Bishops' Register XV, f. 12, XVI, f. 142 (Sir Ralph Hastings, Richard, lord Scrope).

[74] Lancashire Record Office, Dd He 21/1.

[75] *Froissart (K. de L.)*, ii. 8: 'ne poet li gentilz homs venir a parfaite honneur ne a la glore dou monde, sans proece'.

[76] *Scrope and Grosvenor*, i. 143.

of his retinue, it constituted the most powerful of incentives to join his service. In his youth, Gaunt had deliberately sought to foster a chivalric ethos among his followers, riding from Reading to London *cum militibus suis* in May 1359, immediately after his marriage to Blanche of Lancaster, and offering combat to all-comers in the joust.[77] Although this literary posturing was replaced, towards the end of the duke's life, by a wary pragmatism towards the great chivalric issue of the day—the Crusade[78]—the Lancastrian court still continued to provide, in such set-pieces as the jousts held at Hertford in 1393,[79] the opportunity for feats of arms, while the duke himself was internationally recognized as an authority on the law of arms and heard with respect when he pronounced on controverted points.[80] Just as important, John of Gaunt's reputation, influence, and wealth meant that his exploits, and the exploits of his retainers, continued to be recounted to English audiences for many years—'for that is a thing that worldly men desiren greatly, that their name might last long after them here upon earth'.[81] It seems very likely, for instance, that *La Vie du Prince Noir*, by the herald of Sir John Chandos, was written in 1386 under Gaunt's patronage, and at his instigation, with the specific intent of glorifying the chivalric triumphs of the duke and his men in the past.[82] Service in his company was, in consequence, intrinsically more honourable than service with a lesser commander; the voyage of Caux and the voyage of the lord of Lancaster all through France crop up in the Scrope vs. Grosvenor depositions almost as often as the last voyage of the late king or the battle of Spain, as cardinal points in English military experience.[83] Chivalry, too, was one of the disciplines of war, for it gave to the heterogeneous collection of fighting men the duke

---

[77] *Chronica Johannis de Reading et Anonymi Cantuariensis 1346–1367*, ed. J. Tait (Manchester, 1914), pp. 131–2.

[78] *L'Apparicion Maistre Jehan de Meun et le Somnium Super Materia Scismatis d'Honoré Bonet*, ed. I. Arnold (Publications de la Faculté des lettres de l'Université de Strasbourg, 28, 1926), p. 92; N. Valois, *La France et le grand schisme d'occident*, iii (Paris, 1901), pp. 620–3.

[79] DL 28/1/4 ff. 6–8.

[80] Walsingham, *Hist. Ang.*, i. 432–3; *Froissart* (*K. de L.*), xii. 121, 123.

[81] *The Works of Sir John Clanvowe*, ed. V. J. Scattergood (Cambridge, 1975), pp. 69–70; cf. J. Fortescue, *The Governance of England*, ed. C. Plummer (Oxford, 1885), p. 130; *The Boke of Noblesse*, ed. J. G. Nichols (Roxburghe Club, 77, 1860), p. 15.

[82] J. J. N. Palmer, 'Froissart et le Héraut Chandos', *Le Moyen Âge*, 88 (1982), 276–7.

[83] By contrast, Lancaster's own St Malo expedition (*Scrope and Grosvenor*, i. 173) or Buckingham's expedition in 1380 (Ibid. 136, 164, 194, 195) are cited only infrequently, which suggests that the deponents were clear enough in their own minds which were the honourable expeditions and which were not.

gathered around himself a common cause, a shared ethic of duty and service.

3. Profit and Loss

A Lancastrian retainer could thus hope to gain honour by his service abroad with the duke but 'the first, essential point of medieval warfare' was allegedly not honour but profit. If many 'retainers made no pretence of fighting for love of king or lord . . . but for gain',[84] could John of Gaunt's retainers expect such gains in his service? The question is part of a larger problem about the relationship between the magnates' military commitments and the growth of their affinities and, ultimately, about the effects of English involvement in the Hundred Years War as a whole. To this problem no satisfactory answer can be given if the account is confined to a calculation of the disbursements and receipts of treasure, without taking into consideration as well the real costs of the conflict, the total material resources diverted or enlarged by prosecution of the wars.[85] Some consideration of the domestic effects of John of Gaunt's military adventures and the charge they laid upon his estates and affinity in England will, therefore, conclude the chapter. First, it must be established whether, and to what extent, the duke himself could expect to profit from his campaigns abroad; whether, indeed, he was ever in a position to pay his retainers what he promised them in their indentures. Did, in fact, 'the lords make profits, often very large, out of their contracts with the government, and enrich themselves with profit and plunder . . . ?'[86]

(i) The Duke

An examination of Gaunt's dealing with the Exchequer has an importance beyond its obvious relevance to the financing of his indentured retinue. The Crown was constantly committed to paying out far greater sums than were ever available at any one time; delay was consequently inevitable and the relative social and political weight of

---

[84] K. B. McFarlane, *The Nobility of Later Medieval England* (Oxford, 1973), pp. 20–1.

[85] M. M. Postan, 'The Costs of the Hundred Years War', *Past and Present*, 27 (1964), 34.

[86] J. Fortescue, *The Governance of England*, ed. C. Plummer (Oxford, 1885), p. 15.

the creditors often decisive in ensuring preferential payment or assignment.[87] John of Gaunt's position could hardly have been stronger in this respect and he made full use of his privileged status. In 1370, the treasurer and barons of the Exchequer were to allow the duke the wages of those he had retained during the campaign, over and above the numbers specified in his indenture; in 1372 they were to allow him wages and double regard for the whole period of his contractual service, even though the campaign had ended within three months; for his 1373 expedition the duke was simply to account for the total number of men-at-arms he engaged, despite the fact he had failed to meet his full quota of bannerets and knights; in 1376 he was pardoned·all sums owing to the Crown.[88] These privileges were fully reflected in Gaunt's favourable treatment by the Exchequer. Over his whole career, he was paid just over £170,000 in wages of war and diplomatic expenses, of which sum no more than 23 per cent was assigned upon a future source of revenue rather than paid in ready cash. Equally, when Gaunt had to accept tallies of assignation instead of cash, the sources of revenue on which the tallies were assigned were notably secure: the clerical subsidy, which was rarely subject to assignation;[89] farms owed the Crown by the duke's own retainers;[90] best of all, the farms the duke himself owed the Crown for the lands of the countess of Pembroke, which effectively reduced the time-consuming business of cashing a tally to a paper transaction.[91] The number of bad tallies Gaunt suffered was consequently low: tallies worth £3,900 were dishonoured, from a total of £39,040. 8s. 2½d. assigned him throughout his career. It is not, perhaps, surprising that in a moment of anger Richard II once accused the duke of thinking always of his own purse and never of the king's.[92] Yet despite these concessions, a summary examination of the duke's war-finances indicates that, during his most active military period, he was often owed large sums by the Crown, part of which he never managed to

---

[87] G. L. Harriss, 'Preference at the Medieval Exchequer', *BIHR* 30 (1957), 17–40.

[88] Cambridge University Library, MS Dd. III. 53 f. 146 (1370); E. 159/153, Brevia Baronibus, Michaelmas, mm. 5 (1372), 31*d.* (1373), 21 (1376).

[89] E. 401/539 (8 Sept.), 550 (6 May), 563 (31 Oct.); A. B. Steel, *The Receipt of the Exchequer 1377–1485* (Cambridge, 1954), p. 43.

[90] E. 401/514 (7 Feb.), 524 (20 June), 545 (22 May).

[91] E. 401/559 (9 Dec., 30 Jan.), 561 (19 June), 565 (10, 12 May); *Anglo-Norman Letters and Petitions*, ed. M. D. Legge (Anglo-Norman Text Soc., 3, 1941), pp. 134–5 for an example of the difficulties the duke occasionally experienced in cashing his assignments.

[92] Walsingham, *Hist. Ang.*, ii. 132.

recover. If the duke of Lancaster could not obtain full payment for his companies, then it must be doubted whether anyone else did.

The Exchequer certainly made every effort to meet its commitments to the duke. He was promptly paid for his company on the king's expedition against Paris[93] and in 1369 received advance prests of nearly £20,000, almost sufficient to cover the whole cost of his company.[94] The expenses of his forces for the naval expedition of 1372 were paid, perhaps overpaid, in advance[95] and, although the prests of £7,500 the duke received in 1378 were insufficient to meet all the expenses of his St Malo expedition,[96] the deficit was soon made good by the generous provision allowed for Gaunt's journeys to the Scottish March in 1380 and 1381. In April 1382, after many of Lancaster's accounts had been lost in the destruction of the Savoy, the sums he owed for the latter expeditions were held to cancel out the sums still owed the duke from 1378; the wording of the writ to the Exchequer suggests that it was Gaunt, not the Crown, who was the debtor.[97]

The Crown's indebtedness to the duke can thus be narrowed down to two campaigns: those of 1370 and 1373. For the great *chevauchée* of 1373 every effort was made to meet the duke's initial expenses and payments, just over £19,000 in cash having been provided by the time his company left Paris, and to transmit his 'refreshments' promptly, but the duration of Gaunt's service abroad was such that he inevitably returned to England with a large claim to be settled: £9,642. 6s. 5d.[98] Large though this sum was, the 1373 expedition was less serious in its

[93] E. 403/403 m. 39, 408 m. 23, 409 m. 5.

[94] E. 361/4 m. 21; E. 403/438 mm. 19, 20, 21, 24, 38. The duke was still owed £275. 10s. 6d. for this campaign in 1376, when the debt was paid off in two assignations, but that may well constitute the full extent of the *superplusagium*. DL 28/3/1 m. 3; E. 403/461 mm. 3, 4; E. 401/523 (23 Oct.).

[95] E. 403/446 mm. 3, 25, 28, 31. The duke had received £6,155. 18s. 0d. by the time the expedition sailed; the earl of Hereford, who brought a company of 300 men-at-arms and 400 archers, claimed expenses of £4,850. 8s. 5d. for this expedition. E. 364/9 m. 14.

[96] E. 403/462 mm. 15, 19, 468 mm. 15, 18, 19; E. 401/524 (20 June). This included payments for the abortive 1377 expedition.

[97] E. 404/12/78 (5 Sept.); E. 403/478 m. 26; E. 401/539 (8 Sept.) [1380], E. 403/484 m. 3; E. 401/541 (10 May) [1381]; E. 159/158, Brevia Baronibus, Easter m. 12; *The Antient Kalendars and Inventories of the Treasury of His Majesty's Exchequer*, ii. 12 for Gaunt's reciprocal relaxation. It is worth noting that the true cost of Gaunt's force in 1380 (£3,280) was rather less than half the 11,000 marks Thomas Walsingham suggests; Walsingham, *Hist. Ang.*, i. 446–7.

[98] E. 403/447 (5, 23 Mar.), 449 mm. 4, 11; BL Add MS 37494, ff. 2d–7, 38; Cotton Caligula D III, f. 118; E. 159/153, Brevia Baronibus, Michaelmas, m. 31d. for the total *superplusagium*.

financial consequences for the duke than his term of service in Aquitaine as the prince of Wales's lieutenant. Unable for political reasons to levy any impost on the Gascons themselves, Gaunt returned home with a claim of nearly £12,500 outstanding at the Exchequer.[99]

How reliable was the Exchequer in settling these debts? If there is any evidence of default, then the ability to dispose of large sums of Crown revenue that the captains enjoyed in the short term must be balanced by the accumulation of long-standing and unsatisfied claims against the Crown in respect of their military service. In the case of the Aquitaine *superplusagium*, it is true that the duke received steady, if piecemeal, sums in repayment from the Exchequer, but in October 1376, five years after relinquishing his lieutenancy, he was still owed nearly £5,000 when he finally secured a large assignment for the liquidation of the outstanding debt.[100] Such assignments had, throughout, been the Exchequer's favoured method of financing the expedition. Altogether, £13,656. 6s. 4½d. of the £30,975. 19s. 10d. the duke received for his lieutenancy in Aquitaine was initially paid in tallies rather than in cash[101] and, although the level of bad tallies was low,[102] this method of payment further reduced the ready cash at the duke's disposal and rendered him still more dependent on the patience and loyalty of his followers. By contrast, the duke's company for the *chevauchée* of 1373 was financed entirely in ready money but, perhaps as a result, it was not until November 1376 that the barons of the Exchequer were ordered to account with the duke and, although he received £4,669. 18s. 10d. towards a settlement of the sum owed him over the next four years, no further payments towards the outstanding £4,972. 7s. 7d. are recorded.[103] On the face of it, therefore, John of Gaunt's position as chief English war-captain during the 1370s left him with sizeable and long-unsatisfied debts.

Was this, in fact, the case? Even if the accounts Gaunt presented at the Exchequer represent an accurate summary of his expenditure—a large assumption but one that must be made in the absence of any

---

[99] E. 404/10/64 (12 Feb. 1370); *Issue Roll of Thomas Brantingham, 1370*, ed. F. Devon (London, 1835), pp. 444, 494, 99, 140, 157, 165; E. 403/444 mm. 26, 29, for payments for this expedition; E. 364/5 m. 5d. for the total *superplusagium*.

[100] E. 403/447 (25 Jan., 22 Mar.), 449 m. 4, 451 m. 21, 454 m. 14, 461 mm. 2, 3.

[101] E. 401/500 (15 Feb.), 501 (22 May, 15 June), 514 (7 Feb.), 523 (11 Oct.).

[102] Tallies worth only £1,100 of the total issued were dishonoured; E. 403/444 m. 15, 462 m. 3 for their satisfaction.

[103] E. 159/153, Brevia Baronibus, Michaelmas, m. 24d; E. 403/461 m. 24, 468 m. 13, 472 m. 14.

other evidence—the duke could always hope to pass on the burden of Crown debt to his retainers by delaying, or defaulting on, the payment of *their* wages. One chronicler claimed, for instance, that Gaunt delayed paying his troops for so long in 1378 that, *urgente penuria*, they turned to plundering the English countryside.[104] The duke's private accounts certainly reveal the existence of some large debts to his followers, many of whom had a long wait for their money. Roger Wodrington, a Northumbrian esquire, was still owed money for the wages of his company on the expedition of 1359/60 in November 1368, even though the duke himself had been paid in full by October 1361.[105] Members of Lancaster's household were still owed more than £3,500 for the Aquitaine campaign in March 1372, when Sir Michael de la Pole had a claim outstanding from 1369; Thomas, lord Roos, was still being paid for his service in 1373/4 in 1377.[106] Yet although such delays in the payment of his retainers' wages cushioned the effect of the Crown's default, John of Gaunt's own ability to default, whether deliberately or involuntarily, was limited by his need to raise another company for the next campaign; whereas the duke could hardly refuse to serve abroad at the king's command, those who had previously campaigned with him could seek another, and more satisfactory, paymaster.

Before each expedition, therefore, clerks were installed at the Savoy and instructed to meet the outstanding claims of those serving with the duke on his current campaign.[107] The evidence suggests that this practice was carefully observed: Thomas, lord Roos, received payment for his company in 1369 by April 1370; Sir Richard Scrope was paid for his service in Aquitaine in August 1372, as he marched through Canterbury on his way to the duke's muster at Sandwich; the duke ordered in May 1373 that all outstanding debts to Sir Michael de la Pole should be paid off before the coming campaign.[108] His room for financial manœuvre was, therefore, severely limited by his continued military commitments and, while the testimony of his private accounts served to convict Thomas, duke of Gloucester, of malversation,[109] John of Gaunt's effectively clear him of the same charge by

---

[104] *Chronicon Angliae*, p. 195.
[105] DL 29/354/5837 m. 1.
[106] *Reg. I* 969, 1107; DL 28/3/1 m. 7.
[107] BL Harleian MS 3988 f. 39.
[108] Bodl. MS CCC 495, f. 15; E. 403/446 m. 31; *Reg. I* 1320.
[109] McFarlane, *Nobility*, p. 26.

demonstrating the reality of his financial difficulties. In Aquitaine, particularly, the duke was reduced to a variety of expedients in an unsuccessful attempt to keep his company together: sending to his receiver-general in England for 'refreshments', borrowing from the earl of Arundel and from his own retainers, even taking the humiliating step of asking Gaston Fébus, count of Foix, for a loan.[110]

The consequences of these debts were severe and lasting. In 1372, the duke levied a gracious aid from his tenants *'pur la grant necessite que nous avons au present'* and again borrowed money, from the earl of Arundel and John, lord Neville.[111] In 1373, he had to finance his company from payments made by the Exchequer towards the outstanding debts of 1370.[112] One way to avoid such immediate financial embarrassment was for the duke to mortgage his future estate revenues, by offering a preferential lease in lieu of the wages of war he owed. Adam Newsome, a Lancashire esquire, was thus allowed a respite of 10 marks p.a. from the rent he paid for the herbage of the park of Mirescogh until the sum outstanding from his service in Aquitaine was paid off.[113] Newsome was probably happy enough with the arrangement, which gave him a secure reflex assignment for his claim, but for John of Gaunt it meant that his private estate revenues had been diminished in order to meet a debt contracted in the royal service. Far from offering him fat profits, Lancaster's contracts with the Crown during the 1370s seem to have involved him in some substantial financial loss.

Yet if he was not a profiteer, it would be unrealistic to view his actions as the product of a simple-minded patriotism. Strictly financial calculations of profit and loss were less important to the duke than the political advantage to which such claims against the Crown could be turned. He continued to serve abroad because his service there, and still more the debts that accumulated from that service, gave him an invaluable political lever, a potent means to confound his critics at court and in the country. During the Good Parliament, when his associates, Latimer, Neville, and Lyons, all stood accused of reaping illegitimate profits at the Crown's expense, Lancaster himself was owed nearly £15,000 for five years of war service. He, at least, could

[110] *Reg. I* 1038, 941, 919; P. Tucoo-Chala, *Gaston Fébus et la vicomté de Béarn* (Bordeaux, 1959), pp. 353, 403.
[111] *Reg. I* 231–45, 162–3.
[112] Ibid. 1336.
[113] Ibid. 1225, 1233.

not be accused of '*singuler profit et mal governail entour le Roi*'.[114] Similarly, in 1380 the duke was able to effect a swift political coup at the expense of his brother, the earl of Buckingham, by writing off 5,000 marks of Crown debt in return for a grant of the marriage of Mary Bohun, daughter and co-heiress of the last earl of Hereford, which eventually brought estates worth over £900 p.a. to the heritage of Lancaster.[115]

This suggests that there were still profits to be made from warfare in the late fourteenth century but that, at least for John of Gaunt, the connection between service and profit had become indirect and now depended as much upon a captain's political standing in England as upon his success or failure in the field of battle. The connection between domestic politics and the advantages the duke gained from his military service remained as close in the 1380s as it had been in the previous decade, although it now manifested itself rather differently. The March days of 1380 and 1381 were both adequately financed and, although the loss of Gaunt's accounts for the March day of 1383 and his expedition in 1384 preclude any accurate assessment of his financial position, the duke was paid large prests promptly on both occasions.[116] For the king's campaign in Scotland the following year, the initial prests the duke received proved insufficient to meet the costs of his company, but his consequent claim against the Crown was satisfied by an assignation in May 1386[117] while, for the time he spent stationed on the Isle of Thanet in August 1383, ostensibly preparing to go to the aid of bishop Despenser, the duke was not only paid in full, but also received an additional reward from the Crown for his vigilance.[118] John of Gaunt's financial dealings with the Crown thus improved as his political stock dropped. In part, this was due to the generally healthier state of royal finances by the 1380s but, equally, just as Gaunt himself had been careful to give his opponents no pretext

---

[114] G. L. Harriss, 'Cardinal Beaufort, Patriot or Usurer?', *TRHS* 5th series, 20 (1970), 143–5.

[115] *CPR 1377–81*, 537; G. A. Holmes, *The Estates of the Higher Nobility*, p. 25.

[116] 1383: E. 404/13/86 (4 May); E. 403/496 m. 5; E. 401/550 (6 May); 1384: E. 403/499 m. 17; E. 401/553 (3 Mar.). This tally, for £800, was dishonoured but paid in full by 25 Oct. 1384; E. 403/502 m. 16, 505 m. 15; E. 404/13/89 (9 Dec.); E. 403/505 m. 15; E. 401/559 (9 Dec.) for payment to the duke of his arrears on this expedition.

[117] E. 403/508 mm. 12, 13, 22; E. 401/561 (19 June); E. 403/570 m. 6, 572 m. 3; E. 401/563 (31 Oct.), 565 (10, 12 May). The assignations were not, however, entirely satisfactory. £371. 0s. 0d. of the sum assigned 19 June 1385 was never cashed and a new tally was issued 27 Nov. 1400.

[118] E. 101/39/29; E. 403/499 mm. 14, 17: M. E. Aston, 'The Impeachment of Bishop Despenser', *BIHR* 38 (1965), 143–7.

for attack while he controlled the court, so Richard II and his courtiers were now anxious to deny the duke any legitimate ground for complaint. This was a development which reached its culmination in 1386, when Gaunt was effectively paid to go away by the king. Apart from the 20,000 marks the duke received as a gift from the parliamentary subsidy of October 1385, Richard personally loaned him a further 20,000 marks towards the cost of his Castilian expedition. The loan was to be repaid in full if the duke concluded a private peace with Castile but, in the event of his doing precisely that, the obligation was cancelled, which meant that Lancaster had received just over £26,000 from the Exchequer towards the cost of his own dynastic ambitions.[119]

To these sums must, of course, be added the £100,000 indemnity the duke received on his conclusion of the treaty with Castile and the promise of an annual pension of £6,600 p.a.[120] Clearly, the profits that John of Gaunt derived from his military and diplomatic commitments during the 1380s were very substantial, far outweighing the losses he had sustained during the previous decade. Moreover, the duke's prominent role in diplomatic negotiations with the French and the Scots enabled him to go on drawing a steady income from the Exchequer to the very end of his life. Between May 1391 and June 1394, for instance, Lancaster drew over £6,500 in cash from the Exchequer for peace negotiations with the French,[121] for half of which he was granted the unusual privilege of exoneration from account.[122] Equally, after his creation as duke of Aquitaine in May 1391, Gaunt received an annual payment from the Exchequer for the defence of the duchy—varying between 9,000 marks when the duchy was on a war-footing[123] and 5,500 marks at other times[124]—which totalled more

---

[119] E. 403/572 m. 26; *Foedera*, vii. 495; *A Calendar of the Register of Henry Wakefield, Bishop of Worcester 1375–1395*, ed. W. P. Marett (Worcs. Hist. Soc., NS 8 1972), no. 807. In order to make the loan, the king had to borrow over £5,000, at 33% interest, from the Bardi and a group of Iberian merchants; *CPR 1385–9*, 147. *Rot. Parl.*, iii. 313 for the earl of Arundel's protest against the cancellation of this obligation.

[120] P. E. Russell, *The English Intervention*, p. 506.

[121] E. 403/533 m. 6, 536 mm. 13, 21, 22, 541 mm. 17, 22, 543 mm. 5, 14, 546 m. 22, 548 mm. 1, 6, 13.

[122] £3,287. 6s. 8d. to be exact. DL 42/11 f. 73; E. 159/173, Brevia Baronibus, Trinity, m. 6d. For earlier exonerations from accounts granted to the duke in Feb. 1385 and Nov. 1386; E. 159/161, Brevia Baronibus, Trinity, m. 2, 162, Brevia Baronibus, Michaelmas, m. 20d.

[123] E. 403/532 m. 15 (1391); 548 m. 20, 549 mm. 6, 14; E. 401/596 (7 Dec. 1394).

[124] E. 403/559 m. 5; E. 401/609 (22 May 1398). £1,000 dishonoured and reassigned 8 Jan. 1399; E. 403/561 m. 11; E. 401/611.

than £27,000 in all.[125] Precisely what happened to this large sum remains something of a mystery. £4,000 was paid directly into the hands of Sir Henry Percy, appointed the duke's lieutenant in the duchy in 1393,[126] but the fate of the remainder is hard to trace. While there is no evidence that the money was put to any purpose but the defence of the duchy,[127] the duke of Lancaster enjoyed, at the very least, a rare and privileged flexibility in disposing of large sums from the Exchequer for which he did not have to render strict account.

Taking his career as a whole, therefore, it seems plain that John of Gaunt's gains of war far outweighed the losses he sustained during the 1370s, although these losses were serious enough to cause him temporary financial embarrassment and to create genuine difficulties over the payment of his retainers for their service. The duke's gains were, moreover, rather the result of his abilities as a diplomat and politician than as a soldier, made at the expense of the Exchequer as much as of the French. It remains to be seen if warfare could be as profitable for those less adept at winning the peace.

---

[125] Aquitaine payments not specified elsewhere: E. 403/536 m. 7; E. 401/584 m. 7; E. 403/541 m. 2; E. 401/589 (22 Oct.); E. 403/541 m. 4; E. 401/589 (6 Nov.); E. 403/541 mm. 8, 12, 543 mm. 12, 19; E. 401/592 (4 June, 23 July), 602 (7 July); E. 403/555 (12 May); E. 401/606 (12 May).

[126] E. 403/543 mm. 9, 19, 546 m. 24; E. 401/592 (23 July), 593 (11 Mar.); *Anglo-Norman Letters and Petitions*, pp. 254–5.

[127] 'Annales Ricardi Secundi et Henrici Quarti', J. de Trokelowe et anon., *Chronica et Annales*, ed. H. T. Riley (Rolls Series, 1866), p. 188; Walsingham, *Hist. Ang.*, ii. 219 for the huge sums the duke is said to have spent in Gascony. The evidence of Gaunt's private accounts seems, at first sight, to contradict this assertion. In 1392/3 the receiver-general accounted for £2,773. 3s. 5½d. received for the custody of Aquitaine and £243. 15s. 0d. expended for the defence of the duchy (DL 28/3/2 ff. 4, 4v, 14v). In 1394/5 £7,298. 19s. 8d. was received from the Exchequer in payments to the duke for his Calais negotiations and the custody of Aquitaine, but no payments for Aquitaine appear in the receiver-general's certificate of account (DL 28/32/21). The case is not as damning as it looks. The receipts recorded in 1392/3 were all Crown arrears on the previous year's custody, running from 1 June 1391. The receiver's financial year ran from 2 Feb. 1392, so that his expenditure on Aquitaine represents a period of only four months. The account for 1394/5 presents a more difficult problem, but the exceptionally high level of household expenditure (£5,955 compared to just under £2,500 in 1396/7) and the rapid escalation in the treasurer of the household's expenses in the second half of the year, during which time the duke and his company left for Aquitaine (£5,146. 0s. 0d. compared to £708. 5s. 0d.) points to the treasurer doubling as treasurer of war, as Thomas Ampcotes had done in 1370. This hypothesis would explain why no receipts for Aquitaine appear in the receiver-general's account for 1396/7 (DL 28/3/5) although £2,000 in cash and tallies was issued at the Exchequer. The money was paid into the hands of Nicholas Usk, then Treasurer, who must have accounted separately (E. 403/555 (12 May)).

(ii) His Retainers

Did the men under his command fare as well as their captain? It seems, at first sight, unlikely. Most of the duke's military career took place after the golden age of easy pickings had passed, when the tide of war was running against the English. After Nájera, Lancaster and his men took part in no more great victories and the duke's campaigns in 1373 and 1386 ended, in the chroniclers' eyes at least, in *débâcles* of desertion and heavy mortality.[128] As individuals, his retainers did not possess, in relation to the duke, the privileged position that Gaunt possessed in relation to the Crown. In consequence, they were exposed to a double danger: default by the Exchequer, which meant that the duke inevitably passed on the debts of the Crown to his own men, and default by the duke himself. Yet if there was little profit to be drawn from the wars, it is possible that the obligation of military service on which the duke insisted was neither welcomed nor willingly accepted by his retainers. Evidence from the early fifteenth century suggests that service in the companies of the nobility, in particular the cost of horses and war-harness, constituted a heavy call upon the incomes of the gentry.[129] In the case of those who were already retainers of the duke this problem could, admittedly, be met by advance payments from the treasurer of war[130] but this did no more than postpone the very considerable expenditure necessary for those going on campaign.[131]

The first source from which a retainer might hope to recoup this expenditure, and the one for which most information survives, was his wages of war. The terms John of Gaunt offered his men were, in this respect, consistently generous. His indentures invariably offered a retainer the same wages of war as the duke himself received for his retainer's service from the Crown, in contrast to some other captains who sought to make an additional profit when they raised their companies by paying the troops they engaged less for their service than

---

[128] R. Delachenal, *Histoire de Charles V* (Paris, 1909–31), iv. 499–500 (1373); López de Ayala, *Crónica del rey Don Juan I*, ed. E. Llaguno y Amirola (Madrid, 1780), ii. 251, 263; F. Lopes, *Crónica de Dom Joao I: segunda parte*, 229–30, 259 (1386).

[129] A. Goodman, 'Responses to Requests in Yorkshire for Military Service under Henry V', *Northern History*, 17 (1981), 240–52.

[130] PRO 30/26/71, no. 17 (1370); *Reg. I* 445, 934 (1372).

[131] e.g. the duke lent his bachelor, Sir Richard Abberbury, £200 in order to allow him to accompany Henry of Derby to Prussia. DL 28/3/2 f. 6v.

the sum they received from the Exchequer.[132] In addition, a Lancastrian retainer could be sure that, by virtue of his lord's position as a royal duke, the campaigns on which he served would be both prestigious and well paid. By the 1370s, a clear scale of both payment and esteem had been worked out for the various types of military service available. Bottom of the list came garrison-duty, for which accustomed wages and regard were paid;[133] slightly above these rates were those offered for service at sea, accustomed wages with regard and a half,[134] which Gaunt's companies received for the St Malo expedition and his privately financed Castilian campaign.[135] More lucrative, as well as more prestigious in chivalric terms, were the great expeditions against mainland France and Lancaster's position in England ensured that he would often receive command of such campaigns. The precise rate of payment varied: soldiers serving in 1369 received accustomed wages and regard and half as much again; those serving in 1372 and 1373 wages and double regard, which was the rate Gaunt was offered by the Crown for his projected campaign in 1388 as well.[136] Only service in Aquitaine, which offered double wages and regard, was more lucrative but the length of service demanded there was usually longer and the fighting harsher—a theatre of combat best left to the professional.[137]

On top of the wages and regard paid by the Crown must be added the premium Gaunt was prepared to pay in order to secure the services of a retainer. This could be very substantial: John, lord Neville, received a regard of 500 marks a year for himself and a company of 40; Sir Hugh Hastings was promised 250 marks for a company half that size; Sir Walter Penhergerd, a Cornishman with considerable experience in the principality of Aquitaine, received an annual regard of 40 marks

[132] J. W. Sherborne, 'Indentured Retinues and English Expeditions to France, 1369–1380', *EHR* 79 (1964), 742–3; S. Walker, 'Profit and Loss in the Hundred Years War: The Subcontracts of Sir John Strother, 1374', *BIHR* 58 (1985), 100–6.

[133] e.g. E. 101/68/6 (143), 7 (168), 8 (175). From *c.*1375, this was increased to accustomed wages and regard and a half; E. 101/68/9 (219), 10 (228).

[134] E. 101/68/7 (149, 150, 153), etc.

[135] E. 101/37/27 (43); E. 101/68/10 (250*B*).

[136] 1369: E. 101/68/4 (87); 1372: E. 101/68/5 (95); 1373: E. 101/68/6 (120, 121, 126); 1388: E. 159/166, Brevia Baronibus, Trinity, m. 16*d*.

[137] John, earl of Pembroke, was to receive this rate for six months service in Aquitaine in 1372, then wages and double regard for a further six months service in France. E. 364/5 m. 5*d*; E. 101/68/5 (103). For the quality of the fighting in Aquitaine cf. *Froissart* (*K. de L.*), vii. 435: 'Or retourons nous un petit as besoignes des lointaines marches, car li chevalier et li escuier i avoient plus souvent a faire . . . pour les guerres i estoient plus caudes.'

from the duke in time of war, on top of his accustomed wages, but was paid no peacetime fee at all.[138] The payment of a higher fee in war than peace was an incentive the duke frequently offered a new retainer—out of a total of 157 extant indentures, 39 offer a higher fee in war than peace and 14 offer no fee other than accustomed household wages, which effectively constitutes a higher rate of pay in time of war.[139] Most contracts of this type date from 1372, when Gaunt was making plans for the invasion of Castile to which his recent alliance with Portugal had committed him.[140] It was a time when military manpower was much in demand and the duke was forced to bid high to secure the experienced military service he needed. Once concluded, however, an indenture was binding for life, so a number of the duke's retainers were able to enjoy, on a long-term basis, advantages that had served only a temporary purpose for the duke himself.

John of Gaunt was thus, in theory, a generous captain. In practice his payment of war-wages to his men was often dilatory and erratic and the income to be gained from this source was never to be relied upon. The reasons for this state of affairs have already been examined; during the 1370s Gaunt was owed considerable sums for past expeditions by the Exchequer, with grave consequences for his own financial position. With the best will in the world the duke could hardly be prompt or full in his payments. After 1388, however, the case was altered; the duke's Castilian indemnity and pension provided him with ample means to meet the claims against him promptly. This did not always happen. Some retainers were fortunate and received relatively rapid settlement of their claims[141] but the duke's general practice was to assign these debts, even very small ones, on an English receivership,

---

[138] Lewis, no. 3; Appendix III, no. I; *Reg. I* 784. The regards of Neville and Hastings were offered, exceptionally, instead of, rather than in addition to, those offered by the crown. They were, nevertheless, well above the Crown rate, which would have been 265⅔ marks in Neville's case; A. E. Prince, 'The Indenture System under Edward III', *Historical Essays in Honour of James Tait*, ed. J. G. Edwards, V. H. Galbraith, and E. F. Jacob (Manchester, 1933), p. 293.

[139] *Reg. II* 31, 33–7, 42–4, 50–2; Appendix III, nos. 3, 18.

[140] E. Perroy, *L'Angleterre et le grand schisme d'occident*, p. 212; P. E. Russell, *The English Intervention*, p. 192.

[141] e.g. Sir John Trailly was paid £154 of the £213 owed him for his wages of war within a year; Sir Robert Rockley had received all but £100 of the £441. 7s. 0d. owed him by 1392/3. In all, receivers on the Lancastrian auditors' southern circuit paid out £1,319. 13s. 8d. in wages of Spain in 1387/8 alone. DL 29/728/11975 m. 1; DL 28/3/2 f. 14.

where they would be met as swiftly as the other demands on the receiver's resources allowed.[142] This was not, as it happened, very swift, and it was clearly a long time before some of his retainers saw the money owing to them—Sir Thomas Fogg received £20 in wages of Spain from the duke's receiver in Sussex during his first year back in England, a small proportion of the £575. 14s. 10d. of debts owing to him that were assigned on the lordship.[143]

Even under the most favourable circumstances, therefore, when the duke was in a position to fulfil his financial undertakings, the gains a retainer could expect to make from his wages of war alone were uncertain and, in the difficult financial conditions of the 1370s, they might be non-existent. Paradoxically, the surest way to gain preferential repayment for the last campaign was to serve with the duke on the next. Sometimes, this was the *only* way: in July 1373, Gaunt ordered his treasurer of war to cease honouring all bills from the Aquitaine campaign, save to those accompanying him on his current voyage.[144] On the evidence available, it seems unlikely that any of the duke's followers made a living, let alone a fortune, from their wages of war. The one certain payment was the first quarter of a year's wages and regard, and much of that might be absorbed in the purchase of new armour and harness of war. Beyond that, experience taught that it was foolish to expect too much. It may be said, in mitigation, that a Lancastrian retainer enjoyed a better chance of repayment while serving under the duke than with some other commanders.[145] Nevertheless, an indenture of retainer served, in this respect, less to maximize the profits than to cushion the losses occasioned by service abroad with the duke.

Wages of war were not, of course, the only, nor the most important source of gain open to the duke's retainers. A tidy sum could, in theory, be cleared by those Lancastrians who brought companies of their own on the duke's expeditions, provided they could persuade

[142] Sir Thomas Neville's outstanding claim was, for instance, paid over a five-year period; DL 43/15/6 m. 6; DL 29/728/11980 m. 2.

[143] *Reg. II* 1236; DL 29/728/11975 m. 1.

[144] *Reg. I* 1749.

[145] Sir Robert Greenacres, Gaunt's castellan at La Roche-sur-Yon, was still petitioning the king in 1386 for the payment of sums owed him from the Nájera campaign; the duke's esquire, Thomas Maistreson, never recovered the wages of war the prince of Wales owed him; his retainer, Thomas Driffield, was forced to compound a claim for over £2,500 in wages of war against the Crown for a down payment of 400 marks in 1376. *Froissart* (*K. de L.*), viii, 218; C. 81/1353 (72); BL Harleian MS 2119 f. 42d; E. 403/461 m. 20.

their men to serve at wages of war below the Crown rates. Evidence on this score is so scanty that no firm conclusion can be reached, but there is enough to suggest that this kind of profiteering was not always a recourse open to the duke's men. Sir William Mountendre offered Egyn de Nille and his archers the Crown rate in 1373;[146] Sir Hugh Shirley offered his archers the rate he was paid by the duke for service in Spain in 1386.[147] In 1394, however, Sir Matthew Gournay offered Simon Raly, esquire, only £40 for a year's service—an agreement which would have left him with a handsome profit if he received from the duke payment at the standard Aquitaine rate.[148] Much larger sums were, though, to be made at the expense of the enemy, in plunder from the countryside and the ransoms of captured prisoners. The gains to be made under this head have been the subject of considerable speculation among historians but the evidence available for John of Gaunt and his retainers suggests that, here too, the reality was much less enticing.

In principle the duke was, again, a generous captain. Like virtually every other commander, he usually laid claim to a third of all the profits of war acquired by the men under his command,[149] but, in the case of favoured individuals, he was prepared to waive even these customary demands. His indenture with Sir Thomas Percy in 1386, for instance, initially included all the standard ransom provisions, with the added stipulation that the duke was to have all prisoners worth over 10,000 francs in ransom, on payment of that sum to his captor, but within a month of the original contract these conditions had been cancelled entirely, except that the duke was to have possession of any commander or member of the Castilian royal family captured.[150]

Were the duke's retainers able to turn this generosity to practical advantage? In general terms, a number of John of Gaunt's campaigns seem to have been profitable ones. In 1369, plunder from the devastated French countryside was loaded on to the ships that followed the duke on his raid along the Normandy coast; fortresses were gained

[146] E. 101/68/6 (130).

[147] Leicestershire Record Office, 26 D 53/2543.

[148] Somerset Record Office, DD Wo 25/1.

[149] D. Hay, 'The Division of the Spoils of War in Fourteenth-Century England', *TRHS* 4th series, 4 (1954), 96–8; *Reg. I* 782, 788, 789, 868, Lewis, nos. 10–14, 18 specifically assign a third to the duke. In two cases, the duke claims a half of his retainers' profits but, on both occasions, this higher proportion is only to be paid if the retainer claimed compensation for horses lost in the duke's service; if he did not, the duke would claim only the customary third. *Reg. I* 832; Lewis, no. 2.

[150] E. 101/68/10 (250*B*); SC 1/51/26.

and granted out and some wealthy prisoners taken.[151] In 1370 the sack of Limoges produced a heavy crop of captives to be ransomed and the duke's subsequent lieutenancy in Aquitaine certainly brought his men some plunder from the countryside.[152] The *chevauchée* of 1373 went down in English tradition as a profitable one; some valuable prisoners were taken and the duke's treasurer of war was able to issue some small 'refreshments' from the countryside.[153] Gaunt's attack on St Malo in 1386 was thought to have brought him 'great booty' and even Castile, considered a less satisfactory campaigning-ground than France by the duke's soldiery, yielded some prisoners and profitable *appatis* from the towns of Galicia.[154] There are, therefore, reasonably good grounds for supposing that the gains of war still offered some chance of profit to those retainers obliged by their indenture to serve abroad with the duke, but it is hard to be more precise, for concrete evidence of such gains is noticeably thin. Gaunt himself was lucky enough to capture the *mayordomo* of the Aragonese king at Nájera; his retainer, Sir John Dageney, took Sir Jean de Neufville, a nephew of the Maréchal d'Audrehem, in the same battle and sold him to the duke for a large sum.[155] Sir William Beauchamp took a valuable prisoner on the *chevauchée* of 1373 and the duke purchased a number of other prisoners from members of his company.[156] Yet even in these cases, when the captors were assured of *some* profit from their engagement, the size of this profit could be disappointingly small. Gaunt eventually sold his claim on Don Pedro Jordan, the *mayordomo*, to Sir Hugh Calveley for a tenth of the 10,000 gold *doblas* he had originally claimed and, having purchased Sir Jean de Neufville from Dageney, found considerable difficulty in getting any ransom out of him.[157]

---

[151] Pierre Cochon, *Chronique Normande*, ed. C. de Robillard de Beaurepaire (Société de l'histoire de Normandie, Rouen, 1870), pp. 123–4; *CPR 1367–70*, 297; E. 30/256; C. 81/936 (47), 938 (29).

[152] F. Lehoux, *Jean de France, Duc de Berri* (Paris, 1964), i. 246 n. 1; *Calendar of Papal Registers, Letters 1362–1404*, 95–6.

[153] *The Brut*, ed. F. W. D. Brie, (EETS, os 126, 1908), ii. 326; *CPR 1374–7*, 138; E. 368/9 mm. 9*d*, 13, 10 m. 1. The sums are very small, adding up to £242. 14*s*. 6*d*., but this takes no account of how much never reached the treasurer of war.

[154] Walsingham, *Hist. Ang.*, ii. 143, *Chronicon Henrici Knighton*, ii. 209; Lopes, *Crónica de Dom Joao I: segunda parte*, 239–40; Froissart (K. de L.), xi. 386–7, xii. 86–7, 90, 297; *Reg. II* 1231–2.

[155] A. Gutierrez de Velasco, *Los Ingleses en España (Siglo XIV): Estudios de edad media de la corona de Aragón: Sección de Zaragoza*, iv (Saragossa, 1950), pp. 284–8; *Chandos Herald*, 1. 3409; Bodl. MS CCC 495, f. 15.

[156] C. 61/86 m. 8; *Reg. I* 76, 171.

[157] Gutierrez, op. cit. 286; C. 76/57 m. 5—he eventually sold out his claim to William, lord Latimer.

Against such uncertain gains of war must be set the evidence that many of the duke's retainers had themselves been taken prisoner, and suffered financial hardship in consequence. Gaunt's banneret, Sir Michael de la Pole, reminded the Commons that he had twice been taken prisoner in the French wars and Sir Robert Swillington, Sir Edmund Pierrepoint, and Sir John Botiller had all been put to ransom at some stage in their careers.[158] The duke's own campaigns were no exception: Sir Hugh Hastings was captured in Spain in 1367; Sir Thomas Fogg and a number of other English captains fell into the hands of the enemy in 1373 and were still unable to pay their ransoms three years later; some of the duke's company in Spain were taken prisoner and compelled to pay heavily for their release.[159] Nor was the Scottish border a happier theatre of operations for Gaunt's men: Sir William Swynburn was captured by the Scots at the taking of Wark castle and Ralph, baron Greystoke, put to a ransom of 1,000 marks by the earl of Dunbar while in the duke's service.[160] Such misfortunes directly affected the duke himself for, as captain of a company, he was under a moral obligation to contribute towards the ransom of those captured under his command,[161] yet his provisions for their aid could involve him, as well as his retainer, in financial loss; having paid 4,000 francs in aid of Sir Matthew Gournay's ransom from the French in 1395, for instance, he had great difficulty in recovering the money from Gournay's sureties.[162] The duke continued to pay, however,[163] for the obligation upon him was as much prudential as moral and the consequences could be severe if he did not. Thus, when the duke's Poitevin clerk, Guyon Grassin, was captured in Picardy during the *chevauchée* of 1373 and put to a ransom of 120 francs, Gaunt's failure to redeem his retainer within a month, as he had undertaken to do in his indenture with Guyon, was used by the clerk as a pretext for defecting to the French and, more seriously, revealing enough of the

---

[158] *Rot. Parl.*, iii. 217*a*; *Issues of the Exchequer, Henry III–Henry VI*, ed. F. Devon (Record Comm., 1837), p. 157; W. Dugdale, *The Baronage of England* (1675), ii. 458; W. Beamont, *Annals of the Lords of Warrington* (Chetham Society, os 86, 1872), i. 213; cf. SC 6/773/6 m. 2*d* for a payment towards this ransom.

[159] *Froissart* (*K. de L.*), vii. 179; *Anonimalle Chronicle*, p. 74; *Rot. Parl.*, ii. 343; *Collectanea Topographica et Genealogica*, ed. J. G. Nichols (London, 1836), iii. 101.

[160] J. Hodgson, *A History of Northumberland*, II. i (Newcastle, 1827), p. 215; *Northern Petitions*, ed. C. M. Fraser (Surtees Soc., 194, 1981), nos. 115–17; BL Harleian MS 3988, ff. 41*d*–42.

[161] M. H. Keen, *The Laws of War in the Late Middle Ages* (London, 1965), pp. 150–1; SC 8/118/5878 for an invocation of this obligation, addressed to Lancaster.

[162] DL 28/3/5 f. 4v.

[163] *CPR 1389–92*, 309; DL 28/3/5 f. 19 for more examples of Gaunt's aid towards the ransoms of his men.

duke's plan of campaign to earn a full remission of his ransom from Charles V.[164]

No final balance of profit and loss can be struck from such scraps of information but they yield, at the least, some grounds for scepticism over the gains of war available to John of Gaunt's retainers. In one area of the duke's activities, Aquitaine, these doubts can be more thoroughly substantiated. Lancaster spent four tours of duty in the duchy—in 1370, 1374, 1388/9, and 1394/5—but he was unable, on any of these occasions, to draw the same rewards from his service there as his brother, the prince of Wales, had done. The prince was himself largely to blame for this, for Froissart alleges that one of the chief grievances of the Gascons against his rule was the pride of his officials and the monopoly of office in the duchy by the English. Both these abuses continued to create friction after the prince's return to England[165] and the duke's grants of office and pension during his lieutenancies were, in consequence, more concerned to maintain the often fickle loyalty of the Gascons than to provide for his own followers.[166] The problem of Gascon allegiance became, if anything, even more acute after the duchy passed into the duke's hereditary possession in 1390 and the business of keeping the great feudatories of Aquitaine loyal,[167] keeping the borders of his principality intact,[168] and building up a following among those native Gascons with a proven record of loyalty to the English, against a background of spiralling taxation and financial crisis,[169] left little enough with which to reward the men who had followed him from England. What pickings there were seem, in any case, to have gone to his administrators rather than his indentured retainers.[170]

---

[164] 'Recueil des documents concernant le Poitou contenus dans les registres de la chancellerie de France', ed. P. Guérin, *Archives Historiques du Poitou*, 19 (1888), 319–22; *Reg. I* 783.

[165] SC 1/56/70.

[166] E. 36/80 ff. 401, 428; C. 61/107 m. 24; E. 28/6 (unnumbered); *Calendar of Papal Registers, Letters, 1362–1404*, 136.

[167] SC 8/252/12596, 12597; C. 61/106 mm. 1–3, 107 m. 27 (petition of, and grants to, Nompar de Caumont, seneschal of the Agenais); C. 61/108 m. 25 (grant to Guillaume-Amanieu de Madaillon, lord of Lesparre).

[168] P. Tucoo-Chala, *Gaston-Fébus et la vicomté de Béarn*, pp. 365–7; E. 30/1356, 1238 (accord with the count of Foix on payment of 30,000 gold francs); E. 28/4, 1 Feb. 1394 (grant of the castle of Mauleon to Charles of Navarre).

[169] C. 61/101 m. 9, 107 mm. 20, 23, 24, 108 mm. 7, 10, 25; K. A. Fowler, 'Les Finances et la discipline dans les armées anglaises en France au XIVe siècle', *Les Cahiers Vernonnais* (1964), 61.

[170] C. 61/101 m. 11 (William Kettering, the duke's secretary), 105 mm. 8, 12 (Master Henry Bowet).

Thus, it seems that while the expectation of profit might still serve to induce a man to campaign abroad with John of Gaunt, it was an expectation frequently disappointed. Moreover, the experience of some individual retainers suggests that, even when genuine gains of war did materialize, they all too often disappeared as swiftly as they had arrived. Sir Geoffrey Workesley, whom the duke first retained in August 1381, had reaped some handsome profits and a good marriage, to the daughter of the seneschal of Gascony, from a military career that had included service with the king before Paris, with the prince of Wales at Nájera, and, in between, a lucrative interlude as the leader of a free company in Brittany.[171] With the resumption of official hostilities in 1369, however, his fortunes took a rapid turn for the worse. Chosen as one of the captains of Knolles's expedition in 1370, he was ambushed and captured at Pont-Vellain and subsequently put to ransom.[172] His attempts to find the necessary money appear to have ruined him; forced to borrow heavily, his estates were eventually sequestered and awarded to his creditors.[173] After 1370, therefore, Workesley continued to fight abroad because he had to; a military career offered the only hope of a revival in his fortunes and the only means of survival in the interim. He continued to play an important part in some of the great expeditions, serving in Brittany with Montfort in 1375 and Buckingham in 1380, but an increasing amount of his time was spent on the unglamorous, and hardly lucrative, business of garrison duty: at Calais in 1376; as Calveley's lieutenant in the Channel Islands in 1377; at Cherbourg in 1379, where he was acting as Thomas Holland's lieutenant just before his death in 1385.[174]

Even for this highly competent professional—'*miles et manu promptus et bello strenuus*'—warfare was no longer an obviously enviable or profitable occupation; at the height of his prosperity, Workesley seems to have been no more than a modest county landowner, deriving an income of c.£65 p.a. from his two manors.[175] His case can be matched by the careers of some of his companions in Lancastrian service. Thomas Driffield, another man retained by the duke on the

---

[171] SC 8/103/5709; *Foedera*, III. ii. 731; M. C. E. Jones, *Ducal Brittany, 1364–1399*, p. 216.

[172] *Froissart* (*K. de L.*), viii. 19; *Rot. Parl.*, ii. 343.

[173] PL 14/154/3 (33, 34); CP 40/462 m. 98*d*.

[174] C. 81/961 (10); *Froissart*, (*K. de L.*), ix. 244; C. 81/972 (26); C. 76/60 m. 4; Walsingham, *Hist. Ang.*, i. 398–9; PL 3/1/142.

[175] CP 40/462 m. 98*d*. His inquisition post-mortem characteristically undervalues the property at £36. 13s. 4*d*. *Abstracts of Inquisitions Post-Mortem*, ed. W. Langton (Chetham Soc., os 95, 1875), i. 23, 46.

strength of his military experience, had cleared some large sums from
the principality of Aquitaine during the 1360s,[176] but he, like
Workesley, ended his career obtaining false letters of protection in
order to defraud his creditors.[177] Sir Thomas Fogg had been equally
fortunate in Normandy and Brittany,[178] but, after his indenture with
John of Gaunt in 1372, much of his subsequent campaigning proved
less lucrative. If his later claim that his service with the duke of
Lancaster had cost him 10,000 marks sounds hyperbolic,[179] it was
hyperbole with more than a grain of truth: his capture on Lancaster's
chevauchée in 1373 cost him a claim of 1,700 marks against the crown
while the duke's Castilian expedition left him with a further claim of
more than 2,000 marks against his commander.[180]

Thus, in the balance of advantage struck between lord and man, the
retainer's military service weighs heavily in favour of the duke. It was
essential that John of Gaunt should maintain a large indentured
retinue, capable of fulfilling a variety of military functions. For most of
his retainers, on the other hand, the profession of arms was not an
inevitable or essential calling and, by the late fourteenth century, an
increasing number of the English gentry seem to have been staying at
home happily enough.[181] The inducements the duke offered for
service abroad were, admittedly, generous but the gains a Lancastrian
retainer could hope to make by his service nevertheless remained
equivocal and uncertain.

If this was the case, why did the duke's retainers continue to obey
his summons? While the available administrative evidence suggests
that overseas warfare was rarely a profitable enterprise for the man-at-
arms by the late fourteenth century, the literary evidence is equally
adamant that it was precisely the men-at-arms who stood to lose most
by a permanent peace with France. Froissart asserts as much; Thomas,
duke of Gloucester, opposed the peace negotiations of 1391 on behalf
of the poor knights and esquires of England; Langland and Hoccleve

[176] E. 101/68/4 (68–70); E. 403/422 m. 31.
[177] C. 81/1019 (18); *CCR 1381–5*, 452, 552.
[178] *Chronicon Henrici Knighton*, ed. J. R. Lumby (Rolls Series, 1895), ii. 109; P.-C.
Timbale, *La Guerre de Cent Ans vue à travers les registres du Parlement* (Paris, 1961),
pp. 457, 463; *CPR 1361–64*, 126; *Recueil des actes de Jean IV, Duc de Bretagne*, ed. M.
Jones (Paris, 1980), i. 19, 103.
[179] *Anglo-Norman Letters and Petitions*, no. 309.
[180] SC 8/46/2292; E. 159/157, Brevia Baronibus, Hilary m. 13; E. 403/460 m. 10;
Reg. II 1235.
[181] See above, p. 45 n. 24.

bemoan their fate.[182] In the face of this contemporary testimony it must be accepted that rewards of one kind or another were still available from regular war-service, but it may be suggested that the rewards now came, not from the Crown or the French, but increasingly from the individual captains themselves, in the form of annuities, stewardships, and indentures of retainer. The greatest prize to be won overseas was access to lordship at home. Warfare formed an important point of access, sometimes the sole and necessary point, to John of Gaunt's esteem and it was for this reason that so many of his retainers remained willing to fight abroad, despite the financial loss this might entail.

The domestic advantages to be gained by winning the duke's patronage abroad were considerable. Service overseas brought temporary immunity from the investigations of the duke's officials in England[183] and, more important, protection against all legal actions during the term of service; the duke was willing to obtain such protections for a retainer, often at short notice,[184] and to ensure his servants every legitimate legal aid while they were abroad in his service, even to the extent of asking the Chancellor to look favourably on the affairs of one of his valets.[185] Early in the duke's career, the legal protection he offered might even extend to a pardon for any felonies committed—at least 57 men out of his company of 400 in 1359 took the opportunity of obtaining one[186]—although this was a benefit rarely accorded after the renewal of hostilities in 1369.[187] Such benefits were, in any case, only of use to a minority of the duke's followers. What most of his retainers wanted from their service abroad was money; either directly, by the grant of an annuity, or indirectly, by appointment to an office in the Lancastrian administration. Froissart

[182] *Froissart (K. de L.)*, xiv. 314, 384, xvi. 3, 108–9; *The Vision of Piers Plowman, Text C.*, ed. W. W. Skeat (EETS, os 54, 1873), iv. 248–50; Hoccleve, *The Regement of Princes*, ed. F. J. Furnivall (EETS, es, 72, 1897), ll. 869–903; *Nicolai Uptoni de Studio Militari*, ed. Sir E. Bysshe (London, 1654), p. 258.

[183] *Reg. I* 292, 1360.

[184] *CCR 1377–81*, 201; C. 81/1715 (2): the duke requests letters of protection for Sir Thomas Symond, who has forgotten to purchase them.

[185] C. 81/1730 (56).

[186] *CPR 1358–61*, 374–527, *passim*; ibid. *1361–4*, 179, 320, 379.

[187] Military service is never again given as a reason for the issue of a pardon at the duke's supplication, although the duke did occasionally continue to seek them and it is sometimes possible to infer a connection, as in the case of Adam Franceys, pardoned at the duke's request soon after serving with him on the St Malo campaign: *Reg. I* 55; *CPR 1377–81*, 297; C. 76/62 m. 18.

describes how, at the siege of Orense in 1387, the vigour of the attack redoubled as the duke rode up, because all there wished to win the greatest praise and reward from him.[188]

The records of the Lancastrian administration provide many examples of those who succeeded. The good fortune of Sir John de Ipres and Sir Walter Urswick, both knighted on the field of Nájera, both high in the duke's favour and esteem,[189] was exceptional, but many lesser men were able to share in the same bounty. The end of each campaign was the natural time for the duke to reward good service and to fill in the gaps created in his retinue by death and desertion; hence the 24 surviving indentures actually concluded abroad;[190] hence the many grants, of annuities, offices, lands, and franchises made at the same time.[191] As the opportunities for profiting at the expense of the enemy gradually contracted, so the number of these grants, especially for service in Aquitaine, increased.[192] In consequence, the duty to reward good service in warfare was becoming one of the principal charges on the Lancastrian estates and revenues by the 1390s. In 1389/90, the first year after the duke's return from Spain, the receiver at Tutbury paid out £140. 4s. 5d. in annuities newly granted (an increase of 35 per cent on the previous year's total) while at Halton £43. 6s. 8d. of the receiver's modest annuity bill of £52. 10s. 0d. consisted of grants made in Spain.[193] At the same time, grants of offices on the ducal estates in England were made to those who had distinguished themselves by their loyalty abroad. Sir Robert Standish was granted the shrievalty of Lancashire in July 1387 for his service in Spain; Roger Waryn, valet, was appointed his bailiff in Penwortham; four months later, Sir Richard Aston, also with the duke in Spain, was made steward of the honour of Halton.[194] Grants made in this way, on the duke's personal authority, took precedence over all others; the man appointed to be master forester of Ashdown forest by the ducal council in London was, for example, superseded in his post

---

[188] *Froissart (K. de L.),* xii. 194: '*car tous les compagnons s'avanchoient affin qils eussent plus grand los et pris*'.

[189] Lewis, no. 1; *Registrum Honoris de Richmond,* ed. R. Gale (London, 1722), pp. 190–1.

[190] See above, p. 43, n. 12.

[191] e.g. in 1386: DL 42/15 ff. 40, 41, 49, 50v, 16 f. 16 (dated '*a nostre logges sur le champ pres de Benovent deinz nostre roialme de Castile*').

[192] DL 42/15 ff. 42, 59; DL 28/32/22 (15, 17).

[193] DL 29/728/11975 m. 1, 11977 m. 1 (Tutbury); DL 29/16/202 (Halton).

[194] *Reg. II* 1237; DL 42/15 f. 41; DL 29/16/202 m. 1.

by Roger Bradshawe, who obtained the duke's patent for office while serving with him in Gascony.[195]

Consequently, in some honours the duke's estate administration became preoccupied with rewarding his large corps of military retainers, with the result that the stewardship of many honours developed into an increasingly honorific post while the daily burden of administration fell upon the receiver. This was certainly the case at Monmouth, where the marshal of Gaunt's host in 1386, Sir Richard Burley, was succeeded in office by Sir William Lucy, who obtained his patent of appointment in Spain.[196] At Halton, Sir Richard Aston continued to absent himself for long periods of service in Gascony.[197] Most of the Yorkshire stewardships came to be monopolized by the duke's military retainers in the same way: at Knaresborough, the duke's banneret Sir John Marmion held the office of steward until his death in Spain, when he was succeeded by Sir Robert Rockley, who also accompanied the duke in 1386; at Pickering, the Rowcliffe family, Sir Richard and Sir David, dominated the estate administration; at Pontefract, Sir Robert Swillington's duties as steward were largely discharged by the receiver, Robert Morton.[198]

Two opposing pressures were thus simultaneously at work. The effect of repeated service abroad was, on the one hand, to forge a stronger bond between lord and man, adding to the material inducement of a retaining fee the sentiment of chivalric duty, but, on the other hand, to accentuate the differences of wealth between the two. Magnates like John of Gaunt, with sufficient political weight behind them, could continue to derive an adequate profit from the war with France but the benefits derived by his retainers directly from their service abroad seem far more questionable. Yet this process of economic differentiation was offset by the social arrangements of the period, by which the magnates distributed to the knights and esquires, upon whose services they depended, a proportion of their profits, in the form of fees and annuities. To say of this distribution 'no wonder lords were impoverished and the gentry flourished'[199] is to misunderstand

[195] DL 28/32/22 (12); DL 29/727/11945 m. 3.

[196] R. R. Davies, 'The Bohun and Lancaster Lordships in Wales' (unpub. Oxford Univ. D.Phil. thesis, 1965), pp. 49–50.

[197] DL 28/3/5 f. 11.

[198] Somerville, pp. 378, 380, 383.

[199] McFarlane, 'Bastard Feudalism', 177.

its nature. The traffic was not all one way; it was aimed, rather, at redressing an already existing imbalance. Military service was increasingly unpopular among the gentry[200] and, if they were to be persuaded to continue to fight abroad, such a redistribution of income was essential. The spread of clientage and lordship in England was thus a necessary, not a contingent, condition of the English war-effort in France. The case of John of Gaunt and his retainers illustrates this contention with particular clarity, for this chapter has demonstrated that the consequences of the duke's military commitments were twofold: firstly, to create many claims òn his largesse; secondly, to leave him with an exceptional surplus of income after 1388. The duke's response was to finance the running expenses of his household from the Castilian indemnity, while allowing an increasing proportion of his estate revenues to be absorbed in rewarding an ever-growing affinity.[201] The growth of the Lancastrian retinue in England was, therefore, directly connected with the scope and nature of the duke's commitments overseas.

Contemporaries were fully alive to the connection. One of the French ambassadors at Bruges, the abbot of St Vaast, explained that the duke of Lancaster did not wish for peace because he was a great captain of the war and so attracted to his service all the nobles and great men of England. Only with their arms and their loyalty behind him could he return, like Julius Caesar from Gaul, and attain his true ambition—succession to the English throne on the death of his father.[202] The abbot's argument was shrewd, even if his conclusion was false. It is to the duties and activities of the duke's retainers in England, and in peacetime, that attention must now be turned.

---

[200] The ratio of men-at-arms to archers, which was held at 1 : 1 as late as 1373, had increased to 1:3 by the early fifteenth century and went still higher in Henry VI's reign. J. W. Sherborne, 'Indentured Retinues and English Expeditions to France, 1369–1380', *EHR* 79 (1964), 728; M. R. Powicke, 'Lancastrian Captains', *Essays in Medieval History Presented to Bertie Wilkinson*, ed. T. A. Sandquist and M. R. Powicke (Toronto, 1969), pp. 371, 379.

[201] See above, p. 24.

[202] E. Perroy, 'The Anglo-French Negotiations at Bruges, 1374–1377', *Camden Miscellany* 19 (3rd series, 80, 1952), p. 60.

4

THE LANCASTRIAN AFFINITY: COHESION, REWARD, AND LOYALTY

1. Reward

The rights and duties of a Lancastrian retainer in time of war were carefully specified and, it would seem, carefully adhered to, but his indenture was vague over what was expected in peacetime, insisting only that he should attend the lord wherever and whenever summoned.[1] The commitment a retainer made to the duke was, therefore, primarily one of time: he had to be ready to attend the duke in the Lancastrian household or to accompany him around the country in his riding retinue. This obligation could comprehend a wide variety of duties. Retainers were dispatched to garrison the duke's Welsh castles during an invasion scare, summoned to attend the duke at Richard II's coronation, to provide a bodyguard during the Peasants' Revolt, to prosecute his feud with the earl of Northumberland on the streets of London.[2] They were also required, from time to time, to provide the imposing escort by which the duke was always accompanied on his frequent diplomatic missions abroad; behind the expensive splendour of Lancaster's suite at Leulingham in 1384 and Amiens in 1393 lay the more permanent physical resources of his indentured retinue.[3]

Exactly how often a retainer was called upon to perform duties of this sort is unclear but such evidence as there is suggests that his peacetime duties were, on the whole, light. At the top of the Lancastrian administrative hierarchy, the chamberlain of the household could expect to spend just over half his time at court and the duke's chief stewards were occupied on his business for about a third

---

[1] Part of the argument of this chapter has appeared in S. Walker, 'John of Gaunt and his "Affinity": A Prosopographical Approach to Bastard Feudalism', *Prosopographie et génèse de l'État moderne*, ed. F. Autrand (Paris, 1986), pp. 209–22.

[2] DL 28/3/1 m. 7; *Chronicon Henrici Knighton*, ii. 149; Walsingham, *Hist. Ang.* ii. 44.

[3] Walsingham, *Hist. Ang.*, ii. 115; *Chronicon Henrici Knighton*, ii. 318; *Chronique du Religieux de Saint-Denys*, i. 299, 735. C. 81/1018 (11), 1062 (43), 1063 (17) for retainers taking out letters of protection to accompany the duke on these missions.

of the year.[4] These are maximum figures, however; even a highly favoured retainer like Sir Richard Burley spent only ten days at court during five months in 1381 and six of the duke's sixteen household knights did not attend the court at all during this period.[5] An esquire without many duties in his own county might spend rather more time at court[6] but the check-rolls of the household suggest the unsurprising conclusion that attendance in the duke's court stood in inverse proportion to a man's independent standing—the more important he was, the less time he was likely to spend waiting on the duke and his family.

When a retainer was in his home county, how much time was he expected to spend on the duke's concerns? Formal obligations extended no further than the duty of attending the duke in his riding-retinue, which was usually staffed by retainers from the area through which the duke was passing. Thus, two Lincolnshire knights, Sir William Hauley and Sir Thomas Swynford, attended Gaunt in the chapter house of Lincoln when Henry of Derby was admitted to the fraternity of the cathedral in 1386; two of Gaunt's Shropshire esquires, William Chetwynd and Richard Chelmeswyk, were admitted with him to the fraternity of Lilleshall abbey while the duke lay ill there in 1398.[7] This was not, however, the sum of a retainer's responsibilities. The duke kept in touch with his retinue by letter[8] and a retainer could easily be called out to attend a local assize in which the duke was concerned, even asked to give evidence against the duke's opponents.[9] All the same, the sum of these various commitments cannot have been, for many retainers, very onerous and there remains a real question as to the means by which the cohesion and identity of the Lancastrian affinity was maintained in the intervals between the duke's campaigns, if, indeed, it was maintained at all. In turn, this

---

[4] As chamberlain, Sir Robert Swillington spent 66 out of 112 days *infra curiam* in 1381; Sir Walter Blount 96 out of 176 days in 1392. As chief steward, Sir Philip Tilney spent 122 days on the lord's business in 1392–3; Sir John Bussy 126 days in 1396–7. East Sussex Record Office, GLY 3469 mm. 1–5, 6–11; DL 28/3/2 f. 12, 5 f. 11.

[5] East Sussex Record Office, GLY 3469 mm. 1–5.

[6] e.g. John Topclyf, a member of the household by 1375, spent 51 days out of 112 there in 1381; he appears only infrequently on commissions in his native Cambridge-shire—*Reg. I* 1675; East Sussex Record Office, GLY 3469 mm. 1–5; *CPR 1381–5*, 139, 246, 589.

[7] *Chaucer Life—Records*, ed. C. C. Olson and M. M. Crow (Oxford, 1966), pp. 92–3; *VCH Shropshire*, ii. 76.

[8] e.g. *Reg. I* 1687; DL 29/212/3247 m. 2; DL 28/3/2 f. 17v.

[9] See below, p. 229.

raises the further question of the true extent of a Lancastrian retainer's commitment to the cause of his lord, of the strength of the bond of lordship within the local communities from which the duke's followers were drawn and to which they inevitably returned when they were not engaged in his service. It is with the resolution of these two questions that this chapter will principally be concerned.

The difficulties involved in the attempt can best be illustrated by a cautionary example. When the Berkshire esquire, John Englefield, came to make his will in 1393, he had been a retainer of John of Gaunt's for the best part of a decade and he still spent well over half his time on duty in the ducal household.[10] He had campaigned in Spain with the duke; he used a Lancastrian feoffee for the disposal of his estates; above all, he held the manor of Langstock, worth £20 a year, by a life-grant from the duke in lieu of a retaining fee.[11] All this was clearly important to him, but none of it concerned him as he made his will;[12] there his main object was to ensure that his son, William, was not cheated of his inheritance. That done, he remembered the parish church of Englefield, where he wished to be buried; left a bequest to his sister, a nun at Goring, five miles up the Thames, and, because he had known one of the monks there, endowed prayers for his soul at the Buckinghamshire abbey of Missenden, twenty-five miles away. He chose as his executors his wife, a kinsman, and two close friends. An inventory of Englefield's goods, taken a few years earlier, serves to confirm the impression created by his will, for signs of wealth or display are hard to find there; only the great bed with red hangings, the ten silver spoons, and the two Flemish cloths for the high table in the hall provide a pale reflection of the sophisticated ostentation that Englefield encountered during his service at the Lancastrian court.[13] His plough-team of oxen, flock of nearly 300 sheep, and net for fishing in the Kennet suggest, rather, the concerns of a yeoman farmer still cultivating his own demesne lands. Two different types of source-material thus present two radically different pictures of the same man. Looked at from one angle, John Englefield is a loyal Lancastrian retainer, whose life seems to revolve around his lord; looked at from another, he is an independent gentleman, determinedly parochial in his outlook, pursuing his interests and

---

[10] East Sussex Record Office, GLY 3469, mm. 6*d*–14*d*.
[11] C. 76/70 m. 12; *CCR 1385–9*, 139 (Sir Thomas de la Mare); DL 43/15/3 m. 2.
[12] E. 210/6658.
[13] E. 210/6023.

settling his affairs without reference to any authority higher than his own. In order to see the Lancastrian affinity in its proper perspective, a balance has to be struck between these two points of view, between the inducements to service and loyalty the duke could offer and the many concerns of the gentry that lay, apparently, outside the network of bastard feudal relationships.

How did John of Gaunt seek to maintain the loyalty of the large and disparate group of gentlemen who constituted his affinity? The most obvious and traditional means was by the generous distribution of rewards to those who served him well. The duke had many desirable gifts in his hand—land, money, offices, wardships, leases, timber, venison were his to dispose of at will; benefices, corrodies, and pardon of crimes could be obtained at his intercession. These benefits are conventionally described as the duke's patronage, but the act of patronage went beyond the simple distribution of material goods to include the countenance, support, and protection that the duke could offer to his dependants. Such support was particularly important in the competition for royal favour and reward and, at the king's court, the duke was expected to sponsor the petitions of his clients, to obtain for them favours from the king and to provide a bulwark against the schemes of their enemies. In each respect, the extent of Gaunt's lordship could hardly be rivalled by his contemporaries. His wealth and his lands gave him great resources of private patronage; his high birth and his political pre-eminence ensured that few would gainsay his protégés in the courts or refuse his requests on the Council. Second only to the king in his power, he was second only to the king in the advantages expected of him. Nor were these advantages confined to England, for the duke's aspirations as a European prince gave him an international standing that his followers were quick to exploit. If a retainer wanted ecclesiastical preferment for his son, or a dispensation from a consanguineous marriage, the duke would send a petition to Avignon on his behalf;[14] if an Englishman had a grievance against the kings of Aragon, John of Gaunt was the magnate most likely to gain redress for him.[15]

In consequence, he was pursued and besieged by an army of petitioners, demanding from him a whole variety of favours; letters of denization and protection, the issue of bills under the Great Seal, even

[14] *Calendar of Papal Registers, Petitions 1342–1419*, 528–9.
[15] Archivo de la Corona de Aragón, Cartas Reales y Diplomáticas, Juan I, 7/1069. Anthony Goodman kindly brought this document to my attention.

a general remedy for the disputes that arose between executors.[16] For a petitioner to be successful in the face of such competition—the prudent would make an appointment several weeks in advance[17]—he needed friends and influence at the Lancastrian court just as much as he did at Westminster. The prior of Llanthony by Gloucester looked, for instance, to Sir Thomas Hungerford and Sir John Bromwych as his particular allies, asking them to mediate whenever there was a petition to be advanced or a dispute to be smoothed over.[18] Such friends came expensive—the borough of Leicester paid £5. 7s. 2d. to a certain lord to intercede with Katherine Swynford, who would then speak with the duke on the town's behalf[19]—and, in this respect, the Lancastrian retainer enjoyed a double advantage. The most influential of them, the duke's stewards and household officials, themselves received *douceurs* in order to ensure their favour[20] while the rest of the duke's retinue were at least guaranteed access to the lord and a favourable hearing—a head start, though not an assurance of success.

Success was not assured because the duke's position in society did not exonerate even him from going through the proper channels to obtain his requests. Like everyone else, he sought to initiate administrative action by a written request to the Chancellor, for the issue of routine writs, or to the king, for the issue of writs on more important matters.[21] In consequence, Gaunt's value to his retainers did not lie in allowing them to circumvent the normal bureaucratic procedures, but in his ability to guide their petitions to a successful outcome. Typically, when approached by a suppliant he was prepared to sponsor, he would dispatch the original petition to the Chancellor and Treasurer, with a covering note asking that the petitioner be shown as much favour as law and good conscience would allow.[22] Once the normal procedures of government had been initiated, however, the duke's proximity to the king gave him further informal opportunities to advance the cause of his clients—an ability well

[16] SC 8/93/4628; *CPR 1381–5*, 18; SC 8/121/6020, 307/15343; C. 49/16/17 m. 2.

[17] HMC, *Various Collections* (London, 1904), i. 358.

[18] C. 115/K2/6684 f. 106[r–v].

[19] *Records of the Borough of Leicester*, ed. M. Bateson (Cambridge, 1901), ii. 171.

[20] e.g. Sir Godfrey Foljambe, who received fees from monastic houses and lavish entertainments from town corporations by virtue of his office as the duke's chief steward. Bodl. MS Rolls Norfolk 71; *Records of the Borough of Leicester*, ii. 141, 148; HMC, *Manuscripts of the Corporations of Southampton and King's Lynn* (London, 1887), p. 221.

[21] SC 8/300/14971, 121/6046A.

[22] SC 8/103/5111, SC 1/43/40; cf. SC 1/63/244: 'Et ce veuillez faire le plus favourablement . . .'.

recognized by the many petitioners who asked him simply to intercede with the king on their behalf.[23]

This intercession was sometimes very public, as when the duke supported and argued for a petition of Sir William Windsor before the peers of Parliament,[24] but it was more usually private, exercised while the king was in the almost-daily act of considering the petitions before him.[25] It is, in consequence, hard to reconstruct in any detail, but the references by ecclesiastical chroniclers to commissions granted by means of the duke's *auxilium et favorem* and petitions accepted *per bonam mediationem domini Johannis*,[26] the occasional administrative discrepancy between a petition addressed to the king and a note of warranty on the resultant grant, showing that it was issued at the duke of Lancaster's request,[27] the swift legislative remedies occasioned by petitions addressed to the duke[28]—all these indicate that his patronage was as effective as it was sought after. During the Good Parliament, for instance, the abbot of St Augustine's, Canterbury, was induced by the duke to drop a Parliamentary petition against the jurisdiction of the constable of Dover Castle—who happened to be Gaunt's younger brother, Edmund of Cambridge.[29] The abbot agreed, 'partly from fear of the duke, partly to gain advantage for his church', and the sequel proved his compliance wise. Lancaster was soon able to do St Augustine's a good turn, and his enemy William Courtenay a bad one, by abetting the abbey's claim to exemption from the jurisdiction of the archbishop of Canterbury.[30]

On whose behalf did John of Gaunt deploy his administrative influence? More precisely, how much royal patronage could his retainers expect to come their way? An examination of the letters patent which declare a grant to have been made on the information of John, duke of Lancaster, provides some indication. Members of his

---

[23] e.g. SC 8/102/5054, 5059, 5085, 103/5107, 5111, 104/5168.

[24] *Rot. Parl.*, iii. 130*a*; SC 8/146/7280.

[25] A. L. Brown, 'The Authorization of Letters under the Great Seal', *BIHR* 37 (1964), 149, 154.

[26] 'Historiae Croylandensis Continuatio', *Rerum Anglicarum Scriptores Veterum*, ed. W. Fulman (Oxford, 1684), 483; *Gesta Abbatum Monasterii Sancti Albani*, ed. H. T. Riley (Rolls Series, 1869), iii. 137, 241; *Chronicon Henrici Knighton*, ii. 206; Walsingham, *Hist. Ang.*, ii. 199.

[27] SC 8/224/11156; *CPR 1391–6*, 666.

[28] SC 8/147/7347; J. B. Post, 'Sir Thomas West and the Statute of Rapes, 1382', *BIHR* 53 (1980), 24–30.

[29] *Rot. Parl.*, ii. 346; *William Thorne's Chronicle of St Augustine's, Canterbury*, ed. A. H. Davis (Oxford, 1934), p. 611.

[30] *Thorne's Chronicle*, p. 618.

affinity certainly benefited from such grants. An Exchequer pension; a royal manor; custody of an alien priory or a licence to alienate Crown lands: all these could be obtained by Lancastrian retainers at their master's request.[31] Yet a full examination of the notes of warranty on the Chancery rolls suggests, firstly, that the duke was relatively sparing in making applications for royal bounty; secondly, that his retainers and annuitants constituted only one group in a larger mass of suppliants, all of whom had a claim on his generosity, all of whom hoped to be satisfied. This emerges most clearly from the grants made, in the name of the ailing Edward III, on the duke's information between June 1376 and March 1377. Gaunt had no qualms about lining his own pockets[32] but his followers fared, in comparison, less fortunately. Sir John de Ipres, chief of the duke's council, was granted a valuable manor in fee; Juan Gutierez, Lancaster's Iberian expert, received the forfeited goods of a stray Castilian vessel; a rival claimant was ousted from John Wyclif's prebend at Westbury.[33] This, however, was the sum of the benefits the duke obtained for his dependants during a year as *rector et gubernator* of the kingdom, since he had to use his position to meet a variety of other demands: to cement the loyalty of newfound allies, such as the dowager princess of Wales;[34] to reward long-standing courtiers, like the king's butler, William Street, for their services; to attract the sympathetic but uncommitted to his regime; even to reward the needy and deserving.[35] Gaunt's intercessions with the king continued to follow the pattern established in 1376. Besides the grants he obtained for his own dependants detailed above, he sought royal favour on behalf of a wide, and miscellaneous, collection of suppliants: old soldiers,[36] king's clerks,[37] religious houses in danger of sequestration,[38] disgraced Londoners.[39] Thus, although John of Gaunt enjoyed unrivalled opportunities to influence, occasionally to dominate, the distribution of Crown patronage, the use he made of this privilege was neither excessively partisan nor, save where he was himself the beneficiary, excessively rapacious. His restraint was politic,

---

[31] *CPR 1388–92*, 464; ibid. *1374–7*, 475; *CFR 1377–83*, 351; *CPR 1391–6*, 375.
[32] *CPR 1374–7*, 340, 359, 367, 433, 437, 457.
[33] Ibid. 475, 393; *CCR 1374–7*, 416.
[34] Ibid. 406–7; *CPR 1374–7*, 376–7; C. 81/474 (2166).
[35] *CPR 1374–7*, 373, 475, 434, 306.
[36] *CPR 1388–92*, 245; ibid. *1391–6*, 309.
[37] E. 404/14/90 (10 Apr. 1385).
[38] *CPR 1388–92*, 366; ibid. *1391–6*, 215.
[39] Ibid. *1385–9*, 161.

since his influence over the king was always a politically contentious issue and to take too open advantage of it would have been to invite opposition. If this meant that his retainers benefited less, in terms of royal patronage, from their Lancastrian allegiance than they might have hoped, the rest of the benefits the duke could offer were quite generous enough to maintain their loyalty.

These benefits are easy to illustrate, but difficult to quantify. Probably the most sought-after were leases of the ducal estates at a fixed farm for a term of years. In the competition to take up leases after the ending of direct exploitation of the demesne, those who had some prior claim on the duke, whether of blood or service, naturally stood a good chance of success. Indeed, certain offices seem to have brought with them first refusal on adjacent ducal lands—successive constables of Pevensey castle, for instance, leased the demesne lands of the duchy in the marsh of Pevensey.[40] The arrangement carried advantages for both sides: the duke welcomed the opportunity to show favour to the deserving, but he also welcomed the knowledge that a farmer of his lands who was also his retainer was dependent upon him for an annuity as well as a lease, and was the more likely to observe its conditions as a consequence. For the well-placed, the rewards of their reliability could be substantial. Valets and esquires of the household leased pasture, urban property, lead mines;[41] more substantial retainers could take out leases on scattered parcels of ducal lands in order to consolidate their own estates;[42] the most favoured were granted a share in the duke's lordship by the demise of his judicial rights—Sir John Marmion, for instance, leased Gaunt's Richmondshire wapentakes from him.[43]

The persistent and influential were consequently enabled to expand the size and scope of their holdings considerably. Thomas Haselden, controller of the duke's household, took out leases on Lancastrian property all over eastern England, farming the manor of Babraham (Cambs.), the bailiwicks of Boroughbridge (Yorks.) and Snaith (Lincolnshire), and the fens of Bolingbroke (Lincolnshire), besides going into partnership with some colleagues in the ducal administration to buy the reversion of William de Nessfield's lands at Scotton (Yorks.).[44] Sir Thomas Hungerford confined his acquisitions to the

---

[40] East Sussex Record Office, AMS 5592/2; DL 42/15 f. 123v.
[41] DL 42/15 ff. 101v, 120v, 131.
[42] DL 42/15 f. 7v (Sir Robert Urswick).
[43] *Reg. II* 1034.
[44] *Reg. I* 967, 1326; DL 42/1 f. 190; *Reg. II* 1036, 1044.

South-West, farming the Lancastrian manors of Upavon (Wilts.) and Down Ampney (Glos.),[45] while Sir Thomas Metham farmed the duke's demesne lands at Thorner on a preferential lease.[46] Such distinguished lessees were not, however, entirely typical, for, like the estates of Westminster Abbey, the Lancastrian lands were mainly farmed by the yeomanry and richer peasantry, with the gentry constituting only a 'significant minority' among the tenants.[47] Thus, the lessees of Henry of Derby's manors, although they included substantial gentry like Hungerford and Sir Hugh Waterton, were principally drawn from among his ministers and estate officials[48] and it was these ministerial lessees who probably gained most from their tenure of the duke's lands. The case of Richard Brennand, bailiff of the ducal fees at Knaresborough, gives some indication of how much access to the duke's patronage could mean, in material terms, to an aspiring member of the lesser gentry. Anxious to acquire land and lacking the inherited wealth to do so, his purchases could only be financed by repeated borrowings[49] until his position in Lancastrian service and his conspicuous loyalty during the Peasants' Revolt gave him the opportunity to take up a lease on a large parcel of miscellaneous rights in the lordship of Knaresborough and thereby to become an influential local figure.[50]

If the duke's retainers were not the principal beneficiaries of his patronage in the matter of leases, there were other benefits in his gift to which they aspired. Membership of the Lancastrian affinity brought the possibility of acquiring a more permanent stake in the countryside by means of an advantageous marriage. Matches between retainers who attended the duke in his household and the ladies-in-waiting on his wife were inevitably frequent—Sir Walter Blount married Sancha Garcia, one of Queen Constanza's Castilian attendants, for instance, and Edward Gerberge's wife, Alyne, had been nurse to the duke's

[45] DL 28/3/3 m. 1; C. 136/100/2 (2).

[46] DL 29/507/8227 m. 16.

[47] B. F. Harvey, 'The Leasing of the Abbot of Westminster's Demesnes in the Later Middle Ages', *EcHR*, 2nd series, 22 (1969), 20–1.

[48] DL 28/3/3 mm. 1, 2; DL 28/3/4 ff. 2–4. Thomas Whitting, farmer of Ascot, was also the collector of rents there, for instance; Stephen Stutteville, farmer of Soham, was keeper of the Lancastrian fees in Cambridgeshire.

[49] *Feet of Fines for the County of York, 1347–1377*, ed. W. P. Baildon (Yorkshire Arch. Soc., Record Ser., 52, 1915), p. 197; *CCR 1364–8*, 83; ibid. *1369–74*, 200.

[50] DL 29/465/7604, mm. 1–2, 5; *Reg. I* 1617; *Reg. II* 326, 1038; *The Anonimalle Chronicle, 1333–1381*, ed. V. H. Galbraith (Manchester, 1927), p. 159.

daughter, Philippa.[51] Such marriages were encouraged by the duke, since they served to create a true 'affinity' of blood and kinship among his followers. Sir David Rowcliffe was granted £20 p.a. when he married Margery Hesill, the duke's damsel.[52] By a shrewd choice of partner a retainer could, quite literally, make his fortune. For the lucky few, marriage to one of the prosperous dowagers who inhabited the Lancastrian court, the widowed wives of former retainers, transformed their financial position—Sir Richard Burley's marriage to Beatrice, the widow of Thomas, lord Roos, gave him a life-share in the extensive Roos lands; Sir Hugh Waterton laid the foundations of his estates in the Welsh March by marrying Katherine, the widow of Sir John Bromwych, and Sir Thomas Rempston greatly augmented his own holdings in the North Midlands by his marriage to Margaret, the widow of Sir Godfrey Foljambe's son and heir.[53]

In addition, attendance at court brought with it access to another source of income and patronage which John of Gaunt enjoyed, by reason of his right to the wardship and marriage of the heirs of his military tenants. This was a relatively limited source of profit, as far as the duke's retainers were concerned: Gaunt's mistress, Katherine Swynford, was granted the most lucrative wardships available[54] and, after an investigation into the duke's profits conducted in 1374, there was a move towards a directly financial exploitation of his feudal rights that laid more emphasis upon the price a man was prepared to pay than upon his deserts.[55] Nevertheless, a number of his retainers continued to pick up valuable wardships and, although their interest was usually in the profit to be made from exploiting the estates of their ward, a retainer would occasionally use such a purchase to provide a wife for one of his own sons; Sir John Saville's younger son, Henry, was, for instance, married off to Elizabeth, daughter and heir of Simon de Thornton, whom his father had bought, 'for a great sum', in 1374.[56]

Alluring though these benefits of Lancastrian service were, they

[51] Sir Alexander Croke, *The Genealogical History of the Croke Family* (Oxford, 1823), ii. 173–4; *Reg. I* 473.

[52] *CPR 1396–9*, 500.

[53] *Complete Peerage*, XI. 101; *CCR 1385–9*, 286–7 (Burley); *CPR 1388–92*, 100; *CCR 1392–6*, 391 (Waterton); *Collectanea Topographica et Genealogica* (London, 1834), i. 339 (Rempston).

[54] *Reg. I* 181, 446; *Reg. II* 503, 589; DL 28/3/2 ff. 8, 18.

[55] *Reg. I* 1584.

[56] Ibid. 1436; W. P. Baildon, 'Notes on the Early Saville Pedigree', *Yorkshire Archaeological Journal*, 28 (1926), 412.

were both incidental and irregular in their appearance. The mainstay of the retainer's profit from his indenture with the duke remained the money fee he was paid. At the top end of the annuity scale, the fees the duke offered his most favoured retainers and estate officials were very high indeed. Sir Walter Blount and his wife managed to engross pensions and offices worth £176. 13s. 4d. a year; Sir Walter Urswick had lands from the duke worth £123. 6s. 8d.; Sir Thomas Skelton's fees and annuities as chief steward amounted to £120, Sir Richard Burley's to £116. 7s. 6d.[57] and at least ten other retainers enjoyed a fee of 100 marks or more.[58] By any standards, these were substantial sums, roughly equivalent to the annual income of a prosperous knightly family and as generous as all but the most lavish royal annuities. In comparison with the fees offered by other magnates, they were exceptional: only Edward, prince of Wales, offered his men more.[59] Naturally, for the majority of the duke's retainers, the financial rewards of service were rather smaller. Nevertheless, influenced by the example of his elder brother, during the 1370s the duke offered fees still substantially higher than those of some of his contemporaries— £40 p.a. to some knights, £20 or 20 marks to some esquires—and it was not until the early 1380s that the duke's normal retaining fee— £20 for a knight and £10, or 10 marks, for an esquire[60]—stabilized at a level more closely comparable with most other magnates.[61]

What did a sum like that mean to a retainer? What proportion of his annual income did it constitute? Precise income levels varied, not unnaturally, from retainer to retainer. For Sir Robert Swillington, whose lands were valued at over £400 p.a. at his death and were probably worth much more,[62] even the considerable fee he received from the duke was not essential to his prosperity; for Sir Richard

---

[57] *CPR 1396–9*, 547 (Blount); DL 43/15/6 m. 7 (Urswick); DL 28/3/5 f. 8 (Skelton); DL 29/615/9838 m. 2 (Burley).

[58] Sir John Dabridgecourt; Sir Thomas Fogg; Sir Henry Green; Sir Thomas Hungerford; Sir John Marmion; Sir Thomas Morieux; Sir Thomas Percy; Sir John St Lo; Sir Thomas Symond; Sir Robert Swillington. See Appendix I for details.

[59] e.g. *CPR 1377–81*, 161: Sir Aubrey de Vere received £183. 6s. 8d. p.a. from the prince in 1376.

[60] *Lewis*, p. 80.

[61] The earl of Warwick, for instance, offered 20 marks to his knights and £10 to most of his esquires; the earl of Nottingham offered sums between £20 and 10 marks to his knights, with the prospect of an increment on the death of Margaret Marshall; the earls of Stafford rarely paid a fee of more than £10. BL Egerton Roll 8769 m. 1; *CPR 1399–1401*, 28, 196, ibid. *1405–8* 29, Staffordshire Record Office, D. 641/1/2 36 m. 1, 40a m. 1.

[62] C. 136/73 (8); cf. J. Leland, *Itineraries*, ed. L. T. Smith (London, 1906), ii. 19.

Burley, with estates worth about £170 p.a., rewards from ducal service practically doubled his income.[63] Nevertheless, there is enough information to hazard some generalizations. If the minimum financial requirement for gentility was only £10 p.a. of land, most of John of Gaunt's retainers and annuitants clearly commanded incomes higher than that. The majority fell into the category of 'prosperous gentry', with incomes falling somewhere between £40 and £100 a year and probably gravitating towards the upper end of the bracket,[64] while a sizeable minority could be counted among the 'richer knights', with incomes well over £100 a year.[65] Sir Hugh Shirley's lands, for example, were valued at £280 p.a. in the early fifteenth century; bannerets like Sir John Marmion were expected to have an income around £200 p.a.,[66] and a number of the duke's more senior knights could probably command this sort of revenue. Thus, even the inquisitions post-mortem, which notoriously undervalue, estimate Sir John St Lo's lands at £154 p.a. and give Sir Maurice Berkley an income of £123. 6s. 8d., Sir John Dymoke £115, Sir John Trailly £112. 13s. 4d.[67] For such men, an annuity of £20 was a welcome adjunct to their resources but not an essential part of their revenues; even those who experienced some financial difficulties, such as Sir Edmund Appleby, could still dispose of movable goods worth over £200.[68] Paradoxically,

---

[63] *CIM 1387–93*, no. 119.

[64] Retainers assessed as holding more than £40 p.a. of land include: Nicholas Atherton, Sir John Boseville, Sir John Botiller, Thomas Colville of Coxwold, Sir Thomas Erpingham, Sir William Fitzwilliam, Edmund de Frithby, Edmund Gournay, Sir Nicholas Harrington, Richard Holland, Robert de Morton, Sir Edmund Pirpont, Sir Robert Plumpton, Thomas Radcliffe, Robert de Rockley, Sir John Saville, Sir William Scargill, William de Spaigne of Boston. PL 14/154/2 (45); E. 179/130/24 m. 1, 27 m. 1; 149/45 m. 1, 242/26; E. 159/145, Easter, Recorda, m. 26; 'Rolls of the Collectors in the West Riding of the Lay Subsidy (Poll Tax) 2 Richard II', *Yorkshire Archaeological and Topographical Journal*, 5 (1879), 1–52, 241–66, 417–32, 6 (1881), 1–44, 287–342. More precise estimates, which can serve as minimum figures, exist for: Sir John Bagot (£93+); Thomas Berkley of Cobberley (£89); Sir Ralph Bracebridge (£81. 13s. 4d.); Sir Robert Charles (£46); Sir John Oddingsels (£81. 3s. 8d.); Sir William Swynburn (£66. 13s. 4d.); Sir Geoffrey Workesley (£68). *Collections for a History of Staffordshire*, NS 11 (1908), 33; C. 137/46/5, 6/2, 22/2, 42/1; Northumberland Record Office, ZSW 4/89; CP 40/462 m. 98d.

[65] H. L. Gray, 'Incomes from Land in England in 1436', *EHR* 49 (1934), 623–4, 630; T. B. Pugh, 'The Magnates, Knights and Gentry', in S. B. Chrimes, C. D. Ross, and R. A. Griffiths (eds.), *Fifteenth-century England* (Manchester, 1972), p. 97.

[66] Leicestershire Record Office, 26 D 53/2194; N. Saul, *Knights and Esquires* (Oxford, 1981), pp. 9–10.

[67] C. 137/86/10, 23/8; C. 138/8/7; C. 137/7/4.

[68] G. G. Astill, 'An Early Inventory of a Leicestershire Knight', *Midland History*, 2 (1973–4), 274–83.

it was the smaller sums paid to the duke's newly retained esquires which were most effective in binding his followers to his service. Twenty pounds a year was considered an adequate maintenance for the son of a knightly family while his father remained alive and in possession of the estates;[69] a retaining fee of as little as 10 marks consequently constituted an important addition to the young man's income. For the 'esquires of lesser estate', living on a landed income below £40 p.a. with no expectations of inheritance, it was even essential, if the pretensions of gentility were to be maintained.[70]

Fees and annuities were not, of course, all profit. Maintaining the standards of display Gaunt expected from his followers was, in itself, expensive[71] and quite liable to absorb much of the duke's annuity; *some* expenditure on their duties, usually amounting to about a third of the total fee, was required from all but the most negligent constables and master foresters.[72] Nevertheless, the duke's annuity remained, for all his retainers, an important supplement to their income from other sources, not least because it was usually paid promptly and in cash.[73] In a society chronically short of bullion, where the real value of ready money was some way above its face value, this was an important consideration; difficulties of liquidity and the expenses of life at the Lancastrian court were enough to render the financial position of some retainers, even men as prominent as Sir Richard Abberbury, Sir William Croyser, and Sir Thomas Fichet,[74] temporarily embarrassed. A lord with a reputation for reliability in his annuity payments was the more welcome, in consequence. In the value of his annuity payments, therefore, John of Gaunt occupies a point closer to the large fees paid

---

[69] This was the sum Sir Robert Charles stipulated for his son, Thomas; Edward, son of Sir Thomas Banaster, was allowed £20 p.a. until he came of age; Sir Thomas Hungerford settled an annual rent of £20 on his son at the time of his marriage. Sir Philip Tilney's son, Frederick, received a slightly more generous allowance of 40 marks. Norfolk Record Office, NCC Harsyk f. 269; *Reg. II* 578; Bodl. MS Dugdale 18 f. 87; Nottinghamshire Record Office, Dd 4p4/16, 18.

[70] e.g. Nicholas Tournay, a younger son, painstakingly building up a small estate around Glenham and Glentworth (Lincolnshire) during the 1390s. Lincolnshire Archives Office, FL deeds, 3065, 3091, 3103, 3134, 3148; D. and C., C. iii/45/1/6.

[71] *Reg. I* 938: grant of an annuity, 'pur le mielz lour estat maintenir . . .'.

[72] *CPR 1370–4*, 375. Sir John Wood was granted an annuity in compensation for the 20 marks he lost when removed from his post as constable of Knaresborough castle, for which the fee was £20.

[73] See above, p. 23.

[74] Abberbury: E. 159/176 Adhuc Recorda, Hilary m. 16, Easter m. 1; DL 28/3/2 f. 6v. Croyser: C. 131/4/7; *CCR 1385–9*, 497–9; ibid. *1389–92*, 546; *CPR 1396–9*, 128. Fichet: *The Hylle Cartulary*, ed. R. W. Dunning (Somerset Record Soc., 68, 1968), p. xvii.

by most magnates in the early fourteenth century, which could constitute as much as a third of a retainer's annual income, than to the small, often token, sums to which many fifteenth-century lords confined themselves, representing only a fraction of their clients' income,[75] although the general downward movement of the terms the duke offered itself foreshadows this development.

2. Cohesion and Loyalty

These, then, were the considerations that kept a retainer loyal to John of Gaunt: cash in his hand, the chance of a lucrative lease or wardship, a friend at court. Beyond these purely material incentives, however, lay a further series of claims on the loyalty of every Lancastrian servant; the claim of fidelity, honour, and companionship that can be obscured by too nice an assessment of the balance between profit and loss. The most public of these was that imposed by the duke's livery badge—a shared symbol proclaiming a shared loyalty. Best known is Gaunt's device of the linked S, an adaptation of a common ornamental pattern[76] as a personal insignia that was to become the standard Lancastrian badge in the fifteenth century. Both Gaunt and Henry of Derby were using the badge during the 1390s[77] but there is no evidence that it was the only device used by the duke; his son was certainly employing another form of collar—*ad modum de snagge*—in the previous decade.[78] The importance of the Lancastrian livery collar does not, in consequence, lie in the possible significance to be attributed to the choice of letters, but in the incorporation of the letters into a collar and the adoption of this collar as a livery device. Most livery signs took the form of badges, such as the golden crowns Richard II offered to the gentlemen of East Anglia in 1386,[79] so that

[75] J. R. Maddicott, *Thomas of Lancaster* (Oxford, 1970), p. 58; W. H. Dunham, *Lord Hastings' Indentured Retainers, 1461–1483*, Transactions of the Connecticut Academy of Arts and Sciences, 39 (1955), p. 36 n. 11; C. Carpenter, 'The Beauchamp Affinity: A Study of Bastard Feudalism at Work', *EHR* 95 (1980), p. 579.

[76] *Wykeham's Register*, ed. T. F. Kirby (Hampshire Record Soc., 11, 1896–9), ii. 289 for a gold necklace, enamelled and engraven S. bequeathed by Sir John Foxle.

[77] *The Antient Kalendars and Inventories of the Treasury of His Majesty's Exchequer* (London, 1836), iii. 322; DL 28/1/4 f. 15.

[78] DL 28/1/2 f. 14v.

[79] *Westminster Chronicle*, p. 186.

the use of a collar was both unusual and distinctive, serving to set the duke's retainers apart from the servants of other magnates. Although the duke was using the device as early as 1376, references to other collars used as livery badges seem non-existent before the 1390s and they are, even then, confined to members of the royal family.[80]

This invested the collar of SS with a significance that other livery badges lacked. In 1400 Henry IV granted one of his esquires a 10 mark annuity, the better to maintain the dignity of the order of the collar,[81] so that, in Henry's eyes at least, the Lancastrian livery badge was closer in status to the insignia of a continental order of chivalry, such as the Burgundian *toison d'or*, than to the liveries of other English magnates. It was used in much the same way as 'a spectacular but hopeful means of collecting members of an affinity'.[82] Thus, whilst Lancastrian retainers and supporters were the natural recipients of the livery of the collar and it might, in moments of crisis, be handed out to a very large number of people[83] in order to gain their support, it was also issued to foreign notables[84] and to those from whom nothing better than neutrality could be expected. The range of possible recipients is well illustrated by Henry of Derby's gift of collars in 1387/8 to Sir William Bagot, steward of his household; to Philip, lord Darcy, a Yorkshire baron with little discernible political affiliation, and to Sir John Stanley, a rising star of the royal household who had just emerged from a bitter territorial dispute with Derby's father.[85] What, then, did it mean to wear the Lancastrian collar? On the wearer's part, it was a valuable statement of the favour in which he stood with a great lord. Gaunt's followers allegedly thought their badges would give them the earth and sky.[86] If they sometimes failed to satisfy such expectations, they were at least expensive and desirable objects of display worth, by

---

[80] M. V. Clarke, *Fourteenth Century Studies* (Oxford, 1937), pp. 282–3; *Antient Kalendars and Inventories*, iii. 341, 354.

[81] DL 42/15 f. 85v: '*pur tant que nous avons ordenez le predit Johan destre de nostre liveree de le coler . . . afin qil purra maintenir nostre dit ordre*'. M. H. Keen, *Chivalry* (New Haven, 1984), p. 183 points out that this is a confusion between the insignia of a true order of chivalry and a *devise* of clientage; but it was a confusion the Lancastrians were anxious to promote.

[82] P. S. Lewis, 'Decayed and Non-Feudalism in Later Medieval France', *BIHR* 37 (1964), 175.

[83] DL 28/4/1 f. 18v. 192 gilt collars were issued by Derby's receiver-general in the summer of 1399.

[84] DL 41/10/43, no. 15.

[85] DL 28/1/2 f. 14v.

[86] *Chronicon Angliae*, 125.

themselves, a considerable sum.[87] From the lord's point of view, the importance of the collar lay in the *public* statement of allegiance to which it committed the wearer—a man might take many fees but he could wear only one badge of livery at any one time. The statement it made was, nevertheless, a muted one, of mutual good will rather than acknowledged obligation. Richard II expressed it well when he explained that he wore the collar of his uncle *en signe de bon amour d'entier coer entre eux.*[88]

The loyalty of the affinity, fostered by the distribution of a livery badge, found a physical focus in the duke's many castles and his great palace of the Savoy, which stood as a constant and imposing reminder to the Lancastrian retinue of their lord's wealth and power. When the duke was absent, they remained empty and lifeless;[89] within their walls, everything was settled by reference to his desires and commands, whether actual or alleged. In each, the great chamber and the hall provided the physical setting for the communal feasting that gave a visible ceremonial expression to the solidarity of the Lancastrian affinity. Much of the attraction of Lancastrian service lay in the colour and glamour of the duke's life; *bouche of court* was a valued privilege because it granted a passport to the opulent and aristocratic atmosphere of the Savoy, a palace 'unrivalled in the kingdom for splendour and nobility' with a wardrobe as fine as any king's, so full of silver vessels that five carts could not carry them all.[90]

John of Gaunt was careful to foster and encourage, by the considerable sums he spent on his building projects, this solidarity. His earliest undertakings include minor repairs and improvements at Higham Ferrers, Hertford, Pontefract, Tickhill, and the Savoy.[91] By 1377 he was contemplating a more ambitious architectural programme

---

[87] A jury valued one such collar (rather wildly, probably) at £20 in 1400; the £8 Richard Whittington agreed to pay the Exchequer for a collar of SS he had mislaid, at Easter 1402, seems a more accurate figure. *Select Cases in the Court of King's Bench*, ed. G. O. Sayles, vii (Selden Soc., 88, 1971), 103; A. B. Steel, *The Receipt of the Exchequer 1377–1485* (Cambridge, 1954), p. 87.

[88] *Rot. Parl.*, iii. 313.

[89] e.g. when the earl of March stopped at Pontefract in June 1378, he found it deserted, but for builders and carpenters, to whom he gave 13s. 4d. BL Egerton Roll 8728.

[90] Walsingham, *Hist. Ang.*, i. 457; *Chronicon Henrici Knighton*, ii. 135; cf. M. James, *Family, Lineage and Civil Society* (Oxford, 1974), p. 32. The chroniclers' enthusiastic descriptions had a solid basis in fact; a partial inventory of the duke's household chapel shows that its furnishings were worth at least £550. John of Gaunt's own valuation set the contents of the Savoy at £10,000. CP 40/490 m. 252, 491 m. 223; Lincolnshire Archives Office, D. and C., A/4/2/12–14.

[91] W. J. B. Kerr, *Higham Ferrers* (Northampton, 1925), p. 104; *Reg. I* 925–6, 1398

and, although it was not put into action until his return from Spain, Gaunt was spending more than £1,000 p.a. on the project by 1393–4, principally on major new works at Lancaster and Pontefract.[92] Some of this building, at Dunstanburgh, Kidwelly, and Pevensey,[93] was still primarily defensive, but most of it was emphatically civilian in character and purpose, intended as a statement and memorial of the duke of Lancaster's pre-eminence. The centrepiece was the rebuilding of Kenilworth, where an annual assignation of 400 marks was devoted, over twenty years,[94] to constructing a new palace complex, including outer courts capable of accommodating 200 servants and retainers, that briefly outshone any of the king's works. This was a project of architectural magnificence, designed to recreate the splendours of the Savoy in independence of the hostile Londoners, which gave the duke's affinity an added sense of pride in their lord and their allegiance to him, for the identification of his servants with the physical setting of their service was close and intimate, permanently commemorated in the names of 'Dencourtchapel' and Saintlowe tower at Kenilworth, Simeon tower at the Savoy, and Swillington's tower at Pontefract.[95]

Kenilworth was not the only focus for the loyalty of the Lancastrian affinity. By his foundation of the college and hospital of St Mary Newarke at Leicester, Henry of Grosmont had created a domestic, ducal version of the *Sainte Chapelle*, complete with a thorn from the crown of Christ, which was intended to serve as a chantry for the whole Lancastrian affinity: masses were to be said not only for the duke and his ancestors, but also for his friends and well-wishers, and for all those to whom he was bound.[96] At the same time, duke Henry had sought, with some success, to revive popular devotion to the cult of the

(Hertford); 1508–10 (Pontefract); Nottinghamshire Record Office, Dd Fj 9/7/14 (Tickhill); DL 28/3/1 m. 3 (Savoy).

[92] SC 8/223/11132; DL 29/728/11980–3; DL 29/58/1079—1081 for work at Hertford.

[93] L. F. Salzman, *Building in England, down to 1540* (Oxford, 1967), pp. 460–1, 463; R. R. Davies, *Lordship and Society in the March of Wales 1282–1400* (Oxford, 1978), p. 79; DL 43/15/7 m. 6 (Pevensey).

[94] *Reg. I* 1156 (1372); DL 28/3/1 m. 4 (1376); *Reg. II* 92, 206, 279, 422 (1379); DL 43/15/5 m. 4 for a payment of £800 towards the work; WAM 57067 for a request to the abbot of Westminster for timber to be used at Kenilworth.

[95] J. H. Harvey, 'Side-Lights on Kenilworth Castle', *Archaeological Journal*, 101 (1944), 98; 'Accompts of the Manor of the Savoy, temp. Richard II', *Archaeologia*, 24 (1832), 307: *VCH Warwickshire*, vi. 135; G. Fox, *History of Pontefract* (Pontefract, 1827), p. 68.

[96] K. A. Fowler, *The King's Lieutenant* (London, 1969), pp. 188–91. A. H. Thompson, *The History of the Hospital and the New College of the Annunciation of St Mary in the Newarke, Leicester* (Leicester, 1937), pp. 54–5.

murdered earl Thomas at Pontefract and, by establishing a chantry chapel there in 1355, to turn the priory of St John into a shrine for the patron and protector of the Lancastrian cause.[97] John of Gaunt faithfully, if somewhat lukewarmly, maintained these traditions. He showed no great interest in the cult of his grandfather's enemy, but he continued to support a hermit at the shrine[98] and, although his own favoured church was St Paul's, where he established chantries for himself and the duchess Blanche,[99] he carefully set aside 100 marks a year for the completion of his father-in-law's plans at Leicester.[100] In consequence, St Mary Newarke continued to attract the devotions and benefactions of the Lancastrian affinity. Simon Simeon, steward at Bolingbroke, established a chantry for the souls of duke Henry and the healthful estate of duke John in the new college and chose to be buried there himself;[101] Mary Hervey, formerly a lady-in-waiting to duchess Blanche, and Maud, widow of Thomas Hervey, controller of the duke's household, both established chantries there;[102] Sir Robert Swillington left two missals to the foundation, one new and the other an old one 'which I borrowed from the dean',[103] and the dean himself, Richard Elvet, set up a chantry for his brother, John, clerk of the duke's wardrobe, and the souls of the duke and duchess.[104]

Prayers for the dead were a solemn obligation of blood and friendship. 'Instead of a great retinue and throng of followers, their body shall have a throng of worms and their soul a throng of demons', threatened the preachers,[105] but lord and man continued to offer each other protection beyond the grave. Figures as diverse in social standing as Sir John Saville and Richard Gest of Coston, clerk of the duke's kitchen, endowed prayers for the souls of John of Gaunt and his family.[106] In return, the duke obtained for his servants a share in the

---

[97] *Calendar of Papal Registers, Petitions 1342–1419*, 271; *VCH Yorkshire*, iii. 186; *Chronicon Angliae*, p. 41.

[98] *Reg. I* 949; BL Stowe Charter 64.

[99] *Testamenta Eboracensia*, ed. J. Raine (Surtees Soc., 4, 1836), i. 227; *Reg. I* 918; DL 28/3/5 f. 18v.

[100] *Reg. I* 660; DL 29/341/5515 m. 2, 5516 m. 2, 728/11975 m. 2, 11977 m. 2, 11979 m. 1, 11985 m. 1 for payments.

[101] Thompson, op. cit. 87; Lincolnshire Archives Office, Reg. XII f. 347v.

[102] *CPR 1408–13*, 171, 183.

[103] PROB 11/1 f. 59v.

[104] *Calendar of Papal Registers, Petitions 1396–1414*, 272.

[105] G. R. Owst, *Literature and Pulpit in Medieval England* (Cambridge, 1933), pp. 293–4.

[106] C. 143/426/36; PROB 11/2A f. 119.

spiritual benefits that his social position inevitably commanded. When he was admitted to a religious fraternity, his attendants and those he recommended were usually admitted with him;[107] for the family of his confessor he obtained plenary remission of their sins at the hour of death;[108] it was at the Lancaster chantry in St Paul's that Sir Richard Burley wished prayers for his own soul to be said.[109] The duke spared no expense on the ceremonies of the church, spending nearly £600 on the burial of duchess Constance,[110] precisely because they demonstrated publicly the social cohesion of his affinity and, by the public nature of the display, confirmed its legitimacy; the obit of duchess Blanche, in particular, gave him the opportunity for a lavish display of strength in the middle of London in front of a distinguished audience.[111] As a result, shared religious observance provided an additional bond of unity for the affinity, bringing a solidarity that went deeper than the assurance of mutual advantage that gave cohesion to the Lancastrian retinue in the secular world.

Religion was more than an outward show, however, and it did more to unite the Lancastrian affinity around the duke than a concentration on public ceremonial can reveal. Henry of Grosmont's spiritual concerns created a tradition of genuine Lancastrian piety[112] that served to provide his successor with an additional claim on the sentiments and loyalty of his retainers. Gaunt and his retainers shared common attachments to particular religious houses[113] and they shared the same spiritual instructors;[114] in consequence, they shared elements of

---

[107] e.g. BL Cotton Nero D VII f. 132v—admission of Sir William Parr to the fraternity of St Albans, *licet absens*, at the request of duchess Constance.

[108] *Calendar of Papal Registers, Petitions 1342–1419*, 529–30.

[109] *Registrum Johannis Gilbert, Episcopi Herefordensis*, ed. J. H. Parry (Canterbury and York Soc., 18, 1915), pp. 109–10.

[110] DL 28/32/21; cf. *Chronicon Henrici Knighton*, ii. 321; *Annales Ricardi Secundi*, p. 168—*cum magnis sumptibus et solmenitate*.

[111] *Anonimalle Chronicle*, p. 156.

[112] *Testamenta Eboracensia*, ed. J. Raine (Surtees Soc., 4, 1836), i. 202: Mary Roos leaves to Isabella Percy a copy of the 'Livre de Seyntz Medicines'—*uno libro gallico de duce Lancastrie*.

[113] e.g. the abbey of Barlings (Lincolnshire), where Gaunt established an anniversary for himself in 1386. Sir John Rocheford, his steward in Lincolnshire, chose to be buried there, and John Dowedale, one of the valets of the duke's household, left half his movable goods to the abbey. Guildhall Lib., St Paul's, Dean and Chapter, MS A 1944; *The Register of Bishop Philip Repingdon*, ed. M. Archer (Lincoln Record Soc., 57–8, 73, 1963–82), i. 179–80; ii. 210–12.

[114] e.g. Sir Roger Trumpington makes a bequest to Fr. Walter Disse, the duke's confessor; Ivo de Wyram leaves 10s. to Fr. John Feltwell, a clerk of the duke's chapel. Lincolnshire Archives Office, Reg. XII f. 191; PROB 11/2A f. 146v.

an identifiable devotional style. The style was that set by the careerist soldiers and courtiers surrounding Richard II, who combined an ascetic tendency towards funeral austerity and penitential rhetoric in their wills with a new social awareness, manifested in their interest in the foundation of hospitals and poor houses.[115] The duke's own will, his preoccupation with the dissolution of the body, evinced in his insistence that his corpse should not be interred for forty days after his death, his stipulation that no solemnity or feast should be associated with his burial, and his considerable monetary bequests to the poor, amounting to almost £2,000, all demonstrate how closely he was in touch with this current of contemporary piety.[116]

His retainers took their cue from his example. Some of those most intimately concerned in the movement, such as Richard, lord Scrope, or Sir Robert Knolles,[117] were already in his service and there were other members of the Lancastrian affinity in contact with the court, such as Sir Neel Loring and Sir John Dabridgecourt,[118] who show the same conspicuous concern for the poor. The prestige and influence of the court meant that these attitudes were soon disseminated downwards, among the gentry followers of the duke. Some, at least, of his retainers were attracted by the ascetic zeal which led the 'Lollard Knights' towards the rejection of all worldly ceremony and funeral pomp: severest of all, Sir Philip Tilney allowed only two candles to be burnt about his body; Sir Ralph Hastings allowed three, but added a modish contempt for the world—*isto miserrimo seculo*—in his insistence that his body be drawn to Sulby Abbey on a simple cart.[119] Sir Andrew Lutterell concluded his otherwise orthodox will with the characteristically Lollard request that its probate and administration should be carried out without the swearing of

[115] J. Catto, 'Religion and the English Nobility in the Late Fourteenth Century', *History and Imagination*, ed. H. Lloyd-Jones, V. Pearl, and A. B. Worden (London, 1981), pp. 47–52.

[116] *Test. Ebor.*, i. 225, 229; J. B. Post, 'The Obsequies of John of Gaunt', *Guildhall Studies in London History*, 5 (1981), 2–4.

[117] Borthwick Institute, Bishops' Register XVI, ff. 142–3; Lambeth, Reg. Arundel I, f. 245: Scrope left the residue of his goods to build a poor house at Wennesley; Knolles founded an almshouse at Pontefract, to which he bequeathed his whole chapel furniture and 1,000 marks in cash.

[118] Lincolnshire Archives Office, Reg. XII f. 322; *The Register of Henry Chichele, archbishop of Canterbury, 1414–1443*, ed. E. F. Jacob (Canterbury and York Soc., 1937), ii. 57. Loring left money to the leper houses of London; Dabridgecourt provided for an immediate distribution to 120 paupers and 140 'bedredyn'.

[119] Lincolnshire Archives Office, Reg. XII f. 417v; Borthwick Institute, Bishops' Register XV, f. 12.

any oaths.[120] Sir Robert Knolles, Sir Richard Burley, William Balderston, and Sir Robert Berney all made specific injunctions against funeral pomp, Balderston and Berney adding that the money saved should be given to the poor.[121]

In part, the charitable interest that Berney and others displayed sprang from a traditional, unremarkable, awareness of the obligations of lordship: a testator's poor tenants, for instance, were often singled out among his beneficiaries.[122] However, the endowment of specific hospitals[123] and the detailed nature of some legacies suggest a more personal involvement on the part of some testators; Berney, for example, enjoined that two infirm men were to be kept in food and clothing at his expense for a year after his death; William Hoghwyk, Henry of Derby's cook, left money to clothe 23 paupers and gave precise details of the clothes they were to have.[124] Such provisions were common in Lancastrian wills; in all, 28 of the 58 retainers and annuitants whose wills survive provided for the relief of poverty and disease, whereas an examination of the wills of the Yorkshire gentry at much the same period suggests a similar provision in only one case in ten, and a study of charitable bequests among the higher nobility as a whole a proportion of one in three.[125] Interest in the works of mercy was, therefore, unusually common among the duke's retainers; the example of the duke himself and the contact with current fashions of court piety which his service brought combined to impart a common devotional style to the Lancastrian affinity and a shared concern for the same religious issues.

If the wills left by the duke's retainers serve to indicate some of the ways in which the duke's affinity possessed a shared set of interests and ideals, they are also indispensable in illustrating the range of alternative calls upon a retainer's time and in providing the perspective in which to

---

[120] Lincolnshire Archives Office, Reg. XII f. 374v; cf. J. Wyclif, *Opus Evangelicum*, ed. J. Loserth (Wyclif Soc., 1895), i. 49–51.

[121] Lambeth, Reg. Arundel I, f. 245; *Reg. Gilbert*, p. 110; *Reg. Chichele*, iii. 409; Borthwick Institute, Probate Register 3, f. 242.

[122] e.g. PROB 11/1 f. 59v (Swillington), 2B f. 304 (Harcourt); E. 210/6658 (Englefield).

[123] PROB 11/2A f. 74v (Berkley), 2B f. 395v (Bridges).

[124] *Reg. Chichele*, iii. 409; Borthwick Institute, Bishops' Register XVIII, ff. 355v–356.

[125] M. G. A. Vale, *Piety, Charity and Literacy Among the Yorkshire Gentry, 1370–1485* (Borthwick Papers, 50, 1976), p. 28; J. T. Rosenthal, *The Purchase of Paradise. Gift Giving and the Aristocracy, 1307–1485* (London, 1972), p. 103. P. W. Fleming, 'Charity, Faith and the Gentry of Kent, 1422–1529', *Property and Politics in Later Medieval English History*, ed. A. J. Pollard (Gloucester, 1984), p. 46 points out that such particularity in the bequest of alms to the poor was a relatively late development among the Kentish gentry, which does not appear with any frequency until the later fifteenth century.

view the retainers' relations with John of Gaunt. The picture that emerges is a discouraging one for those who maintain the primacy of lordship and magnate service in the lives of the late medieval gentry. At first glance, the hold of the Lancastrian affinity over the lives of its members seems to have been slight. Only three wills mention the duke directly: Sir Robert Swillington left *mon tresgracieuse seigneur* his best horse and finest hanaper, Sir Richard Burley wished to be buried in St Paul's, opposite the duke's tomb, and Richard Gest endowed prayers for the soul of the duke by the Carmelites of Calais.[126] In their different ways, each of these men owed much of their fortune and advancement to the duke and their gratitude is understandable, but they provide the only direct testamentary commemoration of Gaunt in the wills of his retainers, although Sir John Saville's bequest to the chapel of St Clement, within the castle of Pontefract, 'if it should happen that I die there' makes oblique reference to his service of the duke as constable of the castle.[127] By itself, this is not surprising; last wills and testaments were designed as preparations for death and, as an examination of John Englefield's will in relation to his career has already demonstrated, they cannot be expected to reflect all the preoccupations of a lifetime. More significant, however, is the evidence that they provide for the reality of the claims made by other lords on the loyalty and service of the 'Lancastrian' affinity. In general, they contain more bequests to other lords and benefactors than they do to the duke himself. Thus, John of Gaunt was not the only patron Richard Gest chose to commemorate; Edmund, duke of York, was remembered as well. Sir Nicholas Gernoun left a golden buckle to the earl of Buckingham and a silver pyx to the countess of Oxford; Sir Robert Rous made separate bequests to his lord and lady, the earl and countess of Kent.[128] Such knightly retainers were, perhaps, always on the edge of the Lancastrian affinity and should not be expected to entertain any great sense of obligation towards the duke. The argument will not hold for Robert Morton of Bawtry, who acted as Gaunt's chief administrator in Yorkshire for thirty years, but referred to bishop Buckingham of Lincoln as his lord and left him his best goblet. Nor to John Bathe, keeper of the duke's privy expenses over many years, who chose rather to commemorate a more recent connection with the Holland family in his will.[129]

---

[126] PROB 11/1 f. 59; 2A f. 119; *Reg. Gilbert*, p. 109.

[127] Borthwick Institute, Bishops' Register XVI, f. 170.

[128] Norfolk Record Office, NCC Harsyk ff. 27–28; PROB 11/1 f. 1.

[129] Borthwick Institute, Bishops' Register XIV f. 60v; Lambeth Palace Lib., Reg. Arundel II, f. 39v.

This raises an important question about the cohesion of the Lancastrian affinity as a whole and, indeed, about the degree of stability to be attributed to 'bastard feudalism' as a social system. Was it usual for the duke of Lancaster's retainers to be fee'd by other magnates as well? If it was, how did they divide their time and loyalties? Would they desert one lord if a better offer of employment from another came along? If the answer to these questions is affirmative, then bastard feudal society can hardly be characterized as other than 'loosely organized and shamelessly competitive'.[130]

Some exceptions from the investigation must first be made. Every retainer and annuitant was employed by the duke for a specific purpose and, if that purpose could be fulfilled while serving other lords as well, then there was no objection to a retainer doing so and taking his fee at the same time. Lawyers fall most clearly into this category: Sir Robert Plessington was chief of Thomas Woodstock's council, had been the countess of Bedford's chief steward, and took fees from both the Mowbrays and the Staffords, but, as long as he continued to act successfully as the duke's attorney at the Exchequer, there was nothing to be said against these other commitments.[131] Indeed, the duke may have welcomed the opportunity to find out what his peers were thinking and planning. Estate officials enjoyed a similar latitude and often acted as steward for other lords besides Gaunt; the career of Thomas Bridges in Gloucestershire[132] can be matched by the many employers of such well-respected Lancastrians as Robert Morton[133] or William Nessfield.[134] A magnate who fee'd them was paying for their local knowledge and local influence, not buying their allegiance. Their loyalty was the loyalty of a land agent to his client and there is no evidence that it extended, or was

[130] K. B. McFarlane, 'Parliament and "Bastard Feudalism"', *TRHS* 4th series, 26 (1944), 70.

[131] E. 28/3 (14 Feb. 1392); *CPR 1381–5*, 166, 434; Staffordshire Record Office, D. 641/1/2/1 m. 4. For the numerous fees received by Robert Tirwhit, whom Gaunt retained as his serjeant-at-law in 1396/7 see N. Ramsay, 'Retained Legal Counsel, *c.*1275–*c.*1475', *TRHS* 5th series, 24 (1985), 105.

[132] N. Saul, *Knights and Esquires* (Oxford, 1981), pp. 87, 285, 289.

[133] Besides his connection with Bishop Buckingham of Lincoln, Morton was steward and bailiff for life to Alexander Neville, archbishop of York, steward of the Yorkshire lands of Edmund, earl of Cambridge, in receipt of two annuities from the Crown, and a life-tenant of the manor of Eakrigg (Notts.) by the gift of Thomas, lord Roos, of Helmsley. *CPR 1385–9*, 437; ibid. *1381–5*, 320; ibid. *1377–81*, 221; *CCR 1381–5*, 439.

[134] Nessfield took a fee from the Mowbrays; he was chief steward of Edmund, earl of Cambridge's lands and of the lands of the Nuns Preacher at Dartford, king's attorney in the North, and steward of the archbishop of Canterbury's liberties in Yorkshire. *CPR 1358–61*, 268, 357; E. 403/431 m. 12; *CPR 1361–4*, 338; F. R. H. du Boulay, *The Lordship of Canterbury: An Essay on Medieval Society* (London, 1966), p. 396.

expected to extend, beyond the boundaries of the estates they were employed to administer.

Secondly, it is important to distinguish between those who transferred themselves to John of Gaunt's service while their former lord was still alive and those who entered his retinue on the death of their previous master. The second category is relatively large; the first much smaller, despite the undoubted attractions of service with a magnate as powerful as Gaunt. Many of Edward, prince of Wales's former servants made the transition to Gaunt's retinue, for instance,[135] and the duke picked up retainers from his elder brother, Lionel, duke of Clarence,[136] while Henry of Derby's marriage to Mary Bohun opened a path of preferment for a number of the last earl of Hereford's retainers as well.[137] The duke's catchment area was wide; he attracted to his affinity the servants of lesser masters, such as Henry ap Philip, previously in service with Sir Nicholas Audley, or Guyon the clerk, who had been in the household of Sir John Chandos,[138] who were anxious to improve their prospects, as well as veterans of the royal household like William Hervey and Sir Nicholas Dabridgecourt, excluded from preferment in the new king's reign, for whom a Lancastrian annuity was a welcome comfort in lean times.[139]

Such men, simultaneously in receipt of a Crown pension and a Lancastrian annuity, constitute the third and most important category of those who could legitimately serve two masters. The question of divided allegiance could not, in theory, arise and, for the duke, a royal grant to one of his retainers carried with it a number of advantages: it was a reassuring token of the favour his followers enjoyed; by soliciting such grants from the Crown, he could demonstrate to potential recruits his influence and standing with the king; the grant itself increased his

---

[135] e.g. Sir John Kentwood; Sir Andrew Lutterell; Sir Robert Rous; Sir Nicholas Sarnesfield; Sir Walter Urswick; Sir Ralph Paynel. BL Cotton Julius C IV, ff. 288–91; SC 6/772/5 m. 3d. *CPR 1377–81*, 70; *Register of Edward the Black Prince* (London, 1930–43), i. 431.

[136] Sir John Bromwych; Sir Thomas Dale. *CPR 1370–4*, 87; E. 101/28/25, 27.

[137] Robert Fitzralph; Sir William Lucy; Sir Thomas Morieux; Sir Thomas Symond. *CPR 1370–4*, 283, 373; E. 159/157, Brevia Baronibus, Hilary, m. 28d; DL 25/1545.

[138] R. A. Griffiths, *The Principality of Wales in the Later Middle Ages* (Cardiff, 1972), p. 280; *Reg. I* 783.

[139] Hervey left Edward III's household on the king's death and was removed from his office of sealer of the woolsacks by Richard II. *CFR 1377–83*, 51; *CPR 1358–61*, 457; ibid. *1388–92*, 321. Darbrigecourt was granted the constableship of Nottingham castle for life by Edward III but removed in favour of one of Richard II's knights; he lost the custodianship of Stratfield Saye at the same time. *CPR 1374–7*, 349; ibid. 1377–81, 305; *CFR 1377–83*, 395; *CIM 1377–88*, no. 78.

retainer's substance without depleting the duke's. While the value of the annuities the king granted to John of Gaunt's retainers naturally varied enormously, the most generous royal grants were on a scale that even Lancaster could not match: Sir Otes Granson, who received 100 marks p.a. from Gaunt, took £200 p.a. from Richard II;[140] Thomas, lord Roos, paid £50 by the duke, enjoyed a royal annuity of nearly £250 p.a.[141] A favoured confidant of the king could expect even more: Sir Nicholas Sarnesfield, Richard's standard-bearer, enjoyed a life-income of £320 p.a. from various Crown grants.[142] In consequence, a valuable servant could always be lured from the duke's service to the king's by the prospect of richer rewards, but when this happened he did not cease to be of use to Gaunt. Any contact with the king was valuable and any Lancastrian in the royal household was valued as a source of information and advice.

From this point of view, Gaunt was best served during the early 1370s, when three of his retainers occupied important administrative positions in Edward III's household: Sir John Neville as steward between 1371 and 1376; Sir John de Ipres, as controller of the wardrobe from 1368 to 1376, and then as steward in succession to Neville; Sir Richard Scrope as treasurer between 1371 and 1375.[143] Sir John Knyvet, chancellor from 1372 to 1377, was, in addition, one of the duke's justices of the forest in Lancashire.[144] In this context, serving two masters presented few problems. As controller of the household, for instance, Sir John de Ipres spent much of his time on royal business but he still had leisure enough to attend to his duties as sheriff of Lancashire and to sit on the duke's council;[145] while on duty in the household, his position of trust allowed him a measure of informal control over the distribution of royal patronage that was itself invaluable.[146] The Lancastrian presence in the royal administration, therefore, was most influential before John of Gaunt's political predominance began to attract unfavourable notice; however

---

[140] *CPR 1391–6*, 63, 342.

[141] *CPR 1377–81*, 246; *CCR 1377–81*, 17.

[142] *CPR 1377–81*, 70; ibid. *1381–5*, 316, 339; ibid. *1385–9*, 17, 18, 279.

[143] T. F. Tout, *Chapters in the Administrative History of Medieval England* (Manchester, 1920–33), vi. 23, 28, 43,

[144] DL 10/336; DL 42/1 f. 71; cf. SC 1/63/244.

[145] E. 109/396/11 f. 15, 397/5 ff. 36v, 79, 398/9 f. 29; DL 28/3/1 m. 7; E. 101/396/11 f. 19*d* for his presence in Lancashire; he continued to discharge his duties as sheriff after his appointment as controller: JUST 1/451 B m. 6.

[146] SC 1/56/45.

threatening his private power might later appear, his grip on the institutions of government was never again so tight.

In the early years of Richard II's reign, his annuitants remained prominent in the royal administration; Scrope continued to act as steward until May 1378 and then served as chancellor for two short periods between October 1378 and July 1382 while Sir Hugh Segrave, who had been briefly steward of Lancaster's household in 1370–1, acted as treasurer between 1381 and 1386.[147] However, neither of them was as closely identified with the duke and his policies as Ipres and Neville and, as the hostility of the young Richard II and his circle of advisers towards John of Gaunt increased, so the duke's influence on the conduct of government inevitably diminished. A Lancastrian presence in the royal household reappears by 1393, once good relations between the king and the duke had been fully restored, with Sir John Holland acting as chamberlain of the household and Sir Thomas Percy as steward,[148] but this did not mark a return to the easy access to the royal administration that Gaunt had enjoyed at the end of Edward III's reign. Both men were Lancastrian annuitants but, whereas John de Ipres owed his place in the king's household to the patronage and support of the duke of Lancaster, Holland and Percy owed their Lancastrian annuities to the favour they already enjoyed from the king.

Yet even when relations between the duke and his nephew were at their worst, Gaunt kept a foot in the door of the royal household by means of the annuities he paid to some of Richard's chamber-knights: in 1383/4, Sir Thomas Morieux and Sir Nicholas Sarnesfield were both his annuitants and relations with Sir Richard Abberbury, the father of one of the duke's retainers, were cordial.[149] For John of Gaunt, the value of these men lay, above all else, in keeping him informed; chamber-knights like Sarnesfield were usually employed to communicate to the duke the deliberations of the king and council, and he was likely to receive a franker report of proceedings from a messenger whom he fee'd.[150] In addition, the king's household was a centre of gossip and accusations against the duke and it was by having his own men there that Gaunt was best able to thwart the efforts of his

[147] Tout, op. cit. vi. 16, 23.

[148] BL Add. MS 35115, f. 40*d*; E. 101/403/10 f. 43*d*.

[149] E. 101/401/2 f. 42; cf. DL 28/1/2 f. 16v.

[150] E. 404/12/78 (23 Aug. 1380); 13/83 (10 Sept. 1382). Sarnesfield was sent to the North to certify the duke of the council's ordinances concerning the forthcoming March day, and to Leicester to inform him of the bishop of Hereford's report before the council.

enemies. When one such rumour was spreading in August 1394, it was quickly brought to the duke's attention in distant Pontefract and he was able to dispatch a messenger to declare his innocence at once.[151] The messenger himself was carefully chosen; as one of Richard II's diplomatic experts, Sir Richard Abberbury's double standing as a Lancastrian retainer and a royal employee lent his words extra credence and his service to Gaunt added value.[152]

Despite these exceptions, it is not difficult to point out some striking instances of multiple allegiance among John of Gaunt's retainers. Sir Robert Rous counted the king, the earl of Buckingham, and the Fitzalans among his patrons, quite apart from his connection with the Hollands;[153] Sir William Bagot was retained by the Beauchamps and the Mowbrays as well as by Gaunt;[154] Sir Thomas Hungerford had as many as five other lords beside the duke of Lancaster.[155] Many more of the duke's retainers enjoyed at least one other fee, from a wide range of magnate patrons: the earls of Warwick;[156] the duke of Brittany;[157] the Mortimer earls of March;[158] the earls of Kent;[159] John, lord Lovell;[160] Richard, lord Poynings;[161] Margaret, countess Marshal;[162] the archbishops of Canterbury;[163] the bishops of Ely.[164]

---

[151] *Anglo-Norman Letters and Petitions*, ed. M. D. Legge (Anglo-Norman Text Society, 3, 1941), pp. 74–6. The date is suggested by V. H. Galbraith, 'A New Life of Richard II', *History*, NS 26 (1942), 231.

[152] E. 403/546 mm. 13, 16, 549 mm. 2, 6, 556 m. 14 for his missions abroad.

[153] *CCR 1377–81*, 49; *Foedera* III. iii. 96; *CCR 1374–7*, 145; *Testamenta Vetusta*, ed. N. H. Nicolas (London, 1826), i. 105.

[154] BL Cotton Nero D. VII f. 129v; C. 137/81/8.

[155] J. S. Roskell, 'Sir Thomas Hungerford', in *Parliament and Politics in Late Medieval England* (London, 1981–3), ii. 21–7.

[156] Sir Roger Beauchamp; Sir William Beauchamp; Sir Godfrey Foljambe; Thomas Lucy; William Barewell acted as deputy for Thomas, earl of Warwick, in the shrievalty of Worcestershire, 1383–90. *CCR 1360–4*, 570; BL Cotton Charters, XI. 70; *CPR 1350–4*, 425; W. Dugdale, *The Antiquities of Warwickshire* (London, 1656), pp. 397–8; *List of Sheriffs* (List and Indexes, 9), p. 57.

[157] John, lord Neville; Roger Toup. *CFR 1377–83*, 275; C. 81/1343 (24).

[158] Sir John Bromwich; Sir Nicholas Gernoun; Sir John de la Pole of Newborough. *CIPM* XV, 560–1; *CPR 1381–5*, 269; Griffiths, *The Principality of Wales*, 112–13.

[159] John Bathe. Lambeth, Reg. Arundel II, f. 39v.

[160] William Scargill. *CPR 1374–7*, 517.

[161] Hugh Waterton, *CIPM* XVI, 611.

[162] Sir William Frank. *Sir Christopher Hatton's Book of Seals*, ed. L. C. Lloyd and D. M. Stenton (Northants Record Soc., 15, 1950), no. 486.

[163] John Pelham; Richard Perrers. *CPR 1396–9*, 249; *Gesta Abbatum Monasterii Sancti Albani*, ed. H. T. Riley (Rolls Series, 1869), iii. 333–4.

[164] Thomas Braunston; Sir Philip Tilney. *VCH Cambridgeshire*, iv. 250; M. E. Aston, *Thomas Arundel* (Oxford, 1967), pp. 212–13. Cf. below, p. 186 for an analysis of alternative calls on the Lancastrian affinity's loyalty in a single county, Norfolk.

With better information, the list of alternative lords for the duke's retainers would certainly be longer. What is not clear, however, is whether these men were typical of the Lancastrian affinity as a whole. The real question is one of degree: what *proportion* of the duke's following was employed by other masters remains uncertain and, granted the imperfect nature of the surviving evidence, is likely to remain so. Only informed guesswork can provide an answer.

In these circumstances, to estimate the simultaneous pensioners of several lords as a small proportion of the whole affinity may seem to rest too heavily on the argument from silence. Nevertheless, where it is possible to examine the composition of other magnate followings, even those with a close connection with the duke of Lancaster, the degree of duplication in their personnel seems only slight. Thus, Sir William Castleacre, the duke's steward at Hertford, also acted for the duke of Gloucester, while Sir Thomas Percy was a member of Gloucester's council, as he was of Gaunt's; Richard Gest, clerk of his kitchen, farmed some Gloucester manors.[165] Another Lancastrian retainer beside Sir William Bagot, Sir John Peyto, took a fee from Thomas Mowbray, earl of Nottingham.[166] In the case of each retinue, however —and both of them have been investigated in some detail[167]—these are the only examples of simultaneous pensioners that the evidence provides and there are other instances, even for well-documented affinities like those of the earls of Devon[168] or Stafford,[169] where there is no sign of a Lancastrian presence at all. The largest affinity of all, the king's, provides rather more evidence of dual allegiance, but, even here, the signs are that Richard II did not, until the very end of his life, trespass much upon the loyalty of his uncle's retainers. Among 149 identifiable king's knights, some 15 were in simultaneous receipt of a pension from Gaunt,[170] but, once distinguished foreigners, like Sir Otes Granson and Sir Herman Hans, and members of the duke's

---

[165] A. Goodman, *The Loyal Conspiracy* (London, 1971), p. 100; BL Add. MS 40859A m. 4; DL 29/42/815–6.

[166] See below, p. 110, n. 174.

[167] Goodman, op. cit. 87–105, 156 ff; R. E. Archer, 'The Mowbrays: Earls of Nottingham and Dukes of Norfolk to 1432' (unpub. Oxford Univ. D.Phil. thesis, 1984), pp. 339–40.

[168] BL Add. Rolls, 13972; 64320–2; 64803.

[169] Staffordshire Record Office, D. 641/1/2/1–5, 33, 36, 40A.

[170] C. J. Given-Wilson, *The Royal Household and the King's Affinity*, pp. 283–6. Sir John Croft, Sir Hugh Lutterell, and Sir Ralph Radcliffe had, in addition, all been servants of Gaunt at one time, but seem likely to have passed out of Lancastrian service by the time they entered Richard II's affinity.

immediate family, such as John Beaufort and Ralph Neville, are taken into account, the number of Lancastrian retainers whose dual allegiance seems to raise the possibility of a conflict of political loyalties can be reduced to a handful, albeit an influential one—Sir William Bagot, Sir John Bussy, Sir John Cornwall, Sir Henry Green, Sir Richard Hoghton, and, perhaps, Sir John Thornbury. Each of these men was in the duke's service before he entered the king's; Sir Richard Redman of Levens, a king's knight since 1388, seems the only man the duke retained who was already a member of the royal affinity.

The loyalty of Gaunt's retainers was clearly not indivisible and, save in a few exceptional cases, probably never deeply engaged but, for most of his servants, the rule seems to have been one lord at a time. In part, this can be explained by the nature of the service required of an indentured retainer. If the military stipulations in his contract were taken seriously, and there is reason to suppose that they were, then satisfactory service of more than one lord at any one time would have been very difficult for the knightly retainer. Moreover, most lords were in a buyer's market—there were many gentlemen anxious to join their service and a limited number of fees and rewards available. In consequence, only the exceptionally talented or influential could expect to be employed by one lord in the full knowledge that part of their time and energies were committed to another. It was the iron law of supply and demand, not a residual feudal loyalty, that kept the Lancastrian affinity stable in its membership. Indeed, in certain circumstances, multiple allegiances added to, rather than detracted from, the cohesion of the affinity. This occurred when the ties of loyalty created by a shared allegiance to the duke were cemented by the fees one retainer paid to another. Thus, Sir Ralph Hastings took fees from Thomas, lord Roos, and John, lord Neville, in addition to his Lancastrian annuity;[171] in his turn, Neville took a fee from Roos, who also retained two more retainers of the duke: Robert Morton and Sir Ralph Paynel.[172] The network of mutual dependence and protection that such ties created was designed for the sole benefit of the participants but it helped, incidentally, to add structure and stability to the Lancastrian affinity as well. Besides these examples, of course, must be set those retainers of the duke who undoubtedly did manipulate their magnate contacts for their own ends: men like Sir

[171] HMC, *Report on the Manuscripts of the late Reginald Rawdon Hastings*, i. 178; C. 136/100/3.

[172] E. 210/6927, *CPR 1370–4*, 194; *CCR 1381–5*, 219, 435.

William Swynburn, who played one lord off against another in order to secure his own independence of action,[173] or Sir John Peyto, whose search for sufficiently partisan backing to his claim on the estates of the Langley family led him from the service of the earls of Stafford and Salisbury to the Lancastrian retinue and from there to the Mowbray affinity.[174] Nevertheless, these glaring instances of elastic loyalty are too infrequent, in the Lancastrian affinity at least, to substantiate the charge that bastard feudalism disrupted and destabilized existing relations between lords and their followers. On occasion, it could positively strengthen them and, for most of the duke's retainers, one lord at a time was, of necessity, the rule.

Doubts over the loyalty and allegiance of the Lancastrian affinity, raised by a study of their wills, can thus be largely resolved by considering a wider body of evidence. Yet this is not the only question they pose about the cohesion and effectiveness of the duke's following. Sir Robert Swillington, who remembered the duke in his will, also commemorated the social community created by the duke's service in an emphatically Lancastrian series of bequests to the top lay and clerical administrators of the ducal household: Sir Philip Tilney and Sir John Deyncourt; Master William Ashton and William Chusilden. Robert Morton of Bawtry made a more modest one to Nicholas Colne, his subordinate in the receiver's office at Pontefract.[175] Yet, as these examples suggest, such bequests were only common in the wills of those who were involved in the daily running of the Lancastrian household and estates. The constant professional association required in an administrator's life provided a bond of corporate loyalty that the shared allegiance announced in an indenture of retainer could not, apparently, supply. Sir John Plays's commemoration of his former companions-in-arms in the duke's retinue of war, Sir William Beauchamp and Sir John Marmion, provides rare evidence for the same sentiments among Gaunt's military followers, supplemented only by the tokens of friendship between Sir Thomas Dale and Sir Roger Trumpington.[176]

---

[173] See below, p. 253.

[174] P. R. Coss, *The Langley Family and its Cartulary: A Study in Late Medieval 'Gentry'* (Dugdale Soc., Occasional Papers, 22, 1974), pp. 16–17; *CCR 1369–74*, 457; *CPR 1391–6*, 395; *CPR 1388–92*, 51, 280; J. F. Baldwin, *The King's Council in England During the Middle Ages* (Oxford, 1913), p. 491.

[175] PROB 11/1 f. 59; Borthwick Institute, Bishops' Register XIV, f. 61.

[176] Guildhall Lib., MS 9531/3 f. 395; Lincolnshire Archives Office, Reg. XII ff. 190v–191, 197v.

Friendship may seem too delicate an emotion to be recovered by a simple scrutiny of legatees but the provision for the administration of their wills made by the duke's retainers serves to reinforce the suspicion that the Lancastrian service and its demands counted for little in the everyday lives of many retainers. When it came to choosing supervisors and executors to carry out the all-important task of implementing their last wishes, most retainers preferred to confer the responsibility on their immediate family, aided perhaps by some close friends, rather than rely upon the undoubted administrative talent available within the duke's affinity. In general, the Lancastrian connection was better employed providing supervisors, responsible for monitoring the executors' actions and arbitrating any disputes that might arise, than executors: Swillington asked the duke himself to oversee the execution of his will; Robert Whitby chose his successor as receiver-general, John Legbourne; Nicholas Usk, treasurer of the duke's household, chose his father-in-law, John Norbury; William Balderston asked Thomas Langley, formerly his companion in the duke's service, now chancellor of England, to act as guardian for his son.[177] By contrast, acting as an executor was too onerous and personal a task for the sort of relationship created by the affinity to prove very useful; only 6 of the 58 wills left by retainers and officials of the duke included colleagues from Lancastrian service among the executors.[178]

The ties of bastard feudalism were not, therefore, the concerns uppermost in the minds of the duke's retainers as they prepared for death. John Englefield's will has already indicated what was: local charities, family settlements, rewards for the servants. Virtually without exception, the wills they made are narrow in their range of interests and determinedly parochial in the attitudes they evince. It is the local sins, unpaid debts and goods unjustly extorted,[179] oppressions by their bailiffs and injustice to their servants,[180] that weigh most heavily on

[177] PROB 11/1 f. 59; *The Register of Bishop Philip Repingdon, 1405–1419*, ed. M. Archer (Lincoln Record Soc., 57–8, 73, 1963–82), i. 191; PROB 11/2A f. 23. Borthwick Institute, Probate Register 3, f. 242.

[178] Sir Robert Knolles; Sir Robert Swillington; Sir Thomas Dale; John, lord Neville of Raby; Sir Richard Burley; Sir Thomas Erpingham.

[179] Norfolk Record Office, NCC Heydon f. 165 (Wombe), Harsyke f. 84 (Gournay); Lincolnshire Archives Office, Reg. XII f. 417v (Tilney); *Reg. Chichele*, ii. 52 (Dabridgecourt); Borthwick Institute, Bishops' Register XV, f. 12v (Hastings), VA, ff. 334–335 (Rempston); J. Raine, *The History and Antiquities of Hemingborough* (York, 1888), p. 398 (Thomas, lord Roos).

[180] Guildhall Lib., MS 9531/3 f. 395 (Plays); PROB 11/1 f. 59 (Swillington).

their conscience. The most popular choice of burial place is, rather conservatively, a nearby house of religious,[181] and almost every will remembers the parish church and the parish priest, even if they contain no other ecclesiastical bequest.[182] Most confine their charity to churches and hospitals lying within a narrow radius of their own manors; even a man as prominent as Sir Thomas Fogg concentrated his bequests on the churches of Canterbury, where he lived.[183] There is, of course, nothing surprising in this, but it is not the light in which historians are accustomed to see the retainers of a great magnate. If the evidence of their wills is to be believed, the duke of Lancaster's retainers allowed the claims of lordship, whether Gaunt's or anyone else's, only a peripheral part in their concerns.

Since local concerns bulk so large in the lives of the duke's retainers, the part played by the Lancastrian affinity at the local level demands some definition. One way of gauging the relative strengths of lordship and locality is to examine the marriage alliances Gaunt's followers sought for themselves and their children. The choice of suitable spouses was one of the most crucial decisions to confront any gentry family, for upon it might depend the preservation or dissipation of their whole patrimony, the advancement or destruction of their lineage.[184] The duke's service was one source from which a wife might be drawn and, for the fortunate, it held out the prospect of a glamorous and lucrative match. Yet if the attractions of a marriage arranged or purchased by means of the Lancastrian affinity and its social contacts were strong, then so was the pull of the locality. Many of the duke's retainers were happy enough to marry among their neighbours in county society—understood in the social rather than strictly geographical sense, since it is clear that the gentry's horizons were wide enough to comprehend several adjacent counties.[185] If a retainer was of some

---

[181] PROB 11/2A ff. 124 (Bridges), 146v (Wyram); 2B f. 304 (Harcourt); Lambeth, Reg. Arundel I f. 245 (Knolles); Lincolnshire Archives Office, Reg. XII f. 322 (Loring); *Reg. Repingdon*, i. 62 (Berford), 179 (Dowedale); ii. 210 (Rocheford); Borthwick Institute, Bishops' Register XIV, f. 60v (Morton), Probate Register 2, f. 505 (Persay), 3 f. 248 (Usflete); cf. N. Saul, 'The Religious Sympathies of the Gentry in Gloucestershire, 1200–1500', *Transactions of the Bristol and Gloucestershire Arch. Soc.*, 98 (1980), 103–4.

[182] e.g. Lincolnshire Archives Office, Reg. XII f. 197v (Dale).

[183] Kent Archives Office, PRC 32/1/16.

[184] S. M. Wright, *The Derbyshire Gentry in the Fifteenth Century* (Derbyshire Record Soc., 8, 1983), pp. 29–50; C. Carpenter, 'The Fifteenth Century English Gentry and their Estates', *Gentry and Lesser Nobility in Later Medieval Europe*, ed. M. Jones (Gloucester, 1986), pp. 39–45.

[185] e.g. the duke's retainer, Sir William Lucy of Charlecote (Warws.), married a

social standing, he would find little difficulty in providing suitable partners for himself and his children. Even the duke's closest and most trusted advisers—Sir Thomas Hungerford, Sir Godfrey Foljambe, Sir John Marmion, and Sir Robert Swillington, for example[186]—married outside the affinity and the same is true, *a fortiori*, for the bulk of his retainers. In consequence, it was not the established county gentry who stood to gain most matrimonial advantage from their membership of the Lancastrian affinity but those of the duke's servants, who, lacking inherited wealth or status, had risen high in his service by their own talents.

A handful of examples must stand for them all. The duke's retainer, Sir John St Lo of Newton St Lo (Som.), married, firstly, Alice, daughter of Sir Walter Pavely of Brook (Wilts.), and, secondly, Margaret, the daughter of John Clyvedon the younger. His daughters by his first wife married, respectively, Sir Richard Seymour and Sir John Chidiock of Chideock (Dorset); his daughter by his second wife married Sir William Botreaux of Maiden Newton (Dorset).[187] His choice of partner for himself and his children lay, therefore, entirely among substantial West Country families with estates close to his own, and he was sufficiently wealthy to need no other advantage in securing suitable matches. When his daughter Joan, the widow of Sir John Chidiock, remarried, however, she chose as her second husband John Bathe, who had been in John of Gaunt's household, first as a valet and then as keeper of his privy expenses, since 1361.[188] Bathe had thus begun his career in a comparatively humble position and, at the time of his marriage, he still owned no property in the West Country; the instrumentality of the Lancastrian connection in bringing them together seems, in consequence, the more likely. In the same way, Sir William Parr, who came from a background equally obscure, was

---

daughter of Thomas de la Barre of Rotherwas (Herefs.); Lucy's son, Thomas, married Alice, daughter of Sir William Hugford of Apley (Salop). *CIM 1348–77*, no. 766; *CFR 1413–22*, 49.

[186] Hungerford married (1) Eleanor, daughter of John Strug, (2) Joan, daughter of Sir Edward Hussey; Foljambe married into the Irelands of Hartshorn; Marmion married Elizabeth, daughter of Herbert de St Quentin; Swillington married (1) Avora, daughter of Sir Stephen Waleys, (2) Margaret, daughter of Sir Roger Bellers. J. S. Roskell, 'Sir Thomas Hungerford', in *Parliament and Politics in Late Medieval England* (London, 1981–3), ii. 18–19; *CIPM* XIV. 254; *Collectanea Topographica et Genealogica* (London, 1834), i. 336 (Foljambe); *CIM 1387–93*, no. 175 (Marmion); Canon Beanlands, 'The Swillingtons of Swillington', Thoresby Society, *Miscellanea*, 15 (1909), 204–5.

[187] C. 137/86/10.

[188] *Complete Peerage*, V. 457; *Reg. I* 494, *Reg. II* 128.

enabled to marry the heiress of the barony of Kendal by the mediation
of Peter de Roos, her uncle and guardian, who was also a colleague in
the duke's retinue; John Norbury used the social contacts provided by
the affinity to secure for his descendants the position he had gained by
his own precarious career as a *routier* captain: his son was married to
Elizabeth, daughter of Sir William Croyser, formerly steward of the
duke's household; his daughter to Nicholas Usk, currently its
treasurer.[189]

Nevertheless, it would be incorrect to picture the social communities
created by the county and the affinity in competition with each other
for the loyalty of the Lancastrian retainer. In the matter of marriages,
the two complemented and drew strength from one another. The
number of potential partners available in county society was never
unlimited and it was, in consequence, inevitable that some of the
duke's retainers should be linked together by ties of blood—ties which
Lancastrian service had done nothing to create but which nevertheless
served to produce a true affinity of kinship among the duke's servants.
Granted this inevitable occurrence, however, the number of retainers
who married the daughters, or widows, of their colleagues within the
affinity was comparatively, perhaps unexpectedly, small. The precise
picture naturally varies from county to county but the practice of the
duke's servants in the northern Midlands does not seem untypical of
the general pattern. There, most of his retainers in the area themselves
made non-Lancastrian marriages: Sir John Dabridgecourt married
Maud, daughter of Sir Richard Bromhall and widow of Sir John
Tochet; Sir Nicholas Longford married Alice, daughter of Sir Robert
D'Eyncourt; Sir John Loudham's wife was Isabel, daughter and
heiress of Sir Robert Breton of Walton; Sir Thomas Wennesley made
a good match with Juliana, the widow of Sir Richard Vernon of
Haddon.[190]

Where the contacts created by ducal service *did* prove important,
however, was in providing suitable matches for their children—

---

[189] C. 137/50/6; M. A. Rowling, 'William de Parr: King's Knight to Henry IV',
Transactions of the Cumberland and Westmorland Antiquarian and Arch. Soc., NS 56 (1956),
93; M. Barber, 'John Norbury (*c.*1350–1414): An Esquire of Henry IV', *EHR* 68 (1953),
67–9.

[190] *The Visitation of the County of Nottingham*, ed. G. W. Marshall (Harleian Soc., 4,
1871), p. 37; JUST 1/1488 m. 9; W. W. Longford, 'Some Notes on the Family History
of Nicholas Longford, Sheriff of Lancashire in 1413', *Transactions of the Historic Society
of Lancashire and Cheshire*, 76 (1934), p. 60; R. Thoroton, *The Antiquities of
Nottinghamshire* (London, 1677), p. 290; G. Wrottesley, 'A History of the Bagot Family',
Collections for a History of Staffordshire, NS 11 (1908), 54.

membership of the affinity increased the range of suitable partners and provided some assurance that the prospects of the marriage were good ones. Nearly half the matches the duke's retainers made for their children were, in consequence, Lancastrian—two of Sir Alured Sulny's daughters married within the affinity, one to Sir Edmund Appleby and one to Sir Nicholas Longford, while the other two made respectable 'county' matches; Sir Nicholas Montgomery married his son to one of Longford's daughters and a daughter to the son and heir of John Curzon of Kedleston, but the rest of his children married into local gentry families—the Knyvetons, the Clarells of Aldwark, and the Gresleys of Drakelowe; Sir Philip Okeover's son married one of Curzon's daughters; Sir Godfrey Foljambe's younger son, Thomas, married Margaret, daughter of Sir John Loudham; and Peter de Melbourne's son married Elizabeth, daughter and heir of John Merbury.[191] The mere enumeration of these matches demonstrates clearly enough that the network of kinship did have a part to play in drawing the duke's retainers together into a single affinity of blood. If the part marriage played in the creation of the Lancastrian affinity was largely a secondary one, confirming and perpetuating an existing allegiance rather than serving to draw men into the affinity in the first place, it remains true that the claims of local society, so clearly delineated in the wills of the duke's retainers, were, in this respect at least, quite reconcilable with the demands of seigneurial service.[192] His followers had no difficulty in maintaining the two in easy, and advantageous, equilibrium.

Nevertheless, there must remain some doubts, on the evidence presented above, over the importance that the duke's retainers attached to their Lancastrian allegiance. This chapter has suggested that, if the service John of Gaunt required of his retainers in peacetime was hardly onerous, its reward was sometimes insubstantial. The duke certainly had many benefits in his gift, but prudential considerations

---

[191] S. P. H. Statham, 'Later Descendants of Domesday Holders of Land in Derbyshire', *Journal of the Derbyshire Archaeological and Natural History Society*, 49 (1927), 325; Derbyshire Record Office, D. 37 M/RM 1, 2; HMC, *Report on the Manuscripts of the late Reginald Rawdon, Hastings* (1928–47), i. 110; F. Madan, *The Gresleys of Drakelowe* (Oxford, 1899), p. 271; G. Wrottesley, 'An Account of the Family of Okeover of Okeover', *Collections for a History of Staffordshire*, NS 7 (1904), 55; *Collectanea Topographica et Genealogica*, i. 343.

[192] e.g. the close relations that already existed between Sir Philip Okeover, Sir John Cokayn, Sir Thomas Marchington, and Sir Thomas Wennesley before their formal entry into the Lancastrian affinity. Derbyshire Record Office, D. 231 M/T 21, 161, 306; E. 475; D. 158 M/T 16.

alone dictated that his largesse should not be solely directed towards his own clients, while it was often his household attendants and estate officials, not the body of his indentured retainers, who benefited most directly from his patronage. Besides the retaining fee itself, therefore —part of which had, in any case, to be spent on maintaining the state the duke expected in his servants—the advantages to be gained by Lancastrian service might remain alluring but illusory.[193] Precisely for this reason, symbol and sentiment were important adjuncts to the material incentives for loyalty. Yet even these, the religious, ceremonial, and secular splendour with which the duke surrounded himself, might prove insufficient; one chronicler remarks with astonishment how, in a moment of crisis, no knight or esquire dared to declare himself of the retinue of John of Gaunt or to wear his livery in public.[194] This was not because they had found better paymasters elsewhere. The duke offered higher fees and better prospects of preferment than most of his peers; in consequence, few retainers left his service to seek their fortune with any lord other than the king. Rather, it was because, as the evidence of their wills suggests, the local communities in which they lived often claimed a greater share of their concern and loyalty. If the demands of Lancastrian service and the expectations of local society could be kept, for much of the time, in an advantageous equilibrium, there was nevertheless a latent tension between the two that could force the retainer to make some awkward choices. It is to this question—the place of the Lancastrian affinity in local society— that the rest of this book is devoted. Any final estimate of the importance of John of Gaunt and his retainers in late medieval England must largely depend upon the answer to it.

[193] G. G. Astill, 'Social Advancement through Seignorial Service? The Case of Simon Pakeman', *Transactions of the Leicestershire Historical and Arch. Soc.*, 54 (1978–9), 14–25.

[194] 'The Kirkstall Abbey Chronicles', ed. J. Taylor, *Thoresby Society*, 42 (1952), 68; cf. *Chronicon Henrici Knighton*, ii. 145.

5

THE LANCASTRIAN AFFINITY AND LOCAL SOCIETY: SUSSEX AND LANCASHIRE

1. Introduction

The previous chapters have examined in some detail the structure and composition of John of Gaunt's affinity and made a tentative assessment of what it meant, for both duke and retainer, to belong to the same organization. For both parties, the military role of the affinity emerged as its most important feature: the duke was heavily dependent upon his retinue in the vital business of raising his armies and it was still in terms of campaigning abroad that most retainers envisaged their obligation to their lord. The material rewards of this service seem to have been slight enough but the chivalric prestige conferred by fighting in the duke's company did much to compensate for any financial loss. In any case, many retainers fought abroad principally in order to consolidate their standing at home, for to win the duke of Lancaster's attention and esteem on campaign was to secure oneself a position of influence and respect in English local society. Yet it is precisely this direct relationship between military service and civilian life, between employment abroad and reward at home, that constitutes the principal charge against the indentured retinue as a form of social and political organization. In the robust formulation of Plummer: 'when the war was over, they [the temporal lords] returned to England with bands of men accustomed to obey their orders, incapacitated by long warfare for the pursuits of settled and peaceful life and ready to follow their late masters on any turbulent enterprise.'[1]

It is a formulation that has been questioned and, in its more extreme forms, denied by more recent historians of 'bastard feudalism' but it has, at least, the justification of contemporary complaint. If the magnates' specific responsibility for much of the violence of the period

---

[1] Sir John Fortescue, *The Governance of England*, ed. C. Plummer (Oxford, 1885), p. 15.

can now be generally discounted, the influence of their lordship upon local government and politics cannot be so easily disregarded. The second part of this book is principally devoted to an investigation of the Lancastrian affinity and its actions in a variety of local contexts, but it begins with some consideration of the administrative and legal resources available to the duke and his men, for these were the weapons by which a local dominance was best asserted and the processes of government best manipulated. It was upon them, accordingly, that the parliamentary Commons chose to concentrate their fiercest criticisms; one of the concerns of this chapter will be to assess the accuracy and justice of their complaints.

John of Gaunt's own attitude to the problem was clear; he was always obedient to the common law, as he informed the abbot of Whalley, and wished in no way to disturb its course.[2] This was, admittedly, a statement for public consumption and the duke could hardly have been expected to say anything less anodyne. Nevertheless, his recorded remarks and actions on more private occasions lend some colour to his claim. 'Writ you shall have none; advise you amongst yourselves', he told John of Northampton and his allies, and to Alice Perrers, as well, he showed the same unwillingness to interfere illegitimately in the processes of royal government.[3] When approached for help by the plaintiff in a case of alleged maintenance, the duke is on record as advising him to go to the common law.[4] To the Commons at Salisbury, who complained of the illegal protection the magnates afforded their followers, he could have pointed out that, on occasion, he *did* act with severity towards his own men; when Thomas Molyneux of Cuerdale, his feodary in Lancashire, was found guilty of wholesale maintenance, the duke fined him £200 and banned him from his court and presence for life.[5] Nor was this the only contribution the duke made towards the keeping of the king's peace. By his eirenic efforts as a mediator and arbitrator, John of Gaunt also tried to ensure that the quarrels and disputes brought to his attention, both those involving his retainers and those in which he had no direct interest, did not escalate

---

[2] DL 42/1 f. 76v.

[3] *A Book of London English 1384–1425*, ed. R. W. Chambers and N. Daunt (Oxford, 1931), p. 28; *Rot. Parl.*, iii. 13.

[4] J. B. Post, 'Courts, Councils and Arbitrators in the Ladbroke Manor Dispute, 1382–1400', *Medieval Legal Records*, ed. R. F. Hunnisett and J. B. Post (London, 1978), p. 293.

[5] *Reg. II* 302. For further examples of the informal justice exercised within the Lancastrian household, *CPR 1377–81*, 447; *Chronicon Henrici Knighton*, ii. 149–50.

into open violence.[6] The flexibility, simplicity, and speed of arbitration made it a popular means of avoiding the delays and expenses of common law process and, as a powerful and independent figure, possessing sufficient authority to make his judgements stick, the duke was much in demand as an arbitrator.[7] If he was not quite the 'foundation of right, reason and mercy before all others in this kingdom' that one hopeful petitioner claimed,[8] Gaunt's judgements were sought after and respected,[9] so that his willingness to hear and determine the disputes of his own followers constituted, for some of them, one of the additional advantages of Lancastrian service.[10]

Yet arbitration, for all its virtues, was even more open to the illegitimate influence of lordship than mesne process and the duke did not always disdain to avail himself of the advantages his position could confer. When he was appointed in 1392 to resolve a dispute between the citizens of Lincoln and the dean and chapter of the cathedral, Gaunt's own interests as constable of Lincoln castle made him as anxious to restrain the citizens as the chapter themselves, for he had only recently had to seek an oyer and terminer commission against the mayor and bailiffs of Lincoln for their trespasses within the bailey of the castle.[11] His final award in the dispute, delivered within two days, had the virtue of speed, but probably not that of impartiality. Not only was it greatly in the chapter's favour, but the duke had also paid them £40 to help them in their struggle; he got an image of John the Baptist, his patron saint, in gold and silver for his pains.[12]

In the face of such evidence it seems possible that, while careful to appear obedient to the common law, John of Gaunt was as eager as the

---

[6] *Reg. I* 1378; *Reg. II* 578; *CCR 1381–5*, 78; ibid. *1388–92*, 500; *Chronicon Angliae*, p. 394; DL 42/1 f. 189v, 15 f. 45; Norfolk Record Office, NA 44 Le Strange, for disputes arbitrated by the duke and his council.

[7] *Reg. I* 53; SC 8/94/4666; *Reg. II* 294; E. Powell, 'Arbitration and Law in the Late Middle Ages', *TRHS* 5th series, 33 (1983), 49–67.

[8] *Anglo-Norman Letters and Petitions*, p. 6.

[9] *Ancient Petitions Relating to Northumberland*, ed. C. M. Fraser (Surtees Soc., 176, 1966), no. 107; *Rot. Parl.*, iii. 287–8; *CCR 1392–6*, 41 for cases delegated to the duke's arbitration by parliament; cf. C. Rawcliffe, 'The Great Lord as Peacekeeper', *Law and Social Change in British History*, ed. J. A. Guy and H. G. Beale (London, 1984), pp. 34–53.

[10] Nottinghamshire Record Office, Dd Sr 209/169, for the resolution of a dispute between Sir Adam Everingham and Robert Rockley. For Everingham's connection with the Lancastrian affinity, *Treatises of Fistula in Ano, Haemorrhoids and Clysters by John Arderne*, ed. D'Arcy Power (EETS, OS 139, 1910), p. 1.

[11] SC 8/121/6046; *CPR 1388–92*, 220, 270; DL 41/6/17 mm. 1–5; J. W. F. Hill, *Medieval Lincoln* (Cambridge, 1948), pp. 261–4.

[12] Lincolnshire Archives Office, D. and C., 4/2/8–11, 16, 19; Bj 2/8 ff. 5, 10.

rest of his contemporaries to twist it to his own advantage when occasion arose. The resources that he possessed for doing this were, by any standards, formidable, but the one that excited most suspicion and criticism from the parliamentary Commons was the duke's ability to pay retaining fees to the justices of the central courts, the King's Bench and the Common Bench. In 1369, for instance, his council learned in the law included the chief justice of Common Bench, two puisne justices of the same court, and a king's serjeant; in 1384, two justices of Common Bench and a king's serjeant; in 1376, he was paying fees to two justices of each court and the chief baron of the Exchequer.[13] The payment of any fee by a private individual to justices of the central courts was, since the statute of 1346 against the practice,[14] illegal, but, although this was one score on which the parliamentary Commons were justified in their complaints, the duke was far from unique in breaking the law in this way. Most magnates and monastic houses were engaged in the same practice although John of Gaunt's wealth allowed him, as usual, to indulge this illegality on a particularly princely scale.[15] Not only did he fee the justices, but a whole host of minor legal and administrative officials as well—the clerk of the Common Bench, the clerk of the estreats, the under-clerk of the hanaper, the ushers of the Exchequer[16]—who each enjoyed the opportunity of showing favour to their master. Thomas Bedford, the duke's attorney in King's Bench,[17] was also, for instance, a filacer of the court—a double employment that attracted the attention of the Commons, who complained that the clerks of the King's Bench,

---

[13] *Reg. I* 1811; PL 3/1/69; DL 28/3/1 m. 6. Robert Thorp, chief justice of Common Bench 1356–71; William Finchdean, justice of Common Bench 1365–74; John Mowbray, justice of Common Bench 1359–73; Roger Meres, king's serjeant 1362–71 (1369); Robert Belknap, chief justice of Common Bench 1374–88; John Holt, justice of Common Bench 1383–8; John Lockton, king's serjeant 1383–7 (1384); John Cavendish, chief justice of King's Bench 1372–81; Thomas Ingleby, justice of King's Bench 1361–77; Roger Kirton (alias Meres), justice of Common Bench 1372–80; Henry Asty, chief baron of the Exchequer (1376). *Select Cases in the Court of King's Bench*, ed. G. O. Sayles, vi. (Selden Soc., 82, 1965), Appendices II, III, VI, VII, XIV, XV. J. H. Baker (ed.), *The Order of Serjeants at Law* (Selden Soc., Suppl. Series, 5, 1984) pp. 157–8.

[14] *Statutes of the Realm* (London, 1810–28), i. 303–6.

[15] e.g. the earl of March paid fees to only two justices and three king's serjeants in 1374/5, while the earl of Devon granted his livery to four serjeants but no justices in 1384/5. Only Edward, prince of Wales, seems to have been more generous than Gaunt in the distribution of legal fees. BL Egerton Roll 8727 m. 2; Add. Roll 64320; *Register of Edward the Black Prince* (London, 1930–43), iv. 152, 168–9, 264, 266, 301.

[16] *Reg. I* 1788; *Reg. II* 628, 1245; DL 28/3/2 f. 13, 5 f. 9v.

[17] DL 43/15/5 m. 5d; DL 28/32/22 (11).

responsible for writing the records and pleas of the court, altered their enrolments in favour of their own clients.[18]

It was, however, the links between the lords and the justices that drew the most sustained criticism from the Commons, on the grounds that they gave the great magnates and their dependants an illegitimate advantage when they engaged in litigation.[19] Precisely how great an advantage is, by the very nature of the relationship, virtually impossible to estimate but one illustration of the benefits to be won lies in the use the duke made of special commissions of oyer and terminer. For John of Gaunt, such commissions were the most effective means of protecting his local rights and interests from attack;[20] for the Commons, they were more an instrument of aggressive lordship than a positive means of keeping the peace. They were, in consequence, highly unpopular;[21] the duke nevertheless made repeated use of them, suing out nine such commissions during the 1360s and a further eight in the following decade.[22] His liking for them had much to do with the advantages they brought to the litigants who sued them out, the chief of which lay in the plaintiff's ability to nominate the justices appointed to investigate his complaints. Unsurprisingly, John of Gaunt's choice usually fell on his senior estate officials[23] and those justices of the central courts with whom he maintained a formal connection. Sir William Finchdean appeared on nine such commissions between 1362 and 1374; John Mowbray on seven between 1362 and 1370; Roger Meres on five between 1372 and 1380.

Even John of Gaunt had, however, to make some modifications to his practice in the face of the parliamentary Commons' hostility. After 1380, for instance, he sued out only five more special commissions of oyer and terminer and was careful to include among the

[18] J. B. Post, 'King's Bench Clerks in the Reign of Richard II', *BIHR* 47 (1974), 150–1. KB 27/549 m. 13 for Bedford enrolling two cases in which he appears on the duke's behalf.

[19] *Rot. Parl.*, ii. 334, iii. 139, 158, 200, 222. J. R. Maddicott, *Law and Lordship: Royal Justices as Retainers in Thirteenth and Fourteenth Century England* (*Past and Present* Supplement, 4, 1978) treats the whole topic in detail.

[20] See below, pp. 127–41 for a detailed study of one such commission.

[21] R. W. Kaeuper, 'Law and Order in Fourteenth-Century England: The Evidence of Special Commissions of Oyer and Terminer', *Speculum*, 54 (1979), 773–4.

[22] *CPR 1361–4*, 286, 367, 373, 454, 527, 538, 544, 545; ibid. *1364–7*, 69; ibid. *1367–70*, 199, 472; ibid. *1370–4*, 242, 396, 487; ibid. *1374–7*, 321; ibid. *1377–81*, 357, 360, 415.

[23] e.g. Sir Godfrey Foljambe, his chief steward of lands, was nominated to 10 such commissions between 1362 and 1374; Sir Robert Swillington, his chamberlain, appears on 9 between 1363 and 1380.

commissioners a higher proportion of local gentry, many of them without a discernible Lancastrian connection.[24] In addition, the complaints of the Commons were probably instrumental in prompting, from the short-lived Appellant regime, an ordinance that successfully forbade royal judges to take fees from private individuals.[25] Whether this reduced the duke of Lancaster's influence over the course of justice seems, however, more questionable. Justices of the central courts continued to receive payments from the duke, though now in the form of large, occasional gifts rather than small, regular fees;[26] the distinction must have seemed, to his opponents, largely academic. More important, in the palatinate of Lancaster John of Gaunt possessed the perfect institutional means of avoiding any charge of illegality while conveniently continuing to fee a number of central justices. William Thirning, justice of Common Bench since Easter 1388, became a justice at Lancaster in April 1389; John Markham, secondary justice at Lancaster since April 1389, became a justice of Common Bench in July 1396, while continuing to exercise his palatinate office.[27] The rewards these positions commanded were nothing to the rewards available at Westminster, but they were nevertheless substantial—£20 for a chief justice, 26 marks for a secondary justice, with additional payments for every session;[28] certainly enough to constitute a useful adjunct to judicial salaries, particularly at a time when the rest of the nobility appear to have ceased paying fees to the central justices. If there was, indeed, an ordinance against the fee'ing of justices passed in 1388, then one of its unlooked-for effects was to increase still further the duke of Lancaster's hold over the judiciary, at the expense of his fellow peers.

The duke's pre-eminence at court, his proximity to the king, his dominance in the Council, combined with the close ties he maintained with the judiciary and the tidy sums he spent in entertaining and informing the justices assigned to hear his complaints,[29] made him an

---

[24] *CPR 1381–5*, 144, 427–8, 507; ibid. *1385–9*, 395; ibid. *1388–92*, 270.

[25] Maddicott, op. cit. 79–80.

[26] e.g. DL 28/3/2 f. 19—£10 paid to William Thirning and Richard Sydenham, 'justices of the peace of the lord king', for a session of oyer and terminer held at Pontefract. Both were justices of Common Bench at the time.

[27] Somerville, p. 468.

[28] PL 3/1/135, 68, 73—John Davenport was paid 20 marks for holding two sessions, for instance.

[29] *Collectanea Topographica et Genealogica*, i. 334; *Reg. I* 1250; DL 29/212/3247 m. 3.

invaluable ally to his friends, a formidable opponent to his enemies. His dealings with the abbey of Crowland provide a convenient illustration of the kind of influence he could bring to bear on disputes that engaged his attention. At his death, the abbey's chronicler saluted Gaunt as an opportune helper of Crowland in its tribulations and the detailed account he gives of the duke's aid to the abbey during its long battle with Thomas Holland, earl of Kent, bears out the truth of this description.[30] Gaunt's relations with Crowland had not always been as amicable as the chronicler makes out,[31] but, in this case, the duke's tenants in Spalding were as much affected as the abbot's by Thomas Holland's attempts to extend the bounds of his manor of Deeping. In consequence, Crowland was assured of active Lancastrian assistance in the prosecution of its case. John of Gaunt promoted the abbot's cause in the council; publicly contradicted Holland's counter-claim in parliament; forced the men of Deeping to give up what they had stolen from Crowland, and, eventually, presided over the commissions that set precisely the boundaries the abbot had consistently claimed.[32]

In short, the duke produced just the sort of display of overweening personal dominance the parliamentary Commons so disliked. To their criticism Gaunt could answer that his mediation had successfully prevented an escalation of the occasional skirmishes between the two sides into open violence. Even so, the case lends some credence to the complaints of the Commons. The final settlement reached was, after all, the one most favourable to the duke himself and Lancastrian aid to Crowland had not stopped short of violence in order to achieve it. Three men from Henry Bolingbroke's household at Peterborough were behind an attack on the earl of Kent's tenants that led to the death of one of them; it was the rumour that the earl of Derby intended to burn their village to the ground that finally brought the men of Deeping to sue for peace.[33] Threats and covert violence thus went hand in hand with the duke's legitimate public defence of his rights. If

---

[30] 'Historia Croylandensis Continuatio', *Rerum Anglicarum Scriptores Veterum*, ed. W. Fulman (Oxford, 1684), pp. 483–93; E. 163/6/15; SC 8/102/5054, 103/5116, 116/5762 for the course of the dispute; *Rot. Parl.*, ii. 62a, 65b, BL Add. MS 5845 ff. 40v–42 for its background.

[31] *Reg. I* 1434.

[32] *CPR 1388–92*, 219; C. 47/7/7 (10); *CPR 1391–6*, 444—this last commission was directed to Robert, lord Willoughby, but the Crowland chronicler claims that Gaunt presided over it in person.

[33] KB 27/544 (Rex) m. 1; *Records of Some Sessions of the Peace in Lincolnshire, 1381–1396*, ed. E. G. Kimball (Lincoln Record Soc., 49, 1955), i. 56.

the duke could do all this for the abbot of Crowland, who had no greater claim on him than a temporarily common cause, it seems reasonable to assume that, by employing the same methods, he could do as much for his retainers as well.

To find the necessary evidence, however, means setting the duke's affinity within the context of county society. In the relationship created between lord and man by the indenture of retainer, money provided the material nexus between the two contracting parties but it was the exercise of 'good lordship' that provided the real cement and it was within the retainer's own social world, the county, that a magnate was usually called upon to exercise this lordship: by providing a variety of social services, ranging from charter-witnessing to marriage-broking; by securing positions of power and worship in the county administration for his own followers; pre-eminently, by providing aid and comfort, both legal and extra-legal, in the prosecution of his retainers' lawsuits. Without such a local context, there is a danger of disproportion distorting any analysis of the Lancastrian retinue's position. The longer attention is concentrated exclusively on the power of the duke and the size of his affinity the greater both will appear, whereas the central problem in the study of 'bastard feudalism' since the first modern discussion of the subject[34] has, rather, been to strike an adequate balance between the political and economic resources of the magnates and the stubborn independence of the county gentry, whose prejudices had to be respected and their loyalty won. A growing number of local studies reiterate the same point: policy was made at Westminster but it was implemented, or thwarted, in the provinces.[35] In each shire, the Crown, the aristocracy—both absentee magnates and resident local lords—and the body of the shire gentry all possessed legitimate claims to consideration and authority: power lay between them and was never the monopoly of a single group. For the king, relations with the county community were problematic enough

[34] K. B. McFarlane, 'Parliament and "Bastard Feudalism"', *TRHS* 4th series, 26 (1944), 73.

[35] e.g. J. R. Maddicott, 'The County Community and the Making of Public Opinion in Fourteenth-Century England', *TRHS* 5th series, 28 (1978), 27–43; R. R. Davies, *Lordship and Society in the March of Wales 1282–1400* (Oxford, 1978), pp. 249–73; Roger Virgoe, 'The Crown and Local Government: East Anglia under Richard II', *The Reign of Richard II*, ed. F. R. H. du Boulay and C. M. Barron (London, 1971), pp. 218–41; S. M. Wright, *The Derbyshire Gentry in the Fifteenth Century* (Derbyshire Record Soc., 8, 1983), pp. 93–118; I. Rowney, 'Resources and Retaining in Yorkist England: William, Lord Hastings and the Honour of Tutbury', *Property and Politics: Essays in Later Medieval English History*, ed. A. J. Pollard (Gloucester, 1984), pp. 139–55.

but at least he possessed, in the shire court, a convenient means of contact and control. A great magnate like John of Gaunt had no such advantage because the administrative unit of his estates, the honour, was a purely tenurial division which paid little attention to county boundaries.[36] In consequence, the duke was dependent upon individual retainers and estate officials to represent his wishes in each county but this dependence immediately imposed informal restrictions on his authority: his servants were, inevitably, themselves a part of the county community and they were not above mediating his orders in the way that best suited them. If the interests of lord and retainer coincided, all would be well; if they did not, the lord's will was very unlikely to be done.

The situation in Northumberland best illustrates the duke's dilemma. His continental ambitions, as well as his own financial interests, disposed John of Gaunt in favour of the policy of peace with Scotland that he pursued while the king's lieutenant on the March.[37] To see this policy implemented, however, the duke had to bolster his position in the region by recruiting retainers from among the lesser landowners,[38] but the men he engaged showed themselves little influenced by the duke's expressed intentions. Gaunt's eirenic policy had more supporters at Westminster than it did on the March, where the Scots could render a truce more damaging than open war,[39] and his new retainers owed too much of their livelihood to stealing the cattle and ransoming the bodies of the Scots to be ruled by a distant duke of Lancaster.[40] Consequently, both Sir William Swynburn and Sir Thomas Ilderton, whose property in Roxburgh was threatened by the southward advance of Scottish territory,[41] maintained an additional connection with Lancaster's chief rival on the Border, the earl of Northumberland, whose aggressive forward policy they evidently

---

[36] L. Fox, 'The Honour and Earldom of Leicester: Origin and Descent, 1066–1399', *EHR* 54 (1939), 400–2 shows that the component fees of the honour extended into nineteen counties.

[37] J. A. Tuck, 'Richard II and the Border Magnates', *Northern History*, 3 (1968) 38–9. The duke's lordship of Dunstanburgh was charged at £220. 15s. 8½d. at the partition of 1361 and he received most of this sum from his Northumberland estates in 1367/8. By 1388, however, the lordship was worth nothing because the townships had been burnt by the Scots: *CFR 1356–68*, 164; DL 29/354/5837 m. 1; DL 29/728/11974 m. 2.

[38] e.g. Sir Thomas Ilderton; Sir John Fenwick; Sir William Swynburn.

[39] *Northern Petitions*, ed. C. M. Fraser (Surtees Soc., 194, 1981), no. 113.

[40] Northumberland Record Office, ZSW 1/104, 110 (Sir William Swynburn).

[41] *Calendar of Documents Relating to Scotland*, ed. J. Bain (Edinburgh, 1888), iv. 306; *Northern Petitions*, no. 113.

found more attractive.[42] John of Gaunt could pay the gentry of Northumberland their retaining fees but he could not realistically expect their support until his policies coincided with their interests. Moreover, this was only half the duke's problem in his relations with local society. While his policies and decisions were unavoidably modified in their execution by the vested interests of his retainers, each retainer entered the duke's service with a ready-made bundle of alliances and enmities so that, for every new recruit to his retinue, the duke's position within the local community was subtly altered.[43]

Any consideration of the political and social influence of the Lancastrian affinity must, therefore, begin with an examination of its place in local society and involve an assessment of its impact upon the county community, as a collective entity, as well as its relations with individuals within the shire. The nature and extent of the Lancastrian presence varied from county to county and, ideally, the political structure of each shire should be examined and characterized before a true picture of the duke's affinity and the extent of its influence emerges. Clearly, restrictions of time and space make this impossible. Instead, four separate case studies have been used in an attempt to answer the questions raised in this introduction. To begin with, a single incident in Sussex is examined in detail in order to demonstrate the difficulties John of Gaunt experienced in dealing with county society, to illustrate his characteristic method of procedure and to emphasize the close links between obscure local quarrels and the divisions of high politics. This is followed by a study of the duke's palatinate of Lancaster, since it was there that Gaunt was at his most powerful and it is there, in consequence, that the duke's retainers can be observed acting with least constraint. Norfolk was chosen to provide a contrast with the palatinate of Lancaster since, although it was a county with extensive Lancastrian estates, the duke's influence there was counterbalanced by the presence of a number of other magnates and a cohesive gentry community. Finally, the adjoining counties of Staffordshire and Derbyshire were studied together in order to illustrate the contrasting natures of neighbouring shire communities and the variant forms of lordship their differences produced. Throughout, the same series of questions is addressed to the evidence each county provides: how could the duke help his retainers in the

---

[42] Northumberland Record Office, ZSW 1/100, 102 (Swynburn); Walsingham, *Hist. Ang.*, i. 388 (Ilderton).

[43] For the example of William Fifide in Sussex, see below, p. 132.

counties? What did they expect from him and what did they get? What influence did the Lancastrian affinity exercise over the county community? How powerful was the duke of Lancaster at the local level? How did his lordship compare with that of other magnates? Did the exercise of the duke's lordship contribute, as the parliamentary Commons alleged, to the breakdown of public order? How important was magnate lordship and 'bastard feudalism' in the life of later medieval England?

2. Sussex[44]

In June 1384 Sir Edward Dallingridge was attached with his two accomplices, Sir Thomas Sackville and Sir Philip Medstede, at the suit of John of Gaunt, duke of Lancaster, to answer a special commission of oyer and terminer on certain charges brought against him.[45] Lancaster was clearly anxious to gain a conviction, for he proceeded concurrently against them at the trailbaston sessions of the Rape of Pevensey, both by special bill and by jury of indictment.[46] His anxiety is understandable for, whatever the findings of the commission, they could hardly fail to be without a wider political significance. Gaunt was at the height of his unpopularity amongst Richard II's courtiers; during the recent Salisbury Parliament he had been accused of plotting the king's death, and Richard had allegedly reacted by ordering his summary execution. Yet one of his few remaining allies, the earl of Arundel, counted Dallingridge amongst his principal retainers, whilst Sir Edward himself was perhaps the most influential of the Sussex gentry at this period.[47] A servant of the Arundel family, the Despensers and the duke of Brittany, Dallingridge was also a figure of political importance in his own right and, after a long and apparently profitable career in the French wars, he was currently

---

[44] S. Walker, 'Lancaster v. Dallingridge: A Franchisal Dispute in Fourteenth-Century Sussex', *Sussex Archaeological Collections*, 121 (1983), 87–94 gives a less accurate version of the same affair.

[45] JUST 1/947/5. *CPR 1381–5*, 428.

[46] JUST 1/944.

[47] The Marquis Curzon of Kedleston, *Bodiam Castle, Sussex* (London, 1926), pp. 25–8; A. Goodman, *The Loyal Conspiracy* (London, 1971), pp. 115–6, give a biography.

expanding and consolidating his Sussex estates.[48] In 1380 he had been chosen by the Commons as one of the three knights on the committee appointed to examine the state of the realm and his subsequent career shows him to have been an able diplomat and politician.[49] In addition to the intrinsic interest of a dispute between such protagonists, the survival of an unusually full record of the commissioners' proceedings justifies a close examination of the case, for it provides a chance to examine John of Gaunt's method of action in such a dispute whilst casting light on the political community of Sussex in Richard II's reign.

The occasion for the judicial commission sought by John of Gaunt was an outbreak of violence against Nicholas Boyle, his ranger in Ashdown forest, which culminated in the murder of William Mouse, a sub-forester, in March 1384. The real culprit for this crime was Sackville, not Dallingridge: two of the men involved were his servants and Sackville received and sheltered them after the murder.[50] Nevertheless, it was Dallingridge who was the principal target of the duke's vengeance, for the good reason that he had been a thorn in the side of the Lancastrian estate administration for some years past. It emerges from the presentments that the attack on his sub-forester was only the most recent in a long series of attacks on the duke's Sussex estates, dating back to June 1377, when his chase at Ashdown was illegally hunted and his lands in Fletching and East Grinstead despoiled. In March 1380 the duke's under-wood was fired at Ashdown and in April 1381 Dallingridge began a campaign of systematic intimidation against his estates and officials. On Good Friday he drove off livestock belonging to the duke from Fletching. A month later he appeared whilst John Broker, the duke's steward in Sussex, was holding his lord's court at Hungry Hatch and compelled him to swear an oath never to hold a court there again. For good measure, Broker was deprived of his court rolls and book of fees. In June, taking advantage of the confusion created by the Peasants' Revolt, Dallingridge and his accomplices ambushed John Delves, the

[48] *An Abstract of Feet of Fines Relating to the County of Sussex From 1 Edward II to 24 Henry VII*, ed. L. F. Salzman, iii (Sussex Record Soc., 23, 1916), nos. 2480, 2580, 2616; SC 8/209/10442; *CPR 1381–5*, 55.

[49] T. F. Tout, *Chapters in the Administrative History of Medieval England*, iii (Manchester, 1928), 352; J. A. Tuck, *Richard II and the English Nobility* (London, 1973), pp. 141–3; C. M. Barron, 'The Quarrel of Richard II with London', *The Reign of Richard II*, ed. F. R. H. du Boulay and C. M. Barron (London, 1971), p. 192.

[50] KB 27/500 Rex m. 2d; KB 27/502 Rex m. 22. Nicholas Boyle was badly injured in the attack, as well, and eventually received a £40 *ex gratia* payment from the duke for his injuries. DL 29/728/11977 m. 1

Lancastrian feodary in Sussex, at Ringmer, forced him to surrender his commission from the duke and then burnt it in front of him.[51]

The suppression of the great insurrection brought a halt to Dallingridge's open violence, but this was principally because he had succeeded in his object of breaking the resistance of the duke's officials. Faced with a national crisis in his authority, Gaunt chose conciliation rather than confrontation wherever possible. In August 1381 Sir Edward was appointed master forester of Ashdown, at a fee of 10 marks a year, and for the next two years he and his servants seem to have been allowed to hunt the forest at will. The attack on Nicholas Boyle in 1384 must, therefore, be seen against a background of continuing popular unrest in Sussex in the wake of the Peasants' Revolt. At Lewes, the earl of Arundel's castle was stormed and pillaged in 1383; on the Lancastrian estates in the county disorder and disobedience continued unchecked. Sir Thomas Hungerford, Gaunt's chief steward, was unable to levy a fine of 10*s.* from Fletching because the villagers refused to have the lord's minister amongst them.[52]

Despite this disorder Sir Edward might have remained secure in his local predominance, had it not been for the exigencies of national politics. Although removed from his master forestership of Ashdown in August 1383, Dallingridge remained in close contact with the Lancastrian administration. When he went up to Salisbury for the Parliament of April 1384, as a knight of the shire, he carried with him part of the issues of the duke's Sussex lands to deliver to William Everley, the Lancastrian receiver.[53] At that same Parliament, however, the Commons complained for the first time of the violence and extortion practised by the followers of the magnates and demanded a general statute against their oppressions. Lancaster responded to their demand for legislation on the subject by an assurance that the lords of the realm were capable of maintaining discipline amongst their own men, adding that an example would be made of any of his own followers guilty in this respect. The Commons accordingly dropped the matter but, if an example had to be made as an earnest of the lords' good faith, Gaunt's delinquent master forester presented an obvious, perhaps not unwelcome, target. Within a fortnight of the parliament's

[51] JUST 1/944 mm. 1–3; JUST 1/947/5 m. 1.
[52] JUST 1/944 m. 1; A. Reville, *Le Soulèvement des Travailleurs d'Angleterre en 1381* (Paris, 1898), p. cxxxiv; DL 29/727/11938.
[53] DL 29/727/11940 m. 1.

close the judicial commissions against Dallingridge had been issued at Lancaster's request.[54]

Up to this point, Lancaster's policy had been one of inaction and conciliation in the face of considerable and violent provocation. He had, in a sense, little choice for his Sussex estates were of recent acquisition and had yet to acquire the burden of loyalty and expectation that went to constitute a magnate's local standing. Indeed, in expressing so forcibly his hostility towards the duke's officials, Dallingridge was voicing the grievances of many of the Sussex gentry against a powerful but alien newcomer. As earl of Richmond, Gaunt had held the manors of Crowhurst, Burwash, and Bivelham with the rape of Hastings since 1342. In 1372, however, he surrendered these estates in the east of the county and received, in exchange, Queen Philippa's former manors—Willingdon, Grinstead, and Maresfield as well as the forest of Ashdown and the rape and castle of Pevensey.[55] This marked a definite westward shift of Lancastrian territorial interests in Sussex and so brought the duke and his ministers into contact with a powerful new set of neighbours. Chief amongst these were John, lord de la Warr, and Sir Edward Dallingridge. De la Warr was lord of the manors of Wilmington, Arlington, and Folkington, close to Pevensey, and of Fletching, which marched with Maresfield. Dallingridge's lands, like de la Warr's, extended throughout Sussex, but the family originated in Hartfield and Folkenhurst and it was Sir Edward's estates along the northern edge of Ashdown forest— Sheffield and his residential manor of Bolebrook—that formed the core of his inheritance.[56] The evidence suggests that in the past the estates of the Crown in this area had been laxly administered. Farmed for £30 p.a. in Queen Philippa's day, cash liveries from these same properties under Lancastrian supervision were closer to an average £45 p.a.[57] The discrepancy is so large as to suggest that Sir John Seynclere, Queen Philippa's farmer, was receiving a preferential lease in lieu of a retaining fee and the steep rise in the issues of the estates cannot, in consequence, be regarded as direct evidence of the superior efficiency of the Lancastrian administration. Nevertheless, Seynclere's stewardship seems to have been lax, for the foresters under his

---

[54] *Westminster Chronicle*, pp. 80–2; *CPR 1381–5*, 427–8.

[55] *CPR 1364–7*, 333; *Reg. I* 24, 30.

[56] SC 2/206/16; *CCR 1292–6*, 499; *Feudal Aids*, v. 139, 146; *CIPM* VI. 122; *The Earliest Subsidy Returns for the County of Sussex in the Years 1296, 1327, 1332*, ed. W. Hudson (Sussex Record Soc., 10, 1910), pp. 188, 195.

[57] SC 6/1028/4 m. 1; DL 29/441/7082–6.

supervision were themselves guilty of illegal hunting and petty extortion, the manor of Maresfield was in ruinous condition, and its ministers seriously in arrears of their charge. Seynclere himself was later alleged to have detained the profits from quarrying in the forest to his own use, although they were no part of his farm, and to have prevented the ranger from discharging his duties effectively.[58]

Against this background, the characteristically minute supervision exercised by the duke's council over his lands came as an unwelcome contrast, the annual tourns conducted by Sir Thomas Hungerford as an irksome financial innovation, and a spate of outlawries suggests that tighter control was also being kept over the Lancastrian forest rights.[59] From the point of view of the Sussex gentry it was Lancaster who was the aggressor, disrupting the balance of the local community by his intrusive lordship. The bishop of Chichester's long-established rights to the tithes for agistment and pannage in Ashdown forest were, for instance, ignored by the duke's officials when they took over the administration of the forest in 1372. It was only after thirteen years of petitioning, backed by the findings of a local jury, that the bishop eventually managed to recover his rights.[60]

Resentment at the demands of the Lancastrian administration was widespread. The villagers of Folkington withdrew their suit from the duke's hundred court of Longbridge and were maintained in their defiance by John de la Warr's steward, John Brook.[61] Brook was an influential local lawyer, steward of the courts of the abbot of Battle and the bishop of Chichester, as well as an attorney for the earl of Arundel, and his involvement in the attack on Nicholas Boyle demonstrates the depth of local animosity against the Lancastrian estate administration.[62] Even the sheriff consistently refused to hand over the profits of his tourn in the vill of Lindfield, which properly belonged to the duke, unless he was paid a mark a year for his trouble.[63] Dallingridge could, in consequence, command considerable support in his attacks from amongst his immediate neighbours. One of his accomplices, Sir Thomas Sackville, was his son-in-law. The other, Sir Philip Medstede,

[58] *CPR 1370–4*, 179; *Reg. I* 1569, 1654; C. 260/83 no. 88.

[59] e.g. C. 88/58 nos. 17, 58; E. 101/510/28.

[60] *The Chartulary of the High Church of Chichester*, ed. W. D. Peckham (Sussex Record Soc., 46, 1946), nos. 883–5, 887, 889, 891.

[61] JUST 1/944 m. 2.

[62] JUST 3/163 m. 12; JUST 3/216/5 m. 176; JUST 1/943 m. 1; KB 27/502 Rex m. 22.

[63] DL 29/727/11939 m. 1.

was a fellow client of the earls of Arundel, whom Sir Edward had already sheltered after another murder, and the three often acted together in legal transactions.[64] Against a tight-knit little group of this kind, even the greatest of English magnates could not act until he was sure of his ground.

In addition, Lancaster's support among the gentry of Sussex was rather weak. His many retainers did include some resident in the county, such as Robert Beyvill of Little Perching, William Fifide of Shermanbury, and Sir John Seynclere of Brambletye, perhaps retained as a compensation for the loss of his farm of Queen Philippa's Sussex lands, but their support was not always an unmixed blessing. William Fifide, for instance, was already unpopular with both Dallingridge and the earl of Arundel and his violent behaviour can have done little to endear him, or his patron, to his neighbours in Sussex.[65] None was, in any case, as powerful as Dallingridge, nor could the Lancastrian affinity in Sussex (if it can be dignified by that term) draw on the bonds of kinship and the sense of grievance open to the duke's opponents.

In this case, however, Lancaster's lack of an adequate body of local support was amply compensated by his influence on the delegates of central authority. Six justices of oyer and terminer were appointed under a commission dated 16 June 1384, but the proceedings were heard by only three—Reginald Cobham, David Hanmere, and John Holt. Holt was both a justice of Common Bench and John of Gaunt's steward at Higham Ferrers. Hanmere had been in receipt of a fee from the duke since at least 1376/7. For the trailbaston sessions in the rape of Pevensey these three sitting justices were joined by a fourth, the ubiquitous Sir Thomas Hungerford, Lancaster's chief steward.[66] The absentee justices, by contrast, included Richard, earl of Arundel, Dallingridge's principal local patron, and Sir Edward Saint John, a trusted servant of the Arundel family. This is odd, for under normal circumstances Arundel would have been expected to look after the interest of his retainer; the original appointment of justices may even have aimed at impartiality by including the partisans of both protagonists, in the hope that they would bring the opposing parties to

---

[64] *CPR 1381–5*, 444; *Reg. II* 1165; KB 27/502 Rex m. 11; West Sussex Record Office, Firle Place MS 1/204, 206; BL Add. Ch. 30744–5.

[65] SC 8/207/10324; JUST 1/943 m. 1; C. 260/89 (16); *CPR 1374–7*, 492, 495, ibid. *1377–81*, 43; *CCR 1374–7*, 238. Cf. SC 8/111/5516 for a counter-petition by Fifide, in which he claims he has suffered oppressions at the hands of powerful (and anonymous) enemies.

[66] JUST 1/947/5 m. 1; Somerville, 373; DL 28/3/1 m. 6; JUST 1/944 m. 1.

arbitration rather than judgement, for David Hanmere took a fee from the earl of Arundel as well as the duke of Lancaster. In the summer of 1384, however, Arundel was in no position to oppose Gaunt's wishes, for it was only by the duke's mediation that he had been saved from the consequences of his own tactlessness and the king's anger at Salisbury the month before.[67] Political coincidence had thus left Dallingridge unexpectedly exposed to Lancaster's retribution. The duke was swift to seize his opportunity.

Appointed on 16 June, the justices under both commissions sat at East Grinstead from Thursday, 23 June until Wednesday, 29 June. Unusually, Dallingridge appeared in court to defend himself and it is, in consequence, possible to follow the judicial proceedings in detail and hence to identify the motives for his attack on the Lancastrian estates with some precision. The suing of a commission against him and the speed with which the justices acted upon it seem, initially, to have taken Sir Edward by surprise, for his behaviour in court was violent and unruly.[68] On first hearing the charges against him, Dallingridge immediately answered them by a wager of battle— throwing down his gauntlet in court and saying that, unless his accuser was closer in blood to the king than himself, he was prepared to disprove the charges against him by his body. Such a challenge was rare but not unknown as a legal ploy, yet since Dallingridge was accused of trespass alone it was not a recourse open to him, for the wager of battle could only lie in the writ of right or on an appeal of felony.[69] Dallingridge, or rather his counsel, must have known this and his behaviour is puzzling. If his action was not simply bluster, it may have been an attempt to gain time in order to prepare a more adequate defence. On the other hand, Sir Edward's reference to the duke's precedence of blood suggests that he may have been thinking of the procedure of the court of chivalry, where the wager of battle was both permissible and more frequent.[70] Such a possibility is perhaps confirmed by Dallingridge's request, on being presented by the

[67] R. A. Griffiths, *The Principality of Wales in the Later Middle Ages* (Cardiff, 1972), pp. 114–15; Goodman, op. cit. 144–5; *Westminster Chronicle*, pp. 66–8.

[68] JUST 1/944 m. 4.

[69] G. Neilson, *Trial by Combat* (Glasgow, 1890), p. 37; F. Pollock and F. W. Maitland, *The History of English Law Before the Time of Edward I* (Cambridge, 1898, repr. 1968), ii. 632–4.

[70] This is the interpretation of Sir Robert Cotton in *A Collection of Curious Discourses*, ed. T. Hearne (London, 1771), p. 179; M. H. Keen, *The Laws of War in the Late Middle Ages* (London, 1965), pp. 41–2 for the same procedure under the law of arms.

hundred juries, for a copy of the charges against him so that he might answer the presentments by the advice of his counsel. This was common practice in the court of chivalry but the defendant at common law did not enjoy such a right until the nineteenth century.[71] In consequence, the request was refused by the justices, who pointed out that he had already answered the same charges when alleged against him by the duke's counsel, upon which Dallingridge refused to plead at all and was promptly committed to the custody of the sheriff for contempt.

His confinement seems only to have been formal, a change of status rather than an act, for Sir Edward was certainly in court when counsel began his defence.[72] This began impressively enough by entering a waiver stating that the offences of which Dallingridge stood accused had occurred during the great rebellion and he could, in consequence, have claimed the benefit of a general pardon for all trespasses committed at that time,[73] but that he had no wish to do so. Sir Edward, standing in court with his counsel, expressly confirmed this, saying that he had no wish to claim the benefit of any statute in so great a matter, and asked his counsel to reply to the charges against him. It was the common rebels, he explained, gathering together with the intention of killing the duke's officials and destroying his property, who had attacked Delves and Broker. He had indeed been there, but in his capacity as a justice of the peace, doing his best to pacify them. Equally, he was innocent of all the trespasses and hunting offences alleged against him, apart from taking two does and two hinds by the duke's command to deliver to Sir William Croyser's wife. On the other hand, Dallingridge attempted no defence to the accusation that he had prevented the duke of Lancaster's steward from holding his court at Hungry Hatch.[74] He admitted the fact, arguing instead that the court there was an innovation, established by the present duke, and one that drew away suitors from his own hundred court of Dean (i.e. Danehill in Horsted Keynes parish). He had, in consequence, forbidden his tenants to attend the Lancastrian court, even if summoned before it. For the same reason, Dallingridge admitted the charge of carrying off four cows, six oxen, and thirty sheep belonging to the duke from Fletching, stating that as forfeited chattels of John Herlond, a

---

[71] *A Collection of Curious Discourses*, p. 244.
[72] JUST 1/947/5 m. 2*d*.
[73] *Statutes*, ii. 30–1 (6 R.II, st. 2 cl. 4).
[74] JUST 1/944 m. 3.

convicted felon, they were rightfully his as lord of the hundred of Dean, as his ancestors had been since time out of mind.

This was the real crux of Dallingridge's grievance against John of Gaunt. The trespasses and hunting offences of which he stood accused were commonplace, even traditional, misdemeanours amongst the county gentry. His own grandfather had been convicted of very similar offences in Ashdown forest in 1315.[75] A landowner expected, as a matter of courtesy, to be allowed to ride over his neighbour's estates, and the attempt of Richard, earl of Arundel, to establish the inviolability of his Sussex chases in 1377 had led to considerable resentment amongst the gentry, who clearly considered him to have exceeded his rights.[76] The violence of Sir Edward's attacks on Lancastrian property and officials was, by contrast, exceptional, only to be explained as the reaction to a more fundamental challenge to his local standing. Sir Edward's attack may have been prompted by a desire to regain a place in the forest administration lost to his family when the property passed to John of Gaunt. There is some evidence that his father, Roger Dallingridge, had been a forester of Ashdown under Queen Philippa; he certainly received gifts of deer from the forest.[77] The denial of franchisal rights was, however, an altogether more serious matter. The profits of private courts were small, but the possession of private jurisdiction was invaluable, an indispensable adjunct of lordship, both as an instrument of authority and a means of patronage. Dallingridge's possession of the half hundred of Danehill gave him lordship over men as well as lordship over land, a means of coercing and disciplining his tenants that was especially valuable at a time of increasing labour difficulties. It was this that he had sought to defend by his attacks on the Lancastrian officials who allegedly trespassed on his franchise.

Yet his defence of his seigneurial rights, though calculated to win approval amongst the local gentry, proved less successful in legal argument. Thomas Pinchbeck, Lancaster's counsel in this case, replied that the franchisal rights in this dispute were so nearly attached to the dignity of the Crown that they could not be exercised by another without specific royal grant—which, Pinchbeck lost no time in pointing out, the duke of Lancaster certainly possessed and

---

[75] *Sir Christopher Hatton's Book of Seals*, ed. L. C. Lloyd and D. M. Stenton (Northants Record Soc., 15, 1950), no. 356.

[76] JUST 1/943.

[77] *CPR 1351–4*, 156; SC 6/1028/4 m. 1.

Dallingridge's customary claim conspicuously lacked.[78] This was precisely the position adopted by Crown lawyers during Edward I's *quo warranto* inquiries[79] and it was fully supported by two royal letters close, reciting the franchisal grants made to Lancaster in 1372, as well as by the finding of the hundred jury that Henry, late duke of Lancaster, had held a court at Hungry Hatch from three weeks to three weeks, as of the honour of Leicester.[80] The case was not, however, as clear cut as the jury's verdict suggests. Dallingridge's plea of long user, that his ancestors and predecessors as lords of the hundred had always exercised the rights he claimed, had long been recognized at law as sufficient warrant for possession of a franchise. It may be that Dallingridge's objection to the court at Hungry Hatch was not to the novelty of the franchise but to the duke's sweeping interpretation of the rights it gave him, including the ability not only to justice his immediate tenants but also to exercise a supervisory jurisdiction over their courts. It was certainly this claim to which Dallingridge most objected and Pinchbeck's arguments did not address themselves to the question, but protest was unavailing against the combination of judicial favour and royal support that Lancaster could command.[81]

Having lost his principal point, Dallingridge had little better success with his other pleadings. His case was substantially undermined when the justices reconvened on Saturday, 26 June, by the appearance of John Bocche, who came into court and promptly confessed to being an accomplice in all the crimes charged against Dallingridge and his companions.[82] Bocche's appearance in court is surprising when the sheriff could find none of the others indicted. It is so opportune, and his admission of guilt so comprehensive, that it is hard not to suspect a degree of suborning by the Lancastrian administration. Outwardly he was treated with no special leniency by the court since, on failing to appear in King's Bench he was outlawed until his surrender to the Marshalsea in 1388, but he was then paid 36s. towards the cost of his pardon by the duke's receiver in Sussex, which strongly suggests that

---

[78] JUST 1/944 m. 2d.

[79] T. F. T. Plucknett, *The Legislation of Edward I* (Oxford, 1949), p. 44.

[80] JUST 1/947/5 m. 2d. Hungry Hatch was the court of the Liberty of Leicester in Sussex. Cf. L. Fox, 'The Honour and Earldom of Leicester: Origin and Descent, 1066–1399', *EHR* 54 (1939), 402 for a list of Leicester fees in Sussex.

[81] D. W. Sutherland, *Quo Warranto Proceedings under Edward I* (Oxford, 1963), pp. 81–3, 182–4; JUST 1/947/5 m. 1d; JUST 1/944 m. 3.

[82] JUST 1/944 m. 2.

some sort of plea-bargain must have been struck before Bocche appeared in court at all.[83]

As they could hardly fail to do, the jury consequently found against Dallingridge on almost every charge, exonerating him only from the accusation of burning the duke's brushwood at Ashdown in March 1380, and the attack on his servants and property at Ringmer. They also moderated the rather exaggerated estimate of the game taken by Dallingridge and adjudged against him damages of £1,080 rather than the £2,000 originally demanded. Sir Edward once again exacerbated matters by his intransigence, for whilst Sir John Seynclere was giving evidence he declared that it was untrue, threw down his gauntlet in open court, and again wagered battle, this time against Seynclere. His action was certainly without legal justification this time for witnesses, although relatively common in court by the late fourteenth century, had no formal or essential part in proceedings. This suggests that Dallingridge recognized the proceedings for what they were, a challenge to his lordship, and so insisted on treating the case as a matter of honour rather than of legal form. His attitude, embodied in his offer of a judicial duel under the law of arms, graphically illustrates how much of a man's worship and standing was felt to depend on his success or failure at law,[84] but the heroics did him little good. For his contempt of court, Sir Edward was again committed to the custody of William Waleys, the sheriff, and he remained under arrest after conviction, since he refused to make fine with the king for his trespasses. Waleys could be trusted to keep him safe, for he was also Sir John Seynclere's son-in-law.[85]

In the short term, therefore, John of Gaunt's prosecution of Sir Edward Dallingridge had successfully vindicated his seigneurial rights in Sussex, indicated to the county gentry the limits of the earl of Arundel's protection, and provided an object lesson in discipline for the benefit of the Commons. The duke was clearly pleased with the outcome; on Sunday, 27 June, Thomas Pinchbeck was granted a 5 mark annuity for life, presumably as a reward for his labour on the case.[86] Yet the sequel to these events clearly demonstrates how

---

[83] C 88/61 no. 17; DL 29/728/11975 m. 1. He still came to a bad end, murdered on the high road at Sheffield in Sept. 1392. *CPR 1391–6*, 322.

[84] K. B. McFarlane, *The Nobility of Later Medieval England* (Oxford, 1973), p. 113 n. 3.

[85] JUST 1/947/5 m. 2; JUST 1/944 mm. 4, 1d. R. F. Dell, *The Glynde Place Archives, A Catalogue* (Lewes, 1964), p. xii.

[86] DL 29/262/4070 m. 3.

exceptional were the circumstances that enabled Gaunt to bring his opponent to heel. On 16 July, only three weeks after his committal to custody, the sheriff was ordered to release Dallingridge; it has been plausibly conjectured that the earl of Arundel, benefiting from the duke's temporary absence abroad, interceded for him whilst the king was at Arundel castle in July.[87] This was clearly displeasing to Gaunt who, on his return from negotiating a truce with the French, had Sir Edward rearrested in October, but this second imprisonment was again very temporary, since Dallingridge was returned to the Westminster parliament in the following month. Sir Edward's political standing thus suffered little harm from his conviction. The incident gave Richard II a chance to snub his uncle, for Dallingridge's ally, Sir Thomas Sackville, and his servants were pardoned for the crime in June 1385 at the instance of Sir James Berners—'*regi summe familiaris*'[88]—so that, in so far as it brought him into prominence as at odds with the unpopular John of Gaunt, the affair may even have increased Dallingridge's standing amongst the king's courtiers and hence eased his path to rapid promotion in Richard II's service.[89]

In Sussex, as well, Gaunt was careful not to press his advantage too far. The chattels of John Herlond, which Dallingridge had illegally seized in April 1381, were never returned to the duke's ministers; he was still in dispute with the Lancastrian council over their value at the time of his death.[90] John Skinner, Sir Thomas Sackville's parker, successfully followed the example of his masters and refused to pay the fine imposed on him. The tenants of Maresfield were granted two marks towards the cost of a new rental, to replace that destroyed by Dallingridge. The court at Hungry Hatch, which had so outraged him, was re-established in 1385–6 but abandoned in the following year by the advice of the duke's council and, it was specifically stated, at the suit of Sir Edward Dallingridge.[91] It was not the only source of income from the duke's Sussex estates to vanish. The violence in Ashdown meant that the profits of the forest dropped steeply whilst the bailiff of the Lancastrian franchises in the county was unable to levy the estreats imposed during the chief steward's tourn on account of the concerted legal opposition to his demands.[92] For John of Gaunt, the profits of the

[87] *CCR 1381–5*, 449; Goodman, op. cit. 115.

[88] *Westminster Chronicle*, p. 42.

[89] *CCR 1381–5*, 482–3; *Return of members of Parliament, Part I: Parliament of England, 1213–1702* (London, 1878), 225; *CPR 1381–5*, 580.

[90] DL 29/727/11944 m. 1.

[91] DL 29/441/7087 m. 3.

[92] DL 29/728/11985 m. 2d.

court (29*s*. 2*d*. in 1385–6) were a small price to pay in order to maintain good relations with a man of Dallingridge's standing. He had established the principle that he was entitled to hold a court there; in practice he could well afford to abandon it. His concession paid handsome dividends; Sir Edward's son, Sir John, served Henry Bolingbroke as both earl of Derby and king of England with conspicuous loyalty.[93]

Dallingridge was soon in trouble with the law again, appearing in King's Bench in Hilary 1385 for an alleged attack on a jeweller in London, but he had little cause to abandon his violent ways.[94] Besides an uncomfortable couple of months in the summer of 1384 his attack on the Lancastrian estates in Sussex proved remarkably successful. In the short term it bought him the master forestership of Ashdown; in the long term it brought the abandonment of the court at Hungry Hatch. His case thus provides an illuminating commentary on the complaints of the parliamentary Commons at Salisbury. In one sense they were correct to lay the blame for local disorder at the door of the magnates. Even Gaunt chose to wait until the earl of Arundel could not offer Dallingridge his customary protection before settling an old score with him; lesser men were unlikely to have enjoyed even this success. Equally, the means the duke employed to gain a conviction—favourable justices and a bribed witness—do much to confirm the Commons' dark suspicions about the partiality of justice. Yet there was another side to the story, which they chose not to tell. It was Dallingridge who, entirely on his own initiative, had first resorted to violence and, recognizing in his grievances an echo of their own, the gentry of Sussex had rallied to his cause. In the long run it was their continued support for him that made a compromise between the two parties inevitable; the duke still had his estates to run, which he could hardly do unless he were at peace with his neighbours. Dallingridge had powerful friends, but he owed his ability to evade the rigours of the law as much to the protection afforded by the county community as to the intervention of the great. While it is certainly the case that, at the king's Council, 'John of Gaunt ... was obviously more influential than Edward Dallingridge ... though he attended much less',[95] the same cannot be said for Sussex.

---

[93] DL 28/1/4 f. 16; *Expeditions to Prussia and the Holy Land Made by Henry, earl of Derby*, ed. L. T. Smith (Camden Soc., NS 52, 1894), 304.

[94] KB 27/495 Rex m. 53*d*.

[95] A. L. Brown, 'The King's Councillors in Fifteenth-Century England', *TRHS* 5th series, 19 (1969), 101.

Yet although the configuration of power in local and national politics could differ sharply, it would be wrong to draw too clear a distinction between them, for one of the most interesting, if elusive, aspects of the Dallingridge affair is the close connection between the two it suggests. Sir Edward had good reason to resent John of Gaunt's tight hold on English government long before his dispute with the duke's local officials came to a head. In a petition addressed to the Commons in January 1377 Dallingridge recounted how, as chief of the executors of Edward, lord Despenser, he had been unable to obtain payment of £1,700 in wages of war owing to Despenser unless he was prepared to discount half the claim in favour of William Street, controller of the royal household, and a Lombard business-partner. This charge had initially been aired during the Good Parliament, with the result that Street and his colleagues were examined by Gaunt himself, but nothing more was heard of the matter. Dallingridge now called upon the duke to certify his findings and, if necessary, to examine the accused again.[96] His petition was fruitless, for Street was too close an ally for Gaunt to act against him,[97] but this apparent denial of justice was soon followed by Sir Edward's first, isolated, attack on the Lancastrian estates in Sussex, when he hunted the duke's chases on 25 June 1377—a ritualized act of defiance[98] that followed close on the heels of Edward III's death. The long-term consequences of the affair, too, deserve consideration, for Gaunt's brusque exercise of his lordship in Sussex, in disregard of the earl of Arundel's traditional sway over the county, represents the first sign of strain in a relationship that deteriorated rapidly during the rest of Richard II's reign. During the Northern rebellions against the duke and his policies in 1393, Arundel's actions were sufficiently equivocal to prompt accusations of complicity; in the Parliament of January 1394 the earl launched an intemperate attack on Gaunt and was forced into a public apology; Lancaster, for his part, showed no regret when condemning Arundel to death as a traitor in September 1397.[99] The origins of their enmity are clearly complex but it was the clash between Sir Edward Dallingridge and the duke's estate officials in Sussex that first brought them into open conflict.

[96] SC 8/105/5215.

[97] *CPR 1374–7*, 373, 475.

[98] R. I. Jack, 'Entail and Descent: The Hastings Inheritance, 1370–1436', *BIHR* 38 (1965), 6.

[99] 'Annales Ricardi Secundi et Henrici Quarti', p. 162; *Rot. Parl.*, iii. 313–14; *Chronicon Adae de Usk*, ed. E. M. Thompson (London, 1904), pp. 157–9.

John of Gaunt emerges from this analysis of an obscure quarrel in the Sussex countryside as both aggressor and victim, victor and vanquished. His estate officials were the object of consistent and violent attack by the local gentry, for no better reason than their attempt to enforce the duke's legitimate rights. Having gained a public victory over both the local gentry and the earl of Arundel, Gaunt was content with a private compromise; his opponents in national politics nevertheless took advantage of the incident to add insult to the original injury. On the other hand, the county community could, with some justification, view the duke as an unjustified trespasser on their rights and privileges. His interpretation of his franchisal rights was novel, his enforcement of his feudal dues severe, and the combination of political pressure, legal expertise, and straight bribery that he used to defend his position was too powerful to be resisted. When they came into conflict, these were the stark and irreconcilable terms in which the magnates and the county communities viewed each other. Yet what makes the Dallingridge case so valuable is that the battle lines were rarely so clearly drawn. In ordinary circumstances, magnates were an integral and accepted part of the county community[100] and it was to their lordship that many of the local gentry instinctively turned. Having considered a case of resistance to the duke of Lancaster's authority, therefore, it is best to turn to an area of the country where his lordship was welcomed and accepted. Lancashire provides the clearest example.

3. Lancashire

It must be emphasized at once that the position of John of Gaunt and his affinity in Lancashire was entirely exceptional, bearing little relation to the power the duke wielded in the rest of the country. In other English counties Gaunt might be the most substantial landowner, but he was never the only source of patronage and employment available. In Lancashire, this was effectively the case. There were a few magnate families who held land in the county but their estates were small and the families themselves of little importance: the Ferrers of

[100] A. J. Pollard, 'The Richmondshire Community of Gentry During the Wars of The Roses', *Patronage, Pedigree and Power in Later Medieval England*, ed. C. Ross (Gloucester, 1979), p. 52.

Groby held the manor of Bolton-le-Moors, for example, and the Butler earls of Ormond the manor of Weeton. North of the Ribble the Dacres of Gilsland were more substantial landowners but their estates in Lancashire were, significantly, all demised to Sir Robert Plessington, chief steward of John of Gaunt's new palatinate, early in Richard II's reign.[101] The baronies of Warrington and Newton-in-Makerfield were held by the Botiller and Langton families, both scarcely distinguishable from the county's more prosperous gentry, and the Nevilles' castle of Hornby was leased to Sir Michael de la Pole and Sir Robert Swillington, both servants of the duke, so that the De La Warrs of Swineshead (Lincolnshire) were the only magnate family living outside the county to hold an important estate in Lancashire.[102] In consequence, the closest approach to a magnate resident in the county was probably the abbot of Whalley, who retained some of the local gentry and was occasionally dispatched by the community of the shire to petition on their behalf at Westminster.[103] Yet even the abbot of Whalley was glad enough to be taken under the duke's protection and prudent enough to ask his permission before proceeding at law against him.[104]

The county community in Lancashire was, therefore, one that only existed under a mandate from the duke and it was on his lordship that the shire ultimately depended for good government and justice. From 1351, when Henry of Grosmont was first granted palatinate rights within the shire, the jurisdiction of the duke of Lancaster over the men of Lancashire was limited only by the royal prerogative of pardon and the Crown's right to correct errors of justice. John of Gaunt was granted exactly the same rights as his father-in-law in 1377[105] and, even during the period between 1361 and 1377 when the county was theoretically under the jurisdiction of the Crown, the justices at Lancaster continued to exercise a modified form of the palatinate Crown pleas and the duke enjoyed the right to appoint his own sheriff.[106] These were rights that Gaunt insisted should be respected so that, if a lord's power can be judged by 'the amount of delegated (or

---

[101] *VCH Lancashire*, v. 246–7, vii. 176; *CCR 1377–81*, 231, 364.

[102] Lancashire Record Office, Dd He 21/1; M. J. Bennett, *Community, Class and Careerism. Cheshire and Lancashire Society in the Age of Sir Gawain and the Green Knight* (Cambridge, 1983), p. 74.

[103] KB 27/426 m. 15; E. 175/2/27.

[104] DL 42/15 f. 131v, 1 f. 76v.

[105] *The Charters of the Duchy of Lancaster*, ed. W. Hardy (London, 1845), nos. 3, 11.

[106] JUST 1/442A mm. 15–22, 442C; E. 199/21/9.

usurped) royal power he could muster, and the territorial concentration of his lordship'[107] then the palatinate of Lancaster in Gaunt's time bore as much resemblance to the contemporary French *seigneurie* as to any other English lordship.

The consequence of this was that the duke retained a personal responsibility for the whole shire and its inhabitants quite distinct from his role as a good lord to his own followers. There remained in his grants of favour and patronage a quality of personal grace, lacking in the more formalized machinery of royal patronage,[108] that kept John of Gaunt constantly before the minds of his subjects. One suppliant obtained a pardon for his forest offences from the duke by thrusting a draft into his hands 'as he walked in the cloisters between the chamber and the hall immediately after breakfast'; another received his pardon for extortions committed whilst a collector of greenwax by the duke's word of mouth alone. William Rigmaiden, one of Henry of Derby's esquires, placed so much emphasis on obtaining the duke's favour in an assize he was prosecuting that he pursued Gaunt all the way to Gascony in order to obtain it. The harshest punishment the duke could impose was to prohibit a man his court and presence forever.[109] Lancashire in John of Gaunt's time thus presents a 'maximum case' in the study of 'bastard feudalism': an opportunity to observe the operations of a lord's favour almost uninfluenced by the competition of other magnates, almost unrestrained by the operation of royal justice. Inevitably, the duke's retainers and well-wishers will emerge from this examination in an exceptionally favourable position but the limit, if there is a limit, to their influence will serve as a useful indication of the greatest possible pressure that John of Gaunt and his affinity could exert upon a single county community.

It is important to start by defining the operation of favour and patronage within the county a little more closely. Theoretically, the duke's position within his palatinate was all-powerful and, on occasion, he could make full use of these powers, to the extent of ignoring the parliamentary election of the full county court and making his own choice of knight of the shire instead.[110] For most of the time, however,

---

[107] P. R. Hyams, *King, Lords and Peasants in Medieval England* (Oxford, 1980), pp. 234–5.

[108] J. A. Tuck, 'Richard II's System of Patronage', *The Reign of Richard II*, ed. F. R. H. du Boulay and C. M. Barron (London, 1971), pp. 1–21.

[109] PL 14/154/2 (7); PL 3/1/171, 37; *Reg. II* 302.

[110] H. G. Richardson, 'John of Gaunt and the Parliamentary Representation of Lancashire', *BJRL*, 22 (1938), 186.

he was content to allow the daily administration of the shire to remain in the hands of a small group of trusted officials. The duke's direct influence on the running of the shire was not great: grants made under his signet or privy seal, rather than under the seal of the duchy, appear only rarely on the palatinate Patent Rolls[111] and some of these were subject to the assent of his ministers in Lancashire, which implies that they enjoyed a right of dissuasion, if not of veto.[112] Most important of this group of officials was the chief steward, who was called upon to make most of the major decisions within the duchy. When a new sheriff was to be elected, for instance, the receiver, the chancellor, and the justices of the palatinate were required by the duke to provide the names of three or four suitable candidates, but, if their final selection refused to serve, it was up to the chief steward to nominate a substitute.[113] Much of the available patronage in the county, in the form of grants of leases and wardships, was controlled by the same man, whose bill was sufficient to move the great seal of the duchy.[114] These were considerable powers for any one individual to wield, even when the chief steward was chosen from outside the county community;[115] for those stewards who themselves held land in Lancashire,[116] the all-powerful position conferred upon them by the duke's trust and the opportunities for profit the post offered are very clear.

Administrative decisions were not taken solely by the chief steward, however, for the duke called upon a wider group of servants, some without any official standing, for advice and action within the duchy. When a new verderer had to be appointed in 1384, for example, the sheriff was ordered to make an election in the county court, with the full assent of the county, but the successful candidate was, in fact, nominated by Sir Robert Urswick, the master-forester of Amounderness, and Sir Nicholas Harrington; when a coroner was elected in the full county court in 1396, only four men are named as being present, all of them Lancastrian servants—Urswick and Harrington again, Sir Richard Hoghton, and Sir James Pickering.[117] By the 1390s this group

---

[111] e.g. PL 1/1 mm. 7*d*, 9, 11.

[112] PL 1/1 m. 14.

[113] PL 3/1/85, 125

[114] In a sample of 68 such grants, 38 were warranted by the chief steward and 5 by the escheator. PL 14/154/1.

[115] William de Nessfield came from Scotton (Yorks.) and Sir John de la Pole from Newburgh (Staffs.).

[116] Sir Robert Plessington of Ellal and Sir Robert Urswick of Upper Rawcliffe.

[117] DL 37/3 m. 23; PL 14/154/3 (44).

had been formalized into an advisory council, similar but subordinate to the duke's council in London; Richard Hoghton, for instance, was paid a 10 mark fee by the duke, *'esteantz de conseil'*, and in 1393/4 the receiver in Lancashire paid out a total of £40 in such fees.[118] It was this group of councillors and officials which constituted the core of the Lancastrian affinity in the palatinate and the political 'establishment' of the shire. Their position gave them ample opportunity for enrichment and self-advancement, since the administrative institutions of the palatinate, despite their quasi-legal status, retained an *ad hoc* quality that was generally lacking in the more stately processes of royal government—John Scarle, chancellor of the duchy, seals bills as he sits in the church at Preston[119]—and this informality made it all the easier for personal pressure to be exerted and personal favour to be extended.

At the same time, it renders the complicated question of the relations between the duke's affinity, the brokers of power and patronage, and the rest of the county community even more difficult to resolve. If 'one would scarcely expect the gentlemen of . . . the county of Lancaster . . . to refuse the chance of participation in so successful a joint-stock enterprise'[120] as the duke's affinity, how many were given the opportunity in the first place? The great difficulty lies in delimiting the membership of the 'county community'—that is, those gentlemen of the shire with a claim to marks of respect and favour from the duke commensurate with the position to which their wealth and birth entitled them—yet that community lies at the heart of the problems John of Gaunt faced in ruling his palatinate. If he was obliged, as a good lord, to show particular favour to his servants and followers in the county, it was no less his duty to mete out justice and reward to the whole shire. Success in either of these tasks implied a dangerous failure in the other, for the more favour he showed towards his own followers, the more disaffected would grow the rest of the county community; the less partial he was towards his retainers the less he could rely on their loyalty. Yet the rest of the shire was too powerful to be ignored, even by the duke of Lancaster, for collectively it could call on enormous territorial resources. In all, about three-quarters of the identifiable manors in Lancashire were held by resident members of

---

[118] DL 43/15/6 m. 2, 9 m. 2. Bodl. MS Dodsworth 87 f. 80, for a commission to apprehend outlaws issued *per concilium*.

[119] PL 1/1 m. 6.

[120] K. B. McFarlane, 'Bastard Feudalism', *BIHR* 20 (1945), 169.

the gentry, leaving less than a quarter under aristocratic or ecclesiastical control.[121]

There are a number of possible approaches to the problem of defining the community of the county in Lancashire and assessing the place of the duke's following within it. While each has its drawbacks, the evidence they provide, taken together, adds up to a reasonably coherent whole. To begin with the question that would have meant most to contemporaries: how many of those in the county entitled to bear arms were members of the Lancastrian affinity? Calveley's Book, an early fifteenth-century roll of arms which contains a large proportion of coats from the time of Edward III, gives 116 achievements for the Lancashire nobility and gentry.[122] Allowing for repetitions, doubtful identifications, and a number of versions of the royal arms, this total can be reduced to the arms of 52 individuals and a further 28 families, some of them represented more than once. In all, the arms of 70 families are displayed, 25 of whom appeared in the Lancastrian affinity at some stage during John of Gaunt's lifetime. Whilst many of those featured most prominently in the roll—Sir John Botiller of Warrington, Sir Robert Urswick, Sir John Dalton—were also members of the duke's retinue, there remained a number of well-established county families for whom the duke could find no place—the Lathums, Boldes, Keighleys, Singletons, and Farringtons among them. Administrative evidence somewhat refines this picture. Between 1361 and 1399, a total of 52 gentlemen were appointed or elected as sheriff, escheator, MP, or justice of the peace in Lancashire; 29 of these men, generally occupying the most prestigious offices, were in the duke's service at the time of their appointment.[123] But below this group of upper gentry was a larger pool of lesser men who were occasionally called upon to perform administrative tasks and, among them, the hold of the Lancastrian affinity was much less tight; 62 of the 83 men named as collectors of subsidies within the county held no

[121] M. J. Bennett, op. cit. 68–9.

[122] J. P. Rylands, 'Two Lancashire Rolls of Arms', *Transactions of the Historic Society of Lancashire and Cheshire*, 37 (1888), 149–60; A. R. Wagner, *A Catalogue of English Medieval Rolls of Arms* (Oxford, 1950), pp. 63–5.

[123] *List of Sheriffs for England and Wales* (PRO Lists and Indexes, 9, 1898), p. 72; *List of Escheators for England* (PRO Lists and Indexes, 72, 1932), p. 72; *Return of Members of Parliament, Part I* (London, 1878), pp. 166–257; *CPR 1360–4*, 366, ibid. *1367–70*, 418; ibid. *1374–7*, 59, 63; 'Duchy of Lancaster Records. Calendar of Patent Rolls', *DKR* 40 (1879), p. 523; Bodl. MS Dodsworth 87 f. 78v.

other office and, among all 83 in this group, only 5 ever possessed a discernible Lancastrian connection.[124]

An examination of the fragmentary economic evidence available further demonstrates how large and important a section of the county community it was that remained permanently outside the Lancastrian affinity. The surviving returns of the graded poll-tax of 1379 show 10 landowners assessed at the knightly rate of 20s., one at 13s. 4d., and 18 at 6s. 8d., the amount fixed for a landed esquire.[125] Only three of those assessed at 20s. were Lancastrians (Robert Eccleston, Sir John Botiller, and Sir Nicholas Harrington) whilst 4 out of the 18 men assessed as esquires were connected with the Lancastrian affinity and administration. These proportions do not seem untypical: in 1392, when the sheriff of Lancashire was required to distrain all those who held lands worth more than £40 p.a., only 3 of the 17 names he returned were Lancastrian.[126] Thus, whilst Calveley's Book suggests that approximately a third of the county gentry could find a place in the duke's affinity, the administrative and economic evidence suggests that Gaunt maintained links with a slightly higher proportion of the genuinely influential men in the shire but was much more eclectic in his recruitment from the mass of lesser esquires in which a county as poor as Lancashire abounded, picking and choosing as they recommended themselves.

A similar, if more impressionistic, picture of the county community emerges from an examination of some of the deeds and arbitrations entered into by the Lancashire gentry. A general pattern emerges in which Lancastrians consistently occupy the most prominent places in a witness list but are outnumbered by those outside the affinity. When Sir Ralph Radcliffe named 19 sureties prepared to guarantee his proffer for the shrievalty, he chose all 6 of his knightly sureties from within the affinity and only 2 out of the remaining 13 from the same group. When a list of arbitrators was chosen to settle a dispute between Richard Hoghton and William Aghton, it was headed by two of the duke's retainers, Sir John Botiller and Sir Thomas Southworth, and his receiver, William Hornby, and then followed by six

---

[124] *CFR 1369–77*, 112, 127, 192, 229, 269, 388; SC 1/58/43; 'Duchy of Lancaster Records, Calendar of Patent Rolls', pp. 521–4; Bodl. MS Dodsworth 87, ff. 75, 76v, 79.
[125] E. 179/130/24, 27, 28, 240/308 (5).
[126] PL 14/154/2 (45).

non-Lancastrians.[127] There were inevitably arbitrations in which the duke's affinity played little part and an examination of such agreements occasionally highlights the influence of men like Sir Gilbert Halsall or Sir Thomas Fleming, who maintained an important position within the county in independence of the Lancastrian affinity.[128] In other cases, however, an attempt was made to balance Lancastrians and non-Lancastrians in the panel of arbitrators and the importance of the duke's retainers in guaranteeing the permanence of any settlement was recognized by the frequency with which they were called upon to act as witnesses and guarantors, even to agreements in which they played no direct part.[129] The duke's delegated power thus gave to the members of his retinue a predominance in the affairs of the shire which neither their numbers nor their wealth alone warranted.

This predominance was confirmed and institutionalized in the power-structure of the palatinate, in which appointments to the shrievalty and to all the lesser posts in the county's administration, as well as to the commission of the peace, were entirely in the duke's hands after 1377. The command that this gave him over the political life of the shire has been sharply highlighted by the demonstration that, on a number of occasions, the duke sent mandates to the sheriff enclosing the names of those who were to be elected knights of the shire.[130] The evidence for this practice is incontrovertible, yet the impact it had on the parliamentary representation of the county was not excessive. Dividing the 36 Parliaments to which Lancashire returned MPs between October 1362 and September 1397 into three equal samples of twelve, 14 men were returned during the first period (up to January 1377), 14 during the second period (up to November 1384), and 12 during the final period between October 1385 and September 1397. Thus, Gaunt's acquisition of palatinate powers in February 1377 brought no significant attenuation of parliamentary opportunity. If MPs were sometimes returned at his direct behest, his

---

[127] PL 3/1/50; *A Calendar of the deeds and papers in the possession of Sir James de Hoghton, Bart.*, ed. J. H. Lumby (Lancashire and Cheshire Record Soc., 88, 1936), no. 756.

[128] Halsall: Lancashire Record Office, Dd M 34/19; Dd Sc 28/4, 37/10; *The Coucher Book of Furness Abbey*, ed. J. C. Atkinson (Chetham Soc., NS 11, 1887), I. ii. 531–2; *The Cartulary of Burscough Priory*, ed. A. N. Webb (Chetham Soc., 3rd series, 18, 1970), nos. 106, 221. Fleming: Lancashire Record Office, Dd He 6/3, 11/20, 22, 25, 50/28; Dd F 578.

[129] *The Coucher Book of Furness Abbey*, I. ii. 531–2; DL 37/3 m. 23d; Lancashire Record Office, Dd Sc 37/10; *The Cartulary of Burscough Priory*, nos. 106, 221.

[130] Richardson, 'Parliamentary Representation', 175–222.

choice fell widely enough to satisfy those with ambitions to go to Westminster and it was only in the last decade of the duke's life, when Sir Robert Urswick was returned to every Parliament between November 1390 and January 1397, that any contraction in the circle of his choice in favour of the members of his affinity occurred, although such a record of re-election (6 consecutive Parliaments) can be paralleled in many ostensibly 'freer' counties. Nor was the duke's control over the county court ever absolute: in 1379, he nominated three possible candidates but none of them was returned; in May 1382 and February 1383, Sir Robert Clifton of Clifton was elected to successive Parliaments, despite his hostility to the Lancastrian affinity in the shire.[131] Some form of election in the county court must, therefore, have continued under the palatinate, albeit a court whose suitors were sensible of the duke's authority over the county and were usually willing to be swayed by the advice of the small group of Lancastrian retainers and administrators who mediated the wishes of the duke to the political community of the shire. In his turn, John of Gaunt made some effort to include those outside his affinity in the government of the palatinate. When he came to appoint a peace commission in March 1384, only 12 out of the 28 justices had a specific Lancastrian attachment. As with parliamentary representation, however, the political franchise narrowed in the last years of the duke's life: the only other surviving peace commission, issued in 1395, names 8 Lancastrians amongst the 10 justices.[132]

Until then, the duke deployed his political patronage to good effect: the Lancastrian affinity maintained a hold on the administration and representation of the county that was firm but not exclusive. Yet these were only the most public manifestations of his powers and, for many, the duke's favour was most desirably expressed in material terms, in the grants of leases and wardships that John of Gaunt had at his disposal. Economic circumstances served to give this form of patronage a particular importance in late fourteenth-century Lancashire, for, in sharp contrast to the situation elsewhere on his estates, Gaunt's officials in the palatinate experienced little difficulty in leasing out his manors once direct cultivation had ended and there was even considerable competition to take up leases.[133] In consequence, rents rose: some copyhold tenements had their rents doubled; the burgesses

[131] Ibid. 183; McFarlane, 'Bastard Feudalism', 170 n. 1.
[132] PL 1/1 m. 8; Bodl. MS Dodsworth 87, f. 78v.
[133] PL 1/1 m. 15.

of Liverpool were charged two marks more for the farm of the vill; the farm of the vaccaries of Blackburnshire was increased by £20 p.a.[134] The increase in the duke's revenues brought about by these rent-revisions could be very considerable—it was proposed, for example, to add an increment of £140 to the farm of the manors of Eccleston, Leyland, and Ulnes Walton in 1368[135]—and this agrarian evidence agrees well with the conclusion that, untypically, Lancashire was an area of relative demographic vitality in the fourteenth century, with an expanding population that nevertheless remained well below the Malthusian ceiling.[136]

In consequence, county society in Lancashire at this period was exceptionally competitive, for although assarting from the moss was still possible in some areas,[137] an increasing population was competing for a largely unchanging amount of land at the disposal of a single patron. In such a situation, those who enjoyed the duke's favour were in an enviable position. The retaining fee he paid provided them with additional capital resources, which could be used to buy lands and leases or to lend out amongst their less prosperous neighbours,[138] and a safe collateral against which larger sums could be advanced.[139] The material results of this advantage could be striking: Sir Robert Plessington, successively John of Gaunt's attorney at the Westminster Exchequer and his chief steward in Lancashire, came from a family of local freeholders, but, by 1376, he was rich enough to lend the Dacres of Gilsland 1,100 marks[140] and, on the profits of his offices, he built up a sizeable estate for himself in the north of Lancashire by a combination of leasing and outright purchase.[141] Roger Brockholes, the duke's escheator, pursued a similar strategy at a less ambitious level, using the profits of office to build up a compact estate around

[134] DL 29/76/1498; *Reg. I* 1556, 1699; Bodl. MS Dodsworth 87, f. 79v.
[135] DL 42/1 f. 70v.
[136] Bennett, *Community, Class and Careerism*, p. 66.
[137] Lancashire Record Office, Dd Ta 32.
[138] e.g. the loans made by Sir Robert Urswick: *Lancashire Palatine Plea Rolls*, ed. J. Parker (Chetham Soc., NS 87, 1928), pp. 27, 89.
[139] e.g. the duke lent 100 marks to Sir Henry Hoghton, on the security of his annuity: DL 28/3/5 f. 4v.
[140] *CCR 1377–81*, 231; ibid. *1369–74*, 576–7 for another loan by Plessington.
[141] Plessington purchased the manor of Plessington and a third of the manor of Ellal, plus other lands in Lancaster, Comberhall, Kirkham, and Penwortham; he leased the manors of Eccleston, Halton, and Fishwick. *CCR 1377–81*, 216; *Abstracts of Inquisitions Post-Mortem*, ed. W. Langton (Chetham Soc., OS 95, 1875), i. 73; *Final Concords of the County of Lancaster*, ed. W. Farrer (Lancashire and Cheshire Record Soc., 50, 1905), iii. 29; *CCR 1377–81*, 364; *CFR 1369–77*, 335.

Claghton.[142] At the same time, Lancastrian retainers enjoyed an advantage in the allocation of leases and wardships; the duke's steward in Cheshire, for instance, was instructed to allow William Barton of Rydale to have certain lands at farm before all others, paying no more than another would reasonably do.[143] In consequence, the bigger prizes on the land market inevitably tended to go to the inner circle of the duke's supporters: Sir John Botiller and Sir Adam Hoghton jointly took up leases of ducal land worth £120 p.a.; Richard Towneley, steward of the Blackburn wapentake, was granted the custody of Sir William Hesketh's heir; Sir John de Ipres, chief of the duke's council, used his position to purchase the wardship of the Rigmaiden lands.[144] The rent for these properties could be offset against the retainer's fee, which meant that temporary control of the duke's lands in Lancashire was effectively purchased with the duke's own money.[145]

It would be more surprising if John of Gaunt's retainers in Lancashire had *not* enjoyed these sort of favours. Yet, despite their advantageous position, the duke's men never managed to engross all the patronage available[146] and, in assessing the relations between the Lancastrian affinity and the rest of the shire, the important question is really what proportion of the whole they managed to control. Fortunately, the survival of an original file of grants of leases and wardships amongst the Chancery miscellanea of the palatinate at least allows an attempt at an answer. The file[147] covers a period from *c.* Michaelmas 1385 to *c.*1395–6 and appears to be unbroken, so that it may reasonably be assumed to represent all the grants of leases and wardships that passed under the chief steward's seal during this period. If these grants are divided into two categories, those for which an annual render was made and those for which a single lump sum was paid, John of Gaunt's retainers and officials received grants worth £43. 6s. 8d. from a total annual render of £145. 2s. 11d. and paid £134. 13s. 4d. out of a total lump sum payment of £242. 5s. 8d. These

---

[142] Lancashire Record Office, Dd Fz (unnumbered).

[143] *Reg. II* 654.

[144] DL 42/1 f. 70; PL 14/154/1 (69).

[145] Sir Ralph de Ipres, for instance, received as part of his retaining fee an allowance of 100s. on his farm of the mill of Skerton and £7. 11s. 0d. on the rent he paid for the manor of Slyne. DL 43/15/6 m. 2.

[146] e.g. William Farrington was granted the manor of Leyland on a thirty-five-year lease whilst Roger Hulton received the valuable custody of William Bradshagh's lands, worth £100; neither of them had any permanent connection with the Lancastrian affinity. DL 42/1 f. 70; *Reg. II* 1047.

[147] PL 14/154/1.

figures rather underestimate the benefits from membership of the affinity, since the precise value of two major grants to retainers cannot now be recovered,[148] and they take no account of the amount of patronage directed towards the family and kindred of a ducal retainer. Yet even with these qualifications, it is clear that the Lancastrian affinity received roughly a third of the value of one total and half the value of the other. On the assumption that, at best, a third of the county's armigerous families could hope for a place in the Lancastrian affinity, it seems that the duke's retainers were receiving rather more than their strict share of the spoils but that their predominance was never allowed to become a monopoly. In his handling of the material patronage at his disposal, John of Gaunt showed the same circumspection as he did in his manipulation of the political structure of the county. To belong to the Lancastrian affinity was certainly a way to wealth for the gentry of Lancashire, but it was never an inevitable or exclusive one.

How then did the gentry of the county gain entry to the Lancastrian affinity in the first place? In a few cases, the precise means can be indicated[149] but, in general, it is only possible to suggest some of the potential avenues for advancement. Family traditions of service to the house of Lancaster were naturally strong in the county and disposed a number of young men to seek service with the duke: Robert Pilkington's great-uncle and Sir Nicholas Longford's father were both captured at Boroughbridge in Thomas of Lancaster's army and Sir John Dalton's grandfather had been one of earl Thomas's most powerful officials.[150] Yet even in Lancashire, a long tradition of Lancastrian allegiance was never a necessary attribute for a future retainer of the duke's. Against the examples of Pilkington and Longford must be set those of Sir Thomas Banaster, a great-nephew of Adam Banaster, leader of the rebellion against earl Thomas in 1315, and Sir Richard Balderston, whose family profited considerably from remaining loyal to Edward II.[151] More important than the sense of traditional allegiance was the sense of family, for Lancashire retained elements of a clan structure based upon the surname group. In consequence, the tendency for service to the duke to run in families

---

[148] The custody of the manors of Prestwich and Altrington to Sir John Pilkington; the wardship of Adam de Catterall's heir to Sir Ralph de Ipres. PL 14/154/1 (4), (30).

[149] e.g. William Tunstall; see below, p. 158.

[150] *Parliamentary Writs*, ed. F. Palgrave (London, 1827–34), II. ii. 200; *Rot. Parl.*, i. 399b.

[151] *VCH Lancashire*, vi. 103–4, 314.

was more marked in Lancashire than in the rest of the country. Two generations of the Athertons, Banasters, Hoghtons, Ipreses, Radcliffes, Southworths, Tunstalls, and Workesleys each served in John of Gaunt's retinue; by 1399 there were eight members of the extensive Radcliffe family on the Lancastrian payroll.[152] This clannishness was strengthened and perpetuated by a tight network of intermarriage which served to turn the duke's affinity into a large and complex cousinage. To give only two examples: Sir Thomas Banaster married Agnes, a daughter of Sir Adam Hoghton; Banaster's son, Edward, had a daughter who married William, son of Sir Richard Balderston, whose mother was married to Sir William Scargill.[153] Sir Adam Hoghton's son, Sir Richard, married his daughter to John, son of Sir Thomas Southworth; Southworth's sister, Margaret, married Sir Robert Urswick who then chose, as his second wife, Sir John Dalton's mother.[154] All twelve of the men thus linked by the ties of blood and marriage were retainers of the duke. Naturally, this made for considerable cohesion and continuity within the Lancastrian affinity but it also brought disadvantages, for it meant that membership of the affinity, even in its broadest sense, was restricted to relatively few families who monopolized most of the opportunities for recruitment.

There were, it is true, gentlemen such as Sir John Botiller of Warrington or Richard, son of William Radcliffe, whose position in the county was, by itself, sufficiently powerful to command a place in Gaunt's retinue, but they were few in number. Even Robert Urswick, son of the chief forester of Bowland and already an esquire of the king and the earl of Cambridge,[155] was unable to command employment from the duke and resorted to intruding himself (unsuccessfully) into the Lancastrian administration.[156] An easier way into Lancastrian service lay through a prolonged wardship in the duke's hands: Richard Molyneux, John Dalton, and Robert Langley all entered John of Gaunt's retinue in this manner. Molyneux was under the guardianship of one of the ducal clerks, Matthew Assheton, and it is easy to see how prolonged residence at the Lancastrian court, combined with a

[152] DL 29/738/12096 mm. 1–3.

[153] G. F. Beltz, *Memorials of the Most Noble Order of the Garter* (London, 1841), p. 206, *VCH Lancashire*, vi. 26; *Abstracts of Inquisitions Post-Mortem*, i. 14–16.

[154] *VCH Lancashire*, vi. 305; CP 40/433 m. 451; *Calendar of Papal Registers, Petitions 1342–1419*, 528; Lancashire Record Office, Dd B/13/2, *Final Concords of the County of Lancaster*, iii. 43.

[155] *CPR 1364–7*, 313; ibid. *1370–4*, 63.

[156] *Reg. I* 1564, 1688.

guardian's sense of obligation towards his ward, prepared the way for permanent employment by the duke.[157] Nevertheless, in Lancashire (as in nearly every other county), the largest and most easily identifiable group of the duke's retainers were those who had first come into formal contact with him as the result of their military service under his command.[158]

The reasons for this and the rewards that a retainer hoped to gain by his service overseas have already been discussed, but the domestic consequences have still to be assessed. In most counties, where several magnates usually disposed of varying degrees of favour, the primacy of military service in deciding the recipients of ducal patronage and largesse could be disruptive but it was rarely dangerous. In Lancashire, where John of Gaunt was both the fount of justice and a good lord to his followers, the effects could be more severe. Maintaining order in the palatinate, a notoriously disordered part of the country, was bound to prove a more difficult task than regulating the flow of material patronage. Lawlessness in the North, where primitive ties of kinship were stronger and resort to the sword more natural, appears always to have been much wider spread than in the South; family feuds developed quickly and remained bitter. Lancashire was particularly disturbed, for the enmities created by the revolt of Adam Banaster and the suppression of the Contrariants lasted well into Edward III's reign. Continued violence in the 1340s rendered a rapid expansion of the peace commission necessary until, by 1350, it was over sixty strong.[159] It was in these circumstances that the county community devised a system of collective peace-keeping and dispatched an embassy to duke Henry, asking him to adjourn the sessions at Lancaster and come to implement the new system himself. Every common transgressor was to be obliged to enter into a statute merchant towards the duke, of £200 if he was a gentleman or £40 if of lesser estate, which would be executed only if the wrongdoer refused to allow himself to be brought to justice.[160] In consequence, the duke was intimately involved with the

---

[157] *Abstracts of Inquisitions Post-Mortem*, ii. 30; *CFR 1377–83*, 47; *VCH Lancashire*, v. 78; East Sussex Record Office, GLY 3469 mm. 2d, 5d, for Dalton's presence in the household.

[158] e.g. Richard Massy, Thomas Molyneux, John Rixton, John Cansfield, Robert Urswick were all retained by the duke in indentures concluded overseas.

[159] *South Lancashire in the Reign of Edward II*, ed. G. H. Tupling (Chetham Soc., 3rd series, I, 1949), pp. xliii–xlix; *CPR 1348–50*, 533.

[160] *Select Cases in the Court of King's Bench*, ed. G. O. Sayles (Selden Soc., 82, 1965), vi. 89–91; E. 175/2/27.

maintenance of law and order in the county, for his worship depended as much on ruling his own 'country' in peace as on rewarding his followers adequately—the privileges of the palatinate carried with them the heavy obligation of justice. The same system continued to operate under John of Gaunt, with malefactors entering into a recognizance for good behaviour towards the duke or his steward, undertaking either to appear before the justices at Lancaster or to fulfil the conditions imposed on them by the sheriff. Many of the recognizances of debt towards William Hornby, rector of St Michael's on Wyre, recorded in the chancery rolls must in fact have been made towards him in his official capacity as the duke's receiver in the palatinate.[161]

To what extent, then, was John of Gaunt able to use his affinity in Lancashire to maintain the peace of the county? In the formal sense, this duty devolved almost entirely upon the duke's officials. Both the sheriff, who presided over the county court and the special sessions of the hundred courts, and the hundred bailiffs had the power to apprehend on suspicion and to raise the hue and cry. At the same time, the duke's officials had an important and less formal role to play in resolving disputes and quarrels before they reached the stage of open violence. Arbitration was not an exclusively Lancastrian activity, for many of the more prominent knights of the county who remained outside the duke's affinity had an important part to play in such judgements, but the duke's officials sometimes acted as the ultimate court of appeal in the event that the arbitrators chosen by either side could not reach final agreement. In the case of Roger de Fasacrelegh's claim for dower against Edward de Lathum, for example, each side chose two non-Lancastrian arbitrators but added the proviso that the dispute should go to Sir Ralph Radcliffe, the sheriff, if they were unable to come to an equitable judgement. In another case, the arbitrators were given a limited amount of time to do their work; after a fortnight the case would go to Sir John de la Pole, the chief steward, for a decision.[162] Alternatively, the chief steward could act as arbitrator in the first instance and suits might occasionally go to be decided by the duke himself, after due consultation with 'doctors and men wise in

---

[161] DL 37/3 m. 20: a recognizance to Hornby marked *pro Rege et Duce*. Established palatinate practice thus helps to explain the swift growth in the use of recognizances as a means of keeping the peace under the Lancastrian kings. J. R. Lander, *Crown and Nobility 1450–1509* (London, 1976), pp. 277–8.

[162] DL 37/3 mm. 17*d*, 22.

the law of Holy Church, as well as justices, serjeants and others skilled in the law of this land'.[163]

This system of peace-keeping naturally had its shortcomings and Lancashire continued to experience outbreaks of violent crime, although hardly on the scale prevalent earlier in the century. Cattle-rustling was inevitably frequent in an upland county and sometimes led to serious affrays.[164] Ecclesiastical disputes could be no less violent: when the abbey of Whalley was riven with feuding between two rival abbots, one of them occupied and garrisoned the abbey with his supporters, in defiance of the sheriff and the whole *posse comitatus*. At Winwick the vicar, locked in a similar dispute with a rival claimant to the advowson, alleged that he could not approach his church at all because of the maintenance of his opponents.[165] The duke's lands did not escape entirely: there were attacks and trespasses on his Lancashire estates, often minor, but sometimes serious enough to necessitate a special commission of oyer and terminer, as in 1384 when the duke's chases at Bowland and Rossendale were broken and despoiled.[166] At the same time, delegates of the duke's authority remained particularly vulnerable to attack. William Bredkirk, a coroner, was murdered in 1377 and when, in the same year, the palatinate justices came to hold their first sessions at Lancaster, proclamations had to be made against armed bands congregating to impede them.[167] Nor did conditions improve much under the immediate palatinate jurisdiction of the duke: Robert Blakeburn of Capenwra, one of the duke's justices of oyer and terminer, was murdered on the high road at Overkellet in 1394.[168]

Such crimes hardly speak well of the semi-formal system of private peace-keeping devised by the duke and the county community in Lancashire, but this was as much the fault of the public system of legal redress, which the new measures were designed to supplement, as it was due to any defects in those measures. A glance at the operation of royal justice shows the ease with which the course of law could be diverted: murderers found the royal pardon easy to obtain,[169] malicious indictments and counter-accusations turned the legal system

---

[163] DL 42/15 f. 45.
[164] KB 27/453 m. 72, 463 m. 55, 458 m. 64.
[165] KB 27/426 m. 15; PL 3/1/50.
[166] CP 40/418 m. 258*d*, 440 m. 403; PL 1/1 m. 7*d*.
[167] KB 27/463 Rex m. 28*d*; DL 37/3 m. 2.
[168] *CPR 1391–6*, 388.
[169] KB 27/460 Rex m. 14, 464 Rex m. 18*d*.

into an instrument of revenge,[170] and allegations of embracery, the bribing of jurors, were rife. Sir James Pickering, one of the most prominent knights in the county, was said to have bribed five jurors on an assize of novel disseisin to gain possession of some land in Ulverston.[171] Against this background it was understandable that litigants in King's Bench should sometimes prefer to abide by Gaunt's arbitration;[172] any improvement brought about by the peace-keeping of the duke and his followers was welcome.

Inevitably, however, members of John of Gaunt's affinity played some part in these disorders for if, in one sense, the affinity was an additional means of maintaining law and order in Lancashire, the privileged position that the duke's retainers enjoyed by reason of his favour and protection meant that, at times, they were tempted to turn it to their own advantage. The duke was petitioned for redress against Sir John Botiller, the sheriff of the county, and his oppressions;[173] in 1376 Sir Nicholas Harrington, soon to become sheriff, was presented with another Lancastrian, Sir Hugh Dacre, for the murder of Randolph, lord Dacre, at Preston;[174] John Sotheron was also indicted for murder and another retainer, Sir Thomas Southworth, maintained a long-standing feud with Sir Thomas Molyneux of Cuerdale until it was settled by the mediation of friends in 1376. Two years later he was pardoned for a murder and in 1382 he had to give bonds of good behaviour towards many of the major families in the shire—the Radcliffes, Urswicks, Curwens, and Banasters amongst them.[175] These incidents are, in themselves, unremarkable—the misdemeanours of John of Gaunt's retainers could be paralleled by the crimes of gentlemen all over the North—but their disruptive effect on the peace of the county is clear enough. The question is rather the extent to which membership of the duke's affinity protected, even encouraged, his retainers in their crimes and so undermined the good order that the duke had a duty to maintain. Concrete answers are naturally hard to come by—the more successful a criminal, the fewer traces he leaves on the records of justice—but there is some evidence, at least, to

---

[170] KB 27/463 m. 87.

[171] Ibid. mm. 22, 24; JUST 1/1485 m. 8*d* for the original assize. KB 27/464 mm. 28, 36; C. 260/90 no. 18 for more examples of bribery and embracery.

[172] *Reg. I* 53.

[173] W. Beamont, *Annals of the Lords of Warrington* (Chetham Soc., os 86, 1872), i. 201; PL 14/154/5 (7).

[174] C. 260/89 no. 64.

[175] KB 27/469 Rex m. 4*d*; *VCH Lancashire*, vi. 205; KB 27/460 Rex m. 14.

suggest that John of Gaunt showed himself sufficiently lenient to the crimes of his followers as to impede the machinery of justice within his own palatinate.

The murderer of William Bredkirk, the duke's coroner, for example, was Nicholas Atherton, who had been a Lancastrian retainer since 1370.[176] He came to John of Gaunt's service with a reputation for violence already well established and continued to disrupt the peace of the shire consistently over the next twenty years[177] but this did not prevent his rising in the administrative hierarchy of the county to be bailiff of West Derbyshire, where his oppressions understandably aroused widespread complaint.[178] Atherton's pardon for the murder of William Bredkirk was issued at the request of Gaunt's second wife, duchess Constance,[179] so the duke was clearly prepared to accept his violent conduct, probably because Atherton was a frequent campaigner abroad and was consequently more useful as a soldier than a criminal. Sir Thomas Southworth, hardly less turbulent a figure than Atherton in the palatinate, similarly suffered no eclipse in the duke's favour; in August 1377 he was appointed John of Gaunt's deputy as constable and steward of Chester.[180] Equally, William Tunstall managed to escape all the consequences of his crimes, after a year in which he had been convicted of participating in a serious confederacy of maintenance and embracery and had then been involved in a major breach of the truce on the Scottish March, by his faithful service to the duke during the Peasants' Revolt.[181] As the rest of his company melted away, those who remained faithful to Gaunt naturally reaped rich rewards: Tunstall was pardoned all his crimes at Bamburgh on 14 July 1381, as the duke rode back to England, and retained for life at Pontefract ten days later.[182] The effects of this act of grace on the peace of the county were hardly as baleful as in Atherton's case,[183] but

---

[176] KB 27/463 Rex m. 28*d*, 464 Rex m. 5*d*.

[177] *CCR 1364–8*, 179; JUST 3/165A m. 11; PL 16/1/1 m. 2; DL 37/3 m. 1*d*.

[178] *Lancashire Palatine Plea Rolls*, ed. J. Parker (Chetham Soc., NS 87, 1928), pp. 45–6, 57–60. For a more favourable interpretation of Atherton's actions cf. J. S. Roskell, *The Knights of the Shire of the County Palatine of Lancaster, 1377–1460* (Chetham Soc., NS 96, 1937), pp. 96–7.

[179] *CPR 1377–81*, 313.

[180] CHES 29/80 m. 21.

[181] *Reg. II* 302, 388; *Calendar of Documents Relating to Scotland, 1357–1500*, ed. J. Bain (Edinburgh, 1888), no. 299. Lancashire Record Office, Dd Cm 1/12–15, 18–19 for the difficulties one litigant experienced in bringing Tunstall to answer an assize.

[182] *Reg. II* 565, 37.

[183] Roskell, *The Knights of the Shire*, p. 72.

the point that the duke's favour put its recipients beyond the reach of the law was clearly made: as it was again in 1396 when another retainer, Sir John Dalton, was pardoned a charge of conspiracy and murder at the duke's request.[184]

Yet John of Gaunt's own attitude towards breaches of the peace was less irresponsible than these examples might initially suggest. To grant a pardon was not necessarily to disregard the law and its enforcement; it might mark the final stage in a long process of private composition and arbitration. In Tunstall's case, for instance, the duke only obtained a pardon from the king for his retainer's misdemeanours after he had imposed a stringent set of conditions as the price of his favour.[185] Nor was he entirely free to act as he liked, for the prerogative of pardon was one of the few regalian rights the Crown retained within the palatinate. In consequence, obtaining pardons was one of the acts of lordship that John of Gaunt could not extend or withhold at will: if the duke did not issue a pardon, there were always others who would. Thus, when Robert Croft was pardoned in 1394 for the death of Robert Blakeburn, the duke's justice of oyer and terminer, the pardon was issued at the request of Thomas Mowbray, earl of Nottingham.[186] Croft was the son of John Croft of Dalton, a servant of Gaunt's, and the duke would have been the natural man to turn to for such a favour, had the crime not been committed against one of his justices; Mowbray, who had just been appointed a justice of Chester for life by Richard II,[187] was the best available substitute. Significantly, the pardon proved an effective means of detaching the Croft family from their Lancastrian allegiance; Robert Croft was appointed to several royal commissions while his father was retained by the king, at a fee of 20 marks a year, in March 1398.[188] The fact that other influential royalists from Cheshire, such as Peter de Legh of Lyme or the clerk John Macclesfield, could also make use of this loophole in the legal autonomy of the palatinate[189] was, in consequence, a matter of some concern to John of Gaunt, who could ill-afford to be too sparing in his use of the prerogative of pardon or too unforgiving in his attitude towards breakers of the peace. One of Croft's accomplices, William Singleton, who also obtained his pardon

---

[184] PL 14/154/3 (82); *CPR 1396–9*, 177.
[185] *CPR 1377–81*, 505; *Reg. II* 302, 565.
[186] PL 14/154/3 (16); *CPR 1391–6*, 388.
[187] 'Calendar of Recognizance Rolls of the Palatinate of Chester', *DKR* 36 (1875), i. 326.
[188] *CPR 1396–9*, 310, 324, 434, 508.
[189] PL 14/154/2 (50), (60).

at the request of Thomas Mowbray, was later granted an annuity by the duke.[190] The disruption of public order that could arise from his liberality in this respect was not the result of a simple, unthinking abuse of personal lordship to the detriment of a system of public justice; rather, it arose from the ability of several patrons to exercise the same kind of lordship. Even within his own palatinate, John of Gaunt had to act under the constraints of magnate rivalry and political competition.

A clearer picture of the constraints upon his actions and of the impact of his affinity on the legal processes of the palatinate can be gained by examining the course of some of the disputes over land and inheritance that were always a source of conflict in medieval England and, in the atmosphere of sharp competition engendered by the rising population of fourteenth-century Lancashire, were bound to be particularly bitter. At the level of local society, good lordship consisted pre-eminently in the ability to aid and comfort a dependant in the course of such disputes and John of Gaunt naturally kept a careful eye on their conduct. His palatinate justices were sometimes instructed to proceed with a case but come to no judgement without the assent of the duke and his counsel[191] and there is little doubt that, when he wished, the duke could interfere more directly in the course of the law. When the abbot and convent of Whalley wished to pursue their claim to the advowson of the chapel of Clitherhoe castle against the duke at common law, they first took the precaution of petitioning him that they should be allowed to do so 'without any damage or grievance being done them or their counsel'.[192] There is, however, little evidence or complaint that the duke systematically obstructed the course of justice, either to his own advantage or to his retainers', whilst there were very definite limitations on the duke's authority in many such cases.

To take the feud between the Holland and Langley families over the manor of Prestwich as an example: both parties in this dispute could entertain a claim on the manor by marriage but, after some initial hesitation, the duke recognized the right of Roger de Langley as heir and ordered the eviction of Robert de Holland.[193] However, when the sheriff, Sir John Botiller, arrived to take the manor into the duke's hands in 1374 he was attacked by the Hollands and their servants and

[190] *CPR 1391–6*, 388; DL 42/16 f. 171.
[191] DL 37/3 m. 21; PL 14/154/6 (121).
[192] DL 42/1 f. 76v.
[193] *Abstracts of Inquisitions Post-Mortem*, i. 50–3; *Reg. I* 1010.

forced to flee; the Hollands then took possession of Prestwich and maintained themselves there for the next fifteen years,[194] successfully resisting all attempts to oust them. It was only when Robert, the son and heir of Roger de Langley, came of age and reoccupied the manor by force, despite continual harassment by the Hollands,[195] that the decision of the court could finally be put into effect. The fact that the legal decision went the Langleys' way in the first place can be partly ascribed to the favour in which Robert de Langley stood with the duke,[196] but legal right was not enough, and even John of Gaunt and his officials were unable to implement the decision of the courts against determined violence at the local level.

The duke's authority appears in an equally equivocal light during the course of the dispute over the Lathum inheritance, the longest and most important of the property disputes in late fourteenth-century Lancashire. Here, the descent of the inheritance was so complicated by rival claims that, besides the duke himself, the Stanleys, Workesleys, Daltons, and Fasacreleghs all maintained a keen but conflicting interest in the Lathum lands. This was a dispute too large and too comprehensive in its ramifications for the normal controls of the county community, love-day and arbitration, to be effective and the consequence was an outbreak of widespread disorder: in pressing his own claim, Roger de Fasacrelegh enlisted the powerful support of Sir Gilbert Halsall, one of Lathum's executors, but they were both violently opposed by Edward de Lathum, the dead man's bastard brother;[197] Sir John Dalton pursued his wife's claim to lands in Lathum with considerable violence and Sir John Stanley, unwilling to wait upon the fulfilment of his originally rather tenuous hopes of the inheritance, ousted the Lancastrian farmer and occupied the manors by force.[198]

Consequently, John of Gaunt was compelled to intervene but, in the face of so many conflicting interests so aggressively pursued, there was little he could do. The success of Dalton's claim to a larger dower share, despite the technical illegitimacy of his marriage, may have owed something to the duke's favour[199] but the fact that Gaunt had to

---

[194] PL 14/154/5 (26).
[195] *CPR 1401–5*, 96.
[196] PL 14/154/1 (1); *VCH Lancashire*, v. 78.
[197] PL 3/1/74; PL 16/1/1 m. 2; Bodl. MS Dodsworth 87 f. 77v.
[198] PL 14/154/3 (82); *Rot. Parl.*, iii. 204*b*.
[199] *Calendar of Papal Registers, Letters 1362–1404*, 412–13. A divorce between Dalton

petition in parliament for the removal of Sir John Stanley from the
disputed manors—a voluntary but nevertheless humiliating surrender
of his palatinate independence—suggests, once again, that he lacked
the power to enforce his will against determined local opposition even
within his own duchy. In the end, a characteristic compromise was
reached; having vindicated his right to the disputed lands, the duke
granted them to Katherine Swynford who, in her turn, sold them to Sir
John Stanley. As a mark of favour, he was forgiven 50 marks of the
price and, when he came to convey his new possessions, Stanley was
careful to associate some prominent Lancastrian servants with the
grant.[200]

This makes an apparent contrast with the legal battle for the lands of
Sir Geoffrey Workesley, during which a Lancastrian retainer, Robert
Workesley, was able to maintain himself in the disputed manors by
threats and a fraudulent enfeoffment because, so his opponents
alleged, he had no fear of the king or anyone else concerning his right
whilst his lord of Lancaster lived.[201] Yet even here Gaunt's authority
did not pass unchallenged, for, despite the duke's support, Workesley
was ousted from the manors in 1398 and did not regain them until the
accession of Henry IV.[202] If, in this final case, law went as lordship bid,
the duke of Lancaster's lordship was proved insufficient to maintain
the position of his dependant. In the other disputes, Gaunt's favour
may have helped his retainers in vindicating their claims at law, but at
the local level *de facto* possession consistently proved more important
than legal right and *possession* the duke was either unable or unwilling
to guarantee.

John of Gaunt's influence on the course of justice in the palatinate
was, therefore, appreciable but by no means oppressive in its extent or
baleful in its consequences. His servants and retainers did enjoy some
advantage in the course of litigation, but the dangers inherent in this
display of favour were substantially offset by the practical limitations
on the duke's power within his palatinate. If the duke's retainers were

and his wife was insisted upon by the bishop of Lichfield but Fr. Walter Disse,
Lancaster's confessor, granted the couple a dispensation to contract the marriage anew.
Rot. Parl., iii. 204*b*.

[200] DL 28/3/2 f. 18. Lancashire Record Office, Dd Fi/8/5. For the importance this
acquisition of the Lathum lands was to assume in the subsequent rise of the Stanleys cf.
'The Stanley Poem', *Palatine Anthology. A Collection of Ancient Poems and Ballads Relating
to Lancashire and Cheshire*, ed. J. O. Halliwell (London, 1850), pp. 210–22.

[201] CHES 2/69 m. 11; *Rot. Parl.*, iii. 445.

[202] Roskell, *The Knights of the Shire*, pp. 76–7.

sometimes the disturbers of the peace in the county, his affinity provided a means of resolving disputes by agreement, without recourse to the common law or to arms. If the duke was sometimes too lenient towards the misdeeds of his retainers, he was often constrained to be so; even in Lancashire, there were other patrons who would offer their lordship and protection to influential wrongdoers if John of Gaunt refused his. 'Bastard feudalism', in the sense of the duke's conscious exercise of lordship on behalf of his dependants, did not, therefore, constitute a very real threat to the peace of the shire; Gaunt was sufficiently circumspect and sufficiently constrained in his lordship to avoid giving offence to the county community.

More serious, however, was the constant oppression and petty extortion practised by the royal and ducal officials in Lancashire in the names of their masters. By 1376 these were so notorious that a general enquiry was instituted into all extortions and falsities in the county[203] and the prosecutions that arose from the enquiry give a vivid impression of the wide range of abuses that were being practised. William Bredkirk and Gilbert le Norreys, the royal coroners, were called into King's Bench to answer the allegations against them.[204] Henry de Chaderton, the duke's bailiff in West Derbyshire, was accused of a wide range of abuses stretching over twenty years: taking bribes from both sides in lawsuits, sheltering criminals, systematically extorting small sums from both individuals and villages, being the maintainer of every quarrel in West Derbyshire.[205] William de Chorlegh, Sir Richard Radcliffe's sub-sheriff and escheator, was already under investigation for his oppressions in 1371[206]—as escheator, a whole series of complaints against him testify to his high-handed enthusiasm for seizing land into the king's hands, often without sufficient cause;[207] as steward of John of Gaunt's court in Penwortham, he was alleged to have falsified the roll of amercements to his own profit, threatened unjust amercements, harboured felons, extorted £20 p.a. from the common people of the shire and, by virtue of his office, acquired so much wealth that, whereas his lands and rents were worth scarcely 15 marks p.a., it was well known that the annual expenses of his household exceeded 300 marks.[208]

---

[203] *CPR 1374–7*, 320.
[204] KB 27/462 Rex m. 13.
[205] KB 27/454 Rex m. 13.
[206] *CPR 1370–4*, 107.
[207] KB 27/442 Rex mm. 1*d*, 4, 24*d*; 444 Rex mm. 10, 10*d*.
[208] KB 27/455 Rex m. 2; E. 199/21/7, 8.

These two were the most conspicuous offenders in the county but there were complaints against many lesser officials as well[209] and, whilst the enquiry of 1376 brought a temporary halt to the depredations of Chaderton and Chorlegh, it did little to effect a permanent improvement in the conduct of the duke's officials. The abbot of Cockersand complained, for example, that whenever he appeared before the duke's swainmote court to plead his exemption from its jurisdiction, he was prevented from returning home by the master-forester's men; William de Nessfield, the duke's chief steward, was found to have enclosed common land at Urmston to his own advantage; another steward of the duchy, Sir Robert Plessington, was removed from office for his embezzlements and erasures.[210] Nor did the duke's tenants in West Derbyshire have a much easier time after Chaderton's removal from office, for they again petitioned the Lancastrian council for an enquiry into the unjust practices of the bailiff there whilst Sir Nicholas Atherton, holder of the bailiwick in the 1390s, pursued his work with a vehemence that makes it almost impossible to distinguish between legitimate distraint and private vengeance.[211]

Men like Chaderton and Chorlegh were the 'second kings' of the shires whose maintenance and oppressions were the target of attacks by the parliamentary Commons on more than one occasion. They commanded little inherited wealth—Chorlegh was said to have lands worth 15 marks a year, Chaderton's were worth 23 marks[212]—yet their official position gave them an influence quite incommensurate with their social status. Randolph, lord Dacre, the prior of Penwortham, and the abbots of Whaley and Furness were, for instance, all among Chorlegh's victims. In the Commons' eyes, the corruption of such men was the direct result of the protection they received from their magnate masters, symbolized in the gift of livery; only remove this protection and much of the violence and disorder in the counties, which sprang from an inability to obtain adequate redress at law, would be removed as well. Yet there is little sign, in the evidence presented above, that the depredations of the duke's officials were in any way condoned or

[209] JUST 3/155 m. 9; JUST 1/442*B* m. 5, 451*B* m. 1. *Report from the Lords Committees Touching the Dignity of a Peer of the Realm* (London, 1820–9), iii. 633–4; PL 1/1 m. 9.

[210] PL 3/1/174, 155, 83.

[211] PL 3/1/39; *Lancashire Palatine Plea Rolls*, ed. J. Parker (Chetham Soc., NS 87, 1928), pp. 46–7, 57–60.

[212] *Reg. II* 295.

approved by the duke himself. It was, however, particularly hard for the duke to appear blameless in Lancashire, for unauthorized oppression by a ducal official was scarcely distinguishable from the licence allowed a favoured servant by his lord and it was from such unauthorized corruption, rather than Gaunt's conscious exercise of his own lordship, that resentment with John of Gaunt's rule within the palatinate was most likely to spring.

The consequence of this resentment could be far-reaching, as Thomas Molyneux of Cuerdale's feud with Henry Chaderton, the duke's delinquent bailiff, illustrates—a local Lancashire dispute that was eventually to have national repercussions. The feud began with the murder of Richard Molyneux in 1369; the inquest on the body found that he had been killed by John de Leyland, with the maintenance of Henry Chaderton, who received the killer after the crime. The precise facts of the case are characteristically hard to disentangle: in 1376 Chaderton alleged that the findings were maliciously fabricated by the coroners, William Bredkirk and Gilbert Norreys, and that the original inquisition had found nothing against him.[213] Despite his previous record, the Council seemed disposed to believe Chaderton's story and swiftly removed Bredkirk from his office[214] but there is no doubt that the Molyneux clan continued to hold Chaderton responsible for the death of their kinsman. Although he procured a royal pardon in April 1377, Chaderton continued to be pursued by Thomas Molyneux and his family; in a petition to the duke in May 1378 he alleged that he had already been attacked and wounded once and that Molyneux, with a large band of followers, continued to ride around the county in search of him.[215]

The progression from the covert denial of justice to open violence is clear: unable to gain redress at the common law, the Molyneux chose self-help as the best way to avenge their dead kinsman. Yet the real importance of the case lies in the fact that, having formed his confederacy in order to obtain what he saw as justice against a corrupt official, Thomas Molyneux then diversified into maintaining other people's quarrels as well as his own.[216] When he and his accomplices were finally brought to justice in 1380, the names and social standing

---

[213] KB 27/454 m. 2; SC 8/39/1914, 1915, 99/4930, 166/8288.

[214] *CCR 1374–7*, 312.

[215] Ibid. *1377–81*, 125; PL 3/1/168, 180.

[216] Lancashire Record Office, Dd In 53/48–50, Dd M 34/19 for an example of Molyneux's maintenance on his own behalf.

of those pardoned indicate that the confederacy had grown well beyond its original purpose; although three members of the Molyneux family still formed the nucleus of the gang, the other culprits included esquires like William Tunstall, Geoffrey de Osbaldeston, and John Botiller of Marton.[217] None of those involved, with the exception of Molyneux himself, had any connection with the Lancastrian affinity; the confederacy was an attempt by those outside the Lancastrian establishment to fend for themselves against those, like Chaderton, who had the advantage of swift access to the duke and his officers. It was an expression of discontent with the abuses inherent in the ducal administration rather than with the duke himself, yet in seeking a remedy for their grievances Molyneux and his supporters were obliged to undermine the whole basis of the duke's authority, since Chaderton and his colleagues sought refuge behind it. The mayor of Liverpool, for example, had freed Molyneux from his imprisonment in Liverpool castle on his own authority and now refused to act on the duke's mandate for his rearrest.[218]

The Commons' analysis of the reasons for local disorder thus fits the facts of the Chaderton case quite closely, but their preferred remedies hardly seem applicable to it at all. This was because they concentrated principally upon the outward evidence of lordship—on the badges and the liveries by which the magnates distinguished their followers. But the position of men like Chaderton and Chorlegh was too firmly attached to the administrative power they wielded in Lancashire by virtue of their offices ever to be disturbed by such external measures. Hence, although John of Gaunt had to answer for the actions of his servants, there seems no sense in which he was responsible for them. Corrupt officials undoubtedly did both value and abuse the protection of the magnates they served. William de Chorlegh, for example, was able to enhance his social status by leasing quite extensive lands from Gaunt; he used his official position to oust potential rivals from their lands, and his farm of the ducal fishery in the Ribble as the pretext for an attack on the prior of Penwortham and his servants.[219] Against the Commons' demands for specific legislation against this sort of abuse, the magnates maintained that they were capable of disciplining their own men and, within the confines of the

[217] *Reg. II* 302; *CPR 1377–81*, 505.

[218] PL 31/1/180.

[219] DL 25/2096; DL 42/1 f. 94, 16 f. 38; Lancashire Record Office, Dd F/1455A; *Reg. I* 1116.

household or the indentured retinue, they were. On their estates, however, they were too heavily dependent on the efficiency and honesty of their estate officials ever to be effective in rooting out corruption themselves—and their officials were precisely the class of men whom the Commons identified as the worst offenders against the law. The problem was an insoluble one, but it was not a problem created by 'bastard feudalism' in the accepted sense of the phrase. Local violence was an inevitable reaction to the abuse of lordship but the abuse was not practised by the lords themselves, nor was it in their power to control the abuse. Further examination of Sir Thomas Molyneux's career suggests this could be as serious for the magnates as it was for the oppressed poor.

Molyneux was exceptional amongst the confederates of 1380 in having enjoyed a position of some trust in the ducal administration; in disgrace, he was exceptional in his ability to maintain his position within the palatinate in independence of John of Gaunt and his affinity.[220] He had no difficulty in finding new employment in the neighbouring earldom of Chester; vice-justice of Chester by October 1381, as Robert de Vere's deputy, and a justice of Flint by 1385, Molyneux was soon high in Richard II's favour, receiving a life grant of the farm of Middlewich from him in 1387. It was, therefore, as the *precipuum consiliarium* of the duke of Ireland that he earned the chroniclers' tribute to his influence in the North-West: *'qui magnae potestatis erat illo tempore in comitatibus Cestrie et Lancastrie.'*[221] His new-found lordship quickly enabled Molyneux to defy his old patron when, in his capacity as vice-justice of Chester, he refused to accept Gaunt's legitimate claim, as lord of the honour of Halton, to the manor of Barrow.[222] When de Vere called on Molyneux to raise an army from the region in December 1387, the lines of division were, in consequence, as clear cut at the local level as they were in national politics. Robert de Vere was the current broker of royal patronage in the neighbouring county of Cheshire—service with him offered the chance of breaking the hold of the Lancastrian affinity in the palatinate. In consequence, it is hardly necessary to invoke the harsh

---

[220] J. L. Gillespie, 'Thomas Mortimer and Thomas Molineux: Radcot Bridge and the Appeal of 1397', *Albion*, 7 (1975), 164–5 traces his public career.

[221] *Westminster Chronicle*, p. 222; *Chronicon Henrici Knighton*, ii. 251.

[222] P. J. Morgan, *War and Society in Medieval Cheshire 1272–1403* (Chetham Soc., 3rd series, 34, 1987), p. 192. The Lancastrian administration began proceedings to recover the manor in 1388 and eventually regained seisin in 1390. DL 29/16/202 m. 2; SC 6/773/6 m. 3*d*.

coercion alleged against Molyneux by the chroniclers[223] to explain the ease with which de Vere gathered an army. His recruits, in Lancashire at least, were the casualties of bastard feudalism, those who had suffered from the Lancastrian administration of the county, despite John of Gaunt's efforts at even-handed justice.[224] It may well have been the local challenge to his authority Molyneux's recruitment seemed to threaten that persuaded Henry of Derby, *custos* of the palatinate in his father's absence, to abandon the position of neutrality he was maintaining as late as 20 November and side decisively with the Appellants.

Molyneux's principal ally in Lancashire, for instance, was a man who had only recently fallen from the duke's favour: Sir Ralph Radcliffe of Blackburn.[225] Retained as an esquire by John of Gaunt in 1380 and employed on a number of commissions in the duchy, Radcliffe was appointed sheriff by the duke in March 1384 and so became, *ex officio*, one of the most powerful men in the shire.[226] In order to gain office, however, and the opportunities for enrichment that office brought, Radcliffe had preferred £80 for the shrievalty— twice the accustomed farm of the shire.[227] He evidently found an increment of this size impossible to sustain, for within two years Radcliffe had entered into two recognizances towards the duke's officials: one for £160, void if he rendered £80 for the annual farm of his office, and another for £100, void if he rendered a faithful account of all the issues of his office. By 1387 he had been removed from the shrievalty altogether, in favour of Sir Robert Standish, who had been granted the office by the duke himself as a reward for his good service in Spain.[228] Radcliffe probably joined de Vere's army, therefore, because he had a definite grievance against the duke to redress and a place in the sun to regain; similar motives must have impelled Richard Massy of Rixton, who had refused to serve in Spain with the Lancastrian army and had his annuity stopped in consequence.[229]

---

[223] 'Historia sive Narracio de Moda et Forma Mirabilis Parliamenti apud West-monasterium', ed. M. McKisack, *Camden Miscellany* 14 (Camden Soc., 3rd series, 37, 1926), pp. 4–5.

[224] *CCR 1385–9*, 393; DL 37/3 m. 24*d* gives an indication of de Vere's supporters in Lancashire.

[225] *Chronicon Henrici Knighton*, ii. 251.

[226] *Reg. II* 34; Roskell, *The Knights of the Shire*, pp. 83–7 gives a biography.

[227] PL 3/1/50, 51; DL 43/15/6 m. 3.

[228] DL 37/3 m. 3; *Reg. II* 1237.

[229] W. Beamont, *An Account of the Rolls of the Honour of Halton* (Warrington, 1879), p. 22; DL 29/16/202 m. 2.

They represented one strand of discontent in the shire; those who had enjoyed the duke's favour but, by their own fault, were now excluded from the Lancastrian establishment. Their readiness to resort to arms shows how greatly they valued the benefits that membership of the affinity brought.

Perhaps more of a threat to the Lancastrian hold on the county, however, were men like Sir Gilbert Halsall and Sir Robert Clifton; knights from well-established county families who had been prevented, by their exclusion from Gaunt's affinity, from achieving the position in county society for which their birth had apparently fitted them. Halsall had succeeded his father, himself a knight of the shire, in the manors of Halsall and Downholland by 1378,[230] but the lack of opportunity for advancement in Lancashire meant that he had to make a career in the unglamorous business of soldiering in Ireland, where he remained fairly continuously until his death.[231] Friendship and self-interest alike disposed him to look favourably on de Vere's call to arms for, by 1387, he was already a trusted associate of Sir Thomas Molyneux.[232] Clifton's experience was similar, though the consequences of his exclusion from the Lancastrian affinity were harsher. In 1373 he had entered into a statute merchant of nearly £600 towards one of the duke's retainers, Sir Robert Knolles, and, in order to meet his obligation, been forced to mortgage his patrimony to a series of Lancastrian lessees.[233] Unable to find the employment and patronage that would have eased his financial difficulties in the palatinate, Clifton turned to service in Ireland with Sir John Stanley, where he served in the same company as Halsall.[234] Their objection to the Lancastrian affinity's dominance in the county was, therefore, essentially a negative one, concerned with what had *not* been given them rather than with what had been taken from them.

That third and sharper type of grievance did animate some of those who joined Robert de Vere's army. John de Aynesworth, who was ejected from his manor of Middleton in 1366 when he was outlawed for a murder, spent the rest of his life trying to recover his inheritance

---

[230] Lancashire Record Office, Dd Cl /150.

[231] *CPR 1381–5*, 290 (1383); ibid. *1385–9*, 114 (1386), 232 (1387); E. 101/247/1 m. 9 (1390); E. 101/41/18 mm. 1,4,12 (1391); *CPR 1391–6*, 549 (1395). Halsall also took out letters of protection for service in the garrison at Brest in 1382 and to go to Portugal in 1385. C. 81/1011 (8), 1023 (21).

[232] Lancashire Record Office, Dd M 17/39–43, 49/39–40; Dd Cl /174.

[233] Lancashire Record Office, Dd Cl /1253–9; *CCR 1374–7*, 197, 365.

[234] *CPR 1385–9*, 214; cf. Roskell, *The Knights of the Shire*, pp. 51–3.

and this claim automatically brought him into conflict with Gaunt and his clients since, on Aynesworth's forfeiture, the manor had been immediately seized by the duke, who granted it out to a series of his servants.[235] Already a man with a record of violence, Aynesworth took to life as an outlaw easily enough and attracted around himself a large but loosely organized group of confederates, based on Manchester, whose activities were causing considerable concern by 1372, when Aynesworth managed to eject Sir John Botiller, the sheriff, from Middleton by force.[236] His main accomplice in this confederacy, John Radcliffe of Chaderton, provides another example of consistent lawlessness occasioned by his antagonism towards the Lancastrian affinity in the duchy. As an illegitimate son of the rector of Bury, his position on the peripheries of the powerful Radcliffe clan gave him the opportunity for violence but no motive for restraint;[237] his feud with Gaunt's retainer, William Barton of Rydale, to whom the duke had granted the forfeited manor of Middleton,[238] certainly gave him reason enough to wish for the overthrow of Lancastrian domination in the county and he, too, can be found in de Vere's army. For men like this, Radcot Bridge was only one more battle in a war they had been fighting against the Lancastrian affinity for many years.

The problem they posed was an inevitable and insoluble one, as long as John of Gaunt's servants continued to dominate the administrative and political structure of the shire, yet an examination of the numbers and social status of those who declared their hostility to Henry of Derby and his fellow Appellants in 1387 makes it clear that the opposition to Gaunt's rule from within the palatinate was usually more of an unresolved nuisance than a genuine threat. In consequence, it was only under exceptional circumstances, when the political unpopularity of the duke coincided with an access of leadership and patronage from outside the county, that the opponents of the Lancastrian affinity could achieve anything more than minor triumphs. The rise of Thomas Molyneux's confederacy thus coincided with John of Gaunt's temporary withdrawal from politics and his growing unpopularity over

---

[235] SC 8/144/2173; DL 42/1 f. 142v; PL 16/1/1 m. 3 shows he was still contesting possession of the manor in 1388.

[236] KB 9/55c m. 2; KB 27/449 Rex m. 1, 453 m. 72, 460 m. 41.

[237] *VCH Lancashire*, v. 116 n. 20; cf. PL 14/154/1 (28); Bodl. MS Dodsworth 87, f. 76 for his association with the more substantial Radcliffes.

[238] *Final Concords of the County of Lancaster*, iii. 37; KB 27/455 m. 31, 457 Rex m. 63; *CPR 1370–4*, 401.

the conduct of the war with France.[239] In 1387, it was the outbreak of conflict at court that persuaded the palatinate's dissidents to express their local discontents. Equally, the hostility to the duke's predominance in Lancashire expressed in Sir Thomas Talbot's rebellion had as its immediate cause an issue of national policy: the fear that the duke of Lancaster and earl of Derby were bent on giving away the king's claim to the French throne.[240]

The uprising is often described as 'the Cheshire rebellion',[241] but two of the three ringleaders—Sir Thomas Talbot, Sir John Massy of Tatton, and Sir Nicholas Clifton—were Lancashire knights and it is in the context of John of Gaunt's control of the palatinate that this otherwise puzzling episode can best be understood. Talbot himself fits exactly into the pattern of his Lancashire contemporaries, like Halsall and Clifton, who were already hostile to the duke—a knight of some standing in the county who could find no place in the Lancastrian administration. In consequence, he made a name for himself by fighting abroad in the king's service[242] and, while captain of Guines, attracted many Lancashire knights to his company—including known dissidents like Sir Gilbert Halsall, Sir Robert Clifton, Sir Ralph Radcliffe, and John Radcliffe of Chaderton.[243] This command also gave him a specific grievance against the former Appellants and their government,[244] to add to an existing dispute with the duke of Lancaster over the manor of Rishton (Lancs.),[245] but the chroniclers were undoubtedly correct in assigning wider motives, especially opposition to the projected peace treaty, to the rebels. Talbot and his principal accomplice in Lancashire, Sir Nicholas Clifton, were precisely the professional soldiers and garrison captains who would find their occupation gone if a permanent peace was concluded with

---

[239] Walsingham, *Hist. Ang.*, i. 368, 448.

[240] 'Annales Ricardi Secundi et Henrici Quarti', J. de Trokelowe et anon., *Chronica et Annales*, ed. H. T. Riley (Rolls Series, 1866), iii. 159–60.

[241] J. G. Bellamy, 'The Northern Rebellions in the Later Years of Richard II', *BJRL* 47 (1965), 254–74, gives the best account.

[242] Ibid. 262.

[243] C. 76/72 mm. 5, 16; C. 81/1048–55. At a time of truce the command of Guines was a comparatively important military position, putting Talbot on a par with garrison commanders like Sir William Beauchamp and Sir William Scrope, both cadets of noble families.

[244] On appointment to his command at Guines in 1388, he was prevented from taking up the post for six months by the former captain, John Drayton. He was eventually compensated for the financial loss he incurred by Richard II's government in 1391. E. 404/14/96 (22 July 1391); E. 403/533 m. 14.

[245] *VCH Lancashire*, vi. 345; Bodl. MS Dodsworth 87, f. 79; cf. PL 3/1/146.

France. The duke of Lancaster appeared responsible for denying them domestic advancement; now he seemed bent on removing their overseas employment as well.

In Cheshire, the unrest owed much to the heavy financial demands made upon the palatinate for the confirmation of its liberties,[246] but personal issues were involved here too. Gaunt's most prominent retainer in the county, Sir Richard Aston, was currently locked in a dispute with Sir John Massy of Puddington, a former partisan of de Vere's, while Adam Kingsley, an old servant of the Black Prince,[247] was removed from his office of escheator in March 1392 in favour of Thomas Maistreson, another retainer of the duke of Lancaster's,[248] after a sharp struggle for the office.[249] The chroniclers' assertion that the men of Chester feared the deprivation of their liberties finds partial confirmation in the fact that Kingsley's appointments, under the exchequer seal of Chester, were overridden by royal mandates which passed under the great seal.[250] The constitutional implications were, in any case, of less immediate concern than the demonstration that John of Gaunt's servants, already dominant within his own palatinate, could now successfully deploy his lordship in Cheshire as well.

It was this that most disturbed the Cheshire rebels, for the king's envoys to the North-West were specifically instructed to assure them that the duke would reform any abuses undertaken by his servants.[251] Paradoxically, however, only those who had found another patron willing to support their position in the North-West were secure enough to make the protest against the predominance of the Lancastrian affinity that appealed to so many gentlemen in the area, and it is this which gives the rebellion its importance in the high politics of the court. Sir Thomas Talbot had turned his overseas service to advantage and gained a place in Richard II's retinue by 1392; Sir John Massy of Tatton had been appointed sheriff of Chester by the king in October 1389.[252] In consequence, Richard II's actions,

---

[246] T. F. Tout, *Chapters in the Administrative History of Medieval England* (Manchester, 1920–33), iii. 482–3.

[247] *Register of Edward the Black Prince*, iii. 428, 476, iv. 514–15; 'Calendar of Recognizance Rolls of Chester', i. 13, 272; *CFR 1391–9*, 168.

[248] *CPR 1391–6*, 40. The appointment was made 'with the assent of John, duke of Lancaster'.

[249] *CFR 1383–91*, 342; ibid. *1391–9*, 8, 18.

[250] *CFR 1391–9*, 168. His re-appointment, in Nov. 1395, was by letters under the king's privy seal.

[251] C. 47/14/6 (44).

[252] *CPR 1391–6*, 182; 'Calendar of Recognizance Rolls of Chester', i. 330.

or rather his inaction, during the rebellion took on an additional significance, for, despite the disclaimer of involvement he issued,[253] the king showed himself distressingly slow to come to the aid of his uncle when he was attacked by two royal servants—John of Gaunt issued a mandate for a commission to arrest Talbot within his palatinate of Lancaster on 22 August 1393; a similar order within the king's palatinate of Chester was not issued until 22 October.[254]

The third confederate, Sir Nicholas Clifton—whom Walsingham makes the ringleader of the revolt—was less closely connected with the king but he was deep in the counsels of the Holland family, who stood high in Richard's favour,[255] as was his elder brother, Sir Robert Clifton, who was possibly involved in the rebellion as well.[256] Sir Nicholas had been in trouble with the palatinate authorities in Lancashire[257] but his real quarrel with the Lancastrian affinity lay in Derbyshire, and his presence in the rebellion helps to put it into a wider political context as a protest against the predominance of the duke of Lancaster in the counsels of his nephew—a predominance that was felt in the North-West as a constricting monopoly of the available patronage. Yet the protest was not just directed at the particular policies pursued by Lancaster, Gloucester, and Derby on a single issue; as the wording of Richard II's denial of complicity suggests, it was also aimed against the powers of the great magnates in general and their ability to engross much of the available patronage within a single area.[258]

The North-Western rebellion of 1393 serves, therefore, to illustrate the tensions created by Lancastrian lordship in both its legitimate and illegitimate forms. Illegitimate lordship, like the unauthorized depredations of the duke's officials feared by the men of Cheshire, inevitably caused trouble. Yet the violence that broke out was not only the consequence of this abuse of lordship but also the result of its

---

[253] *Foedera*, III. iv. 86.

[254] Bodl. MS Dodsworth 87, f. 77v; 'Calendar of Recognizance Rolls of Chester', i. 330.

[255] See below, p. 231.

[256] Robert Clifton had served with Talbot in the garrison of Guines, was associated with him as a surety before the uprising, and mainprised for the release of a man taken in Talbot's company after the rebellion. C. 81/1049 (49); *CCR 1389–92*, 181; ibid. *1391–6, 335.*

[257] PL 3/1/31: a pardon for trespasses and hunting offences in Simonswood and Croxteth.

[258] *Foedera*, vii. 746; KB 27/532 Rex m. 16 suggests the government feared the spread of the revolt to Yorkshire and Derbyshire as well.

effective and legitimate use. For although John of Gaunt had been at pains to achieve a measure of even-handedness in the distribution of his patronage, the natural advantage his retainers enjoyed could not but lead to an increasing estrangement between the more and less favoured within the palatinate. Yet if, in a sense, the duke's provision for his affinity precipitated the revolt, the affinity nevertheless proved its worth in putting down the uprising, for this was effected less by the formal legal process of arrest and indictment than by the informal social pressure that Gaunt could bring to bear by means of his retainers. Hence, it was through the mediation of 'certain of the wiser knights' of his retinue that the duke managed to convince the insurgents of his innocence and so to pacify them, although these protestations of innocence were accompanied by the renewed promise of advancement—the chronicler's comment that, against the advice of many, Lancaster admitted the more important insurgents to familiar terms with him suggests that they were men of standing with some claim, hitherto unsatisfied, on the duke's time and favour.[259]

In the short term, the discontents of the North-West could be pacified; John of Gaunt even emerged from the rebellion with his national standing enhanced. But the problems which lay at the root of the violence which characterized the region remained unresolved, for the Lancastrian affinity remained the sole brokers of power and patronage in the county palatine. Early in 1394 a statute was passed against the restiveness of Lancashire and Cheshire—the duke himself commented on 'the great malice at present reigning in our duchy by means of false indictments'[260]—but this did predictably little to calm the area; the appointment of a strong commission to apprehend outlaws in 1397 suggests that the county remained chronically disturbed.[261] No less damaging was the distrust created between Richard II and his uncle by the king's equivocal behaviour towards those of his retainers involved in the rebellion. In consequence, however closely John of Gaunt appeared to be associated with his nephew's policies at national level, Richard II's construction of a new court party and his recruitment of an ever-growing band of royal retainers, especially from his own palatinate of Chester, could not fail

---

[259] 'Annales Ricardi Secundi et Henrici Quarti', p. 161; DL 43/15/6 m. 3 shows, in addition, that many of the rebels were pardoned the fines imposed on them by the justices at Lancaster.

[260] *Statutes*, ii. 89; PL 3/1/19.

[261] Lancashire Record Office, Dd To/K/9/6; Bodl. MS Dodsworth 87, f. 80v.

to be viewed with concern by the duke.[262] An examination of the effects of Richard's policy on the position of the Lancastrian affinity within the duke's own palatinate clearly demonstrates the extent to which close attention to the local implications of national politics can qualify accepted judgements on the actions of both Richard II and John of Gaunt.

In the first instance, the intrusion of a royal presence and royal patronage into Lancashire was made through the person of Sir John Stanley, whose rapid rise in the king's favour brought him the controllership of the household by March 1399.[263] As the king's lieutenant in Ireland, Stanley provided a career for many of those in Lancashire who could not find a place in John of Gaunt's service and even attracted to his companies some of the duke's own retainers.[264] Consequently, his growing importance served to qualify the predominance of the duke's affinity within Lancashire but hardly challenged it, for, although Stanley's relations with John of Gaunt remained distant after his quarrel with the duke over the Lathum estates in 1385,[265] they never became hostile. In 1387/8, for instance, Henry of Derby presented Stanley with a livery collar and in 1393 John of Gaunt was sufficiently sure of his support to name him amongst the commissioners appointed to arrest Sir Thomas Talbot.[266] Indeed, in so far as he provided an alternative source of patronage, which eased the pressure of demand on the resources at the duke's disposal without seriously questioning his pre-eminence, Stanley's presence in the North-West could be welcomed, although the use that he made of his new-found authority, gathering 400 men-at-arms and archers from Lancashire for an attack on the city of Chester in July 1394, must have raised some fears for the precarious stability of the region.[267]

During the last two years of the duke's life, as Richard II began a rapid expansion of his household and the recruitment of his 'Cheshire' guard, some of whom certainly came from Gaunt's palatinate,[268] the

---

[262] C. J. Given-Wilson, *The Royal Household and the King's Affinity* (New Haven, 1986), pp. 219–23.

[263] Bennett, *Community, Class and Careerism*, pp. 215–17.

[264] E. 101/247/1; E. 101/23/18; C. 81/1035–9. The latter category includes Sir Robert Hereford, Sir William Hoghton, and John Sotheron of Mitton.

[265] PL 3/1/32: he was indicted before the palatinate justices for forest offences in 1390.

[266] DL 28/1/2 f. 14v; Bodl. MS Dodsworth 87, f. 77v.

[267] *English Historical Documents, 1327–1485*, ed. A. R. Myers (London, 1969), pp. 1222–3.

[268] KB 27/550 Rex m. 18*d*.

royal presence in Lancashire began to look more threatening. A number of those who had served with Sir John Stanley in Ireland were retained by the king[269] but Richard II was concerned to cast his net wider than that: on a single day in March 1398, for example, 5 knights and 22 esquires from Lancashire were retained by the king, the knights at an annual fee of 20 marks, the esquires at 10 marks.[270] On this occasion, Richard did not trespass much upon John of Gaunt's existing followers—3 of the knights and 3 of the esquires were already Lancastrian retainers[271]—but-this extensive recruitment amongst the Lancashire gentry nevertheless poses, in an acute form, the difficult question of how John of Gaunt reacted to Richard II's policy in the last two years of his life. How did he view the erection of an independent principality on his own doorstep? How far did Richard's plans threaten the safety of his own palatinate and its rights?

In one sense, the policy worked to Gaunt's advantage since Richard was careful to associate him with his plans by creating the duke and his heirs male hereditary constables of the enlarged principality of Chester.[272] Yet the systematic extension of the king's patronage and the power of the royal affinity from Cheshire into Lancashire was novel and cannot have been entirely welcome. In particular, some of those now retained by the king had a long history of opposition to the duke and his administrators, so that those who had most cause to resent Lancastrian control of the shire now held a position from which to voice their grievances. Of the group of eight Lancashire gentlemen summoned before the Council in 1388 by the Appellants to answer for their support of Robert de Vere, three were already king's knights by 1398 and another three were retained by the king in the course of the year.[273] A further two esquires—John de Aynesworth and John de Bulkeley—amongst the larger group of contrariants who were required to enter into a recognizance of good behaviour towards the

---

[269] E. 101/42/10 m. 1; 'Calendar of Recognizance Rolls of Chester', i. 215: Sir Gilbert Halsall, John Aldelm, and Nicholas Orell were all retained by the king with annuities on the issues of Chester. E. 101/42/18 mm. 12, 18 for their service in Ireland with Stanley.

[270] *CPR 1396–9*, 321, 324.

[271] Sir John Ashton, Sir Thomas Fleming, Sir Richard Hoghton, Richard Holland, Robert Pilkington, John Southworth.

[272] DL 42/1 f. 49; R. R. Davies, 'Richard II and the Principality of Chester', *The Reign of Richard II*, ed. F. R. H. du Boulay and C. M. Barron (London, 1971), p. 266.

[273] E. 101/42/10 m. 1; *CPR 1396–9*, 324: Sir Gilbert Halsall, Sir Ralph Radcliffe, Sir Robert Clifton. *CPR 1396–9*, 321; 'Calendar of Recognizance Rolls of Chester', i. 407: Richard Massy of Rixton, John Radcliffe of Chaderton, William Rixton.

duke's officials became royal annuitants in 1398.[274] In consequence, John of Gaunt had some legitimate grounds for alarm over the attitudes that the king's new retainers were liable to take towards himself and his men. This alarm was compounded by Richard's patronage of a number of existing Lancastrian retainers. Admittedly, whilst the duke remained alive and the king remained so clearly dependent upon his support for the execution of his policies, the alarm was muted. Yet Gaunt's concern was now concentrated principally upon safeguarding the continuity and integrity of the Lancastrian estates for his exiled son and it was precisely this that the growth of a dual allegiance amongst his retainers most clearly undermined. Thomas Holford of Plumley, for instance, was a Lancastrian retainer and the son of a Lancastrian retainer but his father was retained by the king in October 1397 and by 1399 Holford was one of the seven esquire-commanders of Richard's praetorian guard, the Cheshire watch.[275] He was generously rewarded by the king[276] and, when the Lancastrian inheritance was confiscated in February 1399, the late duke's seneschal and constable at Halton was ousted and replaced, on the warrant of the duke of Surrey, by Thomas Holford.[277]

This was exactly the change of allegiance for which Richard's heavy programme of retaining had prepared and John of Gaunt had been most anxious to avoid; the disquiet that the duke felt at his nephew's policy, in this respect, is best evinced by the number and composition of those he retained in the last two years of his life. Between September 1397 and his death in February 1399, 15 indentures of retainer concluded with John of Gaunt survive[278] and 9 of these were with gentlemen from Lancashire and Cheshire; a further 10 undated grants of annuities assigned on the honour of Lancaster can be tentatively ascribed to the same period.[279] In some cases, the duke's new retainers were, like Sir Richard Redman of Levens, already attached to the royal household, but in the vast majority of cases his new clients were young esquires who had, as yet, no connection with

[274] DL 37/3 m. 24*d*. 'Calendar of Recognizance Rolls of Chester', i. 2, 75: John de Aynesworth, John de Bulkeley.

[275] 'Calendar of Recognizance Rolls of Chester', i. 240; J. L. Gillespie, 'Richard II's Cheshire Archers', *Transactions of the Historic Society of Lancashire and Cheshire*, 125 (1975), 19.

[276] *CPR 1396–9*, 422, 430, 454.

[277] DL 30/41/3 m. 2.

[278] *Lewis*, nos. 34–42; Appendix III, nos. 13–18.

[279] DL 42/15 ff. 6, 12, 21, 25v, 16 ff. 138v, 171, 206, 231.

the king. For the first time in his life, Gaunt now found it necessary to buy the loyalty he had previously taken for granted. It is this programme of retaining, as much as Henry Bolingbroke's prudent generosity in 1399, which explains the massive increase in the cost of the annuities charged on the honour of Lancaster, from £424. 14*s*. 4*d*. in 1394/5 to £1,231. 13*s*. 9*d*. by September 1400.[280] Yet despite the duke's heavy outlay on annuities, the pressure of royal government on the palatinate continued to mount, for, although Richard was content to allow his uncle an honorific position in his new principality of Chester, he was also concerned to sap away at the duke's independence in Lancashire by the exercise of his judicial prerogatives. Cases before the palatinate justices were called into King's Bench with increasing frequency[281] and the number of royal pardons for offences committed within the duke's jurisdiction transmitted from Westminster escalated rapidly: 1 in 1396, 4 in 1397, 18 in 1398.[282]

Richard's assault upon his uncle's lordship achieved its first notable success in the political renaissance of Sir Ralph Radcliffe—a return to power that effectively demonstrated it was no longer John of Gaunt alone who controlled the political destiny of his palatinate. After his dismissal from the shrievalty in 1387 and his arrest in 1388, Radcliffe continued to trouble the ducal administration during the 1390s,[283] but in September 1397, now a king's knight, he was returned to the Shrewsbury Parliament as one of Lancashire's MPs and at the Michaelmas immediately following he regained the shrievalty of the county, at the old render of £40 p.a.[284] As sheriff, he was able to throw the considerable influence of the office behind the nascent royalist party within the palatinate, with the result that some of John of Gaunt's retainers ceased to enjoy the protection the duke's lordship had previously offered. Robert Workesley's opponents, who alleged that he had no fear for his illegally held lands as long as his lord of Lancaster lived, now sought to overthrow him by an overtly political appeal to the new-found strength of the Crown, claiming further that Workesley had ridden against the king at Radcot Bridge. The political line-up was clear and the case was, in a sense, a test of strength: the petitioner in Parliament, Nicholas Workesley, was an archer of the Crown in the

[280] DL 29/738/12096 m. 1.
[281] KB 27/549 Rex m. 17, 552 m. 18.
[282] PL 14/154/3/84, 87–94, 96, 99, 101–5; 6/4, 14, 71–3.
[283] PL 3/1/34; Roskell, *The Knights of the Shire*, p. 84.
[284] DL 42/15 f. 114.

Cheshire guard, whilst his principal maintainer was one of the ringleaders of the 1393 rebellion against Lancaster, Sir John Massy of Tatton.[285] Predictably, Richard II took the part of his servants and ordered the sheriff of Lancashire to arrest Workesley on sight and transfer him to the Tower; he also took the opportunity to demonstrate his indifference to Gaunt's privileges by sending the writ for Workesley's arrest direct to Sir Ralph Radcliffe, without respect for the duke's palatinate rights.[286] Even in the heartland of his power, therefore, John of Gaunt was threatened by the growth of the king's power and ambition, for, despite a heavy outlay on new annuities, the Lancastrian affinity was no longer able to maintain the predominance that had been the condition of political life in Lancashire for the last thirty years. Viewed from the palatinate, the accepted picture of a close and amicable co-operation between the royal and Lancastrian affinities, lasting until Gaunt's death,[287] may need to be heavily redrawn.

What conclusions can be drawn from this study of John of Gaunt's lordship at work in Lancashire? In the first place, it is clear that, even under the most favourable circumstances, 'bastard feudalism' was never an all-embracing form of social organization. Effectively, the duke of Lancaster was the only source of justice and patronage within his palatinate but the bulk of the Lancashire gentry had to do as well as they could without him; no more than a third of the county community could find a place within his affinity. In consequence, the simplest prudential calculation placed some limits upon the duke's exercise of his lordship on his servants' behalf. His retainers occupied most of the important administrative positions in the shire, but they did not entirely monopolize them; in the representation of the palatinate at Westminster some heed was still paid to the voice of the county court; the duke's servants claimed the lion's share of the spoils of office but their claim was never allowed to become exclusive. The ducal service remained a career open to the talents; long traditions of loyalty to the Lancastrian dynasty were common in the palatinate but they were not an essential qualification for membership of the Lancastrian affinity,

---

[285] *Rot. Parl.*, iii. 445; 'Calendar of Recognizance Rolls of Chester', i. 540.

[286] *CCR 1396–9*, 348. Thomas Holford, formerly the duke's retainer, was the man sent to arrest Workesley; E. 403/559 m. 14.

[287] J. A. Tuck, *Richard II and the English Nobility* (London, 1973), pp. 209–10; Bennett, *Community, Class and Careerism*, p. 169.

and the importance of military service in deciding who entered the duke's retinue kept the door of the Lancastrian establishment open to anyone prepared to try his luck abroad. In any case, the gap between the duke's theoretical authority and his actual powers remained considerable and the position of his retainers was never impregnable. In disputes over land and inheritance, possession remained nine points of the law and possession was decided on the ground, often by force of arms, not in the courts. On more than one occasion, the duke's judicial decision in favour of a retainer was successfully thwarted by the violent opposition of the disappointed party.

Nevertheless, the uprisings and disturbances that characterized Lancashire in Richard II's reign make it clear that, whatever the limitations on John of Gaunt's authority, the exercise of his lordship still aroused powerful antagonisms. Yet this was less the consequence of an excess of Lancastrian lordship than of an absence of alternative lords capable of providing employment and reward for those who could not find a place in the duke's service. Active opposition to Lancastrian rule in the county, by those who felt themselves denied their legal rights by the predominance of the duke's men, was sparse and, save in the case of Sir Thomas Molyneux, inconsequential. Passive dissatisfaction, on the part of those who felt themselves denied their rightful consequence, was widespread. In his double role as lord of the whole palatinate of Lancaster and as a good lord to his own followers, John of Gaunt's lapses into partiality were few and relatively venial but their consequences, in both national and regional terms, were serious. By their service with Robert de Vere in 1387, by their support for Sir Thomas Talbot in 1393, by their willing acquiescence in the royalist *revanche* in 1398, the dissatisfied within the palatinate took advantage of every crisis in national politics to undermine the local position of the duke and his affinity. Precisely because the duke's tenurial and territorial pre-eminence in Lancashire was so absolute, this was the only means of opposition available to them; no new patron could be found unless John of Gaunt was first removed.

There is a sense, therefore, in which *more* lordship, not less, was the only answer to the palatinate's problems. A society more purely 'bastard feudal', in the accepted sense of a number of lords each offering their protection and patronage to the gentlemen of the county, would have remedied many of the discontents so violently expressed in Lancashire. Yet it would not have removed the other great cause of offence highlighted by this study: the maintenance and oppression practised by some palatinate officials. These were men who acted in the name of the duke but without his authority or approval; within the confines of a single wapentake they could offer a form of lordship no less effective than the duke's. As the 'second kings' of the shire they were the object of attack by the parliamentary Commons but the remedies suggested by the Commons, principally that the protection of the great should be removed, were hardly applicable to the realities of the situation in Lancashire. Far from encouraging the depredations of his officials, John of Gaunt suffered from them: financially, in terms of lost revenue; politically, as the discontents created by the corruption of officialdom encouraged some of the Lancashire gentry to look outside the county for the lordship that would right their wrongs. In this sense, the duke of Lancaster was as much a casualty of 'bastard feudalism', a victim of his officials' oppressions, as any of the tenants who petitioned him for redress of their grievances.

These are large conclusions to be drawn from the study of a single county, however important in the composition of the duke's affinity; particularly so when Lancashire was an admittedly unique case. If they are to have any general application, they must be tested against the position and actions of the Lancastrian affinity elsewhere, preferably in a shire as different as possible from Lancashire. How large a part did the Lancastrian affinity play in that county community? Can the disorder there be seen as a protest against John of Gaunt's lordship as well? How did the duke's officials use their authority? It is the purpose of the next chapter to provide some answers.

6

THE LANCASTRIAN AFFINITY AND LOCAL SOCIETY: NORFOLK AND THE NORTH MIDLANDS

1. Norfolk

Norfolk provides a strong contrast to Lancashire in geographical, tenurial, and economic terms, and the position of the Lancastrian affinity in the county is predictably very different. Unlike Lancashire, Norfolk was a prosperous and comparatively open society, remaining one of the richest counties in England throughout the later middle ages.[1] A fragmented manorial structure and a long tradition of freehold tenure gave the East Anglian peasantry an exceptional independence whilst, at a higher tenurial level, many magnates held land in the county but none held enough to establish an unquestioned landed pre-eminence.[2] In consequence, the comparative freedom of the peasantry was matched by the independence of the gentry, who had the choice of many lords to serve and the wealth to maintain their independence if they wished. In 1366 the sheriff of Norfolk returned the names of 32 gentlemen in the county with an annual income over £40 p.a. who had not taken the order of knighthood and he was able, when pressed by the Exchequer, to add the names of another 10. The Norfolk and Suffolk Roll of Arms, dating from the end of the fourteenth century, includes more than 150 armigerous East Anglian families.[3]

The roots of the prosperity which supported so many gentry families lay in the mixed sheep/corn husbandry established on the light soils of north and west Norfolk. It was a prosperity which depended upon access to the sea and, in consequence, relations with the great ports of

[1] E. J. Buckatzsch, 'The Geographical Distribution of Wealth in England, 1086–1843', *EcHR*, 2nd series, 3 (1950), 186–7.

[2] Roger Virgoe, 'The Crown and Local Government: East Anglia under Richard II', *The Reign of Richard II*, ed. F. R. H. du Boulay and C. M. Barron (London, 1971), pp. 225–6.

[3] E. 159/145, Easter term, Recorda m. 26*d*; A. R. Wagner, *A Catalogue of English Medieval Rolls of Arms* (Oxford, 1950), p. 73.

Yarmouth and Lynn were close, whilst the county town of Norwich acted as a centre for that conspicuous consumption that defined a gentleman.[4] In turn, the wealthy merchant community, anxious for the social advancement which accrued from the possession of land, provided an important pool of surplus capital to cushion the county's landowners from the effects of declining profits from demesne cultivation.[5] This economic interdependence between the county gentry and the merchant communities of Norfolk was reinforced by strong social and administrative links between the two; the justices of the peace usually sat at either Norwich or Lynn whilst the citizens of Norwich periodically entertained the *nobiles ac gentiles* of the county to breakfast.[6] The result was a cohesive and prosperous county community, whose members were capable of acting together effectively against a magnate as powerful as Henry Despenser, bishop of Norwich.[7]

What position did the duke of Lancaster and his men occupy in this society? The size and wealth of his Norfolk estates alone made John of Gaunt a man of influence in the county. Excluding some manors and franchisal rights granted out for life, his Norfolk lands were valued at just over £900 p.a.[8] Comparative valuations for the estates of other magnates in the county are difficult to find but Michael de la Pole, second earl of Suffolk, could expect no more than £500 from all his East Anglian lands in 1404 whilst Richard, earl of Arundel's Norfolk lands were valued (probably undervalued) at around £200 p.a. at the time of his forfeiture in 1397. The lordship of Rising and the profits of Lynn toll-booth brought the Black Prince just over £100 p.a. from the county.[9] Indeed, only the Mowbray family could outmatch the Lancastrian holdings in Norfolk and Suffolk: Margaret, countess

---

[4] A. Hassell Smith, *County and Court* (Oxford, 1974), pp. 3–15.

[5] John Bolt, one of the *potentiores* of Lynn, became farmer of the duke's manor of Methwold in 1392, for example; in 1400 he received an *ex gratia* grant of 100 rabbits a year for his good conduct as a tenant. DL 29/289/4737, m. 1; DL 43/15/5 m. 5; HMC, *Manuscripts of the Corporations of Southampton and King's Lynn* (1887), p. 192; DL 42/15 f. 27.

[6] 'Norfolk Sessions of the Peace. Roll of Mainpernors and Pledges, 1394–1379', ed. L. J. Redstone, *Norfolk Record Society Publications*, 8 (1936), 3–14; *Records of the City of Norwich*, ed. W. Hudson and J. C. Tingey (Norwich, 1910), ii. 41.

[7] Roger Virgoe, 'The Murder of Edmund Clippesby', *Norfolk Archaeology*, 35 (2) (1972), 302–7.

[8] Valuations in the 1390s fluctuate between £973. 1s. 3d. in 1390/1 and £882. 3s. 0d. in 1393/4. DL 43/15/4 m. 4; DL 29/728/11982 m. 2.

[9] BL Egerton Roll 8776; *CIM 1392–9*, nos. 263, 269, 271, 274; P. H. W. Booth, *The Financial Administration of the Lordship and County of Chester 1272–1377* (Chetham Soc., 3rd series, 28, Manchester, 1981), p. 175.

Marshal, received over £1,400 from her lands in those counties in 1394/5,[10] for example, but the fact that so large a proportion of the Mowbray estates remained for so long in the hands of the dowager countess meant that the family was unable to put this landed wealth to political effect. When the duke of Lancaster visited Norwich in 1385–6, he received a substantial gift of 50 marks from the citizens; Thomas Mowbray, earl of Nottingham, got only 10 marks.[11]

On such occasions, Gaunt was clearly a man to be feasted and placated but his visits to Norfolk were rare and relatively brief. Principally, this was due to the county's geographical isolation—it was not on the way to anywhere which concerned the duke. The shrine of Our Lady of Walsingham provided one of the few reasons for a journey into Norfolk, for Gaunt was certainly there in 1380 and 1394. He may have come to inspect the estates newly granted him in the county in 1372; he was at Norwich in 1378/9 and 1385/6 and he planned a visit, staying at Gimingham, for the summer of 1398, but these are the only indications of the duke's presence in East Anglia that his extensive itinerary provides.[12] In consequence, the Lancastrian affinity in the area lacked the focus for their loyalty that only the duke's personal presence could furnish. Yet this focus and encouragement to loyalty was more necessary in East Anglia than in areas of more traditional Lancastrian concerns for, although extensive, the duke's estates in the region were of recent acquisition. His tenure of the honour of Richmond gave him, it is true, a modest territorial interest in Norfolk almost from birth, centred on the manor of Swaffham and its knights' fees,[13] but he gained far more extensive lands in the county by his marriage to Blanche of Lancaster. These lands had mainly been acquired by earl Thomas from his enemy, the earl Warenne, in a highly advantageous settlement of outstanding disputes in 1318 which brought the house of Lancaster much of its richest property in East Anglia.[14] The tenure of those estates was, however, disturbed; on Thomas of Lancaster's execution for treason in 1322 they reverted to the Warenne family and, in 1330/1, the bailiwick of Lancaster in

[10] College of Arms, Arundel MS 49 ff. 14v–27v.

[11] *Records of the City of Norwich*, ii. 48.

[12] Norfolk Record Office, NRS 3342 m. 3; DL 43/15/7 m. 4; *Reg. I* 1052; *Records of the City of Norwich*, ii. 45, 48; Norfolk Record Office, NRS 15171 m. 2d.

[13] *Registrum Honoris de Richmond*, ed. R. Gale (London, 1722), Appendix, pp. 45–7.

[14] The manors of Gimingham, Methwold, and Thetford as well as the hundreds of Gallow and Brothercross. *CCR 1318–23*, 68; J. R. Maddicott, *Thomas of Lancaster* (Oxford, 1970), pp. 234–7 discusses the circumstances.

Norfolk was worth only £8. 10*s*. 8*d*.[15] It was not until the last earl
Warenne's death in 1347 that Henry of Grosmont was able to make
good his reversionary claims and, even so, the former Warenne lands
retained a separate administrative existence from the rest of the duke's
possessions in the county as late as the 1380s.[16] These possessions
were again enlarged in 1372 when Gaunt surrendered the manor of
Swaffham and the rest of his Richmond lands, receiving in compensation the manors of Wighton, Aylesham, Fakenham, Snettisham, and
Smithdon as well as the hundreds of Erpingham and North Greenhoe;
an 'exchange' that, in fact, greatly extended the duke's territorial
interest in East Anglia.[17] Thus, the creation and consolidation of a
substantial block of Lancastrian lands in the area was effectively
concentrated within a space of twenty-five years, between 1347 and
1372.

Initially, Henry of Grosmont had shown himself anxious to exploit
and consolidate his sudden access of power in the region, for a number
of his most trusted retainers were fee'd from the receivership of
Norfolk and Suffolk; by the time of his death the manor of Tunstead
bore annuity charges very nearly equivalent to its clear value and the
receiver met annuities of £200 p.a. from a total receipt that can hardly
have been more than £600 p.a.[18] The next comparable receiver's
account, that for 1379/80, suggests that John of Gaunt had made little
effort to continue the policy initiated by his father-in-law. By then, the
sum of annuity payments amounted to £193. 10*s*. 5¾*d*.,[19] which
means that expenditure on the Lancastrian affinity in the area had
remained static over a period of twenty years whilst the size and value
of the duke's estates in East Anglia had increased rapidly. Many of
these payments were, in addition, to the pensioners of duke Henry
rather than to men retained by John of Gaunt himself. In consequence,
the Lancastrian affinity still counted for little in Norfolk. The surviving
portions of the poll-tax return of 1379 show eighteen landowners taxed
at the top rate of 20*s*., only two of whom were connected with John of

[15] DL 40/1/11 f. 44v.

[16] *CFR 1344–56*, 43, 52; Norfolk Record Office, NRS 11072 m. 2.

[17] *Reg. I* 34. These estates were charged at £332. 0*s*. 0*d*. in 1393/4; the manor of
Swaffham was farmed from the duke of Brittany at the same time for £100 p.a. DL 43/
15/5 m. 4; *CFR 1383–91*, 67.

[18] DL 29/288/4719, 4720; *CPR 1350–4*, 16, 93; *Reg. II* 581–2 for Henry of
Grosmont's annuitants. They included Sir Nicholas Gernoun, Sir Neel Loring, and Sir
Thomas Uvedale.

[19] Norfolk Record Office, NRS 3342 m. 2.

Gaunt—Edmund Gournay of West Barsham and Eleanora Gerberge, lady of Wickhampton.[20] The rest of the duke's affinity came from more humble surroundings; John Methwold of Langford was assessed at 6s. 8d., for instance, and Thomas Wombe, receiver of the Richmond lands, at only 2s.[21] The families from which Gaunt was soon to recruit —Berney, Erpingham, Groos—were all of a much higher social standing, assessed at 20s. a head;[22] they formed the duke's natural target area in Norfolk, but, in 1379, he had yet to take up the option of their service.

Other magnates were more anxious to make active use of their Norfolk estates. Without offering the opportunity for political dominance, the county provided an ample pool of gentry, on which most of the magnates who held land in the area drew, so that the ties of lordship formed a familiar adjunct to gentry relations within the county community. Thomas Mowbray naturally acquired a number of followers from Norfolk—Sir John Inglesthorpe, John Lancaster of Bressingham, and William Rees of Tharston among them.[23] William Rees was also a retainer of Richard, earl of Arundel, whose steward, John Gournay, came from West Barsham.[24] Both Sir George and Sir Simon Felbrigg were prominent in the service of the earls of March;[25] Edmund, earl of Cambridge, drew successive stewards—Sir Roger Welesham and Sir Thomas Gerberge—from East Anglia;[26] the Lincolnshire family of Willoughby enjoyed many connections with the county, whilst the Staffords were prepared to pay handsomely for the 'friendship' of the Norfolk gentry.[27] For much of his life, John of Gaunt made no greater impact than his fellow magnates upon the loyalties of the county, despite the size of his Norfolk estates, acquiring the service of his retainers there haphazardly as opportunity offered and occasion, chiefly military occasion, demanded. This was certainly the case with the duke's earliest retainers from the area, Sir Hugh Hastings of Elsing and Sir John Plays of Chelsworth, and the

[20] E. 179/149/45 m. 1, 47 m. 1d.

[21] E. 179/149/53 mm. 11, 11d.

[22] E. 179/149/52 m. 1d, 57 m. 3d, 242/26.

[23] *CPR 1399–1401*, 193, 294, 133.

[24] *CPR 1396–9*, 255; D. Gurney, *Records of the House of Gurney* (London, 1848), p. 380.

[25] G. A. Holmes, *The Estates of the Higher Nobility in Fourteenth-Century England* (Cambridge, 1957), p. 63; BL Egerton Roll 8738.

[26] *CPR 1405–8*, 12; E. 403/515 m. 19.

[27] Lincolnshire Archives Office, 5 Anc. 1/1/14, 15, 17, 20; Staffordshire Record Office, D. 641/1/2/4 m. 4.

correlation between indenture and military service remained high throughout John of Gaunt's lifetime.[28] The result was a miscellaneous collection of knightly retainers, scattered over East Anglia, who had little in common except a shared desire to profit from the duke's service. Lancastrian sentiment certainly existed amongst them— Hastings had served on several campaigns with Henry of Grosmont before he was retained by Gaunt, and Plays was keen to draw attention to his descent from Edmund, first earl of Lancaster[29]—but a variety of circumstances ensured that this sentiment was rarely translated into concerted local action on the duke's behalf. Hastings, like Sir Robert Charles of Kettleburgh (Suff.), held lands in Yorkshire which drew his attention away from East Anglia;[30] Sir John Plays's main interests lay further south, in Essex, and he spent much of his time and energy seeking lands in Buckinghamshire to which his family had a claim.[31] Neither Charles nor Sir Philip Deneys of Tannington (Suff.) held an administrative position in his native county; only Sir John Strange of Hunstanton (Norf.) sought any of the traditional employments open to the county gentry, serving as MP for Norfolk in the two Parliaments of 1388.[32] While these were men anxious to turn John of Gaunt's lordship to advantage, the advantage they sought was freedom from, not involvement in, the burdens of local government; at the duke's request, Deneys was exempted from serving on any assize or holding local office against his will while, as a mark of favour, Sir John Strange and his tenants were excused service on juries in the duke's hundred court of Smithdon.[33]

Principally, therefore, the duke used his Norfolk lands as a source of revenue, not retainers, appropriating the surplus of the East Anglian receivership to meet the expenses of his household. Thus, £500 was assigned from Norfolk to the duke's wardrobe in 1378/9 and a further 500 marks assigned for his wife and eldest son. The demand for cash liveries was so insistent that, at times, the duke's retainers suffered in consequence; in 1385/6, for instance, duchess Constance alone received £440. 6s. 8d. from Norfolk whilst £53 in annuities remained

---

[28] With the single exception of Sir Robert Charles, all those retained by the duke before 1388 can be shown to have served abroad with him at least once. Cf. Appendix I.

[29] C. 76/34 m. 14, 38 m. 16; SC 8/20/969, *Rot. Parl.*, iii. 175.

[30] *CCR 1374–7*, 451; *CIPM* XIV. 102, *CCR 1377–81*, 226.

[31] *CPR 1377–81*, 40, 474; ibid. *1381–5*, 85, 139, 246; SC 8/143/7118, 163/8150.

[32] *CCR 1385–9*, 495, 657.

[33] *CPR 1377–81*, 498; F. Blomefield, *An Essay Towards a Topographical History of the County of Norfolk*, 2nd edn. (1805–10), x. 317.

unpaid because of a lack of money in the receiver's hands.[34] The immediate reason for the shortfall was, in that case, one of recalcitrant ministers, but behind the ministers' unwillingness to meet their farms in full lay a more serious decline in the profitability of the lands they managed. Norfolk figures prominently amongst the Lancastrian auditors' reasons for the decline in the duke's estate profits and by 1397 the arrears on his ministers' accounts amounted to over £500.[35] Manors extended at £166 brought in less than half that amount by 1388 and the mills of Fakenham and Aylesham were without farmers, because of the low price of grain. At Tunstead the miller had disappeared as well; at Snettisham the demesne was in the lord's hand for lack of farmers and at Gimingham a similar lack of tenants left many of the bond tenements vacant and ruinous.[36] One way to solve this problem was to grant out decaying properties in lieu of a retaining fee; the manor of Rodmere, about to come into the lord's hand for lack of farmers in 1374, had been granted for life to Fr. John Feltwell by 1385 as his fee.[37] For the duke, therefore, his retinue provided a convenient means of retarding the effects of agrarian decline, but for the recipient it was a less advantageous arrangement, since he might easily find himself with a rapidly wasting asset. Thomas Maundeville, the duke's avener, was granted a marsh and pasture at Tunstead, valued at £12 p.a., in 1381 in lieu of a retaining fee, but by 1393/4 the property was reckoned to be worth only £8 p.a., in 1400 only 10 marks.[38]

Whatever the drawbacks for his retainers, the economic advantages help to explain why, contrary to his normal practice, the duke was prepared to grant out his manors and franchises in Norfolk to his retainers with some freedom. Besides the grant to Maundeville, Sir John Plays received the hundreds of Gallow and Brothercross; Sir Thomas Erpingham, the hundred of South Erpingham; Sir Thomas Morieux and his wife Blanche, the valuable manor of Fakenham.[39] Such life grants had, besides their economic attractions, the advantage of administrative simplicity but they gave the duke less direct control over the actions of his retainers than did the payment of an annual fee,

---

[34] Norfolk Record Office, NRS 3342 m. 2; 11072 m. 2.
[35] DL 29/288/4732 m. 1; Norfolk Record Office, NRS 3345.
[36] Holmes, op. cit. 127–8; DL 29/288/4727 m. 2*d*, 4728 m. 1, 728/11985 m. 2.
[37] *Reg. I* 1570; Norfolk Record Office, NRS 11072 m. 1.
[38] DL 29/288/4724 m. 2, 728/11982 m. 2*d*; DL 42/15 f. 93.
[39] *CPR 1367–70*, 406; DL 42/16 f. 16; *Reg. II* 1010.

which could be withheld at will, and they frequently led to litigation between lord and man. At Gallow, for example, Sir John Plays's farmer was locked in dispute with the Lancastrian steward over the issues of green wax and other casuals, which he had retained in his own hands although they had been specifically reserved to the duke.[40] Diminishing estate returns, which induced John of Gaunt to exploit the social attractions of land as its economic value steadily declined, thus obliged him to surrender a measure of control over his retainers in Norfolk. Political considerations required a further surrender, for in May 1384 the duke demised his manor of Gimingham, worth over £200 p.a., to his brother, Thomas of Woodstock, for an unspecified term of years.[41] In the same year, Woodstock was required to deliver to Henry of Derby the moiety of the Bohun inheritance, worth around £900 p.a., which Henry claimed in the right of his wife.[42] The demise of Gimingham may, therefore, have been intended as partial compensation for this blow to Woodstock's always precarious income, or as a political sweetener in order to gain Thomas's acquiescence to the duke's Spanish plans,[43] but it meant, nevertheless, that for a period of (in practice) six years[44] many Lancastrian annuitants in Norfolk were dependent upon the duke of Gloucester and his ministers for their fee.[45]

As a good lord to the Norfolk gentry, therefore, John of Gaunt displayed some very definite shortcomings. He was hardly ever there; when he *was* there, he showed no great interest in their services, preferring to use his East Anglian revenue for the expenses of his household or to fee annuitants from other parts of the country;[46] when the duke *did* admit them to his affinity, the fees they received were sometimes in arrears, sometimes less valuable than they expected,

[40] DL 29/288/4732 m. 2.

[41] HMC, *Report on the Manuscripts of the Marquess of Lothian* (1905), p. 69; Norfolk Record Office, NRS 11072 m. 1.

[42] *CCR 1381–5*, 511–16; Holmes, op. cit. 24–5.

[43] A similar arrangement was alleged against them in 1394. *Westminster Chronicle*, p. 518.

[44] The manor came back into the duke's hand in 1390. DL 29/728/11977 m. 2*d*.

[45] BL Harleian Ch. 49 H 21. A quittance for his annuity from Sir Thomas Erpingham to the receiver of the duke of Gloucester.

[46] William Wintringham, the duke's carpenter, lived at Southwark but took his fee from Soham (Cambs.); Sir Nicholas Sarnesfield's estates lay in the South-West, although his annuity was assigned on Methwold. Norfolk Record Office, NRS 3342 m. 2; J. H. Harvey and A. Oswald, *English Medieval Architects: A Biographical Dictionary Down to 1550* (London, 1954), p. 297.

sometimes the responsibility of another magnate. This did not mean, however, that the Lancastrian affinity in East Anglia was entirely moribund; rather, that other sections of county society could offer services that the duke was more anxious to exploit.

Like the rest of the county community, he was obliged to maintain an interest in the commercial centres of Norwich, Yarmouth, and Lynn and his affinity in Norfolk shows, in consequence, unusually strong urban links. An annuitant, John Wesenham, named by the Commons as one of the *grantz merchantz* of the recent past, provided contact with the merchant community at Lynn;[47] a retainer, Henry Rose, came from a Yarmouth burgess family who had moved into the countryside and he retained sufficient influence in the town to be appointed captain of Yarmouth in 1371.[48] The duke's shipman, John Hacon, was also a prosperous Yarmouth merchant, one of the four burgesses of the town in 1384 and 1395.[49] His importance to John of Gaunt lay principally in his experience as a commander of naval transports[50] but the duke rewarded him by advancing his position in the town—besides his retaining fee, Gaunt obtained for him a Crown pension assigned on the wool custom of Yarmouth and financed his private trading by periodic loans.[51] No less exceptional was the strong clerical element amongst John of Gaunt's annuitants in East Anglia; in particular the Carmelite friars, who were particularly strong in the region,[52] were the objects of his favour. Fr. Walter Disse, for many years the duke's confessor, and Fr. John Feltwell, a clerk of his chapel, both received annuities assigned on the Norfolk receivership, as did a number of other Carmelites.[53] Clerks such as these were more closely dependent upon the duke for advancement than their lay counterparts, yet they could be no less useful to Gaunt than his gentry followers. John Feltwell, for example, was also a member of the royal chapel[54]

[47] *Rot. Parl.*, iii. 123*b*; HMC, *Manuscripts of the Corporations of Southampton and King's Lynn* (1887), pp. 218, 220.

[48] *Foedera*, III, ii. 925.

[49] F. Blomefield, *An Essay Towards a Topographical History of the County of Norfolk*, 2nd edn. (1805–10), xi. 424.

[50] E. 101/30/13, 18, 29/39; E. 364/13 m. 4v for his commands.

[51] *CPR 1388–92*, 464; DL 28/3/2 f. 5v. *Records of the City of Norwich*, i. 271 for an attempt by the duke to make similar provision for a servant at Norwich.

[52] David Knowles and R. Neville Haddock, *Medieval Religious Houses: England and Wales*, 2nd edn. (London, 1971), p. 234.

[53] Norfolk Record Office, NRS 3342 m. 2—Fr. Martin de Sculthorpe, Fr. Martin Southfield, Fr. Alan Geywood.

[54] E. 101/401/16 mm. 31, 36.

whilst Walter Disse was given special responsibility by the Pope in 1386 for preaching the duke's crusade against the Castilian schismatic.[55] It is a sign of the flexibility and resourcefulness of the Lancastrian administration that it was to these sections of society, usually outside the purlieus of the duke's affinity, that John of Gaunt should turn for his annuitants in East Anglia.

Nevertheless, the absence of a well-defined body of knightly or near-knightly retainers in Norfolk meant that Lancastrian interests in the county lay chiefly in the hands of the duke's ministers, the stewards and receivers of his lands. Socially, such men were of less consequence than the heads of established knightly families to whom Gaunt usually turned for military service, but they came from precisely the group on whom the burden of county administration fell. Edmund Gournay, the duke's steward in Norfolk, served almost continually on the commission of the peace for a period of over twenty years whilst his successor as steward, Sir Robert Cayley, appeared on every commission between 1374 and his death in 1385.[56] John Winter and John Methwold, respectively steward and receiver of the duke's lands in the 1390s, both served as escheator for the county.[57] In consequence, they had every chance to look after the interests of their lord in the execution of their administrative duties, whilst their professional qualification as lawyers gave them an indispensable position in county society as attorneys, trustees, and testamentary executors. Robert Cayley, for instance, was attorney for the citizens of Norwich at the Exchequer; Edmund Gournay, the principal legal adviser to the burgesses of Lynn.[58] Sir Robert Berney, steward of Gimingham by 1398, acted as feoffee for many of his fellow gentry.[59] Such roles undoubtedly brought the lawyers and officials in Lancastrian service considerable influence and created a professional solidarity that rendered the county administrators a recognizable and close-knit group. Edmund Gournay's association with Edmund Clippesby provides an example of particularly close co-operation; fellow justices of the peace and joint-stewards of

[55] *Westminster Chronicle*, p. 164. *Fasciculi Zizaniorum*, ed. W. W. Shirley (Rolls Series, 1858), pp. 506–11 for a fragment of a sermon preached by a Carmelite in support of Gaunt's crusade.

[56] E. L. John, 'The Parliamentary Representation of Norfolk and Suffolk, 1377–1422' (unpub. Nottingham Univ. MA thesis, 1959), pp. 356, 217.

[57] *CFR 1391–9*, 8; *List of Escheators for England and Wales* (PRO Lists and Indexes, 72, 1971), p. 86.

[58] E. 403/478 m. 16; HMC, *Manuscripts of the Corporations of Southampton and King's Lynn* (1887), pp. 221–2.

[59] *CCR 1396–9*, 72, 399; *CPR 1396–9*, 554.

the Lancastrian lands in Norfolk, they acted together on the common council of the city of Norwich and often acquired land together.[60]

In marked contrast to the conditions prevailing in a county like Staffordshire, therefore, some members of the Lancastrian affinity in Norfolk, although few in numbers, were closely involved and highly influential in the running of the shire. Yet the question remains: how much of this influence was deployed upon John of Gaunt's behalf? Did he command their principal loyalty or was he no more than one client among many? The many contacts maintained by the duke's estate officials, even the less prominent among them, with other lords and other institutions strongly suggests the latter view is the more accurate. Thomas Wombe of Swaffham, the duke's receiver, bequeathed three new suits of livery in his will, each from a different donor;[61] both Clippesby and Gournay took fees from the abbey of St Benet's, Holme;[62] John Methwold maintained particularly close relations with the Praemonstratensian house at West Dereham, where he had a private chamber in life and wished to be buried in death;[63] John Winter acted as legal counsel for the citizens of Norwich and as the local agent of the Staffords;[64] Thomas Pinchbeck was steward of the bishop of Ely;[65] Sir Robert Cayley contrived to be steward to both John of Gaunt and bishop Henry Despenser at the time of their bitterest opposition.[66] This multiplicity of ties was not necessarily a disadvantage for the duke; since the county administrators often sat on the councils of several lords, they were in an ideal position to compose seigneurial quarrels rather than to contest them.[67] Nevertheless, the effectiveness which John of Gaunt's ministers in Norfolk possessed by virtue of their administrative prominence was tempered, from the duke's point of view, by the number of rival claims on their attention and abilities. In such circumstances, the tie between lord and man could hardly possess

---

[60] Somerville, p. 377; D. Gurney, *Records of the House of Gurney* (London, 1848), pp. 358–60; CP 25 (1)/167/171 (1361), 173 (1454).

[61] Norfolk Record Office, NCC, Register of Wills, Harsyk, ff. 165–6.

[62] Bodl. MS Rolls Norfolk 71.

[63] KB 9/166/1 m. 69; Norfolk Record Office, NCC, Register of Wills, Harsyk, f. 249.

[64] *Records of the City of Norwich*, ii. 41, 53; Staffordshire Record Office, D. 641/1/2/4 m. 4.

[65] M. E. Aston, *Thomas Arundel* (Oxford, 1967), p. 240.

[66] Somerville, p. 377; *CPR 1381–5*, 380.

[67] R. A. Griffiths, 'Public and Private Bureaucracies in Fifteenth-Century England', *TRHS* 5th series, 30 (1980), 128.

any deeper significance than a contract of employment; it remains to be seen how far such men ever acted together as a single 'affinity'.

Naturally, those in Lancastrian employment provided each other with some useful services, particularly in property matters, where the shared bond of service to the duke gave some guarantee, at least, against fraud or legal chicanery. Besides the long-standing business partnership of Gournay and Clippesby, John Wesenham acted through John Yerdburgh and William Oke, successive clerks of the duke's wardrobe, soon after he had entered Gaunt's service and maintained a long-standing connection with the family of Gaunt's chief steward, Sir Philip Tilney; Edward Gerberge used William Ayrmin, treasurer of the duke's household, while William Caston, the duke's secretary, made use of John Methwold's legal expertise.[68] Nevertheless, prudential, no less than geographical, considerations dictated that for the all-important tasks of enfeoffment and charter-witnessing a wider body of trustees than the Lancastrian affinity alone could provide should be sought. Thus, Sir John Strange chose three Lancastrians amongst the nine feoffees of his Norfolk lands but his relations were closest with Sir Robert Ufford, who came from outside the affinity.[69] As he prepared to join Henry Bolingbroke in exile, Sir Thomas Erpingham conveyed his land to a body of twelve trustees; three of them were Lancastrians but the group also included professional lawyers and royalist partisans, such as the king's standard-bearer Sir Simon Felbrigg.[70] Granted the size of the county community in Norfolk, this was only to be expected; it was only in the lower ranks of John of Gaunt's service that the type of social amenity provided by the affinity was really valued.

A similar pattern emerges from an examination of the marriages made by the duke's retainers and their children. The higher their income or social status, the less likely they were to need to find a wife within the bounds of the affinity. Most Lancastrian retainers in East Anglia married into local knightly families[71] and found no difficulty in

---

[68] CP 25(1)/168/177 (55), 180 (242), 181 (274); Lincolnshire Archives Office, FL Deeds, 3128–30.

[69] Norfolk Record Office, Le Strange MS A 13–15; *CCR 1399–1402*, 496.

[70] *CCR 1396–9*, 399

[71] Edmund Barry married a daughter of Sir Thomas Gerberge, the duke of York's steward; Sir Robert Berney, a daughter of Sir Walter de Walcot; Sir Thomas Erpingham, a daughter of Sir Richard Walton; Robert Fitzralph, a daughter of Sir John Holbrook; Sir John Plays, a daughter of Sir Walter de Norwich; Sir John Strange, a daughter of Sir Richard Walkfare. *The Visitacion of Norffolk*, ed. W. Rye (Harl. Soc., 32,

marrying their children into the same social circle;[72] only Sir Robert Charles, whose son married a daughter of Ralph Ramsey, made use of the social community the affinity provided.[73] For the duke's lesser esquires and administrative officials, by contrast, it was one of the primary inducements to loyalty that John of Gaunt could offer his servants. John Reymes married a sister of John Winter, the Lancastrian receiver in Norfolk; Winter married a sister of John Payn, the earl of Derby's butler; Oliver Groos married a daughter of Sir John White. White himself was the only Lancastrian retainer of knightly status to marry within the affinity; he married Margery, the widow of Robert Hethe of Little Saxham.[74] The Lancastrian affinity in Norfolk thus emerges as an organization which maintained a certain beneficial social solidarity, more effectively at the level of the duke's ministers than of his knightly followers, yet was never exclusive in its demands for loyalty. Sir Thomas Erpingham's famous window in the Austin Friars at Norwich, commemorating the lords and knights, *mortz sans issu male* since the accession of Edward III, strikingly demonstrates his knowledge of, and interest in, the whole county community.[75] When another Lancastrian retainer, John Reymes, came to rebuild the parish church at Overstrand he included a more modest display of armorial glass, showing his own arms and those of his closest associates among the East Anglian gentry—which included the arms of Felbrigg and Clopton, neither of them Lancastrian families, as well as those of Erpingham, Winter, and Groos.[76] Whatever the case in fifteenth-century Norfolk, it seems that, for John of Gaunt's retainers, the 'horizontal' relations of gentry and yeomanry with each other remained just as important to them as the 'vertical' relations of bastard feudalism.[77]

1891), p. 215; F. Blomefield, *An Essay towards a Topographical History of the County of Norfolk*, viii. 120; C. 139/15/2; *CIPM* XIV. 231, X. 598; Norfolk Record Office, Le Strange MS A 12.

[72] Sir John Plays's daughter married Sir John Howard; Sir John Strange's son married Alice, daughter of Nicholas Beman of Paston (Suff.). Guildhall Lib. MS 9531/3 f. 395; *CFR 1383–91*, 295; *CCR 1461–8*, 332.

[73] W. A. Copinger, *The Manors of Suffolk* (London, 1905–11), iv. 301.

[74] A. L. Raimes, 'Reymes of Overstrand', *Norfolk Archaeology*, 30 (1952), 33; W. Rye, *Norfolk Families* (Norwich, 1913), p. 333; Norfolk Record Office, NCC, Register of Wills, Aleyn f. 186–7; *CCR 1399–1402*, 98.

[75] F. Blomefield, *An Essay Towards a Topographical History of the County of Norfolk*, 2nd edn. (1805–10), iv. 86–8.

[76] A. L. Raimes, op. cit., 30–1.

[77] Cf. Roger Virgoe, 'The Crown, Magnates and Local Government in Fifteenth-Century East Anglia', *The Crown and Local Communities*, ed. J. R. L. Highfield and R. Jeffs (Gloucester, 1981), p. 83.

The disparate nature of John of Gaunt's affinity in East Anglia and the intrinsic difficulty of dominating so large and prosperous a county community meant that Lancastrian influence in Norfolk was occasional rather than continuous, designed to protect the duke's existing interests and to enforce his will on particular occasions rather than to exercise a permanent and decisive influence on the politics of the shire. In this it was largely successful, by methods which ranged from the indirect to the nearly illegal. Most directly, county officials were well rewarded for their services to the duke: Edmund Gournay and his fellow justices were liberally entertained at Aylesham when they came to hear a case which concerned John of Gaunt; William Curson, the escheator, received a gift of ten marks in 1384/5 'for his good conduct towards the lord'.[78] These occasional *ex gratia* payments supplemented a more systematic and consistent pressure upon the administrative power-structure of the shire. There were, it is true, some areas of the county administration that remained permanently outside the concerns of the Lancastrian affinity—none of the duke's servants became sheriff, for example, perhaps because it was regarded as an exceptionally expensive and onerous office.[79] On the other hand, Methwold and Winter both served their term as escheators and (after 1370) the duke's affinity always maintained a presence on the commission of the peace. Although Gaunt himself was not appointed to the commission until 1380,[80] the current Lancastrian steward in the county was always a justice of the peace[81] and successive chief stewards of the duke's lands—Sir Godfrey Foljambe, Sir Thomas Hungerford, and Thomas Pinchbeck—also appeared as justices by virtue of their office alone,[82] since only Pinchbeck held any land in the county. This was precisely the kind of appointment most disliked by the Commons and, in the aftermath of the Cambridge Parliament, they succeeded in cleansing the Norfolk peace commission of November 1389 of all Lancastrian taint; within a year, however, both Gaunt and

[78] Norfolk Record Office, NRS 3342 m. 2*d*, 11072 m. 2.

[79] Cf. the petition of Sir John Gildesburgh for an allowance on his account as sheriff of Norfolk and Suffolk, which alleges that the royal franchises granted out to the queen and the duke of Lancaster are the main reasons for the lack of revenue from the county. SC 8/129/6421.

[80] *CPR 1377–81*, 513.

[81] The only exception is the commission of 5 Mar. 1397, to which the duke's steward was not appointed; his receiver, John Winter, was. *CPR 1396–9*, 98.

[82] *CPR 1367–70*, 419; ibid. *1370–4*, 305 (Foljambe); ibid. *1374–7*, 487; ibid. *1377–81*, 96 (Hungerford); ibid. *1388–92*, 345, 524 (Pinchbeck).

his chief steward, Thomas Pinchbeck, were back on the commission[83] and the duke's affinity maintained its presence there throughout the 1390s.

Lancastrian influence upon the county's representation in parliament was less consistent but it could be no less effective. Despite a relatively low overall proportion of Lancastrians amongst the knights of the shire—12 out of 71 MPs returned between 1362 and September 1397—the duke's affinity was noticeably successful in gaining the return of its own at times of political crisis. Hence, at the Parliament of October 1385, when Gaunt's Castilian project came under decisive consideration, the county was represented for the first time by two Lancastrians—Sir Robert Cayley and Sir John White; during the Appellancy crisis, Sir John White was again returned to the two Parliaments of 1388—on both occasions with Sir John Strange, another Lancastrian. In all, over half the county's MPs were Lancastrians between April 1384 and September 1397.[84] John of Gaunt's retainers were, therefore, a fairly constant presence in the administration and government of the county, and, in making any decisions, the duke's interests had always to be considered.

On particular occasions, he could play a more direct part in the politics of the region; the clearest example of this occurs in the aftermath of the Good Parliament, when the duke intervened decisively in favour of the ruling oligarchy of Yarmouth. Impeached as a business partner of Richard Lyons and for his alleged extortions in office, the Yarmouth burgess Hugh Fastolf was vindicated in the following Parliament when the Commons—under the direction of their Speaker and the duke's chief steward, Sir Thomas Hungerford —presented a petition to the lords on his behalf.[85] At the same time, Gaunt moved to restore the oligarchs' position in the county; Thomas Hungerford makes his only two appearances on the peace commission in Norfolk during the following year and, on each occasion, he and Hugh Fastolf were associated with the original commission.[86] The duke continued to take the part of the Yarmouth oligarchy in 1378, supporting their case on the Council during the long struggle with

[83] R. L. Storey, 'Liveries and Commissions of the Peace, 1388–90'. *The Reign of Richard II*, ed. F. R. H. du Boulay and C. M. Barron (London, 1971), p. 140; *CPR 1388–92*, 139.

[84] E. L. John, 'The Parliamentary Representation of Norfolk and Suffolk', p. 24.

[85] *Rot. Parl.*, ii. 375; G. A. Holmes, *The Good Parliament* (Oxford, 1975), pp. 117–18 discusses the impeachment.

[86] *CPR 1374–4*, 387; ibid. *1377–81*, 96.

Lowestoft over the control of Kirkley Roads.[87] Walsingham thought the town had bought the duke's support, but shared interests and shared enemies naturally disposed John of Gaunt in Yarmouth's favour; Lowestoft men had given evidence for the impeachment of Richard Lyons in 1376, while behind the attack on Yarmouth's position stood the London gildsmen, particularly the fishmongers, anxious to gain a larger share in the herring trade.[88] The duke had, in addition, the interests of his own retainers, like Rose and Hacon, to defend; understandably hostile to the appearance of London merchants on the East coast, Hacon was one of the sureties for the group of townsmen who attacked Walter Sibille, a Londoner, at Yarmouth in 1376.[89]

However, support for the burgess oligarchy of Yarmouth and its allies was not a policy calculated to bring John of Gaunt popularity, either in Norfolk or in the country as a whole. During the Peasants' Revolt, Hugh Fastolf's house at Yarmouth was plundered and the town's charter of liberties destroyed; here, as elsewhere, the revolt provided a violent conclusion to the unfinished business of the Good Parliament.[90] It was not to be expected that John of Gaunt's manors should have emerged unscathed from the general upheaval and destruction was, in fact, widespread. One of the few determined attempts at the destruction of manorial records in the west of the county, an area generally distinguished by the aimless quality of its violence, occurred at Methwold, where the duke's muniments and court rolls were burnt.[91] Court rolls were also burnt at North Erpingham, Tunstead, Gimingham, and Hilgay, accompanied by the spoilation of the duke's goods and houses.[92] The destruction of manorial records was, however, a particular feature of the rebellion in East Anglia; the earl of Suffolk, the earl of Nottingham, even such a minor gentry family as the Raimes of Overstrand, all suffered from the same phenomenon.[93] It cannot, in consequence, be construed as the

[87] Ibid. *1377–81*, 188; *Rot. Parl.*, iii. 49; A. R. Saul, 'Local Politics and the Good Parliament', *Property and Politics: Essays in Later Medieval English History*, ed. A. J. Pollard (Gloucester, 1984), pp. 156–71 discusses the dispute in detail.

[88] *Chronicon Angliae*, p. 95; *Rot. Parl.*, ii. 374–5; Saul, op. cit. 165.

[89] C. 47/34/10 mm. 1–32.

[90] E. Powell, *The Rising in East Anglia in 1381* (Cambridge, 1896), p. 32; C. W. Oman, *The Great Revolt of 1381* (Oxford, 1906), p. 100.

[91] KB 9/166/1 m. 71.

[92] Ibid. mm. 52, 62, 91, 103; DL 30/104/1459 m. 1.

[93] KB 9/166/1 mm. 26, 95; CP 40/487 m. 611.

result of a particular animus against the person of John of Gaunt for, in most cases, the destruction was simply a widespread and more violent version of peasant resistance that had been troubling the Lancastrian ministers for some years.[94] In the actions of Geoffrey Litster's *magna societas* there may be a more overtly political edge; Litster was responsible for the destruction on the duke's manor at Gimingham, and William Newlyn of Tunstead, a bondman of the duke's, was brought before Litster's great company on Mousehold Heath and there beheaded. The execution is, however, as likely to have been the result of some obscure personal quarrel as a symbolic act of political defiance.[95]

The animosity displayed towards the duke of Lancaster by the rebels was, therefore, by no means exceptional. He appears even to have been less unpopular in Norfolk than he was with the rebels of Kent and Essex. By contrast, the duke's ministers in the county were the object of more direct and more violent attack than anywhere else in the country. John Methwold's house at Langford was attacked and despoiled; his chamber in the abbey of West Dereham broken into on the same day and £20 in sterling carried away.[96] Sir Robert Cayley's court rolls were burnt at Hempstead and Edmund Gournay's house at West Lexham broken into and robbed.[97] Gournay and Adam Pope, respectively the duke's steward and his receiver, were pursued by the rebels at Burnham on 19 June, with the intention of executing them. With another justice of the peace, Gournay was proclaimed a traitor and a reward offered for his capture; forced to take ship at Holme in order to avoid arrest, he was pursued for twenty leagues by the men of Hunstanton.[98]

It is difficult to establish precisely why Gournay was so unpopular but it seems clear that, in general terms, his unpopularity sprang as much from his prominent position as a county administrator and his

---

[94] There was resistance to the actions of the duke's ministers as early as 1363 and opposition to Edmund Gournay's investigations at Aylesham was envisaged in 1375. The duke's servants were later attacked there and his ministers assaulted at Hunstanton in 1379. *CPR 1361–4*, 373; *Reg. I* 1631; KB 27/495 m. 5; *Proceeding Before the Justices of the Peace in the Fourteenth and Fifteenth Centuries: Edward III to Richard III*, ed. B. H. Putnam (London, 1938), p. 113.

[95] KB 9/166/1 mm. 62, 55. His death went unrecognized by the duke; his widow had to pay an increment on the half acre of free land she inherited from her husband. DL 29/288/4724 m. 1.

[96] KB 9/166/1 mm. 67, 71.

[97] Ibid. mm. 47–9, 63.

[98] Powell, *The Rising in East Anglia*, pp. 135–6.

close association with the ruling oligarchies of Yarmouth and Lynn as from his service with John of Gaunt. It was against such men, the 'second kings' without whom nothing could be done in a shire, that the rebellion was particularly directed,[99] and Gournay was the best example that Norfolk had to offer. By contrast, some of the knightly class in East Anglia occupied a surprisingly ambivalent position towards the rebellion. Besides the outright support lent to the rebels by Sir Roger Bacon and Sir Thomas Cornerd in Norfolk, influential members of the Suffolk gentry, including Sir Roger Scales and Sir Stephen de Hales, played at least an equivocal role.[100] In consequence, John of Gaunt's reliance on his ministers and administrators for the maintenance of his affinity in Norfolk, rather than on the soldiers and courtiers who constituted the bulk of his retinue in many other areas, made him particularly vulnerable to attack. By using prominent local administrators as his officials Gaunt had, in fact, attracted to himself a double hostility, for, to the traditional dislike of the localities towards the agents of central government was added a further, social, antagonism which drew strength from the lowly origins of the men involved. The unpopularity that such men earned themselves by their oppressions[101] rebounded to the detriment of the duke who gave them the position from which they could abuse their authority. John of Gaunt's stipulation, in the aftermath of the crisis, that his stewards should exact no fines from the rebels without prior reference to his council in London[102] suggests that he appreciated the danger and the duke's ministers were, in future, a little more heedful of the customary claims of his tenants.[103]

The duke himself was not always innocent of involvement in the oppressions of his servants, however, and this is particularly clear in the neighbouring county of Cambridgeshire, where Thomas Haselden's manors of Steeple Mordern and Gelden Mordern were sacked by the local peasantry.[104] Haselden's post as controller of the Lancastrian

---

[99] *Rot. Parl.*, iii. 150.

[100] Oman, *The Great Revolt*, p. 102; Powell, *The Rising in East Anglia*, p. 31.

[101] e.g. HMC, *Report on Manuscripts in Various Collections*, vii. 156: a petition of the prior of Bromholm against the oppressions of the bailiffs of the duke of Lancaster at Paston.

[102] *Reg. II* 1109.

[103] DL 29/728/11977 m. 2*d*: the duke's auditors reported in 1390 that the mills of Fakenham and Aylesham could be leased at a great profit but the tenants say that it is not the custom of the manor.

[104] Powell, *The Rising in East Anglia*, pp. 135–7.

household brought him unpopularity on a national scale—his property in Kent was attacked by the rebels as well and the Kentishmen threatened to kill him[105]—but in Cambridgeshire the reasons for his unpopularity can be more precisely stated. Principally, he was an incomer, originally a Yorkshireman from Wakefield,[106] who had lived in the county little more than ten years, although, by a combination of outright purchase and leasing the duke's lands, he had already become a powerful and disruptive figure in local society.[107] The earl of March's auditors, for example, made a memorandum that the people of Mordern were no longer paying their amercements in the lord's court because of the maintenance of Thomas Haselden and other great men of the shire, including Sir Baldwin St George and William Bateman, an apprentice-at-law. To safeguard his position, Haselden had jointly enfeoffed the duke of Lancaster in his newly acquired lands.[108] The duke's protection was being used, or abused, by one of his retainers to advance his own local authority at the expense of a social superior. Such a role can have brought him little popularity in Cambridgeshire, either among the established gentry or among the peasantry, who systematically pillaged the property of both Haselden and his partner, William Bateman.

Haselden was not alone in seeking to turn Gaunt's favour to advantage. His avid acquisition of property has some parallels among the Lancastrian affinity in Norfolk, as the additional capital furnished by the duke's fee allowed more than one retainer to consolidate and expand his holdings—Sir Thomas Erpingham rounded off his family lands; John Raimes speculated on the land market and John Winter's acquisition of the manors of Heylesden and Drayton coincided closely with his appointment as the duke's receiver in Norfolk.[109] At the same time, the comparatively open East Anglian land-market allowed retainers of the duke who came from other parts of the country to buy their way into Norfolk society. Most conspicuously, Sir Robert Knolles used the profits of his campaigns abroad to build up a sizeable estate in the county,[110] but prominent Lancastrian servants like Sir Robert

[105] *Anonimalle Chronicle*, p. 138.
[106] *CCR 1364–8*, 83; *CPR 1374–7*, 398; *CAD* i. A261.
[107] *CCR 1369–74*, 73, 518; ibid. *1377–81*, 502; ibid. *1385–9*, 154; *Reg. I* 967.
[108] BL Egerton Roll 8757 m. 7; cf. J. M. W. Bean, *The Decline of English Feudalism, 1215–1540* (Manchester, 1968), pp. 125–6 for the statute of 1376 against this practice.
[109] Norfolk Record Office, NRS MS 2928 (Erpingham); BL Add. Ch. 14665 (Raimes); CP 25 (1)/168/181 (262) (Winter).
[110] *CCR 1374–7*, 194–5; *Feudal Aids*, iii. 628, 629, 636, 650, 654.

Swillington and Thomas Pinchbeck both picked up Norfolk lands, while Sir John Plays exchanged an outlying estate in Oxfordshire for the manor of Mundford.[111] From the duke's point of view, this was a process to be encouraged since it increased both the number and the standing of his servants in county society and he was, in consequence, willing to distribute the Norfolk patronage at his disposal among a wide geographical range of his retainers; Sir Walter Blount, far from his own country in Derbyshire, acquired the farm of the manors of Gressenhall and East Lexham when he was granted custody of the Hastings estates by the duke and he continued to lease them out once the heir came of age.[112]

Such an exercise of his seigneurial rights on the behalf of his retainers was naturally one of the principal attractions John of Gaunt could offer to the members of his affinity and, in a county lacking long traditions of Lancastrian service or the encouragement provided by the duke's regular presence, it provided a vital means of securing a retainer's loyalty. In consequence, much of the casual feudal income that fell to the duke from escheats, wardships, and outlawries in Norfolk was immediately redirected towards his retainers in the county. Thus, the duke secured 40 marks worth of goods from the property of the outlawed Sir William Clopton; £20 worth were immediately granted as a gift to Sir Thomas Erpingham and the escheator in Norfolk was paid 40s. 'for his good conduct towards the lord', which left John of Gaunt with very little to show, in financial terms, from the transaction.[113] Such grants could occasionally be very valuable indeed, for Sir John Strange estimated the goods of the outlaw Nicholas Willy, which the duke granted him, to be worth 360 marks—eighteen times his annual retaining fee.[114]

The duke's control over the patronage available for distribution in Norfolk was, of course, far less complete than in Lancashire but some valuable properties did pass into his hands and, as in Lancashire, he

---

[111] CP 25(1)/167/174 (1518) (Swillington); 168/179 (184), (197) (Pinchbeck); *CCR 1381–5*, 202 (Plays).

[112] Norfolk Record Office, NRS 3344 m. 2; Le Strange MS NA 47.

[113] DL 29/310/4980 m. 2; DL 43/15/4 m. 4.

[114] BL Add. Ch. 14713. Strange may have been exaggerating, but not by much. He had received £115. 3s. 0d. from the grant by 1397 and a further £65. 16s. 8d. due to him remained in the hands of the duke's ministers. The case provides a surprising example of the effectiveness of outlawry as a legal sanction and an indication of the wealth possessed by an otherwise obscure criminal. Norfolk Record Office, NRS 3345 m. 1; KB 27/494 mm. 12, 12d.

was careful to appear even-handed in granting out the lands at his disposal.[115] Nevertheless, the competition for the duke's favour was fierce enough to provoke some violent clashes between Lancastrian retainers and their opponents; as Sir John Strange explained in a petition to the earl of Derby, the goods of the outlawed Nicholas Willy, granted him by the duke, were subsequently claimed during John of Gaunt's absence in Spain by John lord Lovell. Strange had been attacked by Lovell and his men in London, while he was trying to vindicate his right at the Exchequer, and Lovell now threatened to destroy him by suing out an oyer and terminer in Norfolk.[116] Nevertheless, Strange's membership of the Lancastrian affinity was enough to give him the advantage in the dispute for, with the triumph of Henry of Derby and his fellow Appellants, Lovell was expelled from court and Strange was able to vindicate his claim.[117] His reward for supporting the Appellants in the two Parliaments of 1388 went further than this, for at the end of the Cambridge Parliament he was granted £100 in recognition of his diligence in capturing a French merchant vessel in 1386.[118] At the time, this piece of free-lance piracy had met with less unqualified approval, involving Strange in several appearances before the Council, but this grant effectively vindicated his actions and, in order to gain restitution for the Genoese master of the vessel, Richard II had eventually to overrule his barons of the Exchequer.[119]

Lancastrian lordship could, therefore, be exercised successfully enough on behalf of the duke's retainers in Norfolk and this, no less than John of Gaunt's periodic largesse, was a potent means of maintaining his servants' loyalty. On the other hand, the internal cohesion of the Lancastrian affinity in Norfolk, where many of the duke's retainers maintained ties with other lords and the affinity lacked the single, personal focus provided by the duke's presence, was much less strong than in an area like the palatinate of Lancashire. There, the duke's problem had been to strike some form of political balance between those within and those outside his own affinity. Here, it was to

---

[115] For example, the wardship of the heir of Thomas Bardolf of Spikesworth was granted to John de Yelverton and Geoffrey de Somerton for 200 marks; the custody of the manor of Tanham went to Sir Hugh Hastings IV. None of them possessed any direct connection with the duke. DL 29/288/4729 m. 1*d*.; DL 43/15/5 m. 5.

[116] BL Add. Ch. 14713.

[117] *Chronicon Henrici Knighton*, ii. 257.

[118] E. 403/519 m. 15.

[119] *CCR 1385–9*, 17, 56; *CPR 1385–9*, 323; E. 403/530 m. 5.

impart to his followers an effective sense of unity. In Staffordshire, where the duke's affinity occupied a position in local society roughly analogous to the state of affairs in Norfolk, that sense of unity resulted from the emergence of a well-defined group of retainers, occupying an influential position in county politics, during the 1390s and was signalled by a rapid rise in the value of annuity payments assigned on the receivership of Tutbury.[120] Annuities in East Anglia, which ran at about 14.5 per cent of estate receipts in 1379/80, were absorbing over 30 per cent by 1396/7.[121] Was John of Gaunt buying his way to a new pre-eminence in Norfolk?

On the whole, it seems unlikely; a large proportion of the increase was accounted for by the single grant of 200 marks p.a. to John Holland, earl of Huntingdon.[122] Holland was Lancaster's son-in-law and he had recently acquired estates in Suffolk by royal grant, but his own concerns were too much concentrated on the South-West, where he was seeking to build up a sizeable following in order to challenge the position of the Courtenays, ever to become an important figure in East Anglian politics.[123] As for the rest of the recruits to the Lancastrian retinue during the 1390s, they were principally young esquires, like Oliver Groos, John Raimes, and Edmund Barry, whose fees represented an investment for the future rather than a recognition of their present prominence. This was, in part, the accidental result of the casualties of war; the deaths of Sir Hugh Hastings IV and Sir Thomas Morieux in Spain left a number of gentry without a patron and John of Gaunt certainly attracted the services of some of these.[124] The others rewarded by the duke were principally his household familiars: William Caston, his secretary; Richard Gest of Coston, clerk of his kitchen;[125] John Payn of Helhoughton, butler to his son.[126] Such men were not by themselves influential figures in the county and their offices in any case necessitated regular attendance in the duke's household. Edward Burnell, the son and heir of lord Burnell, who was

---

[120] See below, pp. 224–5.

[121] Appendix IV.

[122] DL 29/310/4980 m. 2: granted 18 Mar. 1391.

[123] *CPR 1388–92*, 91, 423; M. Cherry, 'The Courtenay Earls of Devon: Formation and Disintegration of a Late Medieval Aristocratic Affinity', *Southern History*, i (1979), 90–1; A. Emery, *Dartington Hall* (Oxford, 1970), pp. 42–3.

[124] e.g. John Raimes, who had gone to Scotland in 1385 and Spain in 1386 in the company of Sir Hugh Hastings of Elsing: A. L. Raimes, 'Reymes of Overstrand', 29.

[125] DL 28/3/5 f. 10v.

[126] *Expeditions to Prussia and the Holy Land Made by Henry, earl of Derby*, ed. L. T. Smith (Camden Soc., NS 52, 1894), p. xcii; DL 28/3/4 f. 6v.

retained in February 1397, was potentially more powerful but the bulk of his lands lay in Shropshire.[127] Neither the increasing size nor the changing composition of his affinity, therefore, suggest that John of Gaunt was deliberately seeking support in East Anglia during the last years of his life.

His eldest son, Henry of Derby, had his household headquarters at Peterborough,[128] however, and his residence on the edge of East Anglia helped to bolster the Lancastrian presence in the area. In Cambridgeshire, he maintained and strengthened his father's connection with the Haselden family; Thomas Haselden the younger was retained by Derby and served as the steward of Soham; Richard Haselden, his brother, acted as the steward of Sutton.[129] Thomas Beaumont, a cadet of the Lincolnshire baronial house, and his wife were granted a fee of 50 marks from Soham in May 1398.[130] In Norfolk, as well, Derby attracted some support; Thomas, lord Morley, took his livery while Sir Thomas Hoo of Horsford and Ralph Ramsey of West Somerton, a royal esquire for many years, were both his retainers by 1398.[131] Yet Derby spent little more time in East Anglia than his father did[132] and his inroads upon the loyalty of the region's gentry hardly amount to a concerted attempt to build up a following there. Yet, if the Lancastrian presence in Norfolk underwent no great expansion during the 1390s, there are few signs that the county was of particular interest to any other magnate. Thomas, duke of Gloucester, had always possessed some influence in the area, based principally on his extensive estates in Essex; his moiety of the Bohun inheritance, his temporary possession of Lancaster's manor of Gimingham, and Richard II's grant of the honour of Castle Rising to him in 1386 all served to extend his influence northwards into Norfolk.[133] But although this expansion of

---

[127] *CIPM* XV. 719–29; W. Dugdale, *The Baronage of England* (London, 1675), ii. 61–2; Blomefield, *An Essay Towards a Topographical History*, viii. 193, 280 for his Norfolk lands.

[128] DL 28/3/4 f. 11v; DL 41/10/42.

[129] DL 28/4/1 f. 9v; Somerville, pp. 386–7.

[130] DL 42/16 ff. 142, 144v.

[131] DL 28/1/2/f. 5v; Norfolk Record Office, NRS MS 15171 m. 2; DL 28/4/1 f. 10v.

[132] He was at Walsingham in 1391, departed for Prussia from Heacham in 1392, visited the shrine at Walsingham in 1397, and rode through Norfolk in June 1398, on the last leg of the great circular tour of his father's dominions he undertook that summer: DL 28/3/3 m. 4; *Expeditions to Prussia and the Holy Land*, p. lxxii; DL 28/1/6 f. 46, 10 f. 19.

[133] A. Goodman, *The Loyal Conspiracy* (London, 1971), pp. 95–102; *CCR 1381–5*, 511–6; HMC, *Report on the Manuscripts of the Marquess of Lothian* (1905), p. 69; *CPR 1385–9*, 147.

his East Anglian estates brought him into contact with lesser noblemen like Robert, lord Scales, and provided a number of recruits for his Irish command in 1392, his household and affinity remained predominantly Essex-based.[134]

Richard II, by contrast, could call upon some well-established traditions of loyalty and gratitude in Norfolk and Suffolk, for, as lord of Castle Rising, his father the Black Prince had drawn some of his most important followers from the region, including Sir John Wingfield, governor of his business, Sir Thomas Felton, steward of his household, and Sir Neel Loring, his chamberlain.[135] In consequence, it was to East Anglia that Richard turned instinctively for support in the crisis of 1386; after the impeachment of Michael de la Pole he sent an esquire through the region, offering various gentlemen there the royal livery if they would hold themselves ready to come to him in arms.[136] On that occasion, however, the East Anglian gentry signally failed to answer his call and, when Richard began building up his support among the county élites in a more systematic way during the 1390s, he largely ignored an area that had already failed him. Those gentlemen he did take into his service came, like Sir John Braham and Andrew Botiller, an esquire of the royal household, mainly from the Suffolk/Essex border where Sir Richard Waldegrave, retained by the king in 1394 to be continuously attendant upon his Council, was a major source of royal patronage.[137] In Norfolk, only Sir Edmund Thorpe and Sir Simon Felbrigg, both retained early in 1393, joined the king's affinity. Ivo de Wyram of Thetford, who had been a Lancastrian official for many years, was, in addition, taken on as a royal serjeant-at-arms in 1396.[138]

Neither Lancaster nor Derby, Gloucester nor Richard, then, showed themselves especially anxious to build up a following among the Norfolk gentry. There are some signs, however, that this was the ambition of Thomas Mowbray, who was looking to capitalize upon the extensive East Anglian estates that would come to him on the death of

[134] BL Add. MS 40859A mm. 1–4; Sir John Clifton; Sir Roger Drury; Sir John Lakenheath; Sir Robert Ufford; and Sir John Wilton, all from Norfolk and Suffolk, were amongst the 16 knights who agreed to serve in his company.
[135] T. F. Tout, *Chapters in the Administrative History of Medieval England* (Manchester, 1920–33), v. 432–3.
[136] *Westminster Chronicle*, p. 186.
[137] *CPR 1391–6*, 39; E. 101/403/10 f. 44d; Roskell, *Parliament and Politics in Late Medieval England* (London, 1981–3), iii. 44–6.
[138] *CPR 1391–6*, 206, 227, 700; J. D. Milner, 'Sir Simon Felbrigg, KG: The Lancastrian Revolution and Personal Fortune', *Norfolk Archaeology*, 37 (1978), 84–91.

his grandmother well before his creation as duke of Norfolk in September 1397. William Rees of Tharston and John Lancaster of Bressingham were already long-standing servants of his family;[139] after 1396, they were joined in the Mowbray service by such influential local knights as Sir John Inglesthorp, Sir William Elmham, and Sir George Felbrigg. But, if the eighty esquires and gentlemen who gathered at Lowestoft in October 1398 to watch Thomas Mowbray sail into the sunset are impressive testimony to the growing strength of his following in East Anglia, his condemnation and exile naturally left the nascent Mowbray affinity leaderless.[140] In consequence, the crisis of 1399 saw the county community in Norfolk hesitant and divided. The city of Norwich sought a new patron in Sir Simon Felbrigg, the king's standard-bearer, paying him £10 for his counsel and friendship; King's Lynn optimistically put its trust in the dukes of York and Aumale.[141] Henry Despenser, bishop of Norwich, declared vigorously for Richard, but only Sir William Elmham followed his example.[142] Enthusiasm for the Lancastrian cause was not much more conspicuous. Only two of the old duke's esquires rode northwards to join Henry Bolingbroke's army, although the Lancastrian estate administration, efficient as always, lent unobtrusive aid to his cause.[143] The rest of the Norfolk gentry, quicker than their diocesan bishop to learn that sleeping dogs are best left lying,[144] maintained a characteristic neutrality and did nothing.

If the picture of the Lancastrian affinity in Norfolk that finally emerges from this survey is an ill-defined one, lacking the sharp edge given to Lancastrian allegiance in the palatinate by prolonged local power-struggles and political crisis, the defence must be that, however inconclusive, it is true to the experience of the duke's followers. For a member of the Norfolk gentry, a connection with John of Gaunt was an enviable opportunity for profit and advancement, but, in the context of the shire's politics, the commitment necessary was neither a very deep nor a very partisan one. The duke was rarely present in the county and, when present, he showed no great interest in building up a

---

[139] *CPR 1391–6*, 506; ibid. *1399–1401*, 133 (Rees); *Rot. Scot.*, ii. 99, 103; *CPR 1399–1401*, 294 (Lancaster).

[140] *CPR 1399–1401*, 193; ibid. *1396–9*, 422; *Rot. Parl.*, iii. 384.

[141] *Records of the City of Norwich*, ed. W. Hudson and J. C. Tingey (Norwich, 1910), ii. 52; HMC, *Manuscripts of the Corporations of Southampton and King's Lynn* (1887), p. 223.

[142] E. 403/562 m. 14; 'Annales Ricardi Secundi et Henrici Quarti', p. 246.

[143] DL 42/15 ff. 70, 72v; 16 f. 169.

[144] *Anglo-Norman Letters and Petitions*, p. 115.

following in the shire; his affinity was powerful enough for his own purposes and that was sufficient. It possessed the ability, when occasion demanded, to exert considerable pressure on the power-structure of the county, but, save in the case of parliamentary representation, occasion rarely *did* demand. The affinity maintained a degree of social cohesion at its lower levels, but, the more elevated the status of the duke's retainer, the less dependent he was on contacts provided by his Lancastrian service. Even when John of Gaunt's expenditure on annuities *did* rise during the 1390s, an examination of the men he retained suggests that this was less a response to the gathering atmosphere of political crisis than a necessary provision for his household servants.

On the face of it, this is a surprising conclusion, granted the size and wealth of the Lancastrian estates in Norfolk, but the principal reasons for this state of affairs have already been outlined. The duke's interest in the area was not commensurate with the wealth of his estates there; even if it had been, Norfolk was a large and prosperous county, difficult to dominate, with important urban centres and a number of magnate landowners with a legitimate claim to a stake in the running of the shire. Yet if these conditions were unpropitious for the construction of a powerful Lancastrian affinity, they nevertheless explain the relative stability of the county at a time of political upheaval. The presence of a number of magnates in the shire meant that the opportunities for those who wished to seek service with a lord were comparatively favourable. At the same time, there were few major animosities between the great landowners, hence a lack of issues on which the county was forced to divide; John of Gaunt's relations with Margaret Marshal and the Mowbrays were very cordial[145] and his dispute with Henry Despenser on a matter of national policy had little effect on their local relations. This did not mean that the county remained peaceful or that justice was invariably done; felonies and conspiracies were, in fact, so prevalent that general commissions of oyer and terminer had to be issued in 1376 and 1387.[146] Lancastrian retainers played their part in these disruptions: Sir Philip Deneys was alleged to have extorted robes and gifts from many of the commonalty of Norfolk and Suffolk; the Stranges pursued a long fued with the

---

[145] For exchanges of gifts between the two families: DL 28/1/4 ff. 17v, 18; 5 f. 24; 6 f. 47. Henry of Derby's son, John, spent some time in Margaret Marshall's household: DL 28/1/6 f. 46; 9 f. 15.

[146] *Rot. Parl.*, ii. 374–5; *CPR 1374–7*, 413; ibid. *1385–9*, 388.

Holkham family, and both Thomas Erpingham and Henry Rose were the objects of investigative commissions.[147] But the violence they fomented remained occasional and sporadic, without a definite pattern; although a magnate would protect the interests of his servants, whether guilty or innocent, as John of Gaunt did with Hugh Fastolf and Henry of Derby did with Sir John Strange, 'faction' and factional violence in the county are hard to discern.[148]

If the case of Norfolk in the late fourteenth century cannot quite be described as the 'acceptable face' of bastard feudalism, then at least it demonstrates that the exercise of magnate lordship was not itself enough to plunge a county into competitive violence. When such violence did break out, pre-eminently during the great rebellion of 1381, it was directed less against the magnates themselves than against their servants, who exercised their masters' authority on their own behalf. Lancastrians were sometimes the victims of these oppressions,[149] but, as the Norfolk rebels made clear by their actions in 1381, they were more often identified as the oppressors. In their oppressions, they could call on the protection of the duke's name and, occasionally, on his complicity—whether witting or unwitting—but this is the worst charge that can be levelled against John of Gaunt and his servants in Norfolk. On the whole, the Lancastrian affinity was neither exclusive in its loyalties nor predatory in its actions and it did little, at any stage of the duke's life, to disrupt the peace of the shire. Clearly, this is a very different society from the Norfolk of the mid-fifteenth century, made familiar by the Paston letters, and responsibility for the violence that overwhelmed the region in Henry VI's reign may well lie with the tight little junta of Lancastrian power-brokers who established their hold on the county in the wake of Henry Bolingbroke's usurpation. Nevertheless, John Paston's disingenuous disclaimer—'I suppose ye know that I have not usid to meddel wyth lordis materis meche forther

[147] *CPR 1367–70*, 202 (Deneys); 'Norfolk Sessions of the Peace. Roll of Mainpernors and Pledges, 1394–7', ed. L. J. Redstone, *Norfolk Record Society Publications*, 8 (1936), 4; *CCR 1392–6*, 381; *CPR 1405–8*, 171, 256 (Strange); *CPR 1370–4*, 242 (Erpingham); ibid. 491 (Rose). John Saffrey of Stowe, one of the duke's falconers, seems to have been an equally disruptive figure in Cambridgeshire. *Reg. I* 483–5; *Reg. II* 877; JUST 3/164 m. 22; *Some Sessions of the Peace in Cambridgeshire in the Fourteenth Century*, ed. M. M. Taylor, Cambridge Antiquarian Soc., 55 (1942), pp. lxvii, 52; KB 27/490 Rex m. 18*d*, 491 Rex m. 15.

[148] Contrast Virgoe, 'The Crown and Local Government', p. 227 n. 31; id., 'The Murder of Edmund Clippesby', 302–7.

[149] e.g. SC 8/146/7264: a complaint by John White, the duke's feodary in Norfolk, that John de Yelverton, a prominent local lawyer, had cut and carried away his corn, by the assent and payment of William Curson of Billingford, the sheriff.

than me nedith'[150]—remained a genuine option in the Norfolk of Richard II's reign.

2. North Midlands

The final area chosen for close attention, the northern Midland counties of Staffordshire and Derbyshire, offers the chance to test the conclusions that have emerged from a study of the contrasting county communities of Lancashire and Norfolk in a part of the country that shares in some characteristics of both the counties already studied. Outwardly, Lancastrian influence in the area was nearly as all-pervasive as in Lancashire itself. The original endowment of Edmund, first earl of Lancaster, by Henry III included the manor and lordship of Newcastle under Lyme (Staffs.), and this was soon augmented by the extensive estates, including the honour of Tutbury and forest of Duffield, that were extorted from Robert Ferrers, earl of Derby, in 1269.[151] Thomas, second earl of Lancaster, increased and consolidated the Lancastrian estates in the area by his marriage to Alice Lacy, which brought him much land in southern Staffordshire, and created a tradition of Lancastrian loyalism in the area by his long periods of residence at Tutbury and Melbourne.[152] Less spectacular additions to the ducal lands continued to be made throughout the fourteenth century. In 1343 Henry of Grosmont purchased the manor of Shenston (Staffs.) and in 1372 John of Gaunt received the castle and manor of High Peak in exchange for his surrender of the honour of Richmond's lands in Hertfordshire.[153] These Lancastrian estates, lying principally along the broad alluvial valleys of the Derwent and the Dove, were fertile as well as extensive and, consequently, played an important part in the duke's finances. In 1330/1, the honour of Tutbury had been easily the richest of all the receiverships, and although economic changes and the reorganization of the ducal estates eventually deprived Tutbury of its financial pre-eminence, only the

---

[150] *Paston Letters and Papers of the Fifteenth Century*, ed. N. Davis (Oxford, 1971–6), i. 84–5.

[151] *CChR 1257–1300*, 78, 215; *CPR 1258–66*, 622.

[152] T. F. Tout, 'The Earldoms under Edward I', *TRHS* NS 8 (1894), 146–7; J. R. Maddicott, *Thomas of Lancaster* (Oxford, 1970), pp. 331, 342–7.

[153] DL 42/2 ff. 115–22; *The Charters of the Duchy of Lancaster*, ed. W. Hardy (London, 1845), no. 8.

receiver of Lancaster administered a more valuable collection of lands in the late fourteenth century.[154]

The centre of Lancastrian interests in the area, Tutbury castle, stood close to the border between Staffordshire and Derbyshire and the landed wealth of the honour was divided almost equally between the two counties. The practical effects of this wealth, however, differed markedly between the two county communities, as a cursory examination of their political and administrative structure will demonstrate. In Derbyshire, 73 elections were made to Parliament between January 1361 and September 1397 and 34 of the MPs chosen were Lancastrian annuitants and officials. In Staffordshire, Lancastrians were elected to Parliament on only five occasions in the same period and the earliest of these elections was in February 1388.[155] Appointments to the shrievalty show an identical pattern; no Lancastrian was ever sheriff of Staffordshire during this period whereas six Lancastrians served as sheriff in Derbyshire.[156] This discrepancy appears equally clearly in the composition of the peace commission in the two counties. In Staffordshire, John of Gaunt does not appear as a justice of the peace until May 1380 and even after that date his appointment was never automatic;[157] in Derbyshire, he usually headed the commission[158] and he was able to appoint a deputy to act in his

---

[154] DL 40/1/11 ff. 43v–44. Under John of Gaunt, the lowest figure at which the honour was charged was £1715. 18s. 8d. (1391/2) but the receiver's annual receipts could be as high as £2199. 13s. 3½d. (1382/ 3); DL 43/15/5 m. 1; DL 29/402/6447–8 m. 2.

[155] *Return of Members of Parliament, Part I: Parliaments of England, 1213–1702* (London, 1878), pp. 166–257. In Derbyshire, the Lancastrians returned were: Edmund Appleby (1376); Oliver Barton (1378, 1380); John Cokayn (1361, 1362); John Curzon (1379, Oct. 1382, Oct. 1383); John Dabridgecourt (1393, Sept. 1397); Godfrey Foljambe (1363, 1365, 1369, Feb. 1371, June 1371); Thomas Foljambe (Nov. 1390, 1391); Thomas Marchington (1380, 1381, May 1382, Feb. 1383); Peter Melbourne (1395); Nicholas Montgomery (Jan. 1390); Philip Okeover (May 1382, 1391); John de la Pole (1377, 1394); Alured Sulny (1372, 1379); Thomas Wennesley (Oct. 1382, Nov. 1384, 1386, Jan. 1390, 1394). In Staffordshire, they were: John Bagot (1391, Jan. 1397, Sept. 1397); John Ipstones (Feb. 1388, 1394). Using a rather looser definition of 'Lancastrian', a study of the parliamentary representations of the two counties during Richard II's reign arrives at a similar imbalance: 28 out of 48 Lancastrian returns in Derbyshire, 7 in Staffordshire. J. G. Bellamy, 'The Parliamentary Representation of Nottinghamshire, Derbyshire and Staffordshire in the Reign of Richard II' (unpub. Nottingham Univ. MA thesis, 1961), p. xix.

[156] *List of Sheriffs for England and Wales*, pp. 103, 127. The Lancastrian sheriffs of Derbyshire and Nottinghamshire were: Alured Sulny (1372–3); Robert Morton (1376–7); Hugh Annesley (1380–1); John Loudham (1388–9); Nicholas Montgomery (1391); Thomas Rempston (1393–4).

[157] *CPR 1381–5*, 139; ibid. *1385–9*, 82; ibid. *1388–92*, 135.

[158] Ibid. *1381–5*, 347; ibid. *1385–9*, 82; ibid. *1388–92*, 136 are exceptions.

stead, perhaps even to nominate the whole commission.[159] Even when the Commons secured the appointment of the July 1389 peace commission in Parliament, they were unable to purge the Lancastrian taint from the Derbyshire justices. Two of the six justices named were, in clear contravention of the statutes of the Cambridge Parliament, Lancastrian stewards, and when the commission was increased in size in November 1389, two more Lancastrians were added.[160] In Staffordshire, by contrast, there was never more than one retainer of the duke's among the justices and even this minimal presence was not always maintained.[161]

Much of the imbalance in the public powers of the Lancastrian affinity in these two adjacent counties can be explained by their respective patterns of magnate landholding. In Derbyshire, the duke of Lancaster's position went unchallenged, for the only peers resident in the county were collateral branches of the Grey family, who lived at Codnor and Sandiacre. Besides Gaunt, they were the only magnates to receive administrative appointments in the county with any regularity, but their landed base in the shire was a slender one,[162] so that it was as Lancastrian clients that the Greys enjoyed most of their influence. Relations with the house of Lancaster were always cordial; John, third lord Grey, and his son, Sir Henry, both served abroad in Gaunt's companies,[163] while Richard, fourth lord Grey, was closely associated with several members of the duke's affinity in Derbyshire.[164] Besides the Greys, only two other magnates appear on government commissions in Derbyshire—William, lord Zouche of Harringworth, and Thomas Holland, duke of Surrey.[165] Both were courtiers, with some land in the county, whose principal estates lay elsewhere; both

---

[159] C. 81/1714 (26): 'Ista billa tradita fuit Johanni Knyvet cancellarius domini Regis pro Johanni Regi Castelle, etc. Fiat commissio ad pacem in comitatu Derb' confermand' Johanni Regi Castelle et Legionis et Duci Lancastrie, Thome de Inbleby, Henrico de Braillesford, Roberto de Twyford, Alvredo de Sulny, milites, Olivero de Barton, Willo de Burgh, Johanni de la Pole et Roberto Mau[veisin], cum ista clausula, etc. quod recorda penes ipsum Oliverum, ut locumtenentem ipsius Regis Castelle remanere volumus etc.' The bill clearly refers to the commission of Nov. 1376: *CPR 1374–7*, 314.

[160] *CPR 1388–92*, 136, 139. In the first commission, John de la Pole was currently steward of Tutbury and Peter Melbourne steward of Melbourne.

[161] Sir Godfrey Foljambe (*CPR 1361–4*, 285); Sir John de la Pole of Newborough (*CPR 1367–70*, 195; ibid. *1370–4*, 304, 305; ibid. *1374–7*, 139, 491; ibid. *1377–81*, 45); Sir Walter Blount (*CPR 1377–81*, 514, 571; ibid. *1381–5*, 251; ibid. *1385–9*, 82, 254).

[162] *CIPM* VII. 683, XII. 351.

[163] C. 76/38 m. 6 (1359); *Foedera*, III. ii. 810 (1367); C. 76/52 m. 13 (1369); C. 76/56 m. 20 (1373).

[164] JUST 1/1501 m. 82, 1514 m. 66; SC 8/301/15003.

[165] *CPR 1385–9*, 82; ibid. *1396–9*, 435.

appeared on the Derbyshire peace commission at a time of political crisis, December 1388 and November 1398 respectively, so that their presence can best be explained as an attempt by the court to exercise some surveillance over the justices of a remote and independent shire —short-lived experiments which did little to loosen the grip of the duke of Lancaster and his Grey clients upon the county.

In Staffordshire, the position was less clear cut, for a number of baronial families had their seats in the county; the Staffords at Stafford, the Furnivalls at Alton, the Audleys at Heighley, the Bassetts at Drayton Bassett, and the impoverished Ferrers at Chartley. The county's gentry had, therefore, a rather wider choice before them in their search for a good lord: Sir Thomas Aston of Heywood, like the Lancastrian retainer Hugh Annesley, was closely associated with Ralph, lord Bassett, of Drayton, while Sir Robert Twyford and Sir John Curson were annuitants of the Hastings earls of Pembroke until that family's extinction in 1389.[166] Yet there was little doubt as to who was the most influential of the Staffordshire magnates, for, until the 1390s, the Stafford family maintained a grip on the administration of the county as tight as the Lancastrian hold over Derbyshire. A small group of Stafford servants and annuitants—Sir Nicholas Stafford, their chief steward; John Knightley, steward of the lord's court in the county; John Hinkley, steward of the household; Roger Longridge, and Sir Adam Peshale[167]—represented the county in Parliament eighteen times during Richard II's reign; a member of the Stafford affinity was sheriff of the county on at least eight occasions between 1361 and 1399.[168] In conjunction with Nicholas Bradshawe, the Staffords' receiver-general, and two more annuitants, Robert Burgiloun and Sir Robert Mauveisin,[169] the same group appeared regularly on the Staffordshire peace commission which, until 1380, was always headed by the earl of Stafford. The addition of John of Gaunt to the commission in that year can have made little practical difference since,

[166] *CIPM* XVI. 974 (Aston); Leicestershire Record Office, 26 D. 53/417 (Annesley); *CPR 1381–5*, 313 (Twyford); SC 8/215/10713 (Curson).
[167] Staffordshire Record Office, D. 641/1/2/40A m. 1 (Knightley); D. 641/1/2/33 m. 1, 4 m. 1 (Stafford); D. 641/1/2/4 m. 6 (Hinkley); D. 641/1/2/36 m. 1 (Longridge, Peshale).
[168] *List of Sheriffs of England and Wales*, p. 127. Nicholas Beek (1368–9); Sir Nicholas Stafford (1372–3, 1375–6); Sir Adam Peshale (1380); Sir Humphrey Stafford (1383–4, 1388–9); Sir Robert Mauveisin (1385–6, 1395–6).
[169] Staffordshire Record Office, D. 641/1/2/4 m. 1 (Bradshawe); D. 641/1/2/33 m. 1 (Burgiloun); D. 641/1/2/40A m. 1 (Mauveisin).

unusually for a magnate, the earls of Stafford were regularly found amongst the 'working' justices of the shire and they could, in consequence, keep a close watch over the actions of the bench.[170]

By all the formal measures of influence, therefore, the Staffords maintained a very effective hold over their county, but they did so by means which differ quite markedly from the Lancastrian affinity's. In the first place, their influence was not underwritten by enormous landed wealth, for the real centre of the Staffords' estates lay outside the northern Midlands, in the Marcher lordships of Newport and Caus. In 1400/1 the fifth earl's Staffordshire lands were valued at only £174. 2s. 2d., a small proportion of his clear annual income of c.£2,000, and in neighbouring Derbyshire he held no lands at all. Secondly, the Staffords did not attempt to compensate for this by an extensive distribution of fees amongst the county gentry: the valuation of the fifth earl's lands allows a reprise of only £128. 11s. 8d. for the payment of all annuities, £14. 3s. 4d. of which was assigned on the receivership of Staffordshire.[171] The figure for local annuities had been higher in the recent past, but even the £34. 6s. 8d. paid out in forinsec fees in 1394/5 represents only a tenth of the duke of Lancaster's contemporary expenditure on annuities in the honour of Tutbury.[172] The Staffords' ability to maintain a predominant position in the affairs of their county through an affinity which cost a fraction of the sum spent on the Lancastrian retinue can best be explained by their recent history. By a fortunate combination of marriage and military prowess they had raised themselves in the course of the fourteenth century from the ranks of the prosperous Marcher gentry into the upper reaches of the English nobility.[173] Theirs was a visibly rising star and the Staffordshire gentry did not need much financial inducement to follow it. At the same time, marriages into middling local families by earlier and less-exalted Staffords[174] gave the comital family a number of collateral branches among the gentry of Staffordshire and the neighbouring counties.[175]

---

[170] *Proceedings Before the Justices of the Peace in the Fourteenth and Fifteenth Centuries*, ed. B. H. Putnam (London, 1938), pp. lxxii, 275–89.

[171] Staffordshire Record Office, D. 641/1/2/6, Roll 4.

[172] Ibid. D. 641/1/2/36 m. 1.

[173] C. Rawcliffe, *The Staffords, Earls of Stafford and Dukes of Buckingham, 1394–1521* (Cambridge, 1978), pp. 8–14.

[174] R. H. Hilton, 'Lord and Peasant in Staffordshire in the Middle Ages', *North Staffordshire Journal of Field Studies*, 10 (1970), 5–6.

[175] Stafford Record Office, D. 641/1/2/40A m. 2.

The Staffords' lordship thus represents a rather different form of 'bastard feudalism' to that exercised by John of Gaunt. In place of the huge financial resources which backed the Lancastrian retinue, they relied on a true 'affinity', based on ties of blood and locality, to spread their influence and, by concentrating their interests and resources on a single county, achieved a position in Staffordshire equal to that of the duke of Lancaster in neighbouring Derbyshire at minimal cost. Yet it was a position that depended, to some extent, on the duke's acquiescence, for John of Gaunt possessed a clear territorial predominance in the county: his estates in Staffordshire yielded an income three times as great as the Staffords'.[176] For most of his life, however, Gaunt made no attempt to use this landed wealth to intrude himself and his followers into the Staffords' sphere of influence. Principally, this was because relations between the two families were usually close and friendly. Ralph, first earl of Stafford, was an old companion-in-arms of duke Henry and his eldest son was briefly married to Henry's daughter Matilda.[177] Hugh, the second earl, served abroad under John of Gaunt's command and acted as his deputy at the coronation of Richard II.[178] The advantages to the relationship were not all on one side, however, for both earl Hugh and his uncle, Sir Richard Stafford, were men of political importance, who played a prominent part in the Good Parliament and the minority government, while Ralph, eldest son of earl Hugh, was a particular favourite of Richard II.[179] As long as there were definite dividends to be gained in national politics from their support, John of Gaunt was happy enough to allow the Staffords a free hand in local society.

Unlike Norfolk, therefore, both Staffordshire and Derbyshire were counties with a single dominant magnate, although they lacked the institutional formalization of predominance present in the palatinate of Lancaster. In both counties the Lancastrian affinity was consequently acting in an environment rather different from those already outlined, with some markedly different results. The composition of the duke's

[176] DL 29/728/11987 m. 1. The Staffordshire portion of the honour of Tutbury was audited at a clear annual value of £572. 3s. 5d. in 1399/1400.

[177] K. A. Fowler, *The King's Lieutenant* (London, 1969), pp. 50–1, 61, 202; *Complete Peerage*, XII. i. 177.

[178] *Complete Peerage*, XII. i. 178; L. G. W. Legg, *English Coronation Records* (London, 1901), p. 132.

[179] *Anonimalle Chronicle*, pp. 84, 94; *CPR 1381–5*, 176; *Westminster Chronicle*, p. 123. He was also on good terms with Gaunt, being received into the fraternity of St Benet's, Holme, at the same time as the duke. *Itineraries. William of Worcester*, ed. J. H. Harvey (Oxford, 1969), p. 225.

following itself differed little, however, from the pattern established in other areas. Long service to the house of Lancaster was as much of a help in gaining entry to the ducal retinue as it was in Lancashire,[180] but a record of past loyalty was never a guarantee of future employment and a family like the Mynors of Uttoxeter, once deprived of ducal patronage, rapidly declined in social consequence.[181] Unlike Norfolk, though, the immediate overlap between Henry of Grosmont's affinity in the area and his son-in-law's was slight; annuities totalling only £82. 0s. 0d. p.a. are known to have been granted by duke Henry from his Staffordshire and Derbyshire lands and, of these annuitants, only Sir Alured Sulny can be said to have played an important role in local society after Gaunt's inheritance of the Lancastrian estates.[182] Indeed, the alternative tradition of loyalty and service to the royal house, on which the duke could draw, was probably more important in the northern Midlands in attracting men to John of Gaunt's service than in the other areas studied. Sir Godfrey Foljambe, the dominant Lancastrian figure in Derbyshire in the 1370s, came to the duke's household by his service to Queen Philippa and other members of the royal family, while formerly Lancastrian families like the Longfords and the Okeovers, who had lost much by their loyalty to earl Thomas, had re-established their fortunes in royal, not ducal, service.[183] Nevertheless, the most common route into John of Gaunt's affinity, in this area as in every other, was by military service with the duke: 20 out of the 31 known annuitants who lived in the two counties certainly campaigned abroad with him and Staffordshire, in particular, was one of the duke's principal recruiting grounds, fulfilling for him much the same function as Cheshire for the Black Prince.[184]

Service in peace, the other stipulation in any life indenture, offered another means of entry into Lancastrian affinity for local men but, although lawyers were always welcome in the duke's following,[185] the arts of peace were generally less attractive an accomplishment than

---

[180] Both Sir Walter Blount's father and his uncle had been prominent in the service of Henry, third earl of Lancaster, for example. DL 40/1/11 ff. 46v, 47, 52.

[181] E. Powell, 'Public Order and Law Enforcement in Shropshire and Staffordshire in the Early Fifteenth Century' (unpub. Oxford Univ. D. Phil. thesis, 1979), pp. 288–9.

[182] K. A. Fowler, 'Henry of Grosmont, First Duke of Lancaster, 1310–1361' (unpub. Leeds Univ. Ph.D. thesis, 1961), Appendix J.

[183] *CPR 1354–7*, 548, ibid. *1358–61*, 282; *CCR 1346–9*, 475 (Longford); SC 8/223/12117 (Okeover).

[184] In 1366, for example, Gaunt raised 100 archers for his company from Staffordshire, compared to only 50 from Lancashire. C. 61/79 m. 9.

[185] Sir Godfrey Foljambe had been chief justiciar of Ireland and Sir John de la Pole

military prowess. Whereas John of Gaunt was frequently willing to admit another soldier to his retinue, he seems to have made little attempt to attract the services and loyalty of the influential county administrators, in whose hands day to day authority in the shire largely rested. Foremost among such men in Staffordshire was William Walsall of Rushall, who used his office as marshal of the king's hall to build up a powerful position in the county, which he maintained in complete independence of the Lancastrian affinity.[186] In Derbyshire, Sir Robert Twyford of Kirk Langley occupied much the same position but, although he remained on good terms with the duke,[187] he was never taken into Gaunt's service. This provides a definite contrast with the Staffords' practice in recruiting retainers but it is entirely in keeping with the duke's own preoccupations, for his attention was concentrated on the court, not on the county, and it was to the men who could most readily contribute to his worship and influence there, whether they held lands in the northern Midlands or not, that the largest fees from his Tutbury estates were paid. Sir William Beauchamp, the youngest son of the earl of Warwick, enjoyed a fee of 100 marks from the High Peak, although his own lands lay principally in the Welsh march; Sir John Dabridgecourt, also paid a fee of 100 marks, was the son of a Hainaulter and possessed no hereditary stake in the area at all.[188] Clearly, the duke's affinity in the northern Midlands was never intended as an instrument of political dominance at the level of the shire; it was rather an organic accretion of hopeful soldiers and loyal servants, a product of chance as much as of design and a means of buying off enemies as well as winning friends.

The heterogeneous, almost haphazard, nature of the Lancastrian affinity in the area did mean, however, that it was more dependent upon the personal presence of the duke for its cohesion and self-consciousness than the almost self-regulating group of Lancastrians in the palatinate of Lancashire. Fortunately, John of Gaunt was a regular, if brief, visitor to Tutbury, usually in late summer, and duchess

---

of Newborough was a justiciar of north and south Wales. H. G. Richardson and G. O. Sayles, *The Administration of Ireland 1172–1377* (Dublin, 1963), p. 171; R. A. Griffiths, *The Principality of Wales in the Later Middle Ages* (Cardiff, 1972), pp. 112–13.

[186] J. G. Bellamy, 'The Parliamentary Representation of Nottinghamshire, Derbyshire and Staffordshire in the Reign of Richard II' (unpub. Nottingham Univ. MA thesis, 1961), pp. 176–88.

[187] *CPR 1377–81*, 468, 511.

[188] *Complete Peerage*, I. 24–6 (Beauchamp); G. F. Beltz, *Memorials of the Most Noble Order of the Garter* (London, 1841), pp. 90–2.

Constance spent much of her time there.[189] After a period of neglect since the days of Thomas of Lancaster, the castle was thoroughly refurbished[190] and, in the 1390s, it became one of the more regular residences of Henry of Derby and his sons.[191] The duke's presence in the area possessed an importance quite out of proportion to the time he spent there, by giving a sense of cohesion to his affinity; his visits were a time when both his own retainers and the rest of the county community recommended themselves to their lord, usually combining a gift with a request for favour or a complaint.[192] The duke replied, in his turn, with periodic gifts of game from the well-stocked forests of Needwood and the Peak to the notables of the shire.[193] These occasional contacts with the lord were supplemented by the more permanent link of household service. Because of the duke's relatively frequent presence in the area the number of household servants from Staffordshire and Derbyshire was, in contrast to East Anglia, always appreciable. In the 1380s, Sir Walter Blount was the only chamber knight from the north Midlands, but a number of senior household esquires came from the area and they had their counterparts in the lower levels of the household administration.[194] By the 1390s, Blount had been joined among the chamber knights by Sir Hugh Shirley and Sir John Dabridgecourt whilst their wives, Dame Sanchez Blount and Dame Beatrice Shirley, also had a place in the household as duchess Constance's closest companions.[195]

In the north Midlands, therefore, the presence of the duke and his household provided an effective focus for the loyalties of his affinity

[189] John of Gaunt was certainly at Tutbury in July/Aug. 1362 (DL 42/15 f. 56v, *Reg. I.* 748); at Tutbury in July 1363 (*The Cartulary of Tutbury Priory*, ed. A. Saltman, HMC Joint Publications, 2 (1962), no. 342); at Newcastle under Lyme in Sept. 1364 (DL 42/16 f. 17*d*); at Tutbury in Aug. 1374 and 1375 (*Reg. I* 113, 1742); at Tutbury in Aug. 1380 (*Tutbury Cartulary*, no. 341); at Tutbury and Melbourne in July 1383 (*Reg. II* 900–2); in the High Peak in 1391/2 (DL 28/3/4 f. 11v); at Tutbury in July 1392 (DL 28/3/2 f. 10v) and at Tideswell in Sept. (PL 3/1/22); at Melbourne in July 1394 (DL 42/15 f. 50v). For duchess Constance at Tutbury: *Reg. I* 1276, 1369; East Sussex Record Office, GLY 3469 m. 19.

[190] *VCH Staffordshire*, i. 237–8; DL 29/728/11982 m. 1, 11985 m. 1.

[191] DL 28/1/9 ff. 2, 2v, 10 ff. 16v, 17.

[192] DL 28/1/1 f. 5v, 9 f. 3.

[193] *Reg. I* 1740; SC 6/988/14 m. 4.

[194] East Sussex Record Office, GLY 3469 mm. 1–5. Among the household esquires were William Bagot, William Chetwynd, Roger Coleman, Peter Melbourne, Master John Raynald, the cook. Among the valets: John Ashton, John del Chamber, Simon Estrick, John Stockley, Randolph Tynneslowe.

[195] East Sussex Record Office, GLY 3469 mm. 6–17.

and gave a more immediate meaning to Lancastrian allegiance than was ever the case in Norfolk. Did this mean, as it did to a large extent in Lancashire, that the social contacts established at the duke's court or on overseas service created a separate group of Lancastrians within the broader community of the shire, which itself became the object of envy and, on occasion, the target for violence? At first sight, there is some good evidence for this view, since the duke's concern to maintain his rights, not to mention his profits, caused resentment in both counties. The Sunday market held at Tutbury was, for instance, a constant source of complaint; from the townsmen of Derby and the burgesses of Stafford, whose Saturday market suffered in consequence, as well as from the abbey of Burton-on-Trent, whose rival Sunday fair was proscribed because of the damage it inflicted on the duke's receipts.[196] As in so many other counties, this resentment was compounded by the corruption and extortions of the Lancastrian officials—John Halsweyn, the receiver of Tutbury, was alleged by the jurors of the wapentake of Wirksworth to have levied for his own profit an annual 40s. above the sum they would have rendered the duke[197]— and the ability of the duke's retainers to use the resources of his affinity to circumvent or ignore the sanctions of the law. When Sir Edmund Appleby and his son John were accused of robbing a merchant at Horninglow, they could produce two fellow-Lancastrians as their sureties and, in the following year, a pardon for the crime issued at the request of the duke of Lancaster.[198] Protests against the power and wealth of the Lancastrian affinity, in the form of numerous petty offences, were consequently frequent: concealed wardships,[199] minor thefts,[200] and illegal hunting[201] were the constant objects of Gaunt's litigation.

Indeed, John of Gaunt could call upon an impressive armoury of legal weapons to combat these depredations. When the duke's tenants and officials at Morley were harassed by the gentry family of Stathum, in a dispute over the jurisdiction of his hundred court of Appletree, he took the affront sufficiently seriously to present a schedule of his grievances before the king and council in February 1380. By March, a

---

[196] KB 27/526 m. 9, 478 mm. 22, 33; *CPR 1381–5*, 145, 506.
[197] KB 9/989 m. 12; KB 27/530 Rex mm. 3, 13d.
[198] KB 27/433 Rex m. 17; *CPR 1367–70*, 405. The Lancastrian sureties were Simon Pakeman, steward of Leicester, and Sir John Talbot of Swannington.
[199] CP 40/458 m. 17d.
[200] KB 9/989 mm. 8, 10.
[201] *CPR 1377–81*, 360; CP 40/482 m. 16d.

powerful and heavily Lancastrian commission of oyer and terminer had been issued[202] and Ralph Stathum, the principal offender, compelled to enter into a bond of £100 towards the duke as a guarantee of good behaviour. When the justices finally arrived in September, the duke's receiver was instructed to aid, help, and counsel them in every reasonable way and to pay their expenses.[203] The same method of retribution was used when Roger Coleman, a household esquire of the duke's, was murdered at Handsacre in the course of a long-running dispute between co-heiresses over the division of the manor.[204] It was important to the duke's worship that, even in such domestic matters, an attack upon his servants should not go unpunished. In this case, the killer—Laurence Foster of Frodley— was an experienced wrongdoer with powerful protection and he was soon able to obtain two royal pardons for the crime, but Lancaster's direct intercession at court prevented Foster escaping from justice altogether. Both his pardons were revoked within a month, because the king had granted them 'without recollecting his promise to his uncle . . . before his departure to Spain that he would not grant any such pardon' and Foster had to wait for another until April 1398.[205]

Nevertheless, there were definite limits to the effectiveness of Gaunt's intervention in the process of justice on his retainers' behalf, for even the duke's vengeance could do nothing against Foster's accomplices and protectors, the gentry family of Peshale, who exploited a technicality to have the appeal against them dismissed in Hilary Term 1392.[206] Lancaster, no less than his opponents, was caught in the toils of a legal system that allowed almost interminable delays and evasions—a system that could be as easily exploited against him as on his behalf. When Sir Thomas Ardern attacked his lands and tenants at Lichfield and Barton in 1379, the duke resorted to his favourite means of redress and sued out a commission of oyer and terminer against him but when, in Easter term 1381, Ardern finally appeared in court to answer the indictments, he successfully objected to the panel of the jury, which had been arrayed by the duke of Lancaster's bailiff, and the case failed to reach a conclusion.[207] Even

[202] *CPR 1377–81*, 68, 511. D. Crook, 'Derbyshire and the English Rising of 1381', *BIHR* 60 (1987), 16–18.

[203] *Reg. II* 929, 336.

[204] *CPR 1381–5*, 587; KB 27/498 m. 21.

[205] *CPR 1385–9*, 220, 229, 238; KB 27/549 m. 19d.

[206] KB 27/498 m. 21.

[207] *CPR 1377–81*, 415; CP 40/482 m. 142d.

when John of Gaunt won the judicial arguments, his opponents sometimes resorted to an extra-legal violence that was unanswerable. In the case of his litigation against the Stathum family, the duke's combination of legitimate legal process and doubtful judicial persuasion was temporarily successful in bringing his opponents to heel, but the Stathums refused to acquiesce in their defeat. On 18 June 1381, taking their cue from the disorder and confusion reigning in the South, they went on the rampage, breaking into the duke's park at Morley and killing two of his parkers before going on to sack the Augustinian priory at Bredsall and occupy the royal castle of Horston, from which they flew the banner of St George—the same banner that the rebels at Blackheath and St Albans had displayed less than a week before.[208] This time the duke was unable to obtain either settlement or redress. The Stathums obtained pardons for their part in the insurrection of the commons in December 1381 and they remained irreconcilable. Thomas Stathum led another attack on Gaunt's estates in Derbyshire in December 1387; John Stathum, esquire, was one of the few who rallied to the duke of York to resist the invasion of Henry of Lancaster in 1399; Ralph Stathum treasonably adhered to John Holland, duke of Exeter, in the revolt of 1400.[209]

Despite the exceptional circumstances of the Stathums' uprising, it was not an isolated incident for, on more than one occasion, Lancastrian officials were attacked and killed and the duke proved powerless to avenge them. In 1390 his chief steward of the North, Sir John de la Pole of Newborough, was attacked in the execution of his duties as a justice of the peace by William de Sutton of Rideware and his gang; Sutton subsequently produced a royal pardon and went unpunished.[210] William de Laken, an esquire of Henry of Derby's with lands in Shropshire and Staffordshire, was killed in Fleet Street during the Parliament of September 1397, almost under the nose of his master. His killer, the Cheshire knight Sir John Hawkeston, produced a royal pardon in October 1398 and went without day.[211] The violence and maintenance of which the parliamentary Commons complained so bitterly during the 1380s was, therefore, as prevalent in Staffordshire and Derbyshire as it was in Lancashire, but the

---

[208] KB 9/989 m. 1; KB 27/530 Rex m. 10, 531 Rex m. 20*d*; Crook, 'Derbyshire and the English Rising', 9–12.

[209] *CPR 1385–9*, 395; E. 403/562 m. 15; *CIM 1399–1422*, no. 47.

[210] *CPR 1388–92*, 493–4.

[211] KB 27/550 Rex m. 13, 553 Rex m. 13*d*; *CPR 1396–9*, 427.

Commons' suggested remedies seem no more applicable, for the great lords appear to have borne little direct responsibility for the disorder of the region. Livery badges *were* used as a cover for crime, but it was a minor gentleman such as William de Sutton who used them in this way, not the county magnates, and it was gentry families like the Peshales who were mainly responsible for harbouring and maintaining criminals.

Yet the Lancastrian retinue was not entirely blameless of involvement in the violence of the area, and John of Gaunt's answer to the Commons' request for legislation against the excesses of livery and maintenance, that the great lords were capable of disciplining their own men, loses a little of its plausibility when it is set against the actions of his followers in the northern Midlands. In Derbyshire, dissension and conflict within the duke's retinue was particularly common, for the absence of any rival magnate interest in the county removed the spur of self-interest necessary to the unity and co-operation of a varied group of gentry. Without such a spur, the Lancastrian affinity was soon divided against itself, with individual retainers taking opposite sides in the quarrels of county society. One of the duke's esquires, John Stafford of Eyam, turned up at a loveday arranged in September 1392 with six armed men to maintain one of the parties to the arbitration; his opponent, Sir Roger Leche, arrived with twelve men to support the other party and the affair inevitably ended in violence.[212] In another instance, a number of the duke's retainers even combined against the most influential Lancastrian in the area, Sir Walter Blount. Taking advantage of his position as a justice of the peace, Blount had ridden to Repton with a large band of men to demand the surrender of a townsman, John Moston, who had attacked one of his tenants. The men of Repton replied that Moston had already found security for his good behaviour and refused to give him up, but three days later Blount returned with an armed following and compelled him to enter into a bond for £20 that he would appear at Blount's manor of Barton to make suitable amends. Moston then turned to his own overlord, Sir John Ipstones, for redress and, in the company of a number of other Lancastrians, Ipstones had attacked Blount's manor of Barton Bakepuize and compelled Sir Walter to give up the bond.[213] Ipstones had only just been retained by John of Gaunt;

---

[212] KB 9/989 m. 10; KB 27/531 Rex m. 3.
[213] KB 9/989 m. 3, KB 27/531 Rex m. 17*d*.

Blount was currently chamberlain of the duke's household. Clearly, the internal hierachy of the Lancastrian affinity had little effect on the actions of the duke's retainers while they were on their home territory. Nor did their Lancastrian allegiance, if it was in conflict with their own interests; despite his impeccably Lancastrian background, Sir John Cokayn of Ashbourne, who was alleged to have twenty men of his own retaining, did not spare the duke's estates from his widespread depredations in 1388.[214]

Members of the duke's affinity thus played an active part in the violence that afflicted the northern Midlands. The complaints of the parliamentary Commons are to that extent justified but, whatever their crimes, John of Gaunt's retainers can hardly be held wholly responsible for the disorder. Its real roots lay in the conjunction of three simultaneous developments: the temporary abeyance of other magnate interests in the area; the gradual build-up of the Lancastrian affinity's influence on the basis of a growing territorial stake in both counties; the appearance, on his return from Spain, of some powerful and aggressive new retainers in the duke's service.

The first of these developments meant that, for the last ten years of Richard II's reign, John of Gaunt was to enjoy almost as free a hand in Staffordshire as he already did in Derbyshire. Among the magnates who held land in the county, William, lord Furnivall, had died without male heirs in 1383, Ralph, lord Bassett, died childless in 1390, as did Nicholas, lord Audley, in 1391.[215] More important, the death of Hugh, earl of Stafford, in 1386 inaugurated a series of minorities and early deaths in the Stafford family that was to last until well into the fifteenth century. The Stafford estates were successfully administered and protected during these years by a close-knit group of councillors, but their attention was principally occupied in securing a portion of the Bassett inheritance and the costly litigation this involved necessitated prolonged residence in London; the controlling influence in the politics of the county was, therefore, temporarily removed.[216] As the power of other magnates withered away, so the Lancastrian affinity gradually consolidated the territorial foundations of its influence in the northern Midlands. In part, this was as fortuitous an occurrence as the abeyance of rival magnate interests; in part, it was the inevitable result of the duke's patronage. The bulk of the Bassett inheritance in the area

[214]　*CPR 1385–9*, 463; KB 9/989 mm. 2, 10; KB 27/529 m. 27.

[215]　*Complete Peerage*, V. 587, II. 3–6, I. 339–40.

[216]　*Complete Peerage*, XII. i. 179–81; Rawcliffe, *The Staffords*, p. 12.

ultimately passed to the duke's retainer, Sir Hugh Shirley,[217] for example, and John Beaufort, Gaunt's bastard son, acquired four manors in Staffordshire by a royal grant from the forfeited property of the earl of Warwick.[218] However, these windfalls were less important in augmenting the Lancastrian presence in the area than the gradual accumulation of surplus capital in the hands of the duke's retainers, created by the fees and annuities he paid them. Inevitably, this capital was principally devoted to the purchase of land, hence to acquiring a larger stake in the area and a better claim to a say in its running. Thus Sir Godfrey Foljambe, who enjoyed an income over £100 p.a. from his Lancastrian service,[219] used his wealth to establish his son in Warwickshire[220] and then considerably expanded the family's existing estates in Derbyshire,[221] while John de la Pole of Newborough used his fee as the duke's chief steward of the North Parts to build up his wife's inheritance around Matlock.[222]

The duke's wealth also brought new men and new families into the northern Midlands. His chamberlain, Sir Robert Swillington, originally from Yorkshire, bought an outlying manor in Derbyshire after his inheritance of the Bellers estate in neighbouring Leicestershire, and was granted the keeping of the royal castle of Horston;[223] Sir Walter Blount, the younger son of a Worcestershire family, inherited the Mountjoy estates in Staffordshire in 1374 and, on the proceeds of the enormous fee the duke paid him, bought the Bakepuiz lands around Tutbury in 1381;[224] Oliver Barton, the duke's steward at Tutbury, used his position to buy his way into a county where he had no roots— between his appointment in 1379 and 1386 he bought two manors and

---

[217] Leicestershire Record Office, 26 D. 53/1583; E. P. Shirley, *Stemmata Shirleiana* (London, 1873), pp. 29, 376–86.

[218] WAM, 6045; *CPR 1396–9*, 211.

[219] Foljambe received a retaining fee of £40 p.a., a salary of 70 marks as chief steward of the duke's lands, and a smaller sum as steward of Newcastle and Tutbury, in addition to any profit he made from the farm of the duke's manor of Newcastle. Bodl. MS CCC 495, f. 16; *Reg. I* 1575, 1105, 415.

[220] E. 210/11123; Nottinghamshire Record Office, Dd Fj 1/192/4, 5.

[221] He bought the manors of Hazelwood, Ockbrook, and Chaddesden, besides many smaller parcels of land and pasture. Nottinghamshire Record Office, Dd Fj 1/47/1, 1/62/2, 1/75/1, 1/99/1; BL Wolley Charters, I. 17, II. 22; CP 25 (1)/39/37 (192), (198), 38 (210), (216); *CCR 1369–74*, 564; Sheffield City Library, Bagshawe Collection 1007, 1031–2, 1385.

[222] Derbyshire Record Office, 1233 M/T 35, 47, 77–82.

[223] CP 25 (1)/39/39 (14); C. 136/73/8.

[224] JUST 1/1488 m. 63; Sir Alexander Croke, *The Genealogical History of the Croke Family* (Oxford, 1823), ii. 171, 182–3.

a town house in Derby and took out leases on several sheep runs in the Peak.[225] Influence on the course of local justice and local politics inevitably followed: Barton joined the Derbyshire bench as John of Gaunt's nominee in 1376 and sat continuously for the next ten years; in October 1378 and November 1380 he represented the county in Parliament.[226] In addition to their own purchases, the duke's servants also enjoyed the opportunity of taking up the leases offered on Lancastrian lands and rights in the area[227] and so exercising a little of the duke's influence for themselves. Sir Godfrey Foljambe even leased the whole manor and town of Newcastle under Lyme, by an arrangement which brought him only modest financial advantage but gave him the more valuable privilege of a share in the duke's judicial lordship, of his authority over the people.[228] To that extent, the duke's tacit agreement with the Staffords over their respective spheres of influence was inevitably undermined by the consequences of his generosity to his own followers.

At the same time as the Lancastrian territorial stake in the northern Midlands was increasing, the duke's expenditure on his affinity in the area also rose rapidly. In 1382/3, annuities assigned on the honour of Tutbury totalled £291. 12s. 8d.; by 1387/8 the figure was £398. 16s. 0d. but in the next financial year alone a further £140. 4s. 5d. was granted out in new annuities and by 1391/2 the sum paid in annuities had reached a peak of £632. 19s. 5d., more than double the figure it had been nine years before.[229] To put it another way, in 1382/3 annuities absorbed 13 per cent of the receipts of the honour; by 1391/2 they equalled just over 35 per cent of the receiver's clear annual charge. This increase in the size and cost of the section of the Lancastrian affinity based on Tutbury is striking for two reasons.

[225] CP 25 (1)/39/39 (8), (11), (15), (22), 40 (33); I. H. Jeayes, *A Descriptive Catalogue of Derbyshire Charters* (London, 1906), no. 1493.

[226] *CPR 1374–7*, 314; ibid. *1377–81*, 513, 571; ibid. *1381–5*, 139, 347; ibid. *1385–9*, 82; *Return of Members of Parliament*, pp. 199, 206.

[227] e.g. DL 42/15 ff. 57, 120v, 131, 192v.

[228] *CPR 1361–4*, 202; *Reg. I* 677. Foljambe paid an annual farm of £127 for the manor. In 1386/7 the issues of Newcastle amounted to £136. 5s. 2d. beyond reprises; in 1399/1400 to £138. 13s. 0d., so that Foljambe could only have made a profit of c.£10 a year on the farm. Compared to some of the Black Prince's leases, however, this was a generous margin. T. Pape, *Medieval Newcastle-under-Lyme* (Manchester, 1928), pp. 116–17; P. H. W. Booth, 'Farming for Profit in the Fourteenth Century: The Cheshire Estates of the Earldom of Chester', *Journal of the Chester Archaeological Society*, 62 (1979), 83–90.

[229] DL 29/402/6447–8 m. 2, 728/11975 m. 1, 11977 m. 1; DL 43/15/5 m. 1.

Firstly, it was unique to the region, a development almost without parallel on the rest of the duke's receiverships.[230] Secondly, it came at a time when more and more difficulties were being experienced in maintaining an adequate level of income from the honour. Although stock and dairy farming were generally still profitable, lack of vigilance had brought about a decline in profits from the High Peak while schedules of decayed rents point to a gradual but steady contraction of arable cultivation in the lowland areas of the honour.[231] These difficulties were further compounded by the problem of recalcitrant ministers, who refused to levy their full charge; as early as 1380 the steward of the honour had been forced to imprison some of them in order to obtain payment of the arrears the duke was insistently demanding.[232]

Despite those demands, John of Gaunt was prepared to allow his retinue in Staffordshire and Derbyshire to absorb a rapidly increasing proportion of a slowly declining revenue. Why should this be? One reason was the need to reward the men who had served him in Spain; this was certainly the case with Sir Thomas Beek, Sir John Bagot, Sir John Ipstones, and William Newport and it would explain the great leap in annuity levels between 1387/8 and 1389/90. At the same time Gaunt's son, Henry of Derby, was paying more frequent visits to Tutbury and beginning to build up a following of his own among the local gentry, although it largely continued to be financed by his father. Nicholas Bradshawe, receiver-general of the Stafford estates, Sir Alured Lathbury, and Sir Ralph Braylesford had all become Henry's annuitants by 1398[233] and a number of lesser men from the region also found their way into his service, such as Richard Chelmeswyk of Tasley (Salop.), Thomas Totty of Rolleston (Staffs.), and Ralph Staveley of Staveley (Derby.).[234] This recruitment may have been deliberate, for relations between Lancaster and the Staffords grew appreciably cooler after 1386 when Sir John Holland, the murderer of the earl of Stafford's eldest son, was restored to royal favour by John of Gaunt's intercession.[235] Holland subsequently married one of the

---

[230] See Appendix IV.

[231] G. A. Holmes, *The Estates of the Higher Nobility in Fourteenth-Century England* (Cambridge, 1957), pp. 126–8; DL 29/728/11982 m. 2*d*; DL 43/1/19.

[232] *Reg. I* 207. The problem of mounting arrears was also affecting the Stafford estates: Staffordshire Record Office, D. 641/1/2/3.

[233] DL 28/4/1 ff. 9, 10; DL 42/16 f. 155.

[234] E. 403/533 m. 7; *CPR 1396–9*, 122, 566.

[235] *Chronicon Henrici Knighton*, ii. 206.

duke's daughters and served as constable of his army in Spain. By the 1390s the duke of Gloucester had replaced his elder brother as the Staffords' principal ally and protector.[236] Deliberate or not, the effect of this intensified Lancastrian recruitment was to fill the political vacuum created in Staffordshire by the temporary abeyance of the Stafford interest and to attract those who were casting around in search of a new lord. The results of the duke's increased expenditure soon begin to show, for instance, in the parliamentary representation of the county: the 5 Lancastrian returns to the Commons all occur after February 1388 while there are only 3 'Stafford' returns in the same period.[237]

A less welcome result, however, was the sudden efflorescence of disorder in the north Midlands, in which a small group of new Lancastrian retainers played a major part. The crimes they committed cannot be blamed directly on their new allegiance but they do illustrate the unforeseen and often serious domestic difficulties that were created by John of Gaunt's pursuit of a policy of recruitment to his retinue which laid the greatest emphasis on service abroad and at court, with little consideration for the repercussions of his generosity on county society. The two worst offenders, Sir John Bagot and Sir John Ipstones, already had careers of violence behind them,[238] but their newly acquired Lancastrian allegiance did much to strengthen their position in the area and little to restrain their actions—indeed, Ipstones relied on the help of some of his new colleagues like Sir John Cokayn, Sir Thomas Beek, and Sir Philip Okeover, in the prosecution of his feuds.[239] The duke could hardly prevent this but he was, in a sense, as much the victim of his own retainers' attacks as their more immediate opponents. Sir John Bagot added to the growing coolness between Gaunt and the Staffords by becoming embroiled in a feud with one of their retainers, Sir Robert Mauveisin,[240] and Sir John Ipstones was already involved in a long-running dispute with another family of Stafford clients, the Peshales, when he was first retained by the duke. On his return from Spain, Ipstones took matters into his own

[236] *Complete Peerage*, XII. i. 180–1; Rawcliffe, *The Staffords*, p. 12; Staffordshire Record Office, D. 641/1/2/4 m. 4 for the Staffords wearing Gloucester's livery.

[237] *Return of Members of Parliament*, pp. 234–57. Roger Longridge (Feb. 1388); Sir Nicholas Stafford (Jan. 1390, Nov. 1390).

[238] *Collections for a History of Staffordshire*, ed. G. Wrottesley (William Salt Archaeological Soc., 1892), xiii. 166, 169 (Ipstones); ibid. 69, 127 (Bagot).

[239] KB 9/989 m. 3; KB 27/531 Rex m. 17*d*; *CPR 1388–92*, 339.

[240] *Collections for a History of Staffordshire* (1896), xvii. 22; Staffordshire Record Office, D. 641/1/2/4 mm. 4, 5 for Mauveisin's connection with the Staffords.

hands by forcibly abducting the heiress to the disputed manors of Hopton and Tene, marrying her to his son, and beginning legal proceedings for the seizure of the Peshale estates.[241] Despite suing out a commission of oyer and terminer, the Peshales were unable to gain any redress in the courts and, faced with a *fait accompli*, characteristically turned to violent revenge. Roger Swynnerton, uncle of the abducted heiress, murdered Ipstones in a London street in 1394.[242] Like the Workesley dispute in Lancashire, the affair clearly demonstrates how quickly an unresolved local quarrel could escalate into national prominence and how awkward this could prove for John of Gaunt. Although he was hardly responsible for his retainer's crimes, he could not be unaffected by his murder, nor by his own failure to gain any redress for the crime. Ipstones had been an MP in the Merciless Parliament and an enthusiastic supporter of the Appellant regime;[243] his killer, Roger Swynnerton, appears to have had friends at court, for he was eventually pardoned at the request of Sir Baldwin Raddington, then controller of the household.[244] Political prudence alone dictated that *this* retainer should go unavenged, but the affair had indicated the limits to the protection that the duke of Lancaster could offer.

Protection, whether physical or legal, was one of the attributes of lordship the county gentry most valued in a patron and any limitation upon the duke's power to extend or withhold his at will was naturally a matter for serious concern. No less a cause for concern, though, was the fact that Gaunt had been shown by the incident to be incapable of curtailing the violence that continued to afflict the northern Midlands. 'A magnate who tolerated . . . misrule in his "country" was damaging his own worship and inviting royal intervention',[245] and the presence of the King's Bench at Nottingham in Trinity 1392 and Hilary 1396, as at Derby in Trinity 1393, could be seen as a standing reproach to the duke of Lancaster.[246] It may well be that, far from creating disorder in the region, the duke's increased expenditure on retaining fees assigned to Tutbury was an attempt to staunch it, to contain the

[241] *CCR 1381–5*, 3; JUST 1/814 m. 1.

[242] *CPR 1388–92*, 339; JUST 3/180 m. 48; *Rot. Parl.*, iii. 317.

[243] *CPR 1389–92*, 213.

[244] *CPR 1396–9*, 143.

[245] G. L. Harriss, 'Introduction', in K. B. McFarlane, *England in the Fifteenth Century: Collected Essays* (London, 1981), p. xxi.

[246] *Select Cases in the Court of King's Bench*, ed. G. O. Sayles, vii (Selden Soc., 88, 1971), p. lvi.

actions of unruly gentry like Bagot and Ipstones by offering them a vested interest in the maintenance of the *status quo*. Sir John Cokayn's progress, from breaker of the duke's chases in 1388 to chief steward of the North Parts of his duchy by 1398, suggests that the attempt was a worthwhile one, but Ipstone's murder, no less than the violence he had fomented between Sir Walter Blount and the rest of the duke's affinity in Derbyshire, was an embarrassingly public demonstration to the parliamentary Commons that, contrary to Gaunt's own assurances, the magnates could not always maintain discipline among their own followers, nor peace in the regions where they held sway. The advent of King's Bench was one response to this failure; a second was the growth of royal lordship in the area. For it was the king, with whom John of Gaunt's relations were outwardly so cordial during the 1390s, who did most to challenge the position of the Lancastrian affinity in the northern Midlands during the last years of the duke's life. As early as June 1387, Richard II had used his enforced progress around the country as an opportunity to establish links with several Staffordshire gentlemen[247] and he continued to collect clients in the county in the following decade. Thomas, third earl of Stafford, was retained to stay with the king for life in 1389, and granted custody of his inheritance while still a minor; Sir Adam Peshale became a king's knight in 1390; William Walsall, a king's esquire in 1391; Sir John Bagot showed signs of following his younger brother from the Lancastrian household to the king's.[248] In addition, the deaths and minorities that disrupted the pattern of local politics in Staffordshire gave the Crown an unprecedented opportunity to influence county society through the ability to appoint keepers and guardians of lands in the king's hands: William Walsall, for instance, was both constable of Stafford castle during the young earl's minority and joint-keeper of the Audley barony.[249]

The Crown thus emerged as a third force, besides Lancaster and the Staffords, in the politics of the county, and Richard II's attempt at the manipulation of local society during his 'tyranny' consequently enjoyed some success in Staffordshire. The ubiquitous William Walsall acted as sheriff of the county continuously from 1 December 1396—an illegitimately long term of office—and to the all-important Parliament of September 1397 he returned Sir John Bagot and the French courtier-knight, Sir Rustin Villeneuve. In itself, this was no

---

[247] *Select Cases*, vii, pp. xxv–xxvi.
[248] *CPR 1388–92*, 160, 316; ibid. *1391–6*, 124; ibid. *1396–9*, 462.
[249] *CPR 1391–6*, 124; *CFR 1391–9*, 11

threat to Gaunt's position, for he made no claim to exercise over the political community in Staffordshire the same sort of control as in Lancashire, but it undoubtedly added to his concerns. Thus, Sir William Chetwynd of Ingestre was shown considerable favour by the king in 1387 and at Easter 1388 he revived his family's long-standing claim to the manor of Shenstone against Sir Roger l'Estrange of Knockin.[250] John of Gaunt was obliged to warrant l'Estrange's possession of the manor and, if it was recovered against him, the duke stood to lose heavily in both money and prestige.[251] Chetwynd's chance of success in the plea naturally increased, however, as he rose in royal esteem and Gaunt was taking no chances on the outcome: at the first assize, over £20 was spent in unspecified legal expenses; at the second, Sir Walter Blount, Sir John de la Pole, Sir Nicholas Montgomery, and Sir Philip Okeover were required to attend l'Estrange in court.[252] Even in cases where he had no direct involvement, such disputes were important to the duke for, at the county level, the esteem in which he was held depended to a large extent upon his ability to maintain his clients' part. In this he was usually successful and he was, in consequence, established as a 'good lord' to the Staffordshire gentry when the emergence of a royalist affinity in the county offered the promise of a new and more powerful protector—a promise particularly attractive to those who did not already enjoy Gaunt's favour. In consequence, the inner logic of 'bastard feudalism'—the perennial tendency of the gentry to search for patrons and patrons to acknowledge clients—drove the king and the duke towards opposite sides in the disputes and quarrels that animated the county community.

A more striking example of the same process occurred in Derbyshire, where Thomas Foljambe failed to make good his claim to the manor of Walton, acquired by his marriage to Margaret, daughter of Sir John Loudham. As the heir to his grandfather's wealth and position in the county, himself a lawyer and the duke's steward of the High Peak, Foljambe was in a very strong position in the dispute with his co-heir, Thomas Beckering, over the possession of the manor, but

---

[250] *Select Cases*, vii, pp. xxv-xxvi; C. 260/118 (22); *Collections for a History of Staffordshire* (1894), xv. 8, 60.

[251] WAM, 6039, 6040. The Chetwynd family had already incurred the duke's displeasure by presenting to the rectory of Grendon, which the duke claimed, in 1370. H. E. Chetwynd-Stapylton, *The Chetwynds of Ingestre* (London, 1892), p. 78.

[252] DL 29/728/11979 m. 1, 11982 m. 1.

he experienced unexpected difficulties.[253] This was principally because, faced with so influential an opponent, Beckering had turned to the Lancashire knight, Sir Nicholas Clifton, for assistance and promised a third of the profits of the manor in return for his maintenance in the dispute. In June 1392 Clifton and his ally, Robert Barley, arrived with an alleged 200 men and ejected Foljambe from the manor; in the following August, he returned to carry through a manifestly inequitable division of the disputed estate.[254] Foljambe was powerful enough to take the matter further and he had the backing of the duke of Lancaster at Westminster. By February 1393, Clifton had been ordered to do no harm towards him, under pain of £1,000, to vacate the manor immediately, and to come before the king and Council to explain his conduct.[255] Clifton was the equal to these measures. Secure in his provincial power-base, he ignored all three injunctions and continued his attacks on Foljambe and his lands until June 1393; when summoned before the King's Bench at Derby, near the centre of his own operations, he put himself on the country and was, unsurprisingly, acquitted. His partition of Walton held good until November 1399, when the advent of Henry IV allowed a more Lancastrian version of justice to be done.[256]

Save for the vigour with which it was conducted, the Walton dispute is itself unremarkable, but it does indicate a change in the political balance of Derbyshire. Foljambe was the duke's steward in a heavily Lancastrian county, and a man not afraid of using violence himself,[257] but neither his local position nor his Lancastrian connection availed him against Sir Nicholas Clifton, and even Clifton's lesser accomplice, Robert Barley, escaped retribution.[258] This was partly because Clifton was an exceptionally tough opponent—*militem capitosum et ferocem nimis*, a former *condottiere* whom the ruling council of Florence considered as a possible replacement for Sir John Hawkwood[259]—but principally because he and his brother were long-standing clients of

[253] *Select Cases*, vii. 190–2; Somerville, p. 382; *CFR 1383–91*, 355; ibid. *1391–9*, 50.

[254] KB 9/989 m. 15; KB 27/529 Rex m. 14*d*; Bodl. MS Gough Yorks. 5 f. 26.

[255] *CCR 1392–6*, 109; *CPR 1391–6*, 237.

[256] KB 27/529 Rex m. 14*d*; Nottinghamshire Record Office, Dd Fj 4/2/1. The partition makes provision for a panel of twelve arbitrators to be chosen by the two parties *'a redresser owelement touz les grevances et damages entre eux faites devant ses heures'*.

[257] KB 9/989 mm. 2, 21.

[258] *CCR 1392–6*, 220.

[259] 'Historiae Croylandensis Continuatio', *Rerum Anglicarum Scriptores Veterum*, ed. W. Fulman (Oxford, 1684), p. 488; J. Temple-Leader and G. Marcotti, *Sir John Hawkwood* (London, 1889), pp. 147, 360–1.

the Holland family, the rising stars of Richard II's court.[260] It was as the steward of Thomas Holland, earl of Kent, in the county that Clifton continued his oppressions in Derbyshire, and a result of the Holland connection that, in 1396, he was retained to stay with the king for life and appointed constable of Bolsover castle, six miles away from the scene of his depredations at Walton.[261] Consequently, Clifton was enabled to establish himself in the Lancastrian heartland of the Peak in independence of the duke's affinity and so to offer an alternative source of protection and lordship to those lesser figures, like Beckering and Barley, who were discontented with the duke's hold over office and power in the county. Once again, the local quarrels of their dependants had set the king and the duke of Lancaster, ostensibly allies at the national level, on opposite sides of a dispute and, when it came to a confrontation, Richard II had shown himself prepared to make few concessions to his uncle.

While John of Gaunt stayed alive there was little danger of a serious clash of interests developing between the royal and Lancastrian affinities. Nevertheless, the king continued to make his preparations. Thomas Holland's growing influence in the Midlands was bolstered by a grant of most of the earl of Warwick's forfeited estates and formalized by his appearance on the Derbyshire peace commission in November 1398.[262] On Gaunt's death, the confiscated honour of Tutbury was placed in his hands and old scores began to be paid off: Thomas Foljambe was removed from the stewardship of the High Peak in March 1399 and in April the sheriff was ordered to arrest him and John Calall, another old enemy of Sir Nicholas Clifton's.[263] These events demonstrate clearly enough the far-reaching consequences of some apparently minor local skirmishes but, if they were the preliminaries in Richard II's plan to break the power of the Lancastrian affinity in the north Midlands by establishing Thomas Holland in John of Gaunt's stead, the plan was flawed from its inception. In Staffordshire, the Holland family were pre-eminently the murderers of Sir Ralph Stafford, and Sir Nicholas Clifton the chief accomplice to the crime. Their rise to power was bound to arouse

[260] J. B. Post, 'Sir Thomas West and the Statute of Rapes, 1382', *BIHR* 53 (1980), 28–9; id., 'Courts, Councils and Arbitrators in the Ladbroke Manor Dispute, 1382–1400', *Medieval Legal Records*, ed. R. F. Hunnisett and J. B. Post (London, 1978), pp. 321–2.
[261] KB 27/531 m. 52*d*; SC 8/223/11128–30; *CPR 1391–6*, 222.
[262] *CPR 1396–9*, 200, 435.
[263] *CPR 1396–9*, 489; *CCR 1396–9*, 450; *CFR 1391–9*, 294.

opposition from the Stafford affinity; Sir Nicholas Stafford, chief steward of the family lands, had already been required to enter into a bond of 6,000 marks to keep the peace towards Thomas Holland.[264]

Nor was the king's open partiality for the palatinate of Chester and its inhabitants likely to win him much support in the northern Midlands, where complaints against the incursions of malefactors from Cheshire were bitter and frequent.[265] The arrival of Henry, duke of Lancaster, provided a rare chance to retaliate and the gentry of the northern Midlands seized it eagerly. Staffordshire and Derbyshire declared overwhelmingly for the Lancastrian cause, despite the inroads made by royal patronage on both counties; over half Henry's force was raised and paid from the honours of Tutbury and the Peak, but only the solitary and irreconcilable John Stathum turned out for Richard II.[266] Partly, this was because in choosing the Hollands as his lieutenants, the king had succeeded in offending the sensibilities of the county community, precisely the group he wished to court; partly, it was because the duke of Lancaster had proved, in the long run, a better patron. John of Gaunt's policy of rapidly increasing his expenditure on annuities in this disordered and volatile area had been expensive but it had been successful in maintaining the local gentry in their traditional loyalty to the house of Lancaster.

At first sight, this survey of the place of the Lancastrian affinity within the respective county communities of Staffordshire and Derbyshire lends weight to the older and darker view of 'bastard feudalism' and its effects. In both counties, Lancastrian retainers can be found committing violent crimes and going unpunished. In Derbyshire, Sir John Cokayn pursued his quarrels with the aid and comfort of his colleagues in the Lancastrian retinue; in Staffordshire, the return of Sir John Bagot and Sir John Ipstones from Spain, newly fortified with the assurance of the duke's protection, did much to disturb the peace of the shire. Nor was John of Gaunt able to restrain or redress the crimes of his followers; in the face of the quarrels that broke out between his retainers in Derbyshire, the duke's claim that he and his fellow magnates could keep order among their own servants looks a little hollow. Whereas, in Lancashire, Gaunt had done his best to keep the peace of the shire in the face of the feuds of the gentry, in

[264] KB 9/167 m. 4; *CCR 1389–92*, 563.
[265] SC 8/139/6906, 6922; *Rot. Parl.*, iii. 81; *CCR 1389–92*, 215.
[266] DL 42/15 ff. 70, 70v; E. 403/562 mm. 14, 15.

Staffordshire he was, in a sense, the aggressor—buying his way into a county community that had previously been the preserve of the earls of Stafford and thereby sowing the seeds of the chronic breakdown in public order that was to affect Staffordshire in Henry IV's reign.[267]

Looked at more closely, however, the exercise of Lancastrian lordship in the northern Midlands was a more complicated and less clear-cut business than this. On the one hand, the initial development of a powerful Lancastrian grouping in the area was an accidental one for, although the level of the duke's annuity payments rose sharply in the honour of Tutbury, it was only the most striking instance of a more general increase in the cost of the duke's retinue after his return from Spain, which the particular circumstances of the northern Midlands served to exaggerate. Tutbury was a rich honour with surplus revenue and consequently a convenient place to assign new fees; the temporary abeyance of most other magnate interests in the area meant there was no lack of good candidates recommending themselves to the duke. On the other hand, the ground had been well prepared for such a development by Gaunt's existing servants, who had already used the additional capital provided by their fees from the duke to buy their way to a new importance in county society. In both cases, the important point is that the real impetus behind the growth of the Lancastrian affinity did not come from the conscious decision of the lord but from the independent and uncoordinated actions of his servants and would-be servants. The growth of Lancastrian lordship, in this case, hardly depended upon the initiative of the lord at all.

This conclusion must be set beside the abundant evidence that, no less than in Lancashire, John of Gaunt often had difficulty in enforcing his will in the northern Midlands. Despite the expensive legal expertise at his command, the Stathum and Coleman cases demonstrate that even the duke of Lancaster, the most powerful magnate in the kingdom, could not expect to have things all his own way when in conflict with individual members of the county gentry. At the local level, a fierce guerilla action over familiar terrain was often enough to keep the big battalions at bay. There were, therefore, definite practical limits to John of Gaunt's authority, and if the duke's lordship could be defied by his opponents, it could also be commandeered by his supporters for their own ends. Thus, in both the Chetwynd/L'Estrange

---

[267] E. Powell, 'Public Order and Law Enforcement in Shropshire and Staffordshire in the Early Fifteenth Century' (unpub. Oxford Univ. D.Phil. thesis, 1979), pp. 285–6.

and Clifton/Foljambe disputes, the king and the duke of Lancaster found themselves driven to opposite sides of the issue by the pressure of their respective followers' expectations and saw, in consequence, their conspicuous concord at the level of national politics sapped away by the actions of their local partisans. The violence which afflicted the northern Midlands appears, at first sight, to have sprung from the classic conjunction of bastard feudalism—competing magnates and opportunistic gentry—but it had more to do with the ambitions of the latter than the unfettered lordship of the former.[268]

[268] I. Rowney, 'Government and Patronage in the Fifteenth Century: Staffordshire 1439–1459', *Midland History*, 8 (1983), pp. 49–69 reaches a similar conclusion at a later period.

'BASTARD FEUDALISM' AND THE LANCASTRIAN AFFINITY

'BUT the duke of Lancaster does what he likes without check' complained one bitter chronicler.[1] The most important conclusion to have emerged from each of these county studies is that, in fact, he did not. The limitations on what a magnate, even a magnate as powerful as John of Gaunt, could and could not do at the local level were very considerable. In the palatinate of Lancaster, where the duke was at his most powerful, some prudential limitations were nevertheless placed upon his lordship by the proportion of the county community that remained outside the Lancastrian affinity and, when he tried to enforce a decision given in his own palatinate court, the duke's authority could still be flouted by a determined gentry opponent who was prepared to resort to violence. There were similar constraints on Gaunt's freedom of action in the northern Midlands, where the king and the earls of Stafford presented attractive alternatives to his lordship and the duke had difficulty in restraining the unruly violence of his own retainers. If this was the case in areas where he held a clear landed pre-eminence, it is no surprise that John of Gaunt was unable to make much impact on the prosperous and cohesive county community in Norfolk or many inroads into the traditional loyalties of the Sussex gentry. Instead, the duke's lordship was too often appropriated by the host of minor officials on whom he relied for the administration of his estates and then abused for their personal advantage. Unjust disseisin, petty extortion, and the deliberate obstruction of administrative process were their stock-in-trade,[2] practices that the duke might seek to restrain by the dismissal of delinquent officials,[3] but that he could hardly hope to eradicate. For

---

[1] *Westminster Chronicle*, p. 518.

[2] E. 28/1 (9 June 1389); Magdalen College, King's Somborne 83, for complaints of unjust disseisin against Lancastrian officials. E. 159/171, Trinity, Adhuc Communia, Adhuc Recorda, for extortion by the receiver and bailiff of Leicester; WAM 32777 for the duke's steward in Gloucestershire protecting a fellow Lancastrian against the claims of the abbot of Westminster.

[3] *Reg. II* 621, 827; DL 43/15/2 m. 2 for measures against Henry Don, steward of Kidwelly.

even the staunchest Lancastrian official might turn against his master, if his own vested interests came under threat. The keeper of the ducal fees in the honour of Knaresborough, Richard Brennand, whose loyalty to Gaunt during the Peasants' Revolt earned him the approving notice of the chroniclers, nevertheless joined the confederacy of William Beckwith against the duke's constable at Knaresborough when the latter sought to intrude outsiders into the honorial administration.[4]

This hardly conforms to the traditional view of the magnate's role in the 'bastard feudal' relationship, nor to the well-documented examples of magnate dominance over a region that have contributed to this view; the overweening local power of the Despensers, the duke of Suffolk's mastery over East Anglia in Henry VI's reign, lord Hastings's control of the Midlands under Edward IV.[5] Nor can it be reconciled with the picture of unbridled local oppression by the great lords and their servants that the parliamentary Commons were anxious to paint, or with the belief of many historians that the relations of clientage and dependence created by 'bastard feudalism' did most damage at the local level.[6] It may be, though, that the conditions in the counties so far examined were exceptional and, perhaps, uniquely unfavourable to the creation of a dominant Lancastrian presence in the shire. In order to set these conclusions in a wider context, it is worth attempting a more general estimate of the impact of the duke's affinity on local society by examining its presence within the formal structures of power. 'A lord's control over county government by nominating the local officers' was, it has been suggested, 'a foremost objective of retaining', since it was only by dominating the local administration that a magnate could really help his men and secure their support.[7] Certainly it was in this respect that the legitimate service a magnate's affinity offered its lord shaded off into the illegitimate manipulation of the processes of local justice and government that has become synonymous with the era of 'bastard feudalism'. Was this true in John of Gaunt's case as well?

[4] *Anonimalle Chronicle*, p. 159; *CPR 1391–6*, 273; Bellamy, 'The Northern Rebellions in the Later Years of Richard II', *BJRL* 49 (1964/5), 256.

[5] N. Saul, 'The Despensers and the Downfall of Edward II', *EHR* 99 (1984), 21–6; R. A. Griffiths, *The Reign of Henry VI* (London, 1981), pp. 584–92; W. H. Dunham, *Lord Hastings' Indentured Retainers, 1461–1483*, Transaction of the Connecticut Academy of Arts and Sciences, 39 (1955), pp. 27–46.

[6] e.g. 'it was probably at the local level that retainers were most important. With them the lord could turn his regional primacy into a civil tyranny . . .'; D. Starkey, 'The Age of the Household', *The Later Middle Ages*, ed. S. Medcalf (London, 1981), p. 266.

[7] C. Carpenter, 'The Beauchamp Affinity: A Study of Bastard Feudalism at Work', *EHR* 95 (1980), 517; Dunham, *Lord Hastings' Indentured Retainers*, p. 29.

In formal terms, the standing of an individual and the prestige of his patron at county level was recognized by his election or appointment to one of the three institutions central to the county's governance: Parliament, the shrievalty, and the commission of the peace. It is the role of John of Gaunt and his affinity in the first of these institutions that has been most carefully scrutinized[8] but the extent of magnate influence on the election of the parliamentary Commons remains, in general, obscure. Earlier in the fourteenth century it was, at best, spasmodic and a great magnate like Thomas of Lancaster preferred to have his men on the streets rather than in the debating-chamber. By the mid-fifteenth century, an influential patron like William, lord Hastings, could secure an impressive attendance by his retainers for the more important Parliaments of Edward IV's reign, but, since too heavy-handed an interference in the shire-election quickly offended the sensibilities of the local gentry, it was an ability he exercised only occasionally.[9] Nevertheless, the 'packing' of Parliament was an accusation levelled against the duke by some of his contemporaries[10] and there was, on the face of it, advantage to be gained from the practice by both Gaunt and his retainers. For the duke, it was clearly a help to have some supporters among the Commons, prepared to put his point of view, in debate and informal discussion, to the other knights and burgesses assembled in the chapter house. For his retainers, the benefits were diverse: an opportunity to pursue private business in the capital at public expense; to promote or suppress petitions to Parliament of direct personal concern; a chance to attract the attention of potential patrons.[11] Parliament was also a time when the duke's council, like the king's, met in afforced session to settle legal difficulties, examine recalcitrant ministers, call in overdue debts. In consequence, there were retainers who might wish the expenses of their journey defrayed as well.[12]

How strong, then, is the evidence that John of Gaunt could regularly secure the return of his retainers to Parliament, whether to further his

---

[8] J. C. Wedgwood, 'John of Gaunt and the Packing of Parliament', *EHR* 45 (1930), 623–5; H. G. Richardson, 'John of Gaunt and the Parliamentary Representation of Lancashire', *BJRL* 22 (1938), 175–222.

[9] J. R. Maddicott, *Thomas of Lancaster* (Oxford, 1970), pp. 51–2; Dunham, *Lord Hastings' Indentured Retainers*, pp. 38–9; M. A. Hicks, *False, Fleeting, Perjur'd Clarence* (Gloucester, 1980), pp. 186–9.

[10] *Chronicon Angliae*, p. 112.

[11] Maddicott, 'Parliament and the Constituencies, 1272–1377', *The English Parliament in the Middle Ages*, ed. R. G. Davies and J. H. Denton (Manchester, 1981), pp. 76–80.

[12] DL 28/3/2 f. 12; *Reg. II* 382; Nottinghamshire Record Office, Dd Fj 9/7/20.

own interests, or to advance theirs? The representation of the duke's affinity in the Commons was thickly concentrated in a handful of counties: in Lancashire, where, between June 1369 and October 1397, 41 Lancastrian servants were returned to the 60 available seats; in Yorkshire (21), Lincolnshire (18),[13] Derbyshire (18), and to a lesser extent in Norfolk, where 12 Lancastrians were returned to the 28 available seats after October 1384.[14] These were the only shires in which the Lancastrian presence was consistent and varied in its personnel; in the other counties with a substantial Lancastrian showing among their MPs, it was the result of the prominence of a single individual, such as Sir Thomas Fogge, returned nine times for Kent, or Sir William Bagot, returned thirteen times for Warwickshire, rather than an expression of the collective strength of the affinity in the shire. In total, therefore, the duke's affinity was large enough and influential enough to maintain a consistent influence on the Parliamentary representation of 5 of the 36 counties that returned MPs. Such a figure serves to emphasize the personal predominance John of Gaunt enjoyed among his peers; other magnates could dominate the representation of a single county, as the Beauchamps did in Worcestershire,[15] but no one else could expect his Parliamentary influence to spread so widely. At the same time, the proportion of Lancastrians returned to the Commons in Yorkshire, Lincolnshire, and Derbyshire—one retainer to every three seats—suggests that, even in its heartland, the duke's affinity never monopolized Parliamentary representation. The electoral suffrages of the county gentry could be solicited but they could not be commanded, and the duke was careful not to press his advantage too far.

There was, nevertheless, a sizeable Lancastrian presence in every Parliament—as few as 3 MPs in October 1372, as many as 13 in January 1394 and September 1397.[16] Between these poles the precise

---

[13] J. S. Roskell, 'The Parliamentary Representation of Lincolnshire During the Reigns of Richard II, Henry IV and Henry V', *Nottingham Medieval Studies*, 3 (1959), 63–6.

[14] *Return of Members of Parliament*, pp. 181–257. For full refs. see S. K. Walker, 'John of Gaunt and his Retainers, 1361–1399' (unpub. Oxford Univ. D.Phil. thesis, 1986), p. 83.

[15] J. T. Driver, 'The Knights of the Shire for Worcestershire', *Transactions of the Worcestershire Archaeological Society*, NS 40 (1963), 54.

[16] Oct. 1372: John Botiller (Lancs.); John Dymoke (Lincolnshire); Alured Sulny (Derby.). Jan. 1394: Richard Abberbury (Berks.); William Bagot (War.); Thomas Bedford (Bedford borough); John Bussy (Lincolnshire); Henry Green (Northants); John Ipstones (Staffs.); Robert Neville (Yorks.); John de la Pole (Derby.); John Rocheford

number of the duke's followers present in any one Parliament fluctuated, but the general movement was always upward—5 or 6 in every session in the 1370s, usually 7 or 8 in the 1380s, reaching a peak of 10 to 12 in the 1390s. This was a highly respectable showing, closely comparable with the representation of the royal affinity in the Commons until Richard II's expansion of his following during the early 1390s began to push up the number of his servants in Parliament.[17] With a few exceptions,[18] Gaunt's men were returned as knights of the shire and, since it was the shire knights who always took the leading role in the debates of the Commons, the duke clearly had considerable opportunity to influence their decisions through the advocacy of his followers. Yet it remains uncertain whether this was a state of affairs the duke ever actively sought, and what evidence there is tells against the idea. The Lancastrian presence in the complaisant Parliament of January 1377, around which most of the accusations of 'packing' made against Gaunt have centred, was only slightly greater than among the Commons who, in the preceding Parliament, had given the duke such a turbulent time.[19] Throughout Richard II's reign, there is no sign of the kind of continuity that betokens deliberate policy in the election of the duke's retainers,[20] while the fluctuating number of Lancastrians from Parliament to Parliament bears no discernible relationship to his immediate political concerns. Thus, in Parliaments convened to discuss the duke's proposals for the conduct of the war with France, the turn-out of his retainers was never particularly high—

(Lincolnshire); Robert Urswick (Lancs.); Thomas Walsh (Leics.); John White (Norf.); Thomas Wennesley (Derby.). Sept. 1397: John Bathe (Dorset); John Bagot (Staffs.); William Bagot (War.); John Botiller (Lancs.); John Bussy (Lincolnshire); Richard Chelmeswyk (Salop); John Dabridgecourt (Derby.); John Englefield (Berks.); Henry Green (Wilts.); Robert Morton (Notts.); Thomas Rempston (Notts.); John Rocheford (Lincolnshire); David Rowcliffe (Yorks.). Note, however, that at least seven of these men also received an annuity from the king.

[17] Given-Wilson, *The Royal Household and the King's Affinity*, pp. 246–8.

[18] Thomas Bedford, the duke's attorney in King's Bench, sat for Bedford borough (Jan. 1393, Jan. 1394, Jan. 1395, Jan. 1397); John Hacon, the duke's shipman, represented Great Yarmouth (Oct. 1385, Nov. 1391, Jan. 1393); William Wintringham, his carpenter, sat for Southwark (Oct. 1377, Jan. 1390).

[19] Apr. 1376: Sir Edmund Appleby (Derby.); Roger Brockholes (Lancs.); Thomas Fogge (Kent); John Saville (Yorks.). Jan. 1377: John Botiller (Lancs.); William Chetwynd (Salop); Nicholas Green (Rutl.); Thomas Hungerford (Wilts.); Robert Neville (Yorks.); John Rocheford (Lincolnshire); John Seynclere (Sussex).

[20] N. B. Lewis, 'Re-election to Parliament in the Reign of Richard II', *EHR* 48 (1933), 391.

5 Lancastrians were returned in September 1381, when the duke made his proffer to wage war against the French on his own account, and an average 8 were elected in October 1385, when the Commons were finally persuaded to endorse the 'way of Spain'.[21] Finally, while contemporary accusations of 'packing' concentrated principally on the role of the sheriff in returning his own candidate without the assent of the full county court,[22] the conduct of Lancastrian sheriffs in this regard seems largely, if not entirely, blameless. In all, retainers or ministers of the duke made 108 Parliamentary returns while sheriffs of their respective counties and returned a colleague in the Lancastrian affinity on only 16 occasions. The majority of these 16 returns were, in addition, unexceptional[23] so that it is only the successive Lancastrian returns made in Lincolnshire by Sir Ralph Paynel and the return of a novice MP, William Hervey, by his fellow Lancastrian, Thomas Bridges, in Gloucestershire that look at all suspicious.[24]

Such investigations are, in any case, probably over-ingenious. Membership of the Lancastrian affinity was, by itself, enough to gain a retainer a seat in Parliament, since the knowledge of a man's connection with the duke and his consequently enhanced ability to get things done at Westminster on behalf of the county community could alone be expected to sway the suitors of the shire court in their choice of representative. If John of Gaunt exercised any influence on the composition of the Commons, it lay in his initial decision as to who should receive the endorsement of his standing and abilities implicit in the grant of an annuity or indenture, not in the more complicated but less plausible devices alleged against him by the chroniclers. This conclusion receives some support from an examination of the duke's policy towards the shrievalty. The sheriff's role in Parliamentary elections was only one of the many duties which rendered the office vital to the effective execution of local government. Responsible for

---

[21] *Return of Members of Parliament*, pp. 207–9, 225–7.

[22] *Rot. Parl.*, ii. 355, iii. 235; Walsingham, *Hist. Ang.*, ii. 161.

[23] e.g. Sir Robert Neville of Hornby was returned for Yorkshire by a Lancastrian sheriff on 4 occasions—by Sir Ralph Hastings in Jan. 1377, Oct. 1377, and Sept. 1381; by Sir John Saville in Nov. 1383—but the majority of his 12 returns to Parliament were made by non-Lancastrians. Six more of the 16 returns took place in Derbyshire, where the level of Lancastrian representation was always high.

[24] Paynel returned Sir John Rocheford to the Jan. 1377 Parliament and Sir John Dymoke in Oct. 1377; Hervey was elected an MP for Gloucestershire in Oct. 1386 but did not act as a commissioner in the county until 1388. *CPR 1385–9*, 322; *CIM 1377–88*, no. 387.

commanding the *posse comitatus*,[25] administering and returning all writs, summoning offenders, empanelling juries, and initiating outlawries, his position gave him wide-ranging control over the affairs of the shire and ample opportunity to show favour to his friends or to do the will of his patrons.[26] Magnate influence on the choice of sheriff was, in addition, more direct than it could ever be over the election of shire knights since John of Gaunt, at least, could gain the removal of an unsatisfactory incumbent by direct application to the Chancellor.[27] In consequence, the shrievalty was ideally suited to serve as an instrument of magnate influence over the counties and, if that was ever the duke's intention, the evidence for it is most probably to be found in the personnel of the shrievalty.

In fact, the pattern of Lancastrian influence on the office closely resembles the representation of the affinity in Parliament. Twenty-four of the duke's retainers served as sheriff while in his service, which was enough to give him an appreciable and consistent influence over the counties of Yorkshire (where 4 retainers held office for 7½ years between 1376 and 1399), Lincolnshire (where 4 retainers held office for 6½ years during the same period), and the combined bailiwick of Nottinghamshire and Derbyshire (where 6 retainers held office for 7½ years between 1372 and 1399).[28] In Gloucestershire, where three Lancastrians had engaged in a sharp struggle for the office during 1385, their allegiance to the duke was incidental to the dispute and it

---

[25] E. 404/13/88 (10 June 1384)—Robert Hilton, sheriff of Yorkshire, led 600 archers of the county on John of Gaunt's expedition to Scotland.

[26] *The Stonor Letters and Papers, 1290–1483*, ed. C. L. Kingsford (Camden Soc., 3rd series, 29, 1919), pp. 7–17 give an indication of the range of a contemporary sheriff's duties.

[27] SC 1/40/178; C 81/1355/60. The unsatisfactory sheriff, Thomas Whitton, was a minor official who secured his appointment to the Shropshire shrievalty while representing the county in the Parliament of Nov. 1390. The grounds were probably his failure to fulfil the necessary property qualification—*CFR 1369–77*, 229, 269; ibid. *1377–83*, 55, 143; *CCR 1389–92*, 306; *CFR 1383–91*, 341.

[28] *List of Sheriffs for England and Wales*, pp. 79, 103, 162. Yorks.: Sir Ralph Hastings (Oct. 1376–Nov. 1377, Oct. 1380–Dec. 1381); Sir Robert Neville (Nov. 1378–Nov. 1379, Dec. 1396–Nov. 1397); Sir John Saville (Mar. 1380–Oct. 1380, Nov. 1382–Nov. 1383, Nov. 1387–Dec. 1388); Sir Gerard Usflete (Nov. 1384–Oct. 1385). Lincs: Sir John Bussy (Nov. 1383–Nov. 1384, Oct. 1385–Nov. 1386, Nov. 1390–Oct. 1391); Sir Ralph Paynel (Oct. 1376–Nov. 1377); John Rocheford (Oct. 1391–Oct. 1392); William de Spaigne (Nov. 1378–Nov. 1379, Nov. 1384–May 1385); Notts. and Derby.: Hugh de Annesley (Oct. 1380–Nov. 1381); John Loudham (Dec. 1388–Nov. 1389); Sir Nicholas Montgomery (Mar. 1391–Oct. 1391); Robert Morton (Oct. 1376–Nov. 1377, Nov. 1397–Aug. 1399); Sir Thomas Rempston (Nov. 1393–Nov. 1394); Sir Alured Sulny (Dec. 1372–Nov. 1373).

was to the king, not John of Gaunt, that the contestants looked for support.[29] These figures are impressive, given that a family of minor nobility like the Berkleys could not exert so much influence on the shrievalty of their home county,[30] but as clearly as an examination of the pattern of Lancastrian representation in Parliament, they indicate that even an affinity as large and expensive as John of Gaunt's was limited to three or four counties in the geographical range of its consistent administrative influence.

The shrievalty was influential, but it was also burdensome and expensive, capable of leaving an incumbent seriously out of pocket.[31] It may not, in consequence, have been a post that many retainers were anxious to fill. No such disadvantage attached to the commissions of the peace. A justice did not wield the same power as a sheriff but the appointment allowed him considerable discretion in the administration of local justice and brought with it a certain social prestige, acknowledgement as one of the '*mieux vauteez des contees*', which made the Commons anxious to maintain control of the appointments to the peace commissions themselves.[32] Occasionally their wish was granted, but more usually the justices were nominated by the chancellor and treasurer, in consultation with the Council. In consequence, the composition of each county bench was open to magnate influence[33] and, like his peers, John of Gaunt was not slow to take advantage of this. The chief stewards of the duchy were appointed to commissions of the peace far away from their native counties;[34] stewards of individual honours, such as Leicester, were appointed to the commission in the county where they exercised their seigneurial function[35] and the duke made, in addition, frequent applications to the chancellor to have his men associated with existing commissions.[36]

---

[29] *List of Sheriffs for England and Wales*, p. 50; C 81/1343/75, 1344/8, 1347/20, 1348/5.

[30] N. Saul, *Knights and Esquires* (Oxford, 1981), pp. 153–4.

[31] *Rot. Parl.*, iii. 96, 116, 211–12.

[32] *Proceedings Before the Justices of the Peace in the Fourteenth and Fifteenth Centuries*, ed. B. H. Putnam (London, 1938), pp. xlv–cxii; *Rot. Parl.*, ii. 151.

[33] *Proceedings Before the Justices of the Peace*, p. lxxviii; see above, p. 211.

[34] Sir Thomas Hungerford appeared on commissions of the peace in Norfolk, Lancs., and Lincs.; William de Nessfield on the Lancs. bench after his appointment as chief steward in the North parts. *CPR 1374–7*, 154, 157, 490; ibid. *1377–81*, 46, 96; *DKR* xliii. 363; *CPR 1367–70*, 418, 428.

[35] G. G. Astill, 'The Medieval Gentry: A Study in Leicestershire Society 1350–1399' (unpub. Birmingham Univ. Ph.D. thesis, 1977), p. 165.

[36] e.g. Sir Godfrey Foljambe, Simon Simeon, and Roger Toup were all associated with the Lincs. commissions in the space of two years—*CPR 1367–70*, 429; ibid. *1370–4*, 35, 306.

Lancaster was clearly anxious to see his men on the county benches but, from his own point of view, it is not immediately clear what was to be gained by such appointments. The powers of the justices were admittedly extensive, but they were ineffective as an instrument of lordship since, when indicted before the justices of the peace, the powerful seldom experienced difficulty in getting their cases removed to a higher court.[37] To deal with serious crimes against his estates and officials, the duke preferred to sue out special commissions of oyer and terminer endowed with exceptionally wide powers, such as those he led into Yorkshire in September 1382 and July 1390,[38] rather than to put his faith in the local justices. While lesser offences against his lands could be summarily dealt with by the commissions of the peace,[39] the regular entertainment and occasional payments given by the duke's estate officials to the justices[40] meant that it was hardly necessary to have his own retainers sitting on a case in order to secure a favourable verdict.

Whether the duke's retainers would have sat is, in any case, open to question. Whatever the composition of the commissions issued by the chancery, the actual execution of their work was in the hands of a much smaller group of active justices. In consequence, it is only by examining the composition of this inner circle of county administrators that the *practical* effect of the Lancastrian affinity on the administration of justice in the counties can be gauged. The Lincolnshire evidence well illustrates the gulf between theory and practice. In the parts of Holland, 6 commissions were issued to a total of 23 justices between 1381 and 1396; 7 commissions were issued to 37 justices in Lindsey during the same period. In both cases, there were 11 Lancastrian retainers, estate officials, or palatinate law-officers on the commissions, but the proportion of Lancastrians among the active justices differs markedly. In Holland, 4 out of the 6 justices known to have sat

---

[37] *Yorkshire Sessions of the Peace, 1361–1364*, ed. B. H. Putnam (Yorks. Arch. Soc., 100, 1939), p. xxxv; *Rolls of the Gloucestershire Sessions of the Peace, 1361–1398*, ed. E. G. Kimball (Trans. Bristol and Gloucs. Arch. Soc., 62, 1940), p. 42.

[38] JUST 1/1138, *CCR 1381–5*, 154, J. G. Bellamy, *The Law of Treason in England in the Later Middle Ages* (Cambridge, 1970), p. 149 (1382); *Historia Vitae et Regni Ricardi Secundi*, ed. G. B. Stow (Philadelphia, 1977), p. 131, *Westminster Chronicle*, p. 442 (1390).

[39] e.g. *Records of Some Sessions of the Peace in Lincolnshire, 1360–1375*, ed. R. Sillem (Lincoln Record Soc., 30, 1936), p. 78 (338); *Records of Some Sessions of the Peace in Lincolnshire, 1381–1396*, ed. E. G. Kimball (Lincoln Record Soc., 56, 1962), pp. 79 (229), 97 (284), 135 (306).

[40] *Reg. I* 1697; DL 28/3/2 f. 19; DL 29/212/3247 m. 3; Norfolk Record Office, NRS 3342 m. 2d.

were Lancastrians; in Lindsey only 1 out of 11.[41] Thus, the duke's affinity virtually controlled the sessions of the peace in Holland whereas in Lindsey it hardly appears at all, although the surviving presentments of concern to the duke and most of the Lancastrian lands in Lincolnshire lay there. Elsewhere, the record of the duke's retainers is just as unpredictable. Sir Thomas Metham was the least diligent of the busy Yorkshire justices between 1361 and 1364; in Warwickshire, John Rous of Ragley sat only once in thirty sessions; the surviving records of the justices in Nottinghamshire, Wiltshire, Worcestershire, and the East Riding of Yorkshire during Richard II's reign provide no evidence that the Lancastrians named in the commissions ever sat.[42] In the West Riding, by contrast, Lancastrians dominated the commission and in Lincolnshire much of the bench's work between 1360 and 1375 was done by central justices known to have been fee'd by the duke.[43] A Lancastrian connection might, therefore, get a retainer nominated to the commission of the peace but it seems to have had little further effect on his behaviour. If he was already closely involved in the administration of the county, as an estate official like Edmund Gournay was in Norfolk, then he would continue to be so. If he was not, an indenture with the duke did not entail additional or unaccustomed involvement in the administration of local justice.

This was a state of affairs that suited most of the duke's retainers. For them, a place on the commission of the peace was valuable as an expression of their standing within the county and for the honourable appearance of power it conferred. John Rous of Ragley, for instance, attended his only recorded session of the Warwickshire bench when his lord, the duke of Lancaster, was there as well.[44] Both lord and man drew advantage from the occasion. For the duke, the Coventry session provided a useful opportunity to cement the friendly relations he already enjoyed with the townsmen.[45] For his retainer, it was a public

[41] *Records of Some Sessions of the Peace in Lincolnshire, 1381–1396*, ed. Kimball, pp. xxiv–xxvi.

[42] *Yorkshire Sessions of the Peace, 1361–1364*, pp. xl, xlviii; *Rolls of the Warwickshire and Coventry Sessions of the Peace, 1377–1397*, ed. E. G. Kimball (Dugdale Soc., 16, 1939), p. xliv; *Proceedings Before the Justices of the Peace*, pp. 147–8, 400, 421, 462–3.

[43] *Proceedings Before the Justices of the Peace*, pp. 462–3; *Records of Some Sessions of the Peace in Lincolnshire, 1360–1375*, pp. xxix–xxx.

[44] *Rolls of the Warwickshire Sessions*, pp. xxxiii, 95.

[45] *The Register of the Guild of the Holy Trinity, St Mary, St John the Baptist and St Katherine of Coventry*, ed. M. D. Harris (Dugdale Soc., 13, 1935), p. 26.

demonstration of the favour in which he stood with a great lord that could not but enhance his local standing. Appointment as a justice of the peace and the chance 'to be captaine or a ruler at a session or a shire day'[46] was thus one of the many benefits a retainer looked for from his lord. In consequence, the abundant evidence of the duke's concern for the composition of the peace commissions may be thought to express as much the expectations of his clients as his own needs.

In this area of local government, at least, the duke was in a position to secure for the members of his affinity something they wanted. Yet, in contrast to the Parliamentary presence of the duke's servants, the commissions of the peace saw an absolute decline in the number of Lancastrians appointed to them during Richard II's reign. Thus, when new commissions were issued for every county in December 1382, Gaunt himself headed 13 of them and 35 of his retainers appeared in a total of 29 counties.[47] At the next general overhaul of the peace commissions, made in July 1389, the picture is very different: only 6 Lancastrian retainers were appointed as justices in 5 counties and, when new commissions were issued in the following November, the Lancastrian presence increased only slightly to 9 retainers appearing in 7 counties.[48] This drastic reduction of the number of the duke's retainers on the commissions was largely a result of circumstance, rather than political malice or constitutional principle. The deliberate halving of the gentry membership of each commission in July 1389[49] inevitably thinned the ranks of Lancastrian justices and, since the duke and his household were still out of the country, the remainder of his affinity could not expect a very generous allocation of seats. On the duke's return to England, the number of his retainers acting as justices predictably increased, principally as a result of the repeal of the Cambridge statute excluding magnate stewards from the commissions. When the June 1390 commissions were issued, 16 Lancastrians were appointed in 14 counties and the December commissions, on which the duke himself reappeared in 18 counties, brought the number of his retainers appointed as justices up to 18. The affinity's representation on the peace commissions remained at this level. In June 1394, the

---

[46] *The Boke of Noblesse*, ed. J. G. Nichols (Roxburghe Club, 77, 1860), p. 78.

[47] *CPR 1381–5*, 251–4. For full refs., see S. K. Walker, 'John of Gaunt and His Retainers, 1361–1399', pp. 91–3.

[48] *CPR 1388–92*, 135–9.

[49] R. L. Storey, 'Liveries and Commissions of the Peace, 1388–90', *The Reign of Richard II*, ed. F. R. H. du Boulay and C. M. Barron, p. 138.

next general review of the commissions, 16 Lancastrians were appointed in 15 counties and in November 1397 19 retainers appeared on the commissions in 21 counties.[50]

There are two general conclusions to be drawn from these figures. Firstly, although a reduction in the number of magnate dependants on the commissions of the peace was one of the avowed aims of the Cambridge statute regulating their composition, the Lancastrian affinity was clearly hit particularly hard by the reforms which the statute initiated. The physical presence and political weight of the duke succeeded in restoring to his affinity a reasonable measure of representation but his retainers were never again as ubiquitous on the commissions of the peace as they once had been. The honourable pre-eminence which the Council was prepared to allow John of Gaunt—who headed 13 commissions in 1382, 18 in 1390, 19 in 1394, and 22 in 1397—was not extended to his followers. Secondly, although the Commons' political success on the question of the powers and composition of the peace commission was transitory,[51] their effort to reduce the degree of favouritism and bribery in the choice of justices produced some more lasting effect. Even after Gaunt's return to England restored the numbers of his affinity on the commissions of the peace to an acceptable level, his dependants were never as numerous in the 1390s as they had been in the previous decade. Lancastrian representation was largely restricted to counties where it was justified by the duke's territorial power; his chief stewards were no longer appointed to commissions outside their own counties by virtue of their office; the practice of associating individuals with the original justices was brought to an end. In all probability, the duke's ability to influence the course of justice remained undiminished by these changes. What *was* affected was his ability to nominate his own men to positions of local prominence, coveted by the county gentry, and in so far as the parliamentary Commons' campaign was aimed at controlling precisely this, it may be accounted successful.

A general consideration of the Lancastrian affinity's presence in these areas of local and national government—Parliament, the shrievalty, the commissions of the peace—thus seems to confirm the conclusion arrived at from a close study of that affinity's influence in particular counties. While the duke's servants maintained a definite interest in every aspect of administration that mattered to them, their

---

[50] *CPR 1388–92*, 341–3, 344–5; ibid. *1391–6*, 434–41; ibid. *1396–9*, 230–9.

[51] Storey, 'Liveries and Commissions of the Peace', pp. 148–9.

presence there never constituted a monopoly and their predominance could, at times, be undermined by the corporate protest of an increasingly assertive Commons. The independence the county gentry displayed, at the local level, in their dealings with John of Gaunt and his servants, had its counterpart in the independence of the shires' representatives in Parliament; their considerable local autonomy is reflected, at the national level, in their ability to restrict the opportunities for a display of favour and influence that nomination to a coveted position on the commission of the peace had formerly offered the duke and his fellow magnates. This leaves one central question to be answered: why was Gaunt, pre-eminent though he was in power and wealth, unable to convert his undoubted political and financial resources into effective local authority?

One recent answer to this question has emphasized the courtly, chivalric nature of the duke's ambitions and concluded that they often led him to recruit retainers without much weight or standing in local society. Gaunt's exceptional wealth and the rich store of offices available to him in the palatinate of Lancaster meant, in turn, that the duke was largely capable of satisfying the demands for patronage these retainers made upon him without having to 'politicize' his affinity, either at the national or local level, by resorting to the extra-legal inducements to loyalty some lesser magnates offered their men.[52] While there is certainly some truth in the first part of this analysis, it is far from a complete answer. Despite its primarily military purpose, the Lancastrian affinity still included many knights and esquires of considerable local importance, not all of whom forbore from invoking the duke's lordship on their own behalf. Nor, as we have seen, did John of Gaunt's efforts at containing the private ambitions of his followers within the bounds of legality always meet with success. For this reason, the composition and behaviour of the Lancastrian affinity should not be dismissed as 'old-fashioned and irrelevant'[53] to the development of later medieval lordship. Examined more closely, the reasons for the relative impotence of John of Gaunt and his retainers at the local level have much of interest to say about contemporary English society.

In the first place, allowance must be made for the duke's exalted position within that society. Even his enemies acknowledged him to be

---

[52] A. Goodman, 'John of Gaunt: Paradigm of the Late Fourteenth-Century Crisis', *TRHS* 5th series, 37 (1987), 146–7.
[53] Ibid. 148.

'the greatest lord and most high person in the kingdom after the lord king',[54] but the duke was constrained by his very pre-eminence. A lesser figure, such as John, lord Lovell of Titchmarsh,[55] could afford to flout the law by his local oppressions but John of Gaunt was the object of constant and envious scrutiny and, as uncle to the king, he had to remain above reproach, if not above suspicion. Too public an involvement in local maintenance on a magnate's part could be both temporarily embarrassing and, in the longer run, politically damaging. Although Edward Courtenay, earl of Devon, managed, by throwing himself on the mercy of the king and the lords, to escape with impunity when he was brought before the Council in 1392 on charges of maintenance and embracery, his misdemeanour nevertheless allowed John Holland, earl of Huntingdon, an important opportunity to undermine the Courtenays' long-held ascendancy in Devon.[56]

Secondly, some account must be taken of the nature of the Lancastrian affinity. In size, it was perhaps the largest ever known in medieval England, certainly the largest active during Richard II's reign, but the duke's adherents, like his estates, were scattered all over the country. In consequence, Gaunt was only occasionally able to exercise the dominating influence on the life of a single county that the Courtenays could exercise in Devon, the Percies in Northumberland, or, to a lesser extent, the Berkleys in Gloucestershire.[57] If there is a distinction to be made in the types of late medieval lordship—one type consisting of links between lords and gentry who resided locally, the other a looser network of connections between the great magnates of the realm and gentlemen residing in nearly every county in England— then Gaunt's lordship was clearly of the second sort. Yet in terms of local politics, it was the first type of affinity that proved the most consistently influential. Although no contemporary magnate could match the Lancastrian rent-roll or the duke's expenditure on retaining

---

[54] *Reg. II* 1243.

[55] SC 8/63/3111, 121/6038; BL Add. Ch. 14713; *CPR 1391–6*, 79, 238, for allegations of maintenance against Lovell. K. B. McFarlane, *The Nobility of Later Medieval England* (Oxford, 1973), p. 117 n. 2 for an example of the embracery practised by him.

[56] *Select Cases Before the King's Council 1243–1482*, ed. I. S. Leadam and J. F. Baldwin (Selden Soc., 35, 1918), pp. 77–81; M. Cherry, 'The Courtenay Earls of Devon: Formation and Disintegration of a Late Medieval Aristocratic Affinity', *Southern History*, 1 (1979), 90–1.

[57] Cherry, op. cit. 71–97; J. A. Tuck, 'Richard II and the Border Magnates', *Northern History*, 3 (1968), 33–4; N. Saul, *Knights and Esquires* (Oxford, 1981), pp. 60–105.

fees, the example of the Staffords suggests clearly enough that local residence and constant contact with the shire gentry were more effective in building a county-based affinity than sheer wealth. In the absence of any serious local competitor there *were* some counties, such as Lancashire, Derbyshire, and the West Riding, where the duke could act as the power-broker but, in general, the very nature of the Lancastrian affinity, designed principally to meet the demands of military service abroad and court-ceremonial at home, reduced its effectiveness as an instrument of local politics.

For it was the world of the court, not the county, that primarily interested John of Gaunt. As the titular king of Castile, it was essential that he be surrounded by a large and imposing escort. As Richard II's uncle, there were times when his political position was precarious enough to justify a large armed following—when the Savoy was attacked by the citizens of London in 1377; during his confrontations with the earl of Northumberland in 1381 and with the king himself in 1385.[58] Equally, during the final years of the duke's life the size of his indentured retinue became a form of political insurance, designed to deter the volatile Richard II from any sudden strike against his family.[59] It was principally for such services that John of Gaunt was prepared to maintain so large a following. This did not mean that he could neglect the local standing of his affinity, only that it was not his overriding concern; county quarrels and national politics could never be entirely divorced. Those who resented the duke's local pre-eminence were eager to take advantage of any weakness in his national standing; political considerations might determine Gaunt's own attitude to the disputes of his followers.

The political role of the Lancastrian affinity needs, though, to be carefully defined. It used to be suggested that the duke's great retinue was the essential precondition of his political dominance, since his policies would have carried little weight 'unless supported by a strong Lancastrian party in the country', the nucleus of which 'was Gaunt's own household and retinue'.[60] Such a view now seems to rest on a misunderstanding of both the nature of fourteenth-century politics and the duke's own ambitions. No 'Lancastrian party', in the sense of a

---

[58] *Chronicon Angliae*, pp. 123–4; Walsingham, *Hist. Ang.*, ii. 44–5, *Anonimalle Chronicle*, p. 155; *Westminster Chronicle*, pp. 112–14.

[59] See above, pp. 36–7, 177–8.

[60] M. V. Clarke, 'The Lancastrian Faction and the Wonderful Parliament', *Fourteenth Century Studies* (Oxford, 1937), pp. 36–7.

permanently organized political grouping, ever existed.[61] John of Gaunt's considerable influence over the decisions of government was dependent upon his strength of character and pre-eminence of birth among the English nobility rather than any coherent or continuous political support. Indeed, one of the benefits of maintaining so large a following was that it exempted the duke, to some extent, from the need to engage in politics at all. During his adult life, Gaunt managed to fall out with, or insult, a remarkably high proportion of the upper nobility —Richard, earl of Arundel; Henry Percy, earl of Northumberland; Roger Mortimer, earl of March; Thomas Mowbray, duke of Norfolk; Edward, lord Despenser, and the family of the Courtenay earls of Devon.[62] Even his own brothers were, at times, in bitter dispute with him; Thomas of Woodstock over the disposition of the Bohun inheritance, Edmund of Langley over the duke's abrupt and unilateral surrender of their joint-rights to the throne of Castile.[63] Much of this acrimony must be ascribed to Gaunt's overbearing personality—the temporal lords went in constant fear of him; his demeanour in Council was said to be so threatening that no one else dared speak.[64] But it was the size of his rent-roll and affinity, and the assurance of adequate support even in the face of royal displeasure that they brought with them, that allowed the duke to indulge his dislikes so freely.

Yet when John of Gaunt and his fellow peers, so dominant at the national level, sought to impose their wills on a particular locality, they often found their lordship confined and constrained by the very nature of the local communities in which they had to involve themselves. Each county contained a considerable body of gentry who could claim, on the grounds of wealth alone, some say in the running of the shire. Exactly how large this body was is problematic; estimates of the size of the county community have fluctuated very considerably and it is hard to establish any uniform standard of assessment.[65] The graded poll-tax

---

[61] R. H. Jones, *The Royal Policy of Richard II* (Oxford, 1968), pp. 187–90.

[62] Arundel: see above, p. 140; Northumberland: S. Armitage-Smith, *John of Gaunt* (London, 1904), pp. 252–9; March: W. Dugdale, *Monasticon Anglicanum* (London, 1846–9), vi. 354; Norfolk: *Chronicon Adae de Usk*, p. 169; Despenser: *Chronica Johannis de Reading et Anonymi Cantuariensis*, p. 175; Courtenay: *Chronicon Angliae*, p. 120; *Westminster Chronicle*, p. 37.

[63] G. A. Holmes, *The Estates of the Higher Nobility*, p. 25; SC 8/103/5145.

[64] *Westminster Chronicle*, p. 112; *Rot. Parl.*, iii. 313.

[65] A rough estimate of around 50 gentlemen active in most counties at any one time could, nevertheless, be hazarded. The incomplete subsidy assessment for Staffordshire in 1332 shows 44 families with an estimated income over £20 p.a.; Saul estimates there were about 50 gentry families in mid-fourteenth-century Gloucestershire; Astill

returns of 1379 establish the necessary distinctions of status but their survival is so fragmentary that the best indication available for the size of the county communities in Richard II's reign is provided by the assessments for the 1412 subsidy.[66] The assessments themselves were made by the hundred juries and are consequently liable to err on the parsimonious side but they reveal, none the less, impressively large numbers of men with incomes over £20 p.a. in most counties: 144 in Somerset, 122 in Kent, 95 in Devonshire, 90 in Wiltshire. These counties were, admittedly, exceptional; Kent shared in the prosperity of London, and the counties of the South-West were benefiting from the expansion of the rural cloth industry. But the number of gentlemen in more exclusively agricultural counties was still substantial: 70 in Sussex, 61 in Northamptonshire,[67] 51 in Cambridgeshire. Even a poor northern county like Derbyshire could produce 44 gentlemen with land worth more than £20 p.a. The returns of the graduated income tax of 1436 tell much the same story; below the rank of baron, 933 gentlemen enjoyed incomes over £40 p.a., with approximately 1,200 more gentry in the £20 to £40 bracket.[68]

Taken in conjunction with the estimates given for the size of the county communities in Norfolk and Lancashire, these figures suggest that, at a conservative estimate, there were between 50 and 70 substantial to middling gentlemen active in most counties most of the time. If this is the case, it means that even the most prodigal of magnates could have little expectation of employing more than a small fraction of the politically significant within a shire. In the West Riding of Yorkshire, for instance, the returns of the graded poll-tax of 1379

identifies 47 knightly families active in Leicestershire during the century; Virgoe suggests there were between 40 and 50 active administrators in Norfolk and Suffolk, drawn from a group of gentry approximately twice that size, in Richard II's reign; Wright calculates there were 52 families of 'upper gentry' status in fifteenth-century Derbyshire; Bennett estimates that there were around 40 knightly families 'of the first rank' in late fourteenth-century Lancashire, and rather more in Cheshire. R. H. Hilton, 'Lord and Peasant in Staffordshire in the Middle Ages', *North Staffordshire Journal of Field Studies*, 10 (1970), 2; N. Saul, *Knights and Esquires*, p. 34; G. G. Astill, 'The Medieval Gentry: A Study in Leicestershire Society 1350–1399' (unpub. Birmingham Univ. Ph.D. thesis, 1977), p. 6; Roger Virgoe, 'The Crown and Local Government: East Anglia under Richard II', *The Reign of Richard II*, ed. F. R. H. du Boulay and C. M. Barron (London, 1971), p. 228; S. M. Wright, *The Derbyshire Gentry in the Fifteenth Century* (Derbyshire Record Soc., 8, 1983), p. 5; M. J. Bennett, *Community, Class and Careerism* (Cambridge, 1983), p. 82.

[66] *Feudal Aids*, vi. 391–501, 503–51.

[67] The returns for Northamptonshire were incomplete.

[68] H. L. Gray, 'Incomes from Land in England in 1436', *EHR* 49 (1934), 630.

show 30 knights, 22 esquires eligible for knighthood, and 5 widows of knights-bachelor paying the tax at the top rate of 20*s*. a head. Only 5 of the knights, 2 esquires, and 1 widow of a knight-bachelor had a Lancastrian connection, despite the presence of the twin duchy honours of Pontefract and Tickhill within the Riding.[69] Most noblemen were, in any case, far less lavish than John of Gaunt in their distribution of fees. If the payment of annuities rarely absorbed more than 10 per cent of a late-medieval magnate's income,[70] the following that could be maintained on that sort of a sum was not large. Richard, earl of Warwick, paid fees to 6 knights and 33 other servants in 1396–7, for instance, while the retinue of John, lord Talbot, was about 20 strong while he was a young man, expanding to 35 in the last years of his life. Even Edmund, duke of York, uncle to Richard II, apparently had fewer than 40 retainers.[71] Some magnates, moreover, used these fees to attract yeomen, rather than gentlemen, to their service.[72]

Numbers alone, therefore, made it difficult for any magnate to control and dominate a county single-handed and these substantial bodies of gentry were also bound together by a spirit of corporate solidarity born of the administrative and judicial chores the men of the county had long been required to perform.[73] The 'vertical' relations between magnates and gentry were only one element in the pattern of county politics; the demands of family, kindred, and locality could be as strong, often stronger. 'To follow, not to force, the bent of the county . . .'[74] was already the only realistic solution when dealing with the local gentry who, left to themselves—and it seems that in many counties the gentry *were* left to themselves[75]—were quite capable of

[69] 'Rolls of the Collectors in the West Riding of the Lay Subsidy (Poll Tax) 2 Richard II', *Yorkshire Archaeological and Topographical Journal*, 5 (1879), 1–51, 241–66, 417–32, 6 (1881), 1–45, 129–71, 287–342, 7 (1883), 6–31, 145–86.

[70] See above, p. 21.

[71] BL Egerton Roll 8769 m. 1*d*; A. J. Pollard, 'The Family of Talbot, Lords Talbot and Earls of Shrewsbury in the Fifteenth Century' (unpub. Bristol Univ. Ph.D. thesis, 1968), pp. 216–17; C. D. Ross, 'The Yorkshire Baronage, 1399–1435' (unpub. Oxford Univ. D.Phil. thesis, 1951), pp. 338–50, citing the work of T. B. Pugh.

[72] Ross, op. cit. p. 395 shows this to have been so in the case of the Percies. In 1403–5 they could count on the support of about 20 knights and a much larger number of yeomen.

[73] J. R. Maddicott, 'The County Community and the Making of Public Opinion in Fourteenth-Century England', *TRHS* 5th series, 28 (1978), 27–30.

[74] L. B. Namier, *The Structure of Politics at the Accession of George III* (London, 1929), p. 91.

[75] K. S. Naughton, *The Gentry of Bedfordshire in the Thirteenth and Fourteenth Centuries* (Leicester, 1976), p. 11; G. Platts, *Land and People in Medieval Lincolnshire* (Lincoln, 1985), pp. 39–43.

regulating their own affairs.[76] Consequently, a magnate's intervention in a shire that did not traditionally fall within his sphere of influence could arouse widespread resentment, as the plight of John of Gaunt's estate officials in Sussex so clearly demonstrates. This resentment sprang from a mixture of motives: the gentry's proper pride in the independence of their own 'country';[77] a less-exalted anxiety for their vested interests; a personal independence of outlook and action on the part of individual gentlemen.

Independence took two forms, however. On the one hand, a genuine freedom from all magnate ties, whether by choice or necessity; alternatively, a freedom of action secured by a multiplicity of magnate connections, which allowed the shrewd and enterprising to play off one lord against another—to their own private advantage. Though the county gentry continued to seek the lordship of the great, their search for such lordship was, in itself, a measure of their growing confidence. Whereas, in the early fourteenth century, magnate retainers usually adhered to a single lord, only transferring their allegiance under exceptional circumstances, this was less often the case by the end of the century.[78] As the range of the gentry's interests and activities grew, so did their willingness to seek a wider spread of support and favour, and to exchange the service of one lord for another. In Sussex, Sir Edward Dallingridge could turn to the earl of Arundel for protection against the duke of Lancaster. In Northumberland, Sir William Swynburn could defy the local officers of the duke of York and the archbishop of York because he had the patronage of two more powerful lords—the duke of Lancaster and the earl of Northumberland.[79] On occasion, he could go further and use one of his principal lords to placate the other, as in his petition to the earl of Derby to speak with Northumberland on his behalf;[80] alternatively, he might just ignore his lord's orders entirely.[81]

The first type of independence, from all magnate ties, is naturally

[76] M. J. Bennett, 'A County Community: Social Cohesion Amongst the Cheshire Gentry, 1400–1425', *Northern History*, 8 (1973), 24–44.

[77] *Paston Letters and Papers*, ed. N. Davis (Oxford, 1971–76), ii. 120–1 remains the classic statement of this view.

[78] N. Saul, *Knights and Esquires*, pp. 93–4.

[79] Northumberland Record Office, ZSW 1/81, 96, 91–2, 100.

[80] Northumberland Record Office, ZSW 1/105.

[81] Northumberland Record Office, ZSW 1/101, 102. Such independence of outlook was traditional on the Border. Sir William's father, retained by the earl of Angus in 1334, was arrested and imprisoned by him for his defaults in 1341—Northumberland Record Office, ZSW 1/58, 64.

more difficult to demonstrate and must rest heavily on the argument
from silence, although an examination of the Lancastrian affinity in
Norfolk has already suggested that an established stake in the county
was as important, perhaps more important, in giving men security as
membership of a magnate affinity. If each county contained between
50 and 70 gentlemen of standing, with some consequent claim on a
lord's attention, it is difficult to see how much more than a fraction of
them can have maintained a magnate connection that went any further
than the uncertain promise of future good lordship. Among the 69
surviving indentures that William, lord Hastings, concluded with the
gentry of the northern Midlands during the 1470s, for instance, only
two actually offered the retainer a cash fee; the rest confined
themselves to the promise of Hastings' aid, support, and counsel in his
new retainer's affairs.[82] If such a promise was enough to attract and
maintain the service of the local gentry then, clearly, the magnates
possessed a means of exercising considerable influence in local society
at minimal cost. There are good reasons, however, for thinking that it
was not. Hastings' affinity was constructed, with the king's approval
and encouragement, largely upon the resources of the royal honour of
Tutbury, in an attempt to bring the gentry of the area into closer
dependence upon the king.[83] As the trusted intimate of Edward IV,
Hastings' promise of favour carried a weight that few other magnates
could match. In most cases, though easily and cheaply contracted, such
ties were too easily ignored for either party to put much trust in them.
John Paston's belief that he was the duke of Norfolk's man, and the
duke his good lord, did not, after all, save him from a beating at the
hands of Norfolk's servant, Charles Nowell—'which was to me
strange case'.[84] Assiduous lordship and the territorial concentration of
an affinity could create some exceptions to the rule, but, in general,
there were too many gentlemen chasing too few lords for the ambitions
of all the county community to be satisfied.[85] Even in Lancashire, the
duke's affinity could not comprehend more than a third of the
palatinate's gentry and in Leicestershire, where Gaunt was again the

---

[82] Dunham, *Lord Hastings' Indentured Retainers*, pp. 9–10, 51.

[83] I. Rowney, 'The Hastings Affinity in Staffordshire and the Honour of Tutbury', *BIHR* 57 (1984), 35–45.

[84] *Paston Letters*, i. 67.

[85] Contrast J. G. Bellamy, *Crime and Public Order in England in the Later Middle Ages* (London, 1973), p. 23: 'Few men who owned a little land were able to resist being drawn into one [magnate] camp or another . . .'; C. Carpenter, 'The Beauchamp Affinity', 515: 'only the unimportant would be without a lord'.

major temporal landowner, the proportion of the county's gentry in his service was smaller still.[86]

It would be hard to understand the frequent denunciations of livery and maintenance by the parliamentary Commons if this were not the case. Since the 'commune' petitions could be promoted by small groups within the house,[87] the complaints of the Commons on the subject are best explained as an expression of the grievances of the many unattached gentry of the shire, who found themselves on the receiving end of the abuses practised by the magnates' dependants. Thus, their complaints were not directed against the practice of retaining itself, since a life indenture of service was a state to which many of the petitioners probably aspired, but against its indiscriminate extension and consequent misuse, which guaranteed the safety of men like William de Chorlegh, sub-sheriff of Lancashire, whose ostentatious display of his ill-gotten gains so outraged the hundred juries of the palatinate.[88] Principally, it was to this disruption of the social hierarchy that the Commons objected; that men of low birth, with no inherited wealth or position, were corruptly exercising a power to which they were not entitled. The same social animus lay behind the Commons' vindictive attitude towards Sir Simon Burley, Richard II's favourite, in 1388; it was said that, although his patrimony was worth no more than 20 marks a year, the king's patronage had provided him with an annual income of 3,000 marks, and enabled Burley to issue as many as 220 livery robes every Christmas.[89]

Yet if the county gentry's quarrel with their social superiors on the issue of livery began as a relatively minor one, it eventually opened up a major difference of opinion. This is the real importance of the law-and-order issue in Richard II's reign; it reveals the internal tensions within an outwardly cohesive ruling class. By creating a common self-interest, bastard feudalism could serve to strengthen this cohesion; at other times, such as this one, the abuses of lordship and clientage had precisely the opposite effect, driving a wedge between the peers and the substantial gentry. In reply to the Commons' demands for reform, the temporal lords were adamant in making no concessions and repeatedly insisted that legislation was unnecessary,[90] although the

---

[86] Astill, 'The Medieval Gentry', pp. 223–5.

[87] D. Rayner, 'The Forms and Machinery of the Commune Petition in the Fourteenth Century', *EHR* 56 (1941), 204–5.

[88] See above, p. 163.

[89] *Chronicon Henrici Knighton*, ii. 294.

[90] *Westminster Chronicle*, pp. 82, 356.

evidence for John of Gaunt's difficulties in maintaining discipline within his own affinity suggests that the lords' promise to punish their miscreant followers was one they were manifestly unable to fulfil. In consequence, the propertied and long-established families who traditionally held sway in the counties—'the most sufficient and loyal men of the shires' as they called themselves—closed ranks against an abuse of the patronage system that threatened their own position and, in petitioning that the justices of the peace should be empowered to deal with cases of maintenance, sought to put the means of redress into their own hands.[91] Their quarrel was not with the temporal lords themselves but with their corrupt stewards and officials, yet in order to put through their reforms, it was with the lords they had to take issue. Lordship was to be sought, but the county gentry were quite willing to prune its excesses; their independence at the level of the county had its counterpart in their independent stance on this issue in Parliament.

This attitude serves to resolve the apparent paradox that, on the one hand, a magnate as powerful as John of Gaunt was unable to enforce his will on relatively minor matters at the local level while, on the other hand, the Commons were loud in their complaints against magnate dependants who ruled the shires like 'second kings'. The prolonged debate on lawlessness and the better administration of justice during the 1380s is less a reflection of deteriorating standards of public order than a testimony to the growing power and independence of the gentry. No less than the earlier struggles over the composition and powers of the peace commission,[92] it serves to demonstrate a shift in the balance of political power—the dynamic for reform and legislation now came as much from the shires as from Westminster. In addition, the Commons' campaign on the issue suggests that, as a class, the gentry were growing more, rather than less, independent of magnate authority. Sporadic complaints against the distribution of magnate liveries and the maintenance practised by magnate dependants were a long-standing feature of English political life[93] but the sustained attack the Commons mounted on the abuse during the 1380s betrays a new parliamentary tenacity which brought, for the first time, some concrete success.

---

[91] Ibid. 358; *Rot. Parl.*, iii. 279.

[92] B. H. Putnam, 'The Transformation of the Keepers of the Peace into the Justices of the Peace 1327–1380', *TRHS* 4th series, 12 (1929), 19–48, esp. 47–8; A. Harding, *The Law Courts of Medieval England* (London, 1973), pp. 92–8.

[93] *Rot. Parl.*, i. 183, ii. 62*a*, 165.

The ordinance of 1390 was not the only victory the Commons won on the law-and-order issue: their complaints against the close links between justices of the central courts and local magnates, taken up in October 1382 and reiterated in November 1384, were probably instrumental in prompting an ordinance that forbade the king's justices to take fees from private individuals;[94] their request at the Cambridge Parliament that magnate stewards should be excluded from the commissions of the peace met with temporary success[95] and in 1391 the justices of the peace, the focus of gentry ambitions on this issue, had their powers of summary judgement augmented.[96] In a number of matters displeasing to the Commons, even the duke of Lancaster was forced to mend his ways. After 1380, he sued out special commissions of oyer and terminer only infrequently and was always careful to balance his own nominees by a number of local gentlemen. After 1389, his ability to nominate his own retainers to the commissions of the peace was significantly curtailed[97] while throughout Richard II's reign the number of pardons for felonies issued at his request—another practice criticized by the Commons[98]—diminished noticeably. During the 1370s, the duke had obtained such pardons on sixteen occasions; during the 1380s, eleven times, and, in the 1390s, on only six occasions.[99] The limitations on John of Gaunt's authority highlighted by these local studies cannot, therefore, be regarded as simply the result of the particular constraints imposed on his lordship by the pre-eminence of his political position and the multiplicity of his concerns. Rather, they are evidence that the independence the county gentry had always claimed was now being exercised to increasing effect.

The role of the great magnates and their retainers in creating the violence and disorder undoubtedly endemic in later medieval England needs to be carefully reconsidered in the light of this conclusion. Abuses like maintenance were clearly widespread but the unthinking assumption that the great lords were principally, even exclusively,

---

[94] Ibid. iii. 139, 200; J. R. Maddicott, *Law and Lordship: Royal Justices as Retainers in Thirteenth and Fourteenth Century England*, pp. 79–81.

[95] *Statutes*, ii. 58–9 (12 R.II, *c*.10); R. L. Storey, 'Liveries and Commissions of the Peace, 1388–90', *The Reign of Richard II*, ed. F. R. H. du Boulay and C. M. Barron (London, 1971), pp. 137–9.

[96] *Statutes*, ii. 78 (15 R.II, *c*. 2).

[97] See above, pp. 245–6.

[98] *Rot. Parl.*, ii. 104, 161, 229, iii. 268; *Statutes*, ii. 68–9 (13 R.II st. 2, *c*. 1).

[99] *CPR 1370–4*, 83, 113, 127, 168, 169, 222, 295, 298, 424, 446, 468; ibid. *1374–7*, 432; ibid. *1377–81*, 11, 282, 297, 348, 447, 505, 518, 546, 547; ibid. *1381–5*, 6, 64, 213, 272, 356; ibid. *1385–9*, 158; ibid. *1391–6*, 219, 265, 297, 666, 686, 705.

responsible for them must be rejected.[100] Besides the oppression of magnate officials and their liveried confederates that the Commons blamed must be set a further cause of disorder; the violence and maintenance practised by the county gentry themselves. Indeed, there was a contemporary current of complaint that identified the local gentry, rather than the magnates or their servants, as the principal disturbers of the peace and the well-documented activities of gentleman-criminals like the Folvilles of Ashby Folville, the Derbyshire Coterels, or Sir John Molyns of Stoke Poges do much to confirm this tradition.[101] As the quarrels of John of Gaunt's retainers in Derbyshire suggest, the gentry could maintain as sturdily independent a line in their feuding as in their politics and pay no more heed to the wishes and instructions of their lords than to the admonitions of the king.

A magnate connection often had little bearing on a man's behaviour in his own 'country'. The career of a knight like Sir Ralph Paynel of Castlethorpe (Lincolnshire) shows clearly enough the ease with which a turbulent county squire, prone to violence, could pursue his inclination without effective hindrance, either by the Crown or by his social superiors. Called before the king and Council for his trespasses and excesses in 1355 and 1360, his continual feuds with the rest of the county gentry eventually led to his indictment for complicity in the murder of Sir Nicholas Cantilupe in 1375.[102] Acquitted of the charges against him by juries empanelled by his accomplice, Sir Thomas Kydale, and, in his capacity as sheriff of Lincolnshire in 1377–8, by himself, complaints about Sir Ralph's activities nevertheless continued to flow in from the county until his death in 1383.[103] There was, in truth, little the royal administration could do to restrain him; his services, on a variety of judicial commissions and, ultimately, as sheriff,

---

[100] e.g. Bellamy, *Crime and Public Order*, p. 22: 'The bane of late medieval England above all else was the widespread maintenance that was practised, that is to say the illegal support which *magnates* offered to a lesser man's suit . . .' (my emphasis).

[101] J. G. Bellamy, 'The Coterel Gang: An Anatomy of a Band of Fourteenth-Century Criminals', *EHR* 89 (1964), 698–717; E. L. G. Stones, 'The Folvilles of Ashby Folville, Leicestershire, and their Associates in Crime, 1326–41', *TRHS* 5th series, 7 (1957), 117–36; N. Fryde, 'A Medieval Robber Baron: Sir John Molyns of Stoke Poges, Buckinghamshire', *Medieval Legal Records*, ed. R. F. Hunnisett and J. B. Post (London, 1978), pp. 197–221.

[102] *CCR 1354–60*, 122; ibid. *1360–4*, 144; *CIM 1348–77*, no. 511; *CPR 1364–7*, 144, 281; ibid. *1370–4*, 476; *Records of Some Sessions of the Peace in Lincolnshire 1360–1375*, ed. R. Sillem (Lincoln Record Soc., 30, 1936), pp. 149–51.

[103] Sillem, op. cit. lxx–lxxiv; *CPR 1377–81*, 465; ibid. *1381–5*, 351.

were too valuable to be dispensed with.[104] Equally, although Paynel was the servant of a number of lords—a retainer of John of Gaunt's, he was also the prince of Wales's surveyor of game in Yorkshire and an annuitant of Thomas, lord Roos[105]—his case provides little sign that the lords could discipline their own followers effectively. Although Paynel drew aid and comfort from the Lancastrian affinity when it suited him, his Lancastrian loyalty did not prevent him from procuring the murder of Cantilupe, a colleague in the duke's retinue, in the course of a private feud.[106] Nor was the violence of the gentry solely directed against each other; 'county magnates' like Paynel stood at the apex of a network of clientage and dependence that spread throughout the shire community. Influential local figures, such as Thomas Foljambe, took fees from their social equals as well as from their superiors[107] and substantial gentlemen like Sir Ralph Hastings of Slingsby distributed liveries and annuities[108] on a scale that rendered them, within the circumscribed world of the shire, as powerful as many peers. When knightly families like the Fichets of Spaxton acted as good lords to the lesser gentry of Somerset, even the Courtenay earls of Devon were compelled to recognize their local authority and, in recognition of their 'great labour and diligence' on their clients' behalf, the Fichets reaped exactly the same kind of reward as their social superiors.[109] The result, in terms of maintenance and corruption, was no better: in the Fichets' own county, no one could maintain possession of an estate against them; Sir Ralph Hastings sheltered criminals, even when the crimes they committed were against

---

[104] e.g. *CPR 1361–4*, 213; ibid. *1364–7*, 69, 430; ibid. *1370–4*, 478; ibid. *1374–7*, 52, 409; ibid. *1377–81*, 93, 250, 299, 302, 464, 467, 579; ibid. *1381–5*, 140, 201, 245; *CFR 1369–77*, 368, 404; ibid. *1377–83*, 3, 44, 49, 163, 228.

[105] *Register of Edward the Black Prince* (London, 1930), i. 431, 533; *CCR 1381–5*, 219. Paynel was also on good terms with Sir Michael de la Pole and William, lord Latimer, *CCR 1377–81*, 236, 459.

[106] *Select Cases of Trespass from the King's Courts, 1307–99*, ed. M. S. Arnold (Selden Soc., 100, 1984), i. 82; Sillem, op. cit. 149–51. Paynel's mainpernors at his trial included a number of Lancastrians: Sir William Hauley, William de Spaigne, Oliver Barton.

[107] Nottinghamshire Record Office, Dd Fj 1/112/1: grant of 4 marks a year and a robe at Christmas to Thomas Foljambe by John Tochet of Markeaton.

[108] Huntington Lib., HAP Box 1 (18), HAD 3329.

[109] *The Hylle Cartulary*, ed. R. W. Dunning (Somerset Record Soc., 68, 1968), nos. 122, 156, 158. Thus, Sir Thomas Fichet, one of Gaunt's retainers, acted as patron to the Catecote family, employing their son as his esquire, putting up the money for their daughter's dowry, and aiding them in their claim to the manor of East Harptree. In return, he was granted the reversion of the disputed manor.

Lancastrian servants, and compelled his enemies to submit to his arbitration.[110]

Seen in this light, the Commons' analysis of the reasons for violent crime in the 1380s and, in particular, their ascription of principal responsibility to the maintenance practised and countenanced by their social superiors, looks very like the partial account of an interest group with an axe to grind and a position of advantage to defend. The real target of their campaign proves to be less the abuse of maintenance than its practitioners—the *gentz de petit garisons*, like Henry Chaderton and William Chorlegh, who were using the cloak of magnate authority to challenge the pre-eminence that the established gentry families had long enjoyed at county level. In consequence, the Commons' complaints cannot be treated as evidence of the baleful effects of 'bastard feudalism' as a form of social organization[111] without the considerable qualifications suggested by this study of the Lancastrian affinity in county society. On the evidence of John of Gaunt's dealings with the gentry, the position of the magnates and their dependants at the local level seems, at times, beleaguered—one which was defended against the lawless depredations of the gentry only with difficulty.

This prompts a final reflection. 'Off livelod and poiar like a kyng', as Sir John Fortescue, with pardonable exaggeration, describes him,[112] the duke of Lancaster was the greatest magnate of late medieval England, his affinity the largest and most expensive of its day. Yet this formidable organization could be absorbed without fuss into the fabric of county society. Who a Lancastrian retainer married; who witnessed his charters; who executed his testament—these were choices more usually determined by existing local contacts and loyalties than by his membership of the Lancastrian affinity. Consequently, although they were glad enough to seek John of Gaunt's lordship for the advantages it offered, the county gentry were equally prepared to forego and, if necessary, to flout it. The argument of this book has been that such a situation was not simply the result of the constraints imposed upon the duke of Lancaster's lordship by the variety of his concerns. Rather, it is an accurate reflection of the distribution of power in later medieval

---

[110] *The Hylle Cartulary*, no. 86; KB 9/146 m. 10; KB 27/528 m. 46; SC 8/63/3126.

[111] As e.g. Storey, 'Liveries and Commissions of the Peace, 1388–90', *The Reign of Richard II*, ed. F. R. H. du Boulay and C. M. Barron (London, 1971), pp. 133–5; C. D. Ross, *Edward IV* (London, 1974), pp. 406–13.

[112] Sir John Fortescue, *The Governance of England*, ed. C. Plummer (Oxford, 1885), p. 130.

England. Lordship was never a magnate monopoly; it was delegated, appropriated, mediatized, and diffused throughout a society far more complex in its workings than the starkly contractual terms of an indenture of retainer suggest. Bastard feudalism was no more an affair of 'totalitarian' subordination of the man to the lord than feudalism itself;[113] on examination, the relationship between lord and man that it implies turns out to be as much one of equality as of dependence. For all their wealth and influence, the magnates of later medieval England maintained only a limited control over their men, for, like the knights of the Mâconnais, the gentry possessed other resources, other patrons, other refuge.[114]

[113] F. L. Ganshof, *Qu'est-ce que la féodalité*, 3rd edn. (Brussels, 1957), p. 45.
[114] G. Duby, *La Société aux XIe et XIIe siècles dans la région mâconnaise* (Paris, 1953), p. 195.

APPENDIX I. Retainers and Annuitants of John of Gaunt

THIS Appendix is designed as a composite list, uniting three separate categories of John of Gaunt's servants in an attempt to include all those of any social consequence who took service with the duke. It consists of (i) all known indentured retainers; (ii) all known annuitants paid a fee of 10 marks, the standard sum granted to an esquire in an indenture of retainer, or more; (iii) those members of the ducal household, not comprehended in the preceding categories, who were paid wages while *infra curiam* at 7*d.* a day—the standard esquire's rate. The Appendix is confined to laymen and excludes those estate officials who do not fall into one of the categories outlined above. They are listed in Somerville, pp. 363–85, with the additions and corrections set out in Appendix II below.

Column (*a*) gives the highest peacetime fee enjoyed by the retainer in question; column (*b*) the earliest and latest dates at which he can be shown to have been in receipt of his fee—this is only a fraction of the total period many retainers spent in Lancastrian service; consequently column (*c*) gives the dates of the campaigns for which the retainer took out letters of protection before going overseas in the duke's company—which often provides a more accurate indication of the length of the association between them.

	a	b	c
Abberbury, Sir Richard[1]	£50	1381–99	1370, 1386
Aldrisham, Richard[2]	10 marks	1396–9	none
Annesley, Hugh[3]	£5	1382–92	none
Appleby, Sir Edmund[4]	£20	1372–83	1367, 1369, 1370, 1378
Arnold, falconer[5]	£10	1379–83	none
Ashford, John[6]	35 marks	1368–99	1370
Ashley, John[7]	10 marks	1398–9	none

[1] DL 43/15/3 m. 3; *Reg. II* 613; DL 29/738/12096 m. 8; *Reg. I* 969; C. 76/70 m. 17.
[2] Appendix III, no. 12; DL 29/453/7288 m. 2.
[3] DL 29/402/6447/8 m. 2; *Reg. II* p. 10; DL 43/15/4 m. 3.
[4] *Reg. I* 1220; DL 29/402/6447/8 m. 2; *Foedera*, iii. 810; C. 76/52 m. 15; C. 61/83 m. 3; C. 76/62 m. 4.
[5] *Reg. II* 55, 92.
[6] *CPR 1396–9*, 526; *Reg. I* 465; DL 29/738/12096 m. 6; *Reg. I* 969.
[7] DL 42/15 f. 90v.

	a	b	c
Ashton, Sir John[8]	£20	1382–99	1369, 1378, 1386, 1395
Aston, Sir Richard[9]	£20	1382–99	1386
Aston, Thomas[10]	10 marks	1388–99	1386, 1395
Atherton, Sir Nicholas[11]	£10	1370–99	1369, 1370, 1372, 1373
Atherton, Nicholas[12]	10 marks	1397–9	1386
Bagot, Sir John[13]	40 marks	1387–99	1386
Bagot, William[14]	10 marks	1382–8	none
Balderston, Sir Richard[15]	20 marks	1381–2	1370, 1378
Balderston, William[16]	10 marks	1397	1395
Banaster, Edward[17]		1381–2	none
Banaster, Sir Thomas[18]	90 marks	1372–9	1359, 1367, 1370, 1373
Barber, Geoffrey[19]	£8	1378–84	1370
Barewell, William[20]	none	1383	none
Barley, Thomas[21]		1382	1372, 1378
Barry, Edmund[22]	£10	1396–9	none
Barry, Sir Robert[23]	20 marks	1372–82	1373
Barton, Oliver[24]	£20	1374–82	1369, 1370, 1373
Barton, William[25]		1382	1369, 1372

[8] DL 29/738/12096 m. 1; *Reg. II* p. 8; PL 1/2 m. 1; C. 81/925 (42); C. 76/62 m. 18; C. 81/1039 (25); C. 61/104 m. 7.

[9] DL 29/16/202 m. 2; *Reg. II* p. 12; DL 29/738/12096 m. 3; C. 81/1036 (37).

[10] DL 29/16/202 m. 2; PL 1/2 m. 1; C. 81/1031 (12); C. 61/104 m. 9.

[11] Lewis, no. 2; PL 1/2 m. 1; C. 76/52 m. 10; C. 61/83 m. 1; *Reg. I* 1005; C. 76/56 m. 18.

[12] Lewis, no. 34; DL 29/738/12096 m. 1; C. 81/1033 (8).

[13] DL 29/367/6147 m. 1, 6151 m. 1, 738/12096 m. 6; C. 81/1033 (47).

[14] DL 29/402/6447/8 m. 1; *Reg. II* p. 10; DL 29/584/9239 m. 1.

[15] *Reg. II* 32, p. 8; *Reg. I* 969; C. 76/62 m. 18.

[16] Folger Shakespeare Lib., MS X. d. 91; C. 81/1070 (4).

[17] East Sussex Record Office, GLY 3469 mm. 1–5; *Reg. II* p. 10.

[18] *Reg. I* 849; DL 43/15/6 m. 2; *Reg. I* 1042; *Anonimalle Chron.*, p. 131; C. 76/37 m. 5; C. 61/79 m. 4, 83 m. 3; C. 76/56 m. 18.

[19] DL 29/262/4070 m. 2; *Reg. I* 969.

[20] *Reg. II* 54.

[21] Ibid. p. 11; C. 76/55 m. 21, 63 m. 20.

[22] Norfolk Record Office, NRS 15171 m. 2; *CPR 1396–9*, 542.

[23] *Reg. I* 923; DL 29/212/3247 m. 1, 341/5516 m. 2; *Reg. I* 50.

[24] DL 29/402/6447/8 m. 1; *Reg. I* 226; C. 81/925 (20); C. 61/83 m. 2; C. 76/56 m. 20.

[25] *Reg. II* p. 11; C. 76/52 m. 9, 55 m. 22.

	a	b	c
Bathe, John[26]	£4 11s. 6d.	1372–82	1367, 1369, 1372, 1373
Baynard, Philip[27]		1382	none
Beauchamp, Edward[28]	£20	1372–99	1386
Beauchamp, Sir Roger[29]	40 marks	1373	none
Beauchamp, Sir William[30]	100 marks	1371–4	1367, 1370, 1372, 1373
Beaumont, Sir Thomas[31]		1382	1370, 1372, 1373, 1378
Beek, Sir Thomas[32]	£20	1384–99	1386
Berford, Sir Baldwin[33]	£20	1382–7	1373
Berkley, Sir Maurice[34]	£20	1391–9	1394
Berkley, Thomas[35]	no fee	1381–2	none
Berwick, Thomas[36]	10 marks	1388–99	none
Beyvill, Robert[37]	20 marks	1372–82	1373
Bispham, John[38]	10 marks	before 1399	none
Blackwell, Robert[39]	£12 3s. 4d.	1373–90	1367, 1369
Blount, Sir Walter[40]	£176 13s. 4d.	1372–99	1369, 1370, 1373, 1386, 1395
Bolron, Robert[41]	£10	1393–9	none
Bolton, John[42]		1382	1386
Bondale, John[43]	10 marks	1379–99	none

[26] DL 29/341/5516 m. 2; *Reg. I* 389; *Reg. II* p. 10; C. 61/79 m. 3; C. 76/52 m. 17, 55 m. 21, 56 m. 26.

[27] *Reg. II* p. 11.

[28] *Reg. I* 815; DL 29/615/9838 m. 2, 9839 m. 2, 738/12096 m. 8; C. 81/1033 (45).

[29] *Reg. I* 1209.

[30] Ibid. 832, 883, 1548; *Chandos Herald*, 1. 3198; C. 61/83 m. 3; C. 76/55 m. 22, 56 m. 27.

[31] *Reg. II* p. 7; C. 61/83 m. 3; C. 76/55 m. 21; C. 81/950 (7); C. 76/62 m. 18.

[32] Lewis, no. 7; DL 29/738/12096 m. 6; C. 81/1033 (47).

[33] *Reg. II* 46; DL 29/738/12104 m. 2; C. 76/56 m. 27.

[34] *CPR 1396–9*, 544; C. 61/104 m. 9.

[35] *Reg. II* 35, p. 12.

[36] DL 29/58/1081 m. 1, 1088 m. 2.

[37] *Reg. I* 813; *Reg. II* p. 12; C. 76/56 m. 20.

[38] DL 42/16 f. 206.

[39] *Reg. I* 1180; *Reg. II* p. 10; WAM 32777; DL 29/738/12096 m. 8, 12104 m. 2; C. 81/912 (40); C. 76/52 m. 12.

[40] *Reg. I* 1042; *CPR 1396–9*, 547; DL 29/738/12096 m. 6; C. 81/925 (20); *Reg. I* 969, 1670; C. 76/62 m. 18, 70 m. 19; C. 61/104 m. 5.

[41] Appendix III, no. 7; DL 29/738/12096 m. 3.

[42] *Reg. II*, p. 13; C. 81/1034 (4).

[43] DL 29/262/4070 m. 2, 4071 m. 2.

	a	b	c
Boseville, Sir John[44]	£20	1373–82	1367, 1369, 1370, 1373, 1386
Boseville, Sir Thomas[45]		1382	none
Botiller, Sir John[46]		1371–82	1369, 1370, 1372, 1373, 1378
Botiller, Sir John[47]	£20	1397–9	none
Botquenzelle, Henry[48]	£10	1396–9	none
Boulot, Robert[49]		1382	none
Boyton, Richard[50]	£10	1389–99	1386, 1395
Bracebridge, Sir Ralph[51]	no fee	1385	1386
Bradley, Thomas[52]	20 marks	1372–82	1370
Bradshaw, Sir William[53]	20 marks	1372–4	1370, 1372, 1373
Bradshaw, William[54]	10 marks	before 1399	none
Braunston, Thomas[55]	10 marks	1390	1394
Bray, John[56]	£10	1372–5	none
Brenchley, John[57]	5 marks	1375–81	1386
Bretteville, Sir William[58]		1382	1386
Bridges, Thomas[59]		1382	none
Bromwich, Sir John[60]		1382–8	none
Broxtow, John[61]	no fee	1398	none
Buada, Arnold[62]	20 marks	1391–9	none

[44] *Reg. I* 1221; *Reg. II* p. 8, 277; C. 61/79 m. 4; C. 76/52 m. 15; *Reg. I* 969; C. 76/56 m. 20; C. 81/1034 (32).

[45] *Reg. II* p. 8.

[46] *Reg. I* 8; *Reg. II* p. 8; C. 76/52 m. 7; C. 61/83 m. 3; *Reg. I* 1005; C. 76/56 m. 20, 62 m. 18.

[47] Lewis, no. 33; DL 29/738/12096 m. 1.

[48] DL 28/3/5 f. 6v; C. 266/41 (39).

[49] *Reg. II* p. 12.

[50] Lewis, no. 16; DL 42/16 f. 35v; C. 81/1036 (44); *CPR 1396–9*, 499.

[51] *HMC, Middleton MSS*, pp. 99–100; C. 76/70 m. 17.

[52] *Reg. I* 796; *Reg. II* 26; DL 29/341/5516 m. 3; *Reg. I* 969.

[53] *Reg. I* 793, 1766; *Reg. I* 969; C. 76/55 m. 22, 56 m. 18.

[54] DL 42/15 f. 21; DL 29/738/12096 m. 1.

[55] Norfolk Record Office, NRS 15171 m. 2; C. 81/1069 (27).

[56] *Reg. I* 547, 1706.

[57] *Reg. I* 734; East Sussex Record Office, GLY 3469 mm. 1–5; C. 81/1033 (35).

[58] *Reg. II* p. 9; C. 76/70 m. 20.

[59] *Reg. II* p. 12.

[60] Ibid. p. 9; DL 29/584/9239 m. 1.

[61] Appendix III, no. 18.

[62] Lewis, no. 22; DL 42/16 f. 35.

	a	*b*	*c*
Burford, John[63]	20 marks	1389–99	none
Burgoyne, William[64]	£10	1381–99	none
Burley, Sir Richard[65]	100 marks	1369–87	1367, 1370, 1386
Burley, Sir Roger[66]	20 marks	1379–92	none
Burnell, Edward[67]	20 marks	1397–8	1394
Burton, Thomas[68]	20 marks	1370–82	1369
Bussy, Sir John[69]	£40	1382–97	1378
Camoys, Sir Ralph[70]	£40	1367	1367, 1369
Cantilupe, Sir William[71]	£20	1372	1370, 1372, 1373
Caston, William[72]	£10	1397–9	none
Caunsfield, John[73]	10 marks	1387–99	none
Caunsfield, Matthew[74]	10 marks	1397–9	none
Caunsfield, Robert[75]	£10	1372	1369, 1373, 1386
Cave, John[76]		1382	none
Charles, Sir Robert[77]	no fee	1382	none
Chaucer, Geoffrey[78]	£10	1374–80	none
Chaucer, Thomas[79]	£20	1389–99	1386
Chelmeswyk, Richard[80]	£10	1393	none
Chetwynd, John[81]	10 marks	1394–9	1394
Chetwynd, William[82]	£10	1373–99	1370, 1386

---

[63] Lewis, no. 42; DL 42/15 f. 94v.

[64] *Reg. II* 710; DL 29/738/12096 m. 3.

[65] DL 29/584/9236 m. 1, 738/12104 m. 2; *Political Poems and Songs*, i. 109; *Reg. I* 1042; C. 81/1032 (6).

[66] *Reg. II* 75; DL 29/615/9838 m. 2; East Sussex Record Office, GLY 3469 m. 10*d*.

[67] Norfolk Record Office, NRS 15171 m. 2; C. 61/104 m. 7.

[68] *CPR 1367–70*, 380; *Reg. II* 748; C. 81/925 (20).

[69] *Reg. II* p. 9; DL 28/3/5 f. 8; C. 81/986 (12).

[70] DL 29/615/9836 m. 1; *Chandos Herald*, ll. 2615–16; C. 81/925 (20).

[71] *Reg. I* 833; C. 61/83 m. 3; C. 76/55 m. 21, 56 m. 7.

[72] *CPR 1396–9*, 513.

[73] Lewis, no. 12; PL 1/2 m. 1.

[74] Lewis, no. 35; *CPR 1396–9*, 580.

[75] *Reg. I* 825, 827; ibid. 1058; C. 76/56 m. 18; *DKR* xl. 525.

[76] *Reg. II* p. 11.

[77] Ibid. 50.

[78] *Reg. I* 608; *Reg. II* 296.

[79] *CPR 1396–9*, 490; DL 29/738/12096 m. 6.

[80] DL 29/615/9839 m. 2.

[81] Lewis, no. 29; DL 42/15 f. 20v.

[82] *Reg. I* 809; Lewis, no. 4; DL 42/15 f. 77; *Reg. I* 969; C. 81/1033 (17).

	a	b	c
Cheyne, Sir Roger[83]		1382	none
Clifton, Sir Robert[84]	£20	1373–5	1369, 1373
Clitheroe, Richard[85]	10 marks	1396	none
Cokayne, Sir John[86]	20 marks	1398–9	none
Coleman, Richard[87]		1382	none
Coleman, Roger[88]		1382	1378
Colepepper, John[89]	25 marks	1372–82	1367, 1369
Colville, Sir Thomas[90]	20 marks	1372–3	1369, 1370, 1372, 1373
Cornwall, Sir John[91]	£20	1386–99	1378, 1386
Cornwall, John[92]	20 marks	1395–9	1394
Crancester, Edmund[93]	10 marks	1398–9	none
Crayleboys, John[94]	£10	1382–91	1386
Croke, Richard[95]	10 marks	1398–9	none
Croyser, Sir John[96]		1382	1384, 1386
Croyser, Sir William[97]	£50	1372–82	1369
Curteys, John[98]	£10	1391–9	none
Curteys, Reginald[99]	£10	1396–9	1369
Curwen, Walter[100]	10 marks	1398–9	none
Curzon, Sir Roger[101]	£20	1373–84	1373
Dabridgecourt, Sir John[102]	100 marks	1381–99	1386, 1395
Dabridgecourt, Sir Nicholas[103]	£20	1391	1395

[83] *Reg. II* p. 9.
[84] *Reg. I* 863, 1719; C. 81/925 (23); C. 76/56 m. 26.
[85] Appendix III, no. 11.
[86] DL 29/212/3248 m. 6.
[87] *Reg. II* p. 12.
[88] Ibid. p. 10; C. 76/62 m. 18.
[89] *Reg. I* 830; *Reg. II* p. 10; C. 81/912 (40); C. 76/52 m. 8.
[90] *Reg. I* 1288; C. 76/52 m. 9; C. 61/83 m. 3; C. 76/55 m. 21, 56 m. 20.
[91] DL 29/738/12104 m. 2, 453/7288 m. 2; C. 76/62 m. 3, 70 m. 11.
[92] Appendix III, no. 8; DL 29/738/12096 m. 8; C. 61/104 m. 9.
[93] Appendix III, no. 15.
[94] *Reg. II* p. 13; DL 43/15/3 m. 3; C. 81/1032 (16).
[95] Lewis, no. 40; PL 1/2 m. 1.
[96] *Reg. II* p. 9; C. 71/63 m. 2; C. 81/1038 (7).
[97] DL 29/341/5516 m. 3; *Reg. I* 161; East Sussex Record Office, GLY 3469 mm. 1–5; C. 76/52 m. 6.
[98] East Sussex Record Office, GLY 3469 mm. 6d–14d; DL 42/15 f. 42.
[99] DL 42/16 f. 224; *CCR 1396–9*, 449; DL 28/3/5 f. 12; C. 76/52 m. 12.
[100] Lewis, no. 39; DL 29/738/12096 m. 2.
[101] *Reg. I* 775; DL 29/402/6447/8 m. 1; *Reg. I* 1441.
[102] *Reg. II* 39; DL 42/15 f. 119; C. 76/70 m. 26; C. 61/104 m. 9.
[103] Appendix III, no. 5; DL 43/15/3 m. 3; C. 61/104 m. 9.

	a	*b*	*c*
Dacre, Sir Hugh[104]		1372–82	1369, 1372, 1373
Dageney, Sir John[105]	20 marks	1373	1367, 1369, 1370, 1373
Dale, Sir Thomas[106]	£20	1372–3	1370, 1373
Dale, Thomas[107]	£10	1389–99	1395
Dalton, Sir John[108]		1381–99	none
Daventry, Sir Thomas[109]		1382	1367, 1369
Deincourt, Sir John[110]	£10	1382–92	1367, 1369, 1370, 1386
Deneys, Sir Philip[111]	£20	1372–82	1373
Derby, Adam[112]	£10	1362–99	none
Derby, John[113]	10 marks	1395–9	1395
Dernford, Stephen[114]		1382	none
Dowedale, John[115]	£10	1376–99	1386
Doweville, Sir Thomas[116]	£40	1374–5	none
Driby, Thomas[117]		1382	1372, 1373, 1386
Driffield, Thomas[118]	no fee	1380–2	1373, 1378, 1386
Dymoke, Sir John[119]	20 marks	1370–2	1369
Dutton, Ralph[120]	£10	1387–99	1386
Eccleston, Robert[121]		1382	1386
Elston, Roger[122]		1382	none
Englefield, John[123]	£20	1391–9	1386

[104] *Reg. I* 934; *Reg. II* p. 7; C. 81/925 (4); C. 76/55 m. 21, 56 m. 27.
[105] *Reg. I* 1352; C. 81/912 (40); C. 76/52 m. 21; C. 61/83 m. 3; C. 76/56 m. 18.
[106] *Reg. I* 804, 857; C. 61/83 m. 3; DL 28/3/1 m. 4.
[107] Lewis, no. 18; DL 29/212/3248 m. 5; C. 61/104 m. 7.
[108] East Sussex Record Office, GLY 3469 mm. 1–5; PL 1/2 m. 1.
[109] *Reg. II* p. 8; C. 61/79 m. 4; C. 76/52 m. 15.
[110] DL 29/463/7539 m. 2; *Reg. II* p. 9; East Sussex Record Office, GLY 3469 mm. 6–11; C. 81/912 (40), 942 (3); C. 61/83 m. 1; C. 76/70 m. 28.
[111] *Reg. I* 829; *Reg. II* p. 8; *Reg. I* 49.
[112] *CPR 1396–9*, 567; DL 29/212/3248 m. 5.
[113] DL 28/32/22 mm. 14, 15; DL 29/738/12096 m. 9.
[114] *Reg. II* p. 12.
[115] *CPR 1396–9*, 561; DL 28/3/1 m. 8; C. 81/1033 (31).
[116] *Reg. I* 1662.
[117] *Reg. II* p. 11; C. 76/55 m. 14; *Reg. I* 49; C. 81/1034 (1).
[118] *Reg. II* 28, p. 11; C. 76/56 m. 27, 62 m. 18, 70 m. 17.
[119] *Reg. I* 937; C. 81/925 (20).
[120] DL 29/16/202 m. 2; DL 29/738/12096 m. 3.
[121] *Reg. II* p. 12; *DKR* xliii. 364.
[122] *Reg. II* p. 12.
[123] DL 43/15/3 m. 3; DL 29/738/12096 m. 8; C. 76/70 m. 12.

	a	b	c
Erpingham, Sir Thomas[124]	£40	1380–99	1385, 1386
Eton, Richard[125]	£10	1387–99	1386
Etton, Thomas[126]	£10	1381	1369
Feckenham, John[127]	10 marks	1395–6	none
Fenwick, Sir John[128]		1381–8	none
Fernandez, Sir Juan[129]	£20	1376–82	1373
Ferrers, Sir Robert[130]	100 marks	1392	1378
Fichet, Sir Thomas[131]	£40	1373–87	1385, 1386
Fifide, William[132]		1382	1380, 1385, 1386
Fitzralph, Robert[133]	£20	1373–87	1373, 1386
Fitzwilliam, Sir William[134]		1381–2	none
Flaxman, William[135]	10 marks	1395–9	1395
Fleming, Sir Thomas[136]	20 marks	1398–9	none
Fogg, Sir Thomas[137]	100 marks	1372–99	1373, 1378, 1380, 1386
Foljambe, Sir Godfrey[138]	£40	1362–75	1359, 1369
Frank, Piers[139]		1382	1386
Frank, Sir William[140]	100 marks	1381–4	1373
Freville, Madok[141]		1382	none
Frithby, Sir Edmund[142]	£20	1372	1369, 1372, 1373
Gaskrigg, William[143]	no fee	1380–2	none

[124] *Reg. II* 338; DL 42/15 f. 22; *CCR 1381–5*, 557; C. 81/1036 (32).

[125] Lewis, no. 11; DL 29/615/9839 m. 2.

[126] *Reg. II* 986; C. 76/52 m. 15.

[127] DL 28/32/22 mm. 21, 22.

[128] Leeds Central Lib., Grantley MS 501; Northumberland Record Office, ZSW 1/106.

[129] DL 28/3/1 m. 5; *Reg. II* p. 8; BL Add. MS 37494 f. 5v.

[130] DL 28/3/2 f. 10; East Sussex Record Office, GLY 3469 mm. 6–13; C. 76/62 m. 10.

[131] *Reg. I* 845; DL 29/738/12104 m. 2; *S. & G.*, i. 62; C. 81/1034 (14).

[132] *Reg. II* p. 10; C. 71/60 m. 7, 64 m. 6; C. 76/70 m. 10.

[133] *Reg. I* 844; Norfolk Record Office, NRS 3343 m. 1; *Reg. I* 50; C. 81/1032 (12).

[134] *Reg. II* 561, p. 8.

[135] *CPR 1396–9*, 537; DL 29/738/12096 m. 6.

[136] Lewis, no. 38; *CPR 1396–9*, 593.

[137] *Reg. I* 802; DL 29/453/7288 m. 2; C. 76/56 m. 27, 62 m. 2; *Reg. II* 1080; C. 76/70 m. 20.

[138] Bodl. MS CCC 495 f. 16; *Reg. I* 1721; C. 76/38 m. 13, 52 m. 12.

[139] *Reg. II* p. 13; C. 81/1038 (33).

[140] *Reg. II* 584; DL 29/262/4070 m. 3; C. 81/950 (52).

[141] *Reg. II* p. 11.

[142] *Reg. I* 822; C. 76/52 m. 9, 55 m. 21, 56 m. 11.

[143] *Reg. II* 30, p. 10.

	a	b	c
Geblesen, Piers[144]	20 marks	1382–90	none
Gerard, Sir Thomas[145]	20 marks	before 1399	none
Gerberge, Edward[146]	20 marks	1370–3	none
Gernoun, Sir Nicholas[147]	£20	1361–83	none
Gest, Richard[148]	£10	1392–9	none
Giffard, John[149]	no fee	1381–2	1386
Gissing, John[150]		1381	none
Gloucester, Thomas[151]	10 marks	1391–9	none
Goys, Sir Thomas[152]	£20	1372–80	1370, 1373, 1378
Granson, Sir Otes[153]	100 marks	1374–93	none
Green, Sir Henry[154]	50 marks	1379–99	1372, 1373, 1386
Green, Henry[155]	10 marks	1392–9	1386
Greyndor, Thomas[156]	10 marks	1369–70	1369
Grivere, Sir Jean de[157]	100 marks	1374–83	none
Groos, Oliver[158]	£10	1395–9	1386, 1395
Gynney, John[159]		1382	none
Hacoun, John[160]	£10	1379–96	none
Hale, Sir Frank van[161]	£20	1361–73	1369
Hall, William[162]		1382	1369, 1370, 1372, 1373
Hans, Sir Herman[163]	100 marks	1392	none

[144] *Reg. II* p. 12; DL 43/15/3 m. 3.
[145] DL 42/15 f. 163.
[146] *Reg. I* 509, 843.
[147] DL 29/288/4720 m. 1d; *Reg. II* 807.
[148] East Sussex Record Office, GLY 3469 mm. 7–14; Norfolk Record Office, NRS 15171 m. 2.
[149] *Reg. II* 36, p. 12; C. 81/1035 (34).
[150] East Sussex Record Office, GLY 3469 mm. 1d–4d.
[151] Appendix III, no. 6; DL 29/262/4071 m. 3.
[152] *Reg. I* 933; Norfolk Record Office, NRS 3342 m. 2; C. 61/83 m. 3; C. 76/56 m. 20, 62 m. 3.
[153] *Reg. I* 866; DL 28/3/2 f. 10v.
[154] DL 29/341/5515 m. 2; *CPR 1396–9*, 522; C. 76/55 m. 14, 56 m. 18, 71 m. 22.
[155] DL 29/615/9839 m. 2; DL 29/738/12096 m. 8; C. 76/70 m. 6
[156] DL 29/615/9837 m. 1; C. 81/925 (20).
[157] *Reg. I* 867; *Reg. II* 847.
[158] Norfolk Record Office, NRS 3344 m. 2; DL 29/738/12096 m. 9; C. 76/70 m. 17.
[159] *Reg. II* p. 12.
[160] Norfolk Record Office, NRS 3342 m. 2, 15171 m. 2.
[161] *CIPM* XI. 95; *Reg. I* 1372; *Issue Roll of Thomas Brantingham*, p. 493.
[162] *Reg. II* p. 12; *Reg. I* 1031, 1663; C. 76/55 m. 21; *Reg. I* 49.
[163] DL 28/3/2 f. 10v; East Sussex Record Office, GLY 3469 mm. 6–11.

	a	b	c
Harcourt, Sir Thomas[164]		1382	none
Harley, Sir John[165]		1382	1367, 1369
Haselden, Thomas[166]	£20	1365–82	1367, 1369, 1370, 1373
Hastings, Sir Hugh[167]	£20	1366	1367, 1369
Hastings, Sir Ralph[168]	40 marks	1361–91	1367, 1369, 1370, 1372, 1373, 1385
Hatfield, Robert[169]	£30	1373–99	1369
Hauley, Sir Robert[170]		1382	1359, 1367, 1369
Hauley, Sir William[171]	40 marks	1379–84	1373, 1378, 1386
Havering, Sir Richard[172]		1380–2	1369
Haybere, William[173]	£10	1372–3	none
Haywood, Hugh[174]	no fee	1382	1386
Haywood, Nicholas[175]	10 marks	before 1399	1386
Heyland, Thomas[176]	£10	1398–9	none
Herford, Sir Robert[177]		1382	1386
Hervey, Thomas[178]	£22 15s. 0d.	1381–95	1395
Hervey, William[179]	no fee	1381–2	1386
Hoghton, Sir Henry[180]	£20	1393–9	none
Hoghton, Sir Richard[181]	40 marks	1382–99	none
Hoghton, Sir William[182]	£20	before 1399	none

[164] *Reg. II* p. 8.

[165] Ibid.; C. 61/79 m. 8; C. 76/52 m. 18.

[166] *Reg. I* 506; DL 42/1 f. 190; *Reg. II* 732; C. 81/912 (40); C. 76/52 m. 16; C. 61/83 m. 3; C. 76/56 m. 18.

[167] Appendix III, no. 1; C. 61/79 m. 3; C. 76/52 m. 10.

[168] Huntington Lib., HAD 3325, 3200; C. 61/79 m. 4; C. 76/52 m. 11; C. 61/83 m. 4; C. 76/55 m. 21; *Reg. I* 49; *S. & G.*, i. 103.

[169] *Reg. I* 837; DL 29/738/12096 m. 4; C. 81/926 (42).

[170] *Reg. II* p. 9; C. 76/38 m. 13; C. 61/79 m. 4; C. 76/52 m. 9.

[171] *Reg. II* 24; DL 29/262/4070 m. 3; C. 76/56 m. 18, 62 m. 18; C. 81/1036 (48).

[172] *Reg. II* 287, p. 9; C. 76/52 m. 11.

[173] *Reg. I* 812, 1299.

[174] *Reg. II* 51; C. 81/1031 (13).

[175] DL 42/15 f. 12; DL 29/738/12096 m. 3; C. 61/100 m. 4.

[176] Appendix III, no. 14; DL 29/738/12096 m. 10.

[177] *Reg. II* p. 9; C. 81/1032 (31).

[178] DL 43/15/3 m. 3; East Sussex Record Office, GLY 3469 mm. 1–5; DL 29/728/11986 m. 3; C. 61/104 m. 9.

[179] *Reg. II* 33, p. 10; C. 81/1034 (21).

[180] Lewis, no. 26; DL 29/738/12096 m. 2.

[181] DL 42/15 f. 7v, *Reg. II* pp. 9, 11; DL 29/738/12096 m. 2.

[182] DL 42/15 f. 22v.

	a	b	c
Hoghwyk, William[183]	£10	1392–9	none
Holford, John[184]		1382	1373, 1386
Holford, Thomas[185]		1382	none
Holland, John, earl of Huntingdon[186]	£133 6s. 8d.	1391–7	1386
Holland, Richard[187]	no fee	1381–2	1373
Holme, John[188]	no fee	1372	none
Holt, John[189]	£6 3s. 4d.	1382	none
Hoo, Sir Richard[190]	£20	1372–99	1373, 1378, 1386, 1395
Hudleston, William[191]	10 marks	before 1399	none
Hull, John[192]	£10	1388–99	1386
Hulme, William[193]	10 marks	1382–99	none
Hungerford, Sir Thomas[194]	100 marks	1372–93	none
Hungerford, Sir Thomas[195] (le filz)		1382	none
Huse, Sir Hugh[196]	£20	1395–9	1395
Ilderton, Sir Thomas[197]	£20	1372–82	1369, 1372, 1373
Ipres, Sir John[198]	100 marks	1366–83	1367, 1378
Ipres, Sir John (the son)[199]	£10	1382	none
Ipres, Sir Ralph[200]	£25	1372–94	1369, 1370, 1373, 1386

[183] *CPR 1396–9*, 501; DL 29/738/12096 m. 4.
[184] *Reg. II* p. 13; C. 76/56 m. 5; C. 81/1033 (26).
[185] *Reg. II* p. 13.
[186] DL 29/310/4980 m. 2d, Norfolk Record Office, NRS 15171 m. 2; C. 76/70 m. 17.
[187] *Reg. II* 42, p. 12; CP 40/452 (deeds) m. ii.
[188] *Reg. I* 814.
[189] DL 29/341/5516 m. 3; *Reg. II* p. 11.
[190] *Reg. I* 811; DL 29/738/12096 m. 10; *Reg. I* 49; C. 76/62 m. 18; C. 81/1031 (53); C. 61/104 m. 7.
[191] DL 42/16 f. 138v.
[192] Lewis, no. 15; DL 29/738/12096 m. 8; C. 76/70 m. 20.
[193] *Reg. II* p. 11; DL 29/738/12096 m. 1.
[194] *Reg. I* 360; DL 43/15/6 m. 7.
[195] *Reg. II* p. 8.
[196] Lewis, no. 27; DL 42/15 f. 91v.
[197] *Reg. I* 807; *Reg. II* p. 7; C. 76/52 m. 15, 55 m. 21, 56 m. 27.
[198] *Reg. II* 899; *CPR 1367–70*, 297; C. 61/79 m. 4; C. 76/62 m. 2.
[199] *Reg. II* 49, 711.
[200] *Reg. I* 808; DL 43/15/9 m. 3; *Reg. I* 973; C. 61/83 m. 3; C. 76/56 m. 26; C. 81/1036 (7).

	a	*b*	*c*
Ipstones, Sir John[201]	£10	1387	1386
Iresdale, Waryn[202]	£10	1381–90	1386
Isnell, William[203]	£10	1393–9	1395
Ithel, Eymon ap[204]	10 marks	1396	none
Jouster, Richard[205]	£10	1387–8	1386
Kendal, John[206]	10 marks	1382–99	none
Kentwood, Sir John[207]	20 marks	1386–91	none
Kettering, William[208]	£20	1380–99	1386
Kirkby, John[209]		1382	none
Knolles, Sir Robert[210]		1382	1378
Kynbell, Nicholas[211]	20 marks	1366–75	1367, 1369, 1370, 1373
Laurence, Robert[212]	10 marks	before 1399	none
Leveriche, Thomas[213]	£10 3s. 4d.	1369	1367, 1370
Leyburn, Robert[214]	10 marks	before 1399	none
Longford, Sir Nicholas[215]	£40	1372	1367, 1369, 1370, 1373
Loring, Sir Neel[216]	£20	1361–85	none
Loudham, Sir John[217]		1382	1373
Loudham, Sir John (le filz)[218]	40 marks	1382–8	1386
Lounde, Sir Gerard[219]		1382	1369, 1370, 1378

[201] DL 29/367/6144 m. 1*d*.; C. 76/70 m. 26.

[202] East Sussex Record Office, GLY 3469 mm. 1–5; *Reg. II* p. 10; DL 29/738/12104 m. 2*d*; C. 81/1034 (52).

[203] Lewis, no. 30; East Sussex Record Office, GLY 3469 mm. 12, 13; DL 42/15 f. 47v.

[204] Appendix III, no. 10.

[205] DL 29/738/12104 mm. 1–2; C. 81/1034 (29).

[206] *Reg. II* p. 12; DL 29/212/3248 m. 5.

[207] DL 29/738/12104 m. 2; DL 43/15/3 m. 3.

[208] *Reg. II* 968; DL 29/738/12096 m. 5; C. 76/71 m. 22.

[209] *Reg. II* p. 12.

[210] *Reg. II* p. 7; C. 76/63 m. 18.

[211] DL 42/12 f. 56; *Reg. I* 1708; C. 61/79 m. 3; C. 81/925 (20); C. 61/83 m. 3; C. 76/56 m. 20.

[212] DL 42/15 f. 6.

[213] DL 29/615/9837 m. 1; C. 81/912 (40); *Reg. I* 969.

[214] DL 42/15 f. 21.

[215] *Reg. I* 803; C. 81/912 (40); C. 76/52 m. 3; C. 61/83 m. 3; *Reg. I* 49.

[216] DL 29/288/4719 m. 2; Norfolk Record Office, NRS 11072 m. 2.

[217] *Reg. II* p. 7; C. 76/56 m. 18.

[218] *Reg. II* p. 9; DL 29/728/11975 m. 2; C. 81/1038 (51).

[219] *Reg. II* p. 8; C. 76/52 m. 8; C. 81/931 (46); C. 76/62 m. 18.

	a	b	c
Lucy, Thomas[220]	10 marks	1398–9	none
Lucy, Sir William[221]	£20	1381–99	1385, 1386
Lutterell, Sir Andrew[222]	40 marks	1365–84	1367, 1369
Lutterell, Hugh[223]		1382	none
Lutterell, John[224]	£10	before 1399	1372, 1373, 1395
Maistreson, Thomas[225]	£10	1371–99	1370, 1372
Malet, Sir John[226]	£20	1392–3	none
Manburni, Sir Jean[227]	200 marks	1371–86	1386
Marchington, Sir Thomas[228]		1382	1386
Mare, Sir Thomas de la[229]		1361–82	1367, 1369
Marmion, Sir John[230]	40 marks	1372–87	1367, 1369, 1370, 1372, 1373, 1386
Marshall, William[231]	21 marks	1374–99	1373
Massy, John[232]	10 marks	1387–99	1386
Massy, Richard[233]	£10	1371–99	1370, 1372
Massy, Roger[234]	£10	before 1399	none
Maulevrer, Sir William[235]	10 marks	1376–82	1385
Maundeville, Thomas[236]	£8	1372–99	none
Mautravers, Sir John[237]	£10	1382–6	none
Mayhowe, John[238]	10 marks	1395	none
Meaux, Sir Thomas[239]		1382	1378, 1386

[220] Lewis, no. 41; DL 29/615/9840 m. 2.

[221] *Reg. II* 41; DL 29/615/9840 m. 2; *S. & G.*, i. 66; C. 81/1033 (50).

[222] DL 29/262/4069 m. 2, 4070 m. 2; C. 81/912 (40); C. 76/52 m. 8.

[223] *Reg. II* p. 12.

[224] *CPR 1399–1401*, 549; DL 29/738/12096 m. 8; C. 81/946 (65), *Reg. I* 49; C. 61/104 m. 6.

[225] *Reg. I* 779; DL 29/738/12096 m. 3; *Reg. I* 884; C. 76/55 m. 23.

[226] DL 28/32/2 f. 10v; East Sussex Record Office, GLY 3469 m. 12*d*.

[227] *Reg. I* 786; DL 29/738/12104 m. 1; Lopes, *Dom Joao I*, p. 242.

[228] *Reg. II* p. 9; C. 81/1033 (47).

[229] DL 42/12 f. 56; *Reg. II* p. 8; C. 81/912 (40), 925 (20).

[230] *Reg. I* 819; *Reg. II* 1235; C. 81/912 (40); C. 76/52 m. 15; C. 61/83 m. 1; C. 76/55 m. 21; *Reg. I* 49; C. 81/1036 (3).

[231] *Reg. I* 688; DL 42/15 f. 72v; C. 76/56 m. 20.

[232] Lewis, no. 10; DL 29/738/12096 m. 3.

[233] *Reg. I* 778; DL 29/738/12096 m. 3; *Reg. I* 884; C. 76/55 m. 35.

[234] DL 42/15 f. 25v; DL 29/738/12096 m. 3.

[235] DL 28/3/1 m. 8; *Reg. II* p. 9; *S. & G.*, i. 55.

[236] *Reg. I* 287; DL 42/15 f. 93.

[237] *Reg. II* p. 12; DL 29/738/12104 m. 1.

[238] DL 28/32/22 m. 27.

[239] *Reg. II* p. 8; C. 76/63 m. 20; C. 81/1033 (54).

	a	b	c
Melbourne, Peter[240]	£10	1376–99	none
Merbury, John[241]	10 marks	1395–9	1395
Mersh, John[242]	£11 13s. 4d.	1392–9	1369, 1378, 1395
Messingham, Roger[243]		1382	none
Metham, Sir Thomas[244]	£20	1361–90	1367, 1369, 1370, 1372, 1373, 1378
Middleton, Sir John[245]	£20	before 1399	none
Mikelfield, Richard[246]		1382	none
Mildenhall, Peter[247]	10 marks	1391–9	none
Mohaut, Robert[248]	10 marks	1384–91	none
Mohun, Payn de[249]		1361–75	none
Molyneux, Richard[250]	10 marks	1392	1395
Molyneux, Simon[251]	10 marks	1374	none
Montfort, Sir Baldwin[252]		1382	1386
Montgomery, Sir Nicholas[253]	40 marks	1394–9	1386, 1395
Moresam, John[254]		1382	1386
Morieux, Sir Thomas[255]	£100	1381–5	1386
Morton, Robert[256]	£20	1366–82	none
Mounteney, Thomas[257]	£10	1391–9	none
Mowbray, John,[258] earl of Nottingham	100 marks	1379–82	none

[240] Lewis, no. 5; DL 42/15 f. 1v.

[241] Appendix III, no. 9; DL 29/738/12096 m. 3.

[242] *CPR 1396–9*, 549; East Sussex Record Office, GLY 3469 mm. 7d–12d; DL 29/212/3248 m. 5; C. 81/925 (42); C. 76/62 m. 18.

[243] *Reg. II* p. 12.

[244] Leeds Central Lib., Grantley MS 500; DL 29/507/8227 m. 16; Nottinghamshire Record Office, Dd Fj 9/7/20; C. 61/79 m. 4; C. 76/52 m. 7; C. 61/83 m. 3; C. 76/55 m. 21, 56 m. 20, 63 m. 20.

[245] DL 42/16 f. 25.

[246] *Reg. II* p. 12.

[247] DL 29/310/4980 m. 2d; DL 29/738/12096 m. 9.

[248] DL 29/738/12104 m. 1; DL 43/15/3 m. 2d.

[249] *CPR 1361–4*, 50; *Reg. I* 1741.

[250] DL 28/3/3 m. 3; C. 61/104 m. 7.

[251] *Reg. I* 864.

[252] *Reg. II* p. 9; C. 81/1033 (43).

[253] DL 29/728/11982 m. 1; DL 29/738/12096 m. 6; C. 81/1033 (47); C. 61/104 m. 9.

[254] *Reg. II* p. 13; C. 81/1049 (28).

[255] *Reg. II* 543; Norfolk Record Office, NRS 11072 m. 2; C. 76/70 m. 10.

[256] *Reg. I* 283; Leeds Central Lib., Grantley MS 493–8, *Reg. II* p. 9.

[257] Appendix III, no. 4; DL 29/738/12096 m. 9.

[258] *CPR 1377–81*, 393; *Reg. II* p. 6.

	a	b	c
Mymott, John[259]	£10	1382–99	1373, 1386, 1395
Namers, Sir John[260]		1381–2	none
Nessfield, William[261]		1382	none
Neville, John, lord[262]	100 marks	1366–82	1367, 1369
Neville, Ralph, lord,[263] earl of Westmorland	500 marks	1397–9	none
Neville, Sir Robert[264]	£20	before 1399	1367, 1369
Newmarch, John[265]	80 marks	1361–75	1369, 1370
Newport, William[266]	20 marks	1386–99	1386
Newsome, Adam[267]	10 marks	1372–82	1367, 1370
Newton, Richard[268]	10 marks	1397–9	none
Norbury, John[269]	£10	1398–9	none
Northland, Sir Richard[270]	£20	1372–99	1372, 1373
Notton, William[271]	10 marks	1372–82	1367, 1369, 1373, 1386
Oddingsels, Sir John[272]	£40	1374–80	1378
Oke, John[273]	£10	1392–9	1395
Okeover, Sir Philip[274]		1382–94	1370, 1386
Oliver, Walter[275]	10 marks	1373	1370
Orell, James[276]		1382	1373, 1386
Otteway, Thomas[277]	10 marks	1394–9	1395

[259] *Reg. II* p. 11; DL 29/262/4071 m. 3; C. 76/56 m. 20; C. 81/1031 (24); C. 61/104 m. 9.

[260] East Sussex Record Office, GLY 3469 mm. 2*d*–5*d*; *Reg. II* p. 9.

[261] *Reg. II* p. 13.

[262] *Sotheby's Sale Catalogue*, 14/15 June 1971, no. 1427; ibid. 13 Apr. 1981, no. 98; *Reg. II* p. 7; C. 61/79 m. 4; C. 81/925 (31).

[263] *CPR 1396–9*, 548; DL 29/738/12096 m. 4.

[264] DL 42/15 f. 17v; *S. & G.*, i. 106; C. 76/52 m. 15.

[265] *Reg. I* 398, 1675; *CPR 1358–61*, 543; ibid. *1367–70*, 156; C. 76/52 m. 12; *Reg. I* 969.

[266] Lewis, no. 8; DL 29/738/12096 m. 6.

[267] *Reg. I* 851, 916; *Reg. II* p. 11; *S. & G.*, i. 68; *Reg. I* 1225.

[268] Appendix III, no. 13; DL 42/15 f. 12v.

[269] DL 42/15 f. 43v.

[270] *Reg. I* 806; DL 29/212/3248 m. 6; C. 76/55 m. 21; *Reg. I* 49.

[271] *Reg. I* 816; *Reg. II* p. 12; C. 61/79 m. 2; C. 76/52 m. 9, 56 m. 20; C. 81/1034 (45).

[272] *Reg. I* 869; *Reg. II* 138; C. 81/984 (46).

[273] *CPR 1396–9*, 499; East Sussex Record Office, GLY 3469 mm. 6*d*–12*d*; DL 29/738/12096 m. 8; C. 61/104 m. 7.

[274] *Reg. II* p. 9; DL 29/728/11982 m. 1; C. 61/83 m. 3; C. 81/1033 (47).

[275] *Reg. I* 858, 969.

[276] *Reg. II* p. 12; *Reg. I* 50; C. 76/70 m. 11.

[277] DL 29/728/11982 m. 1; DL 42/15 f. 107; C. 61/104 m. 7.

	a	b	c
Overbury, William[278]	£10	1380–2	none
Palays, Arnold[279]	£10	1392–9	none
Palays, John[280]	£10	1392–8	none
Panetrye, Janyn del[281]		1372–82	1367, 1369, 1373
Parr, John[282]		1381	
Parr, Sir William[283]	£50	1373–99	1370, 1373, 1378, 1395
Paumes, William[284]		1382	none
Payn, John[285]	10 marks	1394–9	none
Paynel, Sir Ralph[286]		1382	1369
Paynewich, Sir Hans[287]		1382	none
Pecche, Sir John[288]		1382	1386
Pelham, Sir John[289]	£25 10s. 0d.	before 1399	1386
Percy, Robert[290]		1382	none
Percy, Sir Thomas[291]	£100	1387–99	1386
Perewyche, Roger[292]	no fee	1382	none
Perrers, Richard[293]		1382	1386
Penhergerd, Sir Walter[294]	no fee	1371	1372, 1373
Peto, Sir John[295]		1382	none
Philip, Henry ap[296]		1382–4	none
Pierrepont, Sir Edmund[297]	£40	1368	1367, 1369, 1370, 1372, 1373

[278] *Reg. II* 1072, p. 10.
[279] DL 28/3/2 f. 10v, 5 f. 6; DL 29/212/3248 m. 6.
[280] DL 28/3/2 f. 10v, 5 f. 6.
[281] Northants Record Office, Fitzwilliam MS 456; *Reg. II* p. 10; C. 61/79 m. 4; C. 81/925 (20), 952 (19).
[282] E. 403/484 m. 15.
[283] *Reg. I* 1596; DL 42/15 f. 161; *Reg. I* 969, 50; C. 76/62 m. 1; C. 61/104 m. 7.
[284] *Reg. II* p. 12.
[285] Norfolk Record Office, NRS 3344 m. 2; DL 29/738/12096 m. 9.
[286] *Reg. II* p. 9; C. 76/52 m. 6.
[287] *Reg. II* p. 9.
[288] Ibid.; C. 81/1033 (43).
[289] DL 42/15 f. 123v; DL 29/738/12096 m. 9; C. 76/71 m. 26.
[290] *Reg. II* p. 13.
[291] *CPR 1399–1401*, 110; C. 76/70 m. 22.
[292] *Reg. II* 52.
[293] *Reg. II* p. 12; C. 81/1034 (8).
[294] *Reg. I* 784; C. 76/55 m. 21; *Reg. I* 49.
[295] *Reg. II* p. 9.
[296] Ibid. p. 12; DL 29/584/9238 m. 2.
[297] DL 29/262/4069 m. 2; C. 61/79 m. 3; C. 76/52 m. 8; C. 61/83 m. 3; C. 76/55 m. 22; *Reg. I* 49.

	a	b	c
Pilkington, Robert[298]	20 marks	1372–82	1369, 1370, 1372, 1373, 1378, 1386
Plays, Sir John[299]	£40	1370–88	1367, 1369, 1370, 1372, 1373, 1378
Plumpstead, William[300]	10 marks	before 1399	none
Plumpton, Sir Robert[301]	20 marks	before 1399	none
Pole, John de la[302]	£10	1381–3	1373, 1386
Pole, Sir John de la[303]		1383–95	1372, 1373
Pole, Sir Michael de la[304]		1369–82	1369, 1370, 1372, 1373, 1378
Popham, Sir Philip[305]	£10	1385–91	none
Popham, Thomas[306]	10 marks	1387–99	1386
Pulham, Stephen[307]	10 marks	1371–87	1370, 1373
Pyrton, Roger[308]	10 marks	1374–82	none
Querneby, William[309]		1372–82	1369
Radcliffe, Sir Ralph[310]	no fee	1380–2	none
Radcliffe, Richard[311]	20 marks	1375	1386
Radcliffe, Robert[312]	10 marks	1398–9	none
Radcliffe, Thomas[313]	100 marks	before 1399	none
Rainford, John[314]	10 marks	before 1399	none
Randolf, William[315]		1382	1370, 1378

[298] *Reg. I* 794; *Reg. II* p. 10; C. 81/924 (3); *Reg. I* 875; C. 76/55 m. 22, 56 m. 18, 62 m. 18; C. 81/1032 (5).

[299] *CPR 1367–70*, 406; DL 29/728/11975 m. 2; C. 81/912 (40), 925 (55); C. 61/83 m. 3; C. 76/55 m. 21, 56 m. 20; C. 81/985 (64).

[300] DL 42/15 f. 125v; DL 29/738/12096 m. 9.

[301] DL 42/16 f. 202v.

[302] *Reg. II* 45; DL 29/402/6448 m. 2; *Reg. I* 50; C. 76/70 m. 26.

[303] DL 29/402/6448 m. 2, 728/11982 m. 1; C. 76/55 m. 29, 56 m. 27.

[304] *Reg. I* 1107; *Reg. II* p. 7; C. 76/52 m. 13; C. 61/83 m. 3; C. 76/55 m. 14, 56 m. 10, 62 m. 2.

[305] DL 29/738/12104 m. 1; DL 43/15/3 m. 3.

[306] Lewis, no. 9; DL 29/738/12096 m. 8; C. 81/1035 (45).

[307] *Reg. I* 777; Norfolk Record Office, NRS 3343 m. 2; *Reg. I* 969, 50.

[308] *Reg. I* 870; *Reg. II* p. 11.

[309] *Reg. I* 902; *Reg. II* p. 11; C. 81/925 (20).

[310] *Reg. II* 34, p. 9.

[311] *Reg. I* 704, 705; C. 81/1034 (11).

[312] Appendix III, no. 17; DL 29/738/12096 m. 2.

[313] *Testamenta Eboracensa*, i. 238; DL 29/738/12096 m. 1.

[314] DL 42/15 f. 153.

[315] *Reg. II* p. 12; *Reg. I* 969; C. 76/63 m. 20.

	a	b	c
Raynald, John[316]	£20	1372–83	1367, 1370
Recouchez, Louis[317]	£40	1372–93	1373
Redman, Sir Richard[318]	£20	before 1399	none
Rempston, Sir Thomas[319]	40 marks	before 1399	none
Reymes, John[320]	£10	1392–9	1386, 1395
Reyner, John[321]	10 marks	1398–9	none
Rither, John[322]	£10 17s. 8d.	1361–94	1369, 1373
Rixton, John[323]	£10	1387–99	1386
Rixton, Richard[324]	£10	1385–99	1386
Robessart, Sir John[325]	40 marks	1392–9	none
Rocheford, Sir John[326]	£50	1361–85	1367, 1369, 1370, 1373
Rocheford, Sir John[327] (the son)	£20	before 1399	1378
Rocheford, Sir Ralph[328]	100 marks	1392–9	1369, 1373, 1378
Rockley, Sir Robert[329]	£90	1373–99	1369, 1370, 1373, 1386
Rondon, Sir John[330]		1382	1386
Rook, Lewis[331]		1382	none
Roos, John[332]		1382	none
Roos, Piers[333]	£10	1382	none

[316] *Reg. I* 797; DL 29/402/6448 m. 2; C. 61/79 m. 8, 83 m. 4.
[317] *Reg. I* 791; DL 28/3/2 f. 11; C. 76/56 m. 20.
[318] DL 42/16 f. 231.
[319] DL 42/16 f. 183; DL 29/212/3248 m. 5.
[320] Norfolk Record Office, NRS 3344 m. 2; East Sussex Record Office, GLY 3469 mm. 7d–8d; DL 29/738/12096 m. 9; C. 81/1040 (24).
[321] DL 42/15 ff. 54v, 103v.
[322] *Reg. II* 999; DL 29/507/8227 m. 14; DL 43/15/6 m. 4; C. 81/925 (20), *Reg. I* 50.
[323] DL 29/16/202 m. 2; Lewis, no. 20; C. 81/1032 (5).
[324] Appendix III, no. 3; DL 29/738/12096 m. 1; C. 76/70 m. 28.
[325] East Sussex Record Office, GLY 3469 mm. 6d–12d; DL 29/212/3248 m. 5.
[326] DL 29/262/4069 m. 2, 4070 m. 2; C. 81/912 (40), 925 (20); C. 61/83 m. 3; *Reg. I* 49.
[327] DL 29/262/4071 m. 3; C. 81/986 (12).
[328] East Sussex Record Office, GLY 3469 m. 12d; DL 29/738/12096 m. 10; C. 81/925 (22); *Reg. I* 49; C. 81/986 (12).
[329] *Reg. I* 1196; DL 29/738/12096 m. 4; C. 81/925 (23); *Reg. I* 1663, 1232; DL 28/3/2 f. 14.
[330] *Reg. II* pp. 9, 12; C. 81/1034 (29).
[331] *Reg. II* p. 12.
[332] Ibid. p. 11.
[333] *Reg. II* 47.

	a	b	c
Roos, Sir Robert[334]	£20	1366–73	1369, 1370
Roos, Robert[335]	£10	1381–3	none
Roos, Thomas[336]		1382	none
Roos, Thomas lord[337]	£40	1370–82	1369, 1370
			1372, 1373,
			1378
Rose, Henry[338]	£10	1375–84	1369, 1373
Roundell, John[339]	10 marks	1397–9	1395
Rous, John[340]		1382	1386
Routhe, Sir Thomas[341]	10 marks	1379–99	1385, 1386
Rowcliffe, Sir David[342]	£40	1382–99	1385
Rowcliffe, Sir Richard[343]		1379–82	1367, 1369
(the son) Rowcliffe, Sir Richard[344]		1379–82	none
Saintowen, Patrick[345]	£10	1392–9	1386
Sanchez, Alfonso[346]	£10	1382–92	none
Sarnesfield, Sir Nicholas[347]	£20	1373–91	1373
Savage, John[348]	10 marks	before 1399	1386
Saville, Sir John[349]	£20	1372–90	1367, 1369,
			1370, 1373
Scargill, John[350]		1380–2	1386
Scargill, Sir William[351]			
(the younger)	20 marks	1372–82	1369, 1370,
			1373

[334] DL 29/262/4069 m. 2; *Reg. I* 1261; C. 76/52 m. 17; C. 61/83 m. 4.

[335] East Sussex Record Office, GLY 3469 mm. 1*d*–5*d*; *Reg. II* 797.

[336] *Reg. II* p. 11.

[337] *Reg. I* 945; *Reg. II* p. 7; C. 76/52 m. 13; C. 61/83 m. 3; C. 76/55 m. 14, 56 m. 18, 62 m. 1.

[338] *Reg. I* 1687; Norfolk Record Office, NRS 3342 m. 2, NRS 11072 m. 2; C. 76/52 m. 9, 56 m. 10.

[339] *CPR 1396–9*, 514; DL 29/738/12096 m. 6; C. 61/104 m. 6.

[340] *Reg. II* p. 11; C. 81/1048 (31).

[341] *Reg. II* 108; DL 29/738/12096 m. 5; *S. & G.*, i. 64; C. 76/70 m. 11.

[342] *Reg. II* p. 9; DL 29/738/12096 m. 5; *S. & G.*, i. 65.

[343] *Reg. II* 72, p. 8; C. 81/912 (40), 925 (20).

[344] *Reg. II* 72, p. 7.

[345] East Sussex Record Office, GLY 3469 mm. 6*d*–12*d*; DL 29/738/12096 m. 8; C. 81/1038 (49).

[346] *Reg. II* 792; East Sussex Record Office, GLY 3469 mm. 6*d*–14*d*.

[347] *Reg. I* 67; *Reg. II* 1030; DL 43/15/3 m. 3; C. 76/56 m. 11.

[348] DL 42/15 f. 149v; C. 81/1036 (19).

[349] *Reg. I* 1037; Notts. Record Office, Dd Sr 231/54, 28/3/5; C. 81/912 (40); C. 76/52 m. 15; C. 61/83 m. 3; C. 76/56 m. 20.

[350] *Reg. II* 27, p. 10; C. 81/1034 (40).

[351] *Reg. I* 920; *Reg. II* p. 8; *Manuscripts of St George's Chapel, Windsor Castle*, ed. J. N. Dalton, p. 88; C. 76/52 m. 13; C. 61/83 m. 3; C. 81/952 (67).

	a	b	c
Scrope, Richard lord[352]	£40	1367–99	1359, 1367, 1369, 1373, 1384, 1385
Seymour, William[353]	no fee	1383	none
Seynclere, Sir John[354]		1372–82	1385, 1386
Seyton, Sir John[355]	20 marks	1377–83	1369, 1378, 1385, 1386, 1395
Sherwynd, Robert[356]	10 marks	1387–99	1386
Shirley, Sir Hugh[357]	£20	1392–9	1386
Simeon, Robert[358]	20 marks	1390–9	1386
Simeon, Simon[359]	£20	1361–84	1369
Singleton, William[360]	10 marks	before 1399	none
Skelton, Sir Thomas[361]	£20	1396–7	none
Skoggan, John[362]		1382	none
Sotheron, John[363]	10 marks	1372–99	1373
Southworth, John[364]	£10	1398–9	none
Southworth, Sir Thomas[365]	20 marks	1372–82	1372, 1373, 1378, 1386
St Lo, Sir John[366]	£100	1372–3	1367, 1369, 1370, 1372, 1373
Stafford, John[367]	£10	1383–99	none

[352] *Reg. I* 600; DL 42/15 f. 55v; C. 76/38 m. 13; C. 61/79 m. 3; C. 76/52 m. 13; *S. & G.*, ii. 15–16.

[353] *Reg. II* 44.

[354] *Reg. I* 487; *Reg. II* p. 9; *S. & G.*, i. 54; C. 81/1032 (14).

[355] DL 29/212/3247 m. 2, 341/5516 m. 2; C. 81/925 (20); C. 76/63 m. 18; *S. & G.*, i. 56; C. 81/1034 (9); C. 61/104 m. 7.

[356] Lewis, no. 13; DL 29/738/12096 m. 8.

[357] East Sussex Record Office, GLY 3469 mm. 6d–14d; DL 42/15 f. 23; Leicestershire Record Office, 26 D. 53/2543.

[358] Lewis, no. 21; DL 29/212/3248 m. 5; C. 81/1036 (8).

[359] DL 29/262/4069 m. 3, 4070 m. 3; C. 81/925 (20).

[360] DL 42/16 f. 171.

[361] DL 28/3/5 f. 8.

[362] *Reg. II* p. 12.

[363] *Reg. I* 810; C. 266/42/41, 82/4; C. 76/56 m. 20.

[364] Bodl., Dodsworth MS 53 f. 17; PL 1/2 m. 1.

[365] *Reg. I* 805; *Reg. II* p. 8; C. 76/55 m. 22, 56 m. 20, 62 m. 18; C. 81/1033 (5).

[366] *Reg. I* 1385, 1679; C. 81/912 (40); C. 76/52 m. 12; C. 81/939 (17), 946 (29), 950 (45).

[367] DL 29/402/6448 m. 2; *CPR 1396–9*, 513; DL 29/738/12096 m. 6.

	a	b	c
Standish, Sir Robert[368]	50 marks	1372–99	1370, 1378, 1386, 1395
Stanes, William[369]	10 marks	1372–84	1369
Staveley, Ralph[370]	10 marks	1392–9	none
Strange, Hamo[371]		1382	none
Strange, Sir John[372]	no fee	1373–82	1386
Strickland, Thomas[373]	10 marks	before 1399	none
Stynt, John[374]		1382	none
Sudbury, William[375]	no fee	1373–82	1370
Sulny, Sir Alured[376]	20 marks	1361–75	1369, 1373
Swell, John[377]	20 marks	1389–99	1386
Swillington, Sir Robert[378]	£70	1362–87	1359, 1367, 1369, 1380
Swillington, William[379]	£5	1382–99	1386
Swynburn, Sir William[380]	£20	1384–96	none
Swynford, Sir Thomas[381]	£106 13s. 4d.	1382–99	none
Swynton, Sir John[382]	£40	1372–84	1373
Symond, Sir Thomas[383]	100 marks	1373–87	1378, 1386
Talbot, Sir Gilbert[384]	20 marks	1383–7	1373, 1386
Talbot, John[385]	£10	1372–5	none
Talbot, Sir John[386]	40 marks	1373–84	1369, 1370
Talbot, Nicholas[387]	20 marks	1387–99	1386

[368] *CPR 1396–9*, 571; DL 42/15 f. 89; *Reg. I* 969; C. 76/62 m. 18; C. 81/1033 (7); C. 61/104 m. 7.
[369] *Reg. I* 799; DL 29/262/4070 m. 2; C. 81/925 (20).
[370] *CPR 1396–9*, 566; DL 29/212/3248 m. 5.
[371] *Reg. II* p. 12.
[372] *Reg. I* 853; *Reg. II* p. 8; C. 76/70 m. 11.
[373] DL 42/15 f. 6.
[374] *Reg. II* p. 11.
[375] *Reg. I* 856; *Reg. II* p. 11; *Reg. I* 969.
[376] SC 6/988/14 m. 4d; *Reg. I* 1714; C. 81/925 (20), 1730 (51).
[377] Lewis, no. 19; DL 29/738/12104 m. 2d; C. 81/1034 (14).
[378] *CPR 1361–4*, 397; *Reg. II* 1239; C. 76/38 m. 13; C. 81/912 (40), 942 (3); C. 71/60 m. 2.
[379] *Reg. II* p. 10; DL 29/738/12096 m. 5; C. 76/70 m. 12.
[380] *Archaeologia Aeliana*, 4th series, 11, 79; Northumberland Record Office, ZSW 1/91, 92.
[381] *CPR 1396–9*, 498; DL 28/3/2 f. 10; *Reg. II* p. 10; DL 29/738/12096 m. 10.
[382] *Reg. I* 789; DL 29/262/4070 m. 2; *Reg. I* 1457.
[383] *Reg. I* 838; DL 29/738/12104 m. 2; C. 81/1715 (2), 1038 (24).
[384] DL 29/738/12104 m. 1; C. 81/960 (35); *Froissart (K. de L.)*, xii. 324.
[385] *Reg. I* 800, 1622.
[386] Ibid. 1297; DL 29/402/6448 m. 2; C. 81/925 (20); C. 61/83 m. 4.
[387] Lewis, no. 14; DL 29/738/12096 m. 8.

	a	b	c
Tebaud, Piers[388]		1382	none
Thoresby, Elys[389]	no fee	1374–80	none
Thornbury, Sir John[390]	no fee	1380–2	1372
Topcliff, John[391]	£10	1374–91	1369, 1370
Torbock, Sir Richard[392]		1382	1384, 1386
Totty, Thomas[393]	10 marks	1392–9	none
Tournay, Nicholas[394]	10 marks	before 1399	none
Travers, Sir Thomas[395]	£20	1373–5	1369, 1370, 1373
Trewennock, Thomas[396]	no fee	1381–2	none
Trumpington, Sir Roger[397]	£20	1371–8	1369, 1370, 1373, 1378
Trumpington, Roger[398]	20 marks	1392–9	none
Tunstall, Sir Thomas[399]	£23 6s. 7d.	before 1399	1395
Tunstall, William[400]	no fee	1381–2	1386
Tutbury, Thomas[401]	20 marks	1361–73	1367, 1369
Tybenham, John[402]	£5	1398–9	none
Typet, Simon[403]	10 marks	1375–99	1386
Urswick, Sir Robert[404]	40 marks	1394–9	none
Urswick, Robert[405]	£10	1395–9	1395
Urswick, Sir Walter[406]	£123 6s. 8d.	1361–94	1367, 1369, 1370, 1372, 1385, 1386
Usflete, Sir Gerard[407]	£20	1370–99	1370, 1372

[388] *Reg. II* p. 12; C. 81/1034 (59)—protection for 1386, revoked,/1350 (7).
[389] *Reg. I* 865; *Reg. II* 353.
[390] *Reg. II* 31, p. 8; C. 76/55 m. 21.
[391] *Reg. I* 614; DL 29/310/4980 m. 2*d*; C. 76/52 m. 15; C. 61/83 m. 3.
[392] *Reg. II* p. 9; *DKR* xl. 522; C. 81/1033 (8).
[393] *CPR 1396–9*, 122; DL 42/15 f. 18v.
[394] DL 42/15 f. 65v.
[395] *Reg. I* 834, 1654; C. 76/52 m. 14; *Reg. I* 1663; C. 76/56 m. 26.
[396] *Reg. II* 43, p. 12.
[397] *Reg. I* 848, 930; *CCR 1377–81*, 201; C. 76/52 m. 15; *Reg. I* 969; C. 76/56 m. 27.
[398] *CPR 1399–1401*, 247; East Sussex Record Office, GLY 3469 mm. 7*d*–14*d*.
[399] DL 25/3480; C. 61/104 m. 9.
[400] *Reg. II* 37, pp. 9, 11; C. 81/1034 (27).
[401] *Reg. I* 852; C. 81/912 (40), 924 (3).
[402] Lewis, no. 37; DL 29/738/12096 m. 10.
[403] *Reg. I* 733; *CPR 1396–9*, 532; DL 29/212/3248 m. 7*d*; C. 81/1033 (33).
[404] *CPR 1396–9*, 547; DL 29/738/12096 m. 1.
[405] Lewis, no. 28; DL 42/15 f. 13v.
[406] *CPR 1367–70*, 77; DL 43/15/6 m. 7; C. 61/79 m. 4; C. 76/52 m. 15; C. 61/83 m. 2; C. 81/947 (11); *S. & G.*, i. 51; C. 81/1034 (61).
[407] Nottinghamshire Record Office, Dd Fj 9/7/16; DL 29/738/12096 m. 5; C. 61/83 m. 2; C. 76/55 m. 22.

	a	b	c
Usk, Nicholas[408]	£20	1377–99	none
Wandesford, John[409]		1382	none
Warde, Henry[410]	20 marks	1372–81	1369
Waterton, Hugh[411]	40 marks	1377–99	1373
Waterton, Robert[412]	10 marks	1392–9	none
Wells, John lord[413]	£20	1372	1369, 1372, 1373
Wennesley, Sir Thomas[414]	20 marks	1384–99	none
Wesenham, John[415]	£20	1381	none
White, Sir John[416]	£20	1382–97	1386
Whitfield, Richard[417]	no fee	1372–82	none
Whitemore, Edmund[418]	10 marks	1398–9	none
Whittingham, Thomas[419]		1392	1386
Wilby, William[420]	10 marks	1389–91	none
Wintringham, William[421]	£20	1373–80	1373
Wirley, Richard[422]	20 marks	1372–3	1370
Workesley, Sir Geoffrey[423]	£20	1381–3	none
Workesley, Robert[424]	£20	1382–99	none
Wrench, John[425]	£15	1377–84	1367, 1369, 1370
Wyram, Ivo[426]	10 marks	1397–9	none

[408] DL 29/212/3247 m. 1; *CPR 1396–9*, 470; DL 29/212/3248 m. 7.
[409] *Reg. II* p. 13.
[410] *Reg. I* 795; East Sussex Record Office, GLY 3469 mm. 1*d*–5*d*; C. 81/925 (20).
[411] DL 28/3/1 m. 7; DL 29/212/3248 m. 5; *Reg. I* 50.
[412] *CPR 1396–9*, 468; DL 29/738/12096 m. 4.
[413] *Reg. I* 788; C. 81/925 (55); C. 76/55 m. 21, 56 m. 24.
[414] Lewis, no. 6; DL 29/738/12096 m. 6.
[415] *Reg. II* 502, 978.
[416] Ibid. p. 12; Norfolk Record Office, NRS 15171 m. 2; C. 81/1032 (27).
[417] *Reg. I* 782; *Reg. II* p. 11.
[418] Appendix III, no. 16, SC 8/148/7377.
[419] East Sussex Record Office, GLY 3469 mm. 6*d*–14*d*; *Reg. II* 1235.
[420] DL 29/738/12104 m. 2*d*; DL 43/15/3 m. 3.
[421] *Reg. I* 854; Norfolk Record Office, NRS 3342 m. 2; C. 76/56 m. 18.
[422] *Reg. I* 820; BL Add. MS 37494 f. 38; *Reg. I* 969.
[423] *Reg. II* 38, 799.
[424] Ibid. p. 11; DL 29/738/12096 m. 3.
[425] DL 29/584/9237 m. 2, 9238 m. 2; C. 81/912 (40); *Reg. I* 922; C. 61/83 m. 3.
[426] Lewis, no. 32; Norfolk Record Office, NRS 15171 m. 2; DL 29/738/12096 m. 9.

APPENDIX II. Central and Estate Officials

Additions and Corrections to Sir Robert Somerville's List

The order of the list in Somerville, pp. 363–85 has been followed and the letter S after an entry indicates that further information on a particular official will be found there. No attempt has been made to improve on the list of the duke's Welsh officials provided by R. R. Davies, 'The Bohun and Lancaster Lordships in Wales in the Fourteenth and Fifteenth Centuries' (Oxford University D.Phil. thesis, 1965), pp. 387–92. Unless otherwise stated the date given is that at which the official appears as holding office.

(i) Household and Central

Chamberlain:

Sir Robert Swillington	Mich. 1383–4	(*BIHR* 13 (1935/6), 155) S
Sir Richard Abberbury	28 July 1388	(*Foedera*, vii. 595)
Sir Walter Blount	Mich. 1394–5	(Norfolk Record Office, NRS 3344 m. 2) S

Steward:

Sir Hugh Segrave, in Aquitaine	1371	(*Reg. I* 1115)
Sir John Dabridgecourt	1399	(*CPR 1396–9*, 534)

Controller:

Thomas Haselden	15 June 1383	(C. 71/62 m. 1) S
John Tutbury	13 Dec. 1391	(E. 403/536 m. 13) A mistake for Thomas Tutbury?
John Oke	Sept. 1397	(DL 28/3/5 f. 14; *CPR 1396–9*, 499)

Treasurer:

John Marthon	date unknown	(*Political Poems and Songs*, ed. T. Wright (Rolls Series, 1859), i. 97)
John Lincoln	1363	(*Calendar of Papal Registers, Petitions 1342–1419*, 423) S
Thomas de Stockton	1364–5	(DL 29/288/4721 m. 3)
John Norfolk	Mich. 1383–4	(*BIHR* 13 (1935/6), 155) S

Robert Whitby	23 July 1393	(E. 403/543 m. 19)
	18 June 1394	(E. 403/548 m. 13)
Nicholas Usk	1395–7	(*Anglo-Norman Letters and Petitions*, no. 283; DL 28/3/5 f. 5) S

Wardrobe:

John Burton, keeper	Mich. 1383–4	(*BIHR* 13 (1935/6), 155) S
John Elvet, clerk	Feb. 1394–5	(DL 28/32/21)
	Mich. 1396	(DL 28/3/5 f. 5)
John Binbrook, clerk succeeding Elvet	21 Dec. 1396	(DL 28/3/5 f. 5)

Secretary:

| John Leventhorpe | 1375 | (*The Anglo-French Negotiations at Bruges, 1374–1377*, ed. E. Perroy, pp. 8, 23) |
| William Ketteryng | Jan. 1390 | (C. 61/101 m. 11) |

Chief Steward of Lands:

| Sir Godfrey Foljambe | 1358, 1366 | (*Collectanea Topographica et Genealogica*, i. 334) S |

Chief Steward—South Parts:

| Sir Thomas Skelton | Mich. 1396–7 | (DL 28/3/5 f. 8v) S |

Chief Steward—North Parts:

Sir William Hauley	Mich. 1383–4	(DL 29/262/4070 m. 3) S
John de la Pole	8 May, 7 Aug. 1387	(*Plumpton Correspondence*, p. xxii; Nottinghamshire Record Office, Dd Fj 9/7/19) S
Sir John Bussy	Mich. 1396–7	(DL 28/3/5 f. 8) S
John Cokayn	4 Mar. 1398	(*Yorkshire Deeds*, i. 155) S

Receiver-General:

| William Bughbrigg | 3 June 1363 | (E. 43/194) S |
| Nicholas Usk | 8 Jan. 1399 | (E. 403/561 m. 11) |

Attorney-General:

| Thomas Haselden, in office before Whitby | c.1382–6 | (DL 28/3/2 f. 12v) |
| Robert Whitby | Mich. 1396 | (DL 28/3/5 f. 8v) S |

Auditor—North Parts:

| Richard Monmouth | 7 Aug. 1387 Mich. 1396–7 | (Nottinghamshire Record Office, Dd Fj 9/7/19; DL 28/3/5 f. 7v) |

(ii) Local Officers

Beds. and Bucks.:

| Richard Shelve, feodary | Mich. 1396–7 | (DL 28/3/5 f. 2) |

Dunstanburgh:

John Querneby, receiver, steward, and constable	1367	(DL 29/354/5837 m. 1)
Thomas Galon, receiver	Mich. 1396–7	(DL 28/3/5 f. 2) S

Halton:

William Nessfield, steward	1380	(W. Beamont, *An Account of the Rolls of the Honour of Halton*, p. 47)
Sir Richard Aston, app. steward and constable	22 Nov. 1387	(DL 29/16/202 m. 1) S
William Dutton, receiver in Cheshire, app.	15 Nov. 1390	(SC 6/773/6 m. 4)

Hertford:

Edward Beauchamp, constable	14 June 1397	(*CPR 1396–9*, 148) S
John Asshewy, receiver	Mich. 1396–7	(DL 28/3/5 ff. 1v, 14) S

Knaresborough:

Sir John Marmion, app. constable	20 July 1377	(*CPR 1377–81*, 294) S
Richard Brennand, guardian of the castle	June 1381	(*Anonimalle Chronicle*, p. 153) S
Sir Robert Plumpton, constable and lieutenant to the master forester	Oct. 1387	(*Plumpton Correspondence*, p. xxii)
Thomas Chaucer, removed from office as constable	1399	(*CPR 1396–9*, 494; *Historical Notices of Swyncombe and Ewelme*, p. 27)

Lancashire:

Sir John Botiller, app. sheriff	27 Nov. 1371	(E. 199/21/9) S
Ralph de Ipres, receiver	Mich. 1396–7	(DL 28/3/5 f. 2) S
Sir John Botiller (of Rawcliffe), receiver under John of Gaunt		(DL 42/15 f. 117v)

Wapentakes

Blackburnshire:

Richard Radcliffe, steward	29 Aug. 1361– 3 Apr. 1364	(*De Hoghton Deeds*, nos. 502, 570, 875, 876)
Gilbert de la Legh, steward	8 Sept. 1374	(Lancs. Record Office Dd Wh 3/3) S
Thomas Radcliffe, steward	11 Apr. 1388 8 July 1394	(*De Hoghton Deeds*, no. 578) S (Lancs. Record Office, Dd Pt 5/63)

Amounderness:

Robert de Singleton, steward	May 1362	(*De Hoghton Deeds*, no. 408)
Sir Adam Hoghton, master forester	20 Dec. 1369	(Bodl. MS CCC 495 f. 15) S
Ralph de Ipres, steward	1395–6	(PL 14/154/1(14)) S

Salford and West Derby:

Matthew Rixton, steward	1368	(KB 27/454 Rex m. 13)
Ralph de Torbok, bailiff of West Derbyshire	1368–9	(JUST 1/442*B* m. 3)
Nicholas de Barmford, bailiff of Salfordshire	1386–7	(PL 16/1/1 m. 2*d*)
Richard Halsall, bailiff of West Derbyshire	Sept. 1394	(*Cartulary of Burscough Priory*, no. 152)
Hugh de Ines, bailiff of Salfordshire	date unknown	(PL 14/154/1/25)

Clitheroe:

Richard Townley, steward	14 Dec. 1365	(*De Hoghton Deeds*, no. 88)

Leicester:

William de Burgh, steward	Mich. 1377–8	(DL 29/212/3247 m. 1) S
Sir Thomas Walsh, constable	Apr. 1394	(*CCR 1392–6*, 212) S
William Chiselden, receiver	Mich. 1396–7	(DL 28/3/5 f. 4) S
Oliver de Kneshale, feodary in co. Northants	Mich. 1381–2	(DL 29/341/5516 m. 2*d*) S
William Bispham, feodary in co. Northants	Jan. 1387 Mich. 1394–5	(Leics. Record Office, 26 D. 53/2047; E. 159/171, Adhuc Communia, Trinity, Recorda) S

Lincoln:

Richard Bradley, receiver and feodary	Mich. 1396–7	(DL 28/32/23; E. 368/170, Adhuc Communia, Trinity, Recorda) S
Hugh Annesley, keeper of Lancaster fees in co. Lincs.	Mich. 1391–2	(DL 43/15/4 m. 3) S

Norfolk and Suffolk:

Edmund Gournay, steward	Mich. 1379–80	(Norfolk Record Office, NRS 3342 m. 1) S
Robert Cayley, steward	Mich. 1384–6	(Norfolk Record Office, NRS 11072 m. 2, 3343 m. 2) S
John de Methwold, steward	20 June 1392 1394–5, 1396–7	(Norfolk Record Office, MR 79 241 X 3, NRS 3344 m. 2, 15171 m. 2)

Sir Robert Berney, steward of Gimingham	Mich. 1398–9	(DL 29/289/4744 m. 4)
John Winter, receiver	Mich. 1396–8	(Norfolk Record Office, NRS 15171 m. 1; DL 29/289/4744 m. 1)
William Farwell, bailiff of the liberty of the honour of Lancaster	Mich. 1396–7	(Norfolk Record Office, NRS 3345 m. 1*d*)
Pickering:		
Sir David Rowcliffe, constable	1393	(KB 9/146 m. 10) S
Pontefract:		
Sir William Finchdean, steward	1364–5	(G. Fox, *History of Pontefract*, p. 28) S
Sir John Saville, constable	1396–7	(CP 40/542 m. 242 d.)
Sir Robert Neville of Hornby, constable	date unknown	(*CPR 1405–8*, 73; *Rot. Parl.*, iii. 449*b*)
Robert Morton, receiver	1366, 1370	(*Collectanea Topographica et Genealogica*, i. 334; Nottinghamshire Record Office, Dd Fj 9/7/16) S
William Kettering, receiver	Mich. 1396–7	(DL 28/3/5 f. 2) S
Thomas Maunsell, bailiff of the liberty	May 1381	(Nottinghamshire Record Office, Dd Fj 1/259/21)
Hugh de Brerelay, master forester	1366	(*Collectanea Topographica et Genealogica*, i. 334)
South Parts:		
William Everley, receiver	May 1384	(DL 29/727/11940 m. 2) S
William Overbury, receiver	12 Mar. 1385 demits 11 July 1396	(Magdalen College, Benham MS 162; DL 28/3/5 f. 4) S
Robert Toly, feodary in co. Somerset	Aug. 1372	(*The Hylle Cartulary*, no. 26) S
John Wolf, feodary in co. Somerset and Dorset	1396	(E. 368/170, Adhuc Communia, Trinity, Recorda; DL 28/3/5
receiver	Mich. 1396–7	f. 3) S
Sussex:		
John Edward, steward	1376	(JUST 3/163 m. 9*d*) S
John Broke, steward	1391–2	(DL 43/15/4 m. 4) S
William Cole, receiver of Surrey and Sussex	Mich. 1396–7	(DL 28/3/5 f. 1v)
John Delves, feodary	Mich. 1377–8 to Mich, 1385 –6	(DL 29/441/7081; JUST 1/944 m.1; DL 29/727/11941) S

John Bradbridge, feodary   Mich. 1387–90 (DL 29/727/11942–3)
John Singleton, bailiff of the 1392–3   (DL 29/728/11979 m. 2)
   franchise
Sir Thomas Symond,   Mich. 1385–6   (DL 29/727/11941 m. 2)
   constable of Pevensey
Roger Ewent, constable   8 July 1389   (*CPR 1396–9*, 14) S
Roger Lewknor, app. master 1395   (DL 29/727/11945)
   forester of Ashdown, but
   displaced on the duke's
   mandate by Bradshawe

Tickhill:
William Normanton, feodary 1396   (E. 368/170, Adhuc Communia,
                                        Trinity, Recorda)

Tutbury:
John Cokayn, steward   26 Sept. 1363   (*Cartulary of Tutbury Priory*, ed.
                            26 July 1367   A. Saltman, nos. 357, 342)
Robert atte More, receiver July 1367   (E. 212/RS 211) S
Thomas Botheby, receiver   Mich. 1396–7   (DL 28/3/5 f. 2) S
Sir Alured Sulny, master-   26 Sept. 1363   (*Cartulary of Tutbury Priory*, nos.
   forester   26 July 1367   357, 342) S
Thomas Foljambe and   1396–7   (*Collectanea Topographica et*
   Thomas Wennesley, joint   *Genealogica*, i. 334)
   surveyors of the forest of
   the Peak
John Hublyn, receiver of   June 1376   (BL Wolley Charter, II. 75) S
   the Peak
Thurstan del Boure, bailiff Hilary 1387   (*Select Cases in the Court of King's*
   of the liberty of the   *Bench*, ed. Sayles, vii. 51)
   Peak
Sir Thomas Wennesley,   Mich. 1392–3   (DL 43/15/7 m. 1) S
   constable of Peak castle

Yorkshire:
William Normanton,   7 Aug. 1387   (Nottinghamshire Record Office,
   feodary   14 Sept. 1390   Dd Fj 9/7/19, 20) S
William Kettering, receiver 16 May 1387   (Nottinghamshire Record Office,
                            May 1395/6   Dd Fj 9/7/18; Northumberland
                                           Record Office, ZSW 1/ 91, 92) S

Richmond:
William Nessfield, steward 25 Mar. 1368   (*Gesta Abbatum Monasterii Sancti*
                                         Albani, iii. 98)
Robert Morton, receiver   Nov. 1363–   (Leeds Central Lib., Grantley
                             Feb. 1368   MSS 493–8)

(iii) Other Local Officers

Stephen Stutteville, keeper of fees in Cambs. and Hunts.	Mich. 1396–7	(DL 28/3/5 f. 4v) S
Stephen Dernford, keeper of fees and franchises in Devon	Mich. 1379–80	(BL Add. Roll 64317 m. 2) S
John Sire, steward of King's Somborne	1 June 1384	(Magdalen College, King's Somborne MS 84 (168))
Thomas Titteshale, feodary in Suffolk	1369–70	(DL 36/2/268) S

APPENDIX III. Unpublished Indentures of Retinue with John of Gaunt, duke of Lancaster

THE indentures transcribed and calendared in this Appendix supplement those published from the two volumes of John of Gaunt's registers and the patent rolls of the royal chancery. They differ in few important respects from the indentures already in print, but they help to provide a clearer picture of the chronological development of the duke's retinue, the changing conditions of service the duke required from his men, and the diplomatic evolution of the indenture itself.

The most important of these indentures is the first, concluded with Sir Hugh Hastings in 1366, which pre-dates all existing contracts with the duke and provides a rare example of the initial, experimental, form of Gaunt's indentures before their standardization during the early 1370s. In the elaboration and detail of its stipulations it stands in strong contrast to the duke's early indenture with Sir John de Ipres,[1] but the combination of the conventional features of an indenture with those of a military subcontract, including a very full enumeration of the conditions of the service to be undertaken by Sir Hugh, gives it many similarities to the duke's indenture with John, lord Neville, in 1370.[2] However, the second indenture printed here emphasizes how brief was this period of experimentation and evolution in the substance of the duke's contracts for, in offering Sir Gerard Usflete a regard of £20 p.a. for the service of two esquires in wartime, it anticipates by two years the provisions of some of the indentures copied into the duke's first register.[3]

The emphasis on a retainer's service in time of war which appears in both Hastings's and Usflete's indentures is still more strongly expressed in the duke's contract with Richard de Rixton (no. 3) which, whilst granting Rixton and the two men-at-arms and six archers he undertook to bring with him their wages of war, grants only Rixton himself wages and bouche of court in time of peace. The purpose of such an indenture is, clearly, almost entirely military, the product of a specific need for manpower in the forthcoming expedition against Scotland and the duke's projected venture in Spain, but the contract also provides an example of the relatively small class of indentures which offer the duke's retainer no annual fee for his services. In another of these indentures, also concluded in April 1385, Sir Ralph Bracebridge was granted wages for himself and an esquire in time of war and, in time of peace, wages and bouche of court only when summoned by the duke and bouche of court

---

[1] Lewis, no. 1.
[2] Ibid. no. 3.
[3] *Reg. I* 803, 833.

alone for his esquire.[4] This restriction on attendance at the duke's court, no less than the absence of an annual fee, contrasts strongly with the large suite of servants allowed Sir Hugh Hastings or John, lord Neville, and clearly illustrates the tendency towards a simplification and standardization of the substance of the duke's contracts, in a way that generally gave greater discretionary powers to the duke and left his retainers with fewer specific rewards and allowances.

The remaining indentures, all dating from the last decade of the duke's life, faithfully reflect this tendency in both substance and wording. John Cornwall's indenture (no. 8) provides a late example of the grant of improved terms of service when the retainer changes his status (in this case, from esquire to knight) and is unique in assuming that the change will definitely take place. It is also unusual in granting Cornwall, although still only an esquire, both wages of war and bouche of court—a privilege normally reserved for those of knightly status. The provisions of the other indentures can be paralleled many times amongst the contracts dating from this period enrolled on the Patent Rolls, and depart in only minor respects from a basic formula by which the retainer is to serve the duke in peace and war, for the term of his life, travelling with the duke wherever he wills, suitably equipped in accordance with the retainer's rank, and attending the duke in his household in time of peace. In return, the retainer receives a fee—£20 in the case of the only knight retained, £10 or 10 marks in the case of esquires —assigned on a particular receivership in addition to wages (with or without board) in wartime or when he is in attendance in time of peace.

More interest attaches to the chronology of recruitment. The fifteen indentures collected here that were concluded during the 1390s reinforce the impression of a steady and continuous recruitment of young men to the duke's retinue during these years, whilst the group of six indentures drawn up between October 1397 and July 1398, when added to the eight published indentures from this period, suggests a deliberate increase in John of Gaunt's recruitment of support in the last months of his life. In particular, John Broxtow's indenture (no. 18)—the only example of a contract without a fee which does not come from the early 1380s—suggests that the duke's retaining policy was once more imposing a severe strain on his financial resources. Equally, the extraordinary nature of the duke's political position at this time can be deduced by a glance at the place-dates of these contracts, for whereas the majority of the indentures concluded before October 1397 were dated at London or Hertford, all those concluded in 1398 are dated from places in the North and Midlands, as if John of Gaunt had finally withdrawn from London and the court in order to seek support in the northern heartlands of the Lancastrian cause.[5]

---

[4] Nottingham University Library, Middleton MS Mi F 10; accurately printed in *HMC Report on the Manuscripts of Lord Middleton*, pp. 99–100.

[5] The indentures published by Lewis, nos. 37–42 conform to this pattern.

In transcribing these indentures, the conventions adopted by Prof. N. B. Lewis have been followed as closely as possible. Doubtful or missing words have been enclosed in square brackets and other emendations of the text described in footnotes. The text has been divided into paragraphs for convenience of reference, contractions have been expanded, punctuation and the use of the letters, u, v, i, and j modernized, and capitals within the sentence restricted to proper names.

1. Sir Hugh Hastings—London, 16 May 1366

Ceste endenture faite parentre mon treshonurez seignur Johan duc de Lancastre, dune part, et mons[ire] Hugh de Hastings, dautre part, tesmoigne que le dit mons[ire] Hugh est demorez devers le dit seignur le duc pur peas et pur guerre a terme de la vie le dit[6] mons[ire] Hugh en manere come ensuit.

Cest assavoir que le dit monsire [   ] prendra par an de mon dit seignur le duc pur la peas vivant le dit monsire Hugh vint livres par an dargent des issues de manoir de Gymyngham en le countee de Norff' par les meines del resceivor illeoqes qi pur le temps y serra as termes de seint Michel et de Pasque par oweles porcions. Et en cas que le dit rent de vint livres soit aderere par une moys apres nulles des termes avantditz, que bien lise a dit monsire Hugh en le dit manoir destreindre et la destresse retenir tanque gree lui soit faite. Et a quele heure que le dit monsire Hugh sera envoiez par mondit seignur le duc, sera a bouche en court en temps de peas ovesque deux esquiers, un chamberlein, six chivalx et troiz garcions et prendra liveree ou gages pur les ditz chivalx et garcions solenc lusage del hostiel le dit duc, et aussint gages pur lui et ses gentz venant [   ] come attient.

Et endroit de guerre lavantdit monsire Hugh est tenuz deservir le dit duc et travaillera ovesque lui ove [   ] darmes, soi le tierz de chivalers, et dix archers a chival bien arraiez, et prendra pur son fee par an deux cent et cinquante marcs et tiels gages pur lui et ses gentz come sera allowez a autres de sa condicion. Et seront ses chivalx convenablement prisez et [   ] le dit pris restorez si nulles deux soient perduz en le service le dit duc. Et avera suffisant eskippesson pur lui et ses ditz gentz et chivalx come reson demande. Et comencera son an de guerre le jour qil prendera son chemyn et qil se remuera de son hostiel devers le dit duc pur le viage, a quele heure il sera prestement paiez de son fee pur le demy an, et pur lautre demy an touz jours par quarters devant la mein durrante la guerre. Endroit des prisoners ou autres avantages pris es ditz parties de guerre par le dit monsire Hugh ou null de soens, le dit duc ferra a luy come il ferra as autres de sa condicion. Et en cas que le dit duc preigne son chemyn sur les enemys Dieux lavandit monsire

---

[6] Interlineated.

Hugh sera a bouche en court ovesque deux esquiers as coustages le dit duc si le dit monsire Hugh soit en [   ] de travailler.

Et en cas que le dit monsire Hugh chaunge son estat destre a banere, il sera a bouche en court ove un chivaler, deux esquiers, deux chamberleinz et garsons et chivalx en manere come desus est dit, et pur la guerre il travaillera ovesque le dit duc ove vint hom[mes] darmes, soi le sisme de chivalers, et vint archers au chival bien arraiez, et prendra par an pur son fee cink cent marcs et tiels gages come [   ] allowez al dit duc depar nostre seignur le roi. Endroit de restor des chivalx, eskippeson pur lui, ses ditz gentz et chivalx, gayn de guerre [   ] comencement del an de guerre et des paiementz de fees et gages pur les avanditz vint hommes darmes et vint archers, serra [   ] monsire Hugh en manere come desuis est dit des ditz hommes darmes et ditz archers al afferant.

En tesmoignance de queux chose a [   ] endenture les parties avantditz entrechaungeablement ount mys lour sealx. Donnee a Loundres le xvi jour de maii lan du regne nostre seignur Edward tierz puis le conqueste quarantisme.

Norfolk Record Office, MR 314 (22) 242 x 5

2. Sir Gerard Usflete—Savoy, 1 April 1370

Cest endenture faite parentre mon[sire] Johan duc de Lancastr', dune part, et mon[sire] Gerard de Usflet, dautre part, tesmoigne que le dit mons[ire] Gerard est demorez et retenuz envers le dit duc pur paes et pur guerre a terme de sa vie, pour quelle demore le dit duc ad grante au dit mons[ire] Gerard vingt livres dargent par an a terme de sa vie apprendra des issues de son honur de Pontfreit par les maines de son receivour illoesques qi pur le temps sera as les termes de Pasque et de saint Michel par ovelles porcions. Et le dit monsire Gerarde sera a bouche en court ovesque un esquier et un chamberlain quel heur qil vendra a la court a lenvoie le dit duc, et lors prendra gages pur luy et ses gentz come autres bachilers del hostiel preignent.

Et pur la guerre le dit monsire Gerard sera tenuz de servir le dit duc et de travailler ovesque luy ove deux esquiers homes darmes convenables et bien arraiez, et prendra pur leur fees vingt livres par an et tieles gages come autres de leur condicion prendront. Et en droit de ses chivalx prisez et perduz en le service du dit duc et auxint des profitz de gurre par le dit monsire Gerard ou les soens waignez le dit duc ferra a luy come il ferra as autres bachilers de sa condicion, et comensera le dit monsire Gerard . . .[7] gages pur luy et ses[8] dit deux esquiers envenantz et retornantz par resonable journes. Et avera covenable eskipson pur luy, ses ditz gentez, chivalx et hernoys come raison demandra.

En tesmoignance du quelle chose les avantditz duc et monsire Gerard as les

---

[7] A line in the original indenture has been omitted by the copyist at this point.

partes de cestes endentures entrechangeablement ont mys leur sealx. Donnee a⁸ la Sauvoye le primer jour davril lan du regne nostre tresdoute seigneur le roy dengleterre quarant quarant.⁹

PRO, DL 42/15 f. 53ʳ⁻ᵛ

3. Richard Rixton, esquire—Rothwell, 30 April 1385[10]

Ceste endenture faite parentre le puissant prince Johan roy de Castille et de Leon, duc de Lancastre, dune part, et Richard de Ryxton esquier, dautrepart, tesmoigne que le dit Richard est retenuz et demorez denvers meisme le roy et duc pur pees et pur guerre a terme de sa vie en manere que sensuit.

Cestassavoir que lavantdit Richard sera tenuz a servir le desusdit roy et duc sibien en temps de pees come de guerre a terme de sa vie et de travailler ovesque lui a queles parties qil plerra a meisme celuy roy et duc ovesque deux ses compaignons gentz darmes et sys archers bien et covenablement arraiez pur la guerre. Et sera le dit Richard lui meismes as gages et bouche de court a ses diverses venues illoeques quant il sera envoiez par les lettres lavantdit roy et duc de son mandement. Et prendra meisme le Richard du dit roy et duc pur la guerre pur lui meismes, ses avantditz compaignons gentz darmes et archers desusnomez autieux gages de guerre come lavantdit roy et duc prendra de nostre seignur le roy pur semblables gentz darmes et archers par les maynes del tresorer meisme celui roy et duc pur la guerre qi pur le temps sera.

Et endroit des chivalx du dit Richard et de ses ditz compaignons gentz darmes preisez et perduz de guerre en la service de lavantdit roy et duc ensemblement et de leskippeson de lui ses ditz compaignons gentz darmes et archers desusnomez, leur chivalx, servantz et hernoises quelconques et aussi del comencement de son an de guerre et des prisoners et autres profitz de guerre prisez ou gaignez par le dit Richard, ses compaignons gentz darmes et archers desusnomez ou par null' de leur gentz et servantz, le dit roy et duc ferra a meisme celui Richard en manere come il ferra as autres esquiers de son estat et condicion pur semblables gentz darmes et archers come desuz est dit.

En tesmoignance de quele chose a ycestes endentures les parties avantdites entrechangeablement ont mys leur sealx. Don a Rothewellhawe le darrein jour davrill lan du regne le roy Richard seconde puis le conquest oytisme.

Lancashire Record Office, Dd Bl 24/1

---

⁸ Interlineated.
⁹ *Sic.*
¹⁰ An English translation of this indenture appears in *English Historical Documents, 1327–1485*, ed. A. R. Myers (London, 1969), no. 653.

4. Thomas Mounteney, esquire—Hertford, 6 February 1391

Ceste endenture fait parentre le treshaut et puissant prince Johan duk de Guyenne et de Lancastre dune part et Thomas Mountenay dautre part tesmoigne que certeines endentures par les queles le dit Thomas fuist retenuz devers le dit duk preignant dys marcz par an susrendues en la chancellerie du dit duk pur estre cancellez, le dit Thomas est retenuz et demorez devers le dit duc de luy servir tant en temps de pees come de guerre a terme de sa vie et pur travailler ovec luy as quelles parties que luy plerra bien et convenablement montez et arraiez pur pees et pur guerre come a son estat appartient.

Et sera le dit Thomas en temps de pees as gages et bouche de court a ses diverses venues quant pur luy sera envoie par lettres dicell duc ou de son mandement, des queles gages il sera paiez par les mayns del tresorer du dit duc qi pur le temps sera. Et prendra le dit Thomas desore pur son fee sibien en temps de pees come de guerre dys livres par an a terme de sa vie del issues de les terres et seigneuries du dit duc as contees de Norff' et Suff' par les mayns de son receivour illoeques qorest ou qi pur le temps sera as termes de seint Michel et de Pasqes par oveles porcions.

Et outre ce prendra mesme le Thomas en temps de guerre autielx gages de guerre ou autrement autielx gages et bouche de court come prendront autres esquiers de son estat du dit duc pur le viage, des queles gages il sera paiez par les mayns del tresorer de lavantdit duc pur la guerre qi pur le temps sera.

Et en droit des prisoners et autres proffitz de guerre par le dit Thomas ou null de ses gentz en le service du dit duc prisez ou gaignez et del comencement de son an de guerre ensemblement et de leskippeson de luy et ses gentz, chivalx et hernoys mesme celuy duc ferra a luy par manere come il ferra a ses autres escuiers de tiel estat et degree.

En tesmoignance de quele chose a ycestes endentures les parties avantdictes entrechangeablement ont mys lour sealx.[11]

Donnee a Hertford le vj jour de feverer lan du regne nostre tresredoute seigneur le roy Richard second puis le conqueste quatorzisme.

PRO, DL 42/16 f. 233

5. Sir Nicholas Dabridgecourt—Hertford, 31 August 1391

Ceste endenteure faicte parentre le puissant prince Johan duc de Guyenne et de Lancastre et monsire Nichol dabriggecourt, dautre part, tesmoigne que le dit monsire Nichol est retenuz et demorez devers le dit duc pur luy servir tant en temps de pees come de guerre a terme de sa vie et pur travailler ovecques

---

[11] Apart from minor verbal changes and differences in the titles of the parties, the formulas for the allowances and corroboration clauses are standard in the succeeding contracts.

luy as quelles parties qil plerra au dit duc bien et covenablement armez come a son estat appartient.

Et serra le dit monsire Nichol en temps de pees as gages et bouche de court du dit duc a ses diverses venues illoesques quant pur luy serra envoiez par lettres du dit duc ou de son mandement, en manere come serront autres bachilers de son estat et condicion.

Et prendra lavandit monsire Nichol pur son fee sibien en temps de pees come de guerre vingt livres par an a terme de sa vie des issues de la seignurie de Aldeburn par les maines del receivour du dit duc illoesques qore est ou qi pur le temps serra[12] as termes de saint Michel et de Pasques par ovelles porcions.

Et prendra outre ce en temps de guerre autielx gages de guerre ou gages et bouche de court come prendront autres bachilers de son estat et condicion, des quelles gages il serra paiez par les maines del tresorer du dit duc pur la guerre qi pur le temps serra.

Normal allowance and corroboration clauses except that (i) 'en le service du dit duc' *is omitted.*

Donnee a Hertford le darrain jour daust' lan du du[13] regne nostre tresredoute seigneur le roy Richard second puis le conquest quinzisme.

PRO, DL 42/15 f. 41

6. Thomas Gloucester, esquire—London, 12 November 1391

Cest endenture fait parentre le puissant prince Johan duc de Guyen et de Lancastre, dun part, et Thomas Gloucestre, escuier, dautre part, tesmoigne que le dit Thomas est retenuz et demores devers le dit duc pur luy server tant en temps de pees come de guerre as terme de sa vie et pur traveiller ovesque luy as quelles parties qil plerra au dit duc bien et covenablement arraiez et mountez come a son estate appartient.

Et sera le dit Thomas en temps de pees as gages et bouche de court de dit duc a ses diverses venuez illoesques quant pur luy serra envoiez par lettres de dit duc ou de son comandement en manur come serront autres escuiers de son estate et condicion.

Et prendra le dit Thomas pur son fee sibien en temps de pees come de guerre dys marcs par an a terme de sa vie des issues des terres et seignuries du dit duc en conte de Nicole par les maines de son receivour illoesques qore est ou qi pur le temps serra as termes de Pasque et seint Michel par ovelles porcions.

Et outre prendra lavandit Thomas en temps de guerre autielx gages de

---

[12] Interlineated.
[13] *Sic.*

guerre come prendront autres escuiers de sa condicion par les maines del tresorere du dit duc pur la gurre qi pur le temps sera.

Normal allowance and corroboration clauses except that (i) 'en le service du dit duc' is omitted.

Donnee a Loundres le xij jour de Novembr' lan de regne nostre tresredoute seigneur le roy Richard second puise le conquest qinzsime.

PRO, DL 42/15 f. 45ᵛ

7. Robert Bolron, esquire—Leicester, 8 January 1393

Ceste endenture fait parentre le treshaut et puissant prince Johan duc de Guyen et de Lancastre, dune part, et Robert Bolron esquier, dautre part, tesmoigne que le dit Robert est retenuz et demorez devers le dit duc pur luy servier tant en temps de pees come de guerre a terme de sa vie et pur travaillier ovesque luy as quelles parties qil plerra au dit duc bien et covenablement montez armez et arraiez pur la pees et pur la guerra come a son estate appartient.

Et sera le dit Robert en temps de pees as gages et bouche de court du dit duc a ses diverses veneuz illoesques quant pur luy sera envoiez par lettres du dit duc ou de son comandement en manere come seront autres esquiers de sa condicion illoesques, des quelles gages il sera paiez par les maines del tresorer de lostel du dit duc pur le temps esteant.

Et prendra lavantdit Robert pur son fee sibien entemps du pees come de gurre dys livres par an a terme de sa vie des issues de noz[14] terres et seignuries du dit duc deinz son duchie de Lancastre par les maines de son receivor illoesques qore est ou qi pur le temps sera as termes de Pasqes et de seint Michel par ovelles porcions.

Et outre ce prendra le dit Robert en temps de gurre autielx gages de gurre ou autrement autielx gages et bouche de court come prendront ses autres esquiers de son estate et condicion pur la viage, des quelles gages il sera paiez par les maines del tresorer du dit duc pur la gurre qi pur le temps sera.

Normal allowance and corroboration clauses.

Donnee a Leycestre le viij jour du Janver lan du regne nostre tresredoute seigneur le roy Richard second puis le conquest sesizsme.

PRO, DL 42/15 f. 58

8. John Cornwall, esquire—Saint-Seurin, Bordeaux, 12 March 1395

Cest endenture fait parentre le treshaut et puissant prince Johan duc de Guyen et de Lancastre, dun parte, et Johan Cornewaylle de Kynlet escuier, dautre

---

[14] *Sic.*

part, tesmoigne que le dit Johan Cornewaylle est retenuz et demores devers le dit duc pur luy servir tant en temps de pees come de guerre al terme de sa vie et pur travailler ovesqes luy a queux parties que plerra a dit duc, bien et convenablement montez et arrayez pur la guerre come a son estate appartient.

Et sera le dit Johan Cornewalle en temps de pees as gages et bouche de court du dit duc come seront autres escuiers famulers de sa condicion. Et prendra lavantdit Johan Cornewelle pur son fee sibien en temps de pees come de guerre vint marcz par an a terme de sa vie des issues del manoir de lavantdit duc de Aldeburne en countee de Wyltshire par les maines del receivour illoesquez le temps esteaunt as termes de Pasqes et seint Michel par ovelles porcions pur tout le temps que le dit Johan Cornewalle sera en lestat descuier.

Et apres qil avera changiez son estate et pris lorder du chivaler, de lors enavant il prendra pur son fee sibien en temps de pees come de guerre a terme de sa vie vingt livres par an des issues du susdit manoir par les maines del receivor du dit duc illoesques pur la temps esteant as termes [et] par manere susdit.

Et outre ceo en temps de guerre prendera et avera le dit Johan Cornewalle a tielx gages de guerre et bouche de court du dit duc come prendront et averont autres ses escuiers famulers de tiel estate et condicion, des gages de guerre il sera paiez par les maines del tresorere du dit duc pur la guerre qi pur la temps serra.

Normal allowance and corroboration clauses, save that (i) the allowance clause refers to gains of war made 'par le suyt du dit Johan Cornewalle ou null de ses gens', (ii) *Cornwall is described as one of the duke's* 'escuiers famulers'.

Donnee a Seint Seuryn de Bourdeux le xij jour de marcz lan de reigne nostre tresredoute seigneur le roy Richard secound puis le conquest dys et oetysme.

PRO, DL 42/15 f. 44ᵛ

9. John Merbury, esquire—Bordeaux, 2 October 1395

Cest endenture fait parentre le treshault et puissant prince Johan duc de Guyen et de Lancastre, dun part, et Johan Merbury son escuier, dautre part, tesmoigne que le dit Johan Merbury est retenuz et demorez devers le dit duc pur luy servir tant en temps de pees come de guerre a terme de sa vie et pur travailler ovesqes luy as quelles parties que plerra au dit duc, bien et covenablement montez et arraiez pur la guerre come [a son estat][15] appartient.

Et serra le dit Johan en temps de pees as gages et bouche de court du dit duc a ses diverses venues illeosques quant pur[16] luy serra envoiez par lettres du dit

[15] Words in brackets omitted by the scribe.
[16] Interlineated.

duc ou par son comandement en manere come serront autres escuiers de son estate et condicion.

Et prendera du dit duc le dit Johan Merbury pur son fee sibien en temps de pees come de guerre dys marcs par an a terme de sa vie des issues del seigneurie de dit duc a Halton en contee de Cestre par les maines de son receivor illeosque qore est ou qui pur le temps sera as termes de Pasque et seint Michel par ovelles porcions.

Et prendra outre du dit duc le dit Johan en temps de guerre autielx gages de guerre ou gages et de bouche de court du dit duc come prendront autres escuiers de son estate pur la viage, de quelles gages de guerre il[17] serra paiez par les maines del tresorere dicelle duc qui pur le temps serra.

Normal allowance and corroboration clauses.

Done a Burdeux le second jour doctobre lan de regne nostre tresredoute seigneur le roy Richard puis le conquest dys et noefisme.

PRO, DL 42/15 f. 46ᵛ

10. Eymon ap Ithel, esquire—London, 7 January 1396

Repeats no. 9 almost verbatim except that (i) 'en contee de Cestre' *is omitted from clause no. 3; (ii)* 'pur le viage' *is omitted from clause no. 4, (iii) wages of war are to be paid* 'par les maines del tresorer del mesme celuy duc pur la guerre'.

PRO, DL 42/15 f. 40ᵛ

11. Richard Clitheroe, esquire—London, 13 January 1396

Repeats no. 9 almost verbatim except that the 10 mark fee is assigned on the honour of Pontefract.

PRO, DL 42/15 f. 47

12. Richard Altricham,[18] esquire—London, 19 May 1396

Repeats no. 9 almost verbatim except that (i) the 10 mark fee is assigned on the issues of the duke's lands in Sussex and Surrey; (ii) in time of war Altricham is offered 'gages de guerre ou gages de bouche de court' *as other esquires of his estate and condition receive them.*

PRO, DL 42/15 f. 43ᵛ

---

[17] 'et' in MS.
[18] The name appears as 'Altryncham' in the indenture itself, but as 'Altricham' in the text of the confirmation and in the margin of the Register.

13. Richard Newton, esquire—Hertford, 3 October 1397

Repeats no. 9 almost verbatim except that (i) Newton is required to serve 'montez armez et arraiez'; *(ii) clause no. 3 begins—* 'Et prendra de lavantdit duc le susdit esquier a terme de sa vie pur son fee . . .'; *(iii) the 10 mark annuity is assigned on the duchy of Lancaster; (iv)* 'en la service du dit duc' *is omitted from the allowance clause and provision made for both* 'leskipson et reskipson'.

PRO, DL 42/15 f. 56ᵛ

14. Thomas Heland, esquire—Pontefract, 24 February 1398

Repeats no. 10 almost verbatim except that (i) the retaining fee is £10 assigned on the honour of Bolingbroke; (ii) Heland is required to serve 'montez armez et arraiez'.

PRO, DL 42/15 f. 56

15. Edmund Crancester, esquire—Newcastle, 22 March 1398

Repeats no. 9 almost verbatim except that (i) Crancester is required to serve 'montez armez et arraiez'; *(ii) the 10 mark fee is assigned on the lordship of Dunstanburgh; (iii) in time of war Crancester is offered* 'gages du gurre ou autrement autielx et bouche de court'.

PRO, DL 42/15 f. 57ᵛ

16. Edmund Whitemore, esquire—Leicester, 5 May 1398

Repeats no. 10 almost verbatim except that (i) Whitemore is required to serve 'montez armez et arraiez'.

PRO, DL 42/16 f. 42

17. Robert Radcliffe of Ordsall, esquire—Pontefract, 24 May 1398

Repeats no. 9 almost verbatim except that (i) Radcliffe is required to serve 'montez armez et arraiez'; *(ii) the amount of the annuity granted is omitted by scribal error; (iii) the fee is assigned on the duchy of Lancaster.*

PRO, DL 42/15 f. 46

18. John Broxtow, esquire—Nottingham, 4 July 1398

Ceste endenture faite parentre le treshault et puissant prince Johan duc de Guyene et de Lancastre, dune part, et son escuier Johan Broxtow, dautre part, tesmoigne que le dit Johan est retenuz et demorez devers le dit duc pur lui servir tant en temps de pees come de guerre a terme de sa vie et pur travailler ovec lui as queles parties quil plaira au dit duc bien et covenablement montez et arraiez come a son estat appartient.

Et serra le dit Johan en temps de pees as gages et bouche de courte du dit duc a ses diverses venues illoeques quant pur lui serra envoie par lettres de mesme le duc ou de son mandement en manere come serront autres ses escuiers de son estat et condicion.

Et prendra de lavandit duc le susdit Johan en temps de guerre autielx fees et gages de guerre ou autrement autielx fees et gages et bouche de courte come prendront autres escuiers du dit duc de son degree pur le viage, des queles fees et gages il serra paie par les maines del tresorer du dit duc pur la guerre qui pur le temps serra.

Et en droit des prisoners et autres profitz de guerre par le susdit Johan ou nul de ses gens en le service du dit duc prisez ou gaignez et del comensement de son an de guerre ensemblement et de leskippeson de luy, ses gens, chivalx et hernois mesme le duc ferra a luy en manere come il ferra as autres ses escuiers de son estat et condicion.

En tesmoignance de quele chose a icestes endentures les parties avantdites entrechangeablement ont mys lour sealx.

Donnee a Notingham le quart jour de Juyl lan du regne nostre tresredoute seignur le roi Richard second puis le conquest vingt et second.

Nottingham University Library, Middleton MS Mi F 10

APPENDIX IV. Annuity Payments by Receiverships

In the tables below, column (1) represents, in the case of receivers' accounts, the total annual receipts, including arrears of the previous year; in the case of auditors' valors, it represents the receiver's clear annual charge, with all casuals included but all reprises, except the annuities themselves, deducted. Column (2) represents the sum of annuities paid, plus those paid by the receiver but disallowed on his account by the auditors for technical reasons, such as the lack of an aquittance.

Halton

	£	s.	d.	£	s.	d.	
1379/80	689	11	8	33	10	0	DL 29/16/201
1388/9	385	17	2	72	0	0	DL 29/16/202
1389/90	596	0	3½	82	10	0	DL 29/728/11976
1391/2	424	1	8	66	13	4	DL 29/728/11978
1392/3	335	3	6	66	13	4	DL 43/15/6
1393/4	332	10	7	78	17	4	DL 43/15/9
1394/5	307	11	11	95	0	0	DL 29/728/11984

Hertford

	£	s.	d.	£	s.	d.	
1380/1	74	11	5½	—			DL 29/58/1079
1381/2	104	13	2	—			DL 29/58/1080
1387/8	110	7	3	29	2	6	DL 29/728/11975
1389/90	95	8	2½	21	7	11[1]	DL 29/728/11977
1390/1	105	4	8	21	15	3	DL 43/15/4
1391/2	145	1	10½	18	0	0	DL 29/728/11979
1392/3	106	11	6	22	0	0	DL 43/15/7
1393/4	109	16	4¾	20	6	8	DL 29/728/11982
1394/5	111	19	10¾	21	0	0	DL 29/728/11985
1395/6	105	0	8	18	6	8	DL 29/58/1085
1396/7	94	18	4	20	6	8	DL 29/58/1086
1398/9	67	12	11	18	6	8	DL 29/58/1087

[1] Includes temporary annuities, paid during the lord's pleasure.

Kidwelly (with Iscennen, Ogmore, Ebboth)

	£	s.	d.	£	s.	d.	
1369/70	360	14	3	31	0	0	DL 29/584/9236
1381/2	784	1	5½	15	0	0	DL 29/584/9237
1383/4	449	11	8	96	13	4	DL 29/584/9238
1384/5	—			207	10	0	DL 29/738/12104
1385/6	657	14	5	68	13	4	DL 43/15/1
1386/7	732	1	0	2	0	0	
1387/8	—			2	0	0	DL 29/738/12104
1388/9	993	4	0	2	0	0	DL 43/15/2
1389/90	—			2	0	0	DL 29/738/12104
1390/1	672	5	2	23	15	0	DL 43/15/3
1393/4	638	1	5½	73	10	5[2]	DL 29/728/11983
1394/5	790	14	11	13	12	6	DL 29/728/11986

[2] This figure includes the fees and wages of ministers, which amounted to £60. 6s. 8d. in the following year.

Knaresburgh

	£	s.	d.	£	s.	d.	
1389/90	370	4	7	198	6	8	DL 29/728/11976
1391/2	339	7	1	198	6	8	DL 29/728/11978
1392/3	321	9	8	198	6	8	DL 43/15/6
1393/4	313	9	1	188	6	8	DL 43/15/9
1394/5	348	0	10	208	6	8	DL 29/728/11984

Lancashire

	£	s.	d.	£	s.	d.	
1389/90	1434	12	3	234	12	0	DL 29/728/11976
1391/2	1611	7	11	278	2	0	DL 29/728/11978
1392/3	1669	8	4	298	14	4	DL 43/15/6
1393/4	1415	15	2	399	7	8[3]	DL 29/728/11980
1394/5	1741	9	8	424	14	4	DL 29/728/11984

[3] DL 43/15/9, covering the same financial year, gives a slightly lower figure for expenditure on annuities: £383. 16s. 8d.

Leicester and Higham Ferrers

	Leicester						Higham Ferrers						Combined Annuity		
	(1)			(2)			(1)			(2)			Total		
	£	s.	d.	£	s.	d.	£	s.	d.	£	s.	d.	£	s.	d.
1377/8	522	19	7	149	12	8	—			—			—		
1380/1	379	17	2	120	15	10	280	18	10	173	0	1	293	15	11
1381/2	408	11	5	110	4	7	273	18	0	167	13	5	277	18	0
1390/1	578	1	4	236	13	4	296	10	3	89	12	9	326	6	1
1391/2	540	12	7	283	10	4	276	18	3	95	14	1	379	4	5
1392/3	591	17	9	261	9	4	306	10	9	144	4	7	405	13	11
1393/4	691	0	6	268	14	4	316	17	11	142	7	11	411	2	3
1394/5	534	3	8	322	1	0	276	18	3	242	10	0	564	11	0

Sources:

1377/8:	DL 29/212/3247	1391/2:	DL 43/15/5
1380/1:	DL 29/341/5515	1392/3:	DL 43/15/7
1381/2:	DL 29/341/5516	1393/4:	DL 29/728/11982
1390/1:	DL 43/15/4	1394/5:	DL 29/728/11985

Lincoln

	£	s.	d.	£	s.	d.	
1368/9	2282	19	9	82	10	0	DL 29/262/4069
1383/4	1494	15	4	240	4	7	DL 29/262/4070
1392/3[4]	1274	11	0	210	7	11	DL 43/15/6
1393/4[4]	1214	18	2	181	4	7	DL 29/728/11980
1394/5[4]	1227	8	8	189	11	3	DL 29/728/11984

[4] This figure is a sum of the receipts from (i) the honour of Bolingbroke; (ii) Lancaster fees in Lincolnshire; (iii) towns of Huntingdon and Godmanchester at fee farms.

Monmouth

	£	s.	d.	£	s.	d.	
1367/8[5]	948	19	11	71	5	5[6]	DL 29/615/9836
1369/70[5]	947	14	9	76	12	7[6]	DL 29/615/9837
1384/5	704	15	6	197	17	6	DL 29/615/9838
1385/6	612	19	11	147	17	6	DL 43/15/1
1386/7	603	3	0	97	7	1	

Monmouth

	£	s.	d.	£	s.	d.	
1387/8	623	6	0	53	10	0	DL 43/15/2
1388/9	—			60	3	4 ⎫	DL 29/738/12096
1389/90	—			61	3	4 ⎭	
1390/1	583	13	11	62	3	8	DL 43/15/3
1394/5	757	2	4	112	3	4	DL 29/615/9839

[5] Includes the receipt from Three Castles.
[6] Includes fees and wages of ministers.

Norfolk

	(1)			(2)			Combined cost of annuities and grants of land		
	£	s.	d.	£	s.	d.	£	s.	d.
1379/80	1369	10	0¼	193	10	5½	233	5	10½
1384/5	752	6	6¾	158	0	0	292	2	6
1385/6	743	5	4	171	0	0	305	2	6
1390/1	1003	4	8	245	18	3	308	11	7
1392/3	938	0	10¾	253	15	0	289	15	0
1393/4	882	3	0	251	0	0	287	0	0
1394/5	921	4	6	242	10	0	278	10	0
1396/7	919	19	3¾	277	15	0	313	5	0

Sources: 1379/80: Norfolk Record Office, NRS 3342
1384/5: Norfolk Record Office, NRS 11072
1385/6: Norfolk Record Office, NRS 3343
1390/1: DL 29/310/4980
1392/3: DL 43/15/5
1393/4: DL 29/728/11982
1394/5: Norfolk Record Office, NRS 3344
1396/7: Norfolk Record Office, NRS 15171

Pickering

	£	s.	d.	£	s.	d.	
1389/90	270	17	11	105	13	4	DL 29/728/11976
1391/2	238	8	10	55	13	4	DL 29/728/11978
1392/3	324	18	2	75	13	4	DL 43/15/6
1393/4	257	4	5	72	13	4	DL 43/15/9
1394/5	321	13	0	72	13	4	DL 29/728/11984

Pontefract

	£	s.	d.	£	s.	d.	
1389/90	581	2	9	199	17	11	DL 29/728/11976
1391/2	380	16	1	346	4	7	DL 29/728/11978
1392/3	692	5	8	529	14	1	DL 43/15/6
1393/4	655	8	6	531	10	9	DL 43/15/9
1394/5	630	7	1	507	2	10	DL 29/728/11984

Parts of the South

	£	s.	d.	£	s.	d.	
1384/5	—			268	13	1½ ⎫	
1385/6	—			167	13	1 ⎬	DL 29/738/12096
1386/7	—			125	16	5½ ⎭	
1387/8	546	5	4	161	13	1½	DL 43/15/2
1388/9	—			156	13	1½ ⎫	DL 29/738/12096
1389/90	—			182	11	5½ ⎭	
1390/1	762	8	10	179	9	9	DL 43/15/3
1393/4	522	2	7½	227	6	5½	DL 29/728/11981
1394/5	592	9	2½	191	3	1½	DL 29/728/11986

Sussex

	£	s.	d.	£	s.	d.	
1387/8	282	3	3	100	13	4	DL 29/728/11975
1389/90	331	17	0½	119	11	8	DL 29/728/11977
1390/1	293	19	10	117	6	8	DL 43/15/4
1391/2	320	10	0	117	6	8	DL 29/728/11979
1392/3	463	15	10	123	0	0	DL 43/15/7
1393/4	311	8	2½	97	13	4	DL 29/728/11982
1394/5	300	15	10½	110	11	8	DL 29/728/11985

Tutbury

	£	s.	d.	£	s.	d.	
1382/3	2199	13	3½	291	12	8	DL 29/402/6447–8
1387/8	1768	7	3½	398	16	0[7]	DL 29/728/11975
1389/90	1779	11	1	592	8	2[7]	DL 29/728/11977
1390/1	1762	13	0	600	9	2	DL 43/15/4

Tutbury

	£	s.	d.	£	s.	d.		
1391/2	1715	18	8	632	19	5½	DL	43/15/5
1392/3	1768	18	10	628	18	6	DL	43/15/6
1393/4	1838	2	0	587	5	2[7]	DL	29/728/11982
1394/5	1724	11	3	593	18	6	DL	29/728/11985

[7] Includes annuities assigned on the castle of Melbourne.

APPENDIX V. The *Nomina militum et scutiferum*

THE list of men printed in *Reg. II*, pp. 6–9 as the *Nomina militum et scutiferum* poses problems of purpose and dating which must be resolved if the full value of the document is to be appreciated. In general terms, the statement that it represents 'a list of the men, all of whom were probably retained for life in his [Gaunt's] service between 1379 and 1383' is incontrovertible, and the warning that the *Nomina* presents, in consequence, a slightly inflated picture of the actual size of the duke's affinity at any one time is certainly accurate.[1] It should, however, be remembered that the *Nomina* is only a list of the inner core of the duke's following, of those *de retinentia domini* who could be summoned at his discretion for military service. It does not include all the duke in 1368, appears in the *Nomina*, for instance, because both enjoyed their annuity in 1383, nor Sir Nicholas Sarnesfield, first granted an annuity by the duke in 1368, appear in the Nomina, for instance, because both enjoyed their grants by the lord's letters patent rather than by an indenture of retainer.[2]

An examination of the original manuscript suggests it is possible to be a little more specific about the date of this list of retainers.[3] Both the names of the knights and of the esquires were compiled in a single, identical, hand as far as Sir Baldwin Berford (among the knights) and Thomas Trewennok (among the esquires). Additions to both lists were then made in another, possibly two other, hand or hands: one set of additions in the case of the knights, two for the esquires. This suggests that the *Nomina* was initially the result of a single act of compilation, followed by periodic revision, rather than of a long process of piecemeal addition.

If this is the case, it should be possible to estimate when it was compiled. The original list of names was certainly not drawn up any earlier than August 1380, since indentured retainers like Sir John Oddingsels, in receipt of his fee in January but dead by 27 August 1380, or Elys Thoresby, who died between August and December 1380, do not appear in it.[4] Indeed, since Thomas Trewennok was retained as late as December 1381 and Sir Baldwin Berford in February 1382, its compilation can hardly be dated before the latter month.[5] Nor can it have been drawn up any *later* than October 1382 since the first datable indentures among the additional names (Sir Robert Charles and

---

[1] K. B. McFarlane, 'Bastard Feudalism', *BIHR* 20 (1945), 165.

[2] *Reg. II* 807; Norfolk Record Office, NRS 3342 m. 2; *Reg. I* 67, 1178.

[3] DL 42/14 ff. 8–9.

[4] *Reg. II* 138; *CIPM* XV, 330–2 (Oddingsels); *Reg. II* 353; *CPR 1377–81*, 550 (Thoresby).

[5] *Reg. II* 46, 43.

Hugh Haywood) were both concluded in that month.[6] A date for the compilation of the original *Nomina* between February and October 1382 seems, therefore, unavoidable; the appearance of Sir Robert Barry, who was certainly dead by Michaelmas 1382, among the knights may suggest that it was drawn up earlier rather than later within that period.[7]

How are the additional entries to be dated? Among them are the names of Sir Ralph Bracebridge and Richard Rixton, both retained in April 1385,[8] which strongly suggests that the *Nomina* was the object of periodic revision until that date; the deletions and corrections made to the list also indicate currency until mid-1385. Among those marked *mortuus*, or with their names cancelled, Sir William Frank was dead by Easter 1384; Sir Richard Balderston, Edward Banaster, and William Barton by December 1384; John Wrench was in receipt of his annuity at Michaelmas 1384 but *not* by Michaelmas 1385; Roger Coleman was killed in January 1385 and Sir Geoffrey Workesley died between 28 February and 30 March 1385.[9]

On the argument outlined above, therefore, the *Nomina militum et scutiferum* may be taken as a list of the duke's indentured retainers early in 1382, with the names of all those he retained over the next three years added, at intervals, to it.

[6] *Reg. II* 50, 51.

[7] DL 29/341/5516 m. 2.

[8] Appendix III, no. 3; HMC, *Report on the Manuscripts of Lord Middleton* (1911), pp. 99–100.

[9] DL 29/262/4070 m. 3; 'Calendar of Rolls of the Chancery of the Duchy of Lancaster', *DKR* 32 (1871), 356, 357; G. F. Beltz, *Memorials of the Most Noble Order of the Garter* (London, 1841), p. 209 n. 2; DL 29/584/9238 m. 2, 738/12104 m. 1; KB 27/495 Rex m. 21; C. 81/1023 (40); *Abstracts of Inquisitions Post-Mortem*, ed. W. Langton (Chetham Soc., os, 95, 1875), i. 23.

BIBLIOGRAPHY

I. Manuscript Sources

(a) England

(i) Public Record Office

CHANCERY

C. 47	Chancery Miscellanea
C. 61	Gascon Rolls
C. 66	Patent Rolls
C. 71	Scotch Rolls
C. 76	Treaty Rolls
C. 81	Chancery Warrants
C. 88	Chancery Files, Records upon Outlawry
C. 115	Duchess of Norfolk Deeds
C. 131	Extents for Debts
C. 136–139	Inquisitions Post Mortem
C. 143	Inquisitions Ad Quod Damnum
C. 260	Chancery Files, Recorda
C. 266	Cancelled Letters Patent

EXCHEQUER

E. 28	Council and Privy Seal Records
E. 30	Diplomatic Documents
E. 36	Exchequer Books
E. 37	Court of the Marshalsea
E. 43	Ancient Deeds, series WS
E. 101	King's Remembrancer, Accounts Various
E. 159	King's Remembrancer, Memoranda Rolls
E. 163	King's Remembrancer, Miscellanea
E. 175	Parliamentary and Council Proceedings
E. 179	Subsidy Rolls
E. 199	Sheriffs' Accounts
E. 210	Ancient Deeds, series D
E. 212	Ancient Deeds, series DS
E. 361	Wardrobe and Household Accounts
E. 364	Foreign Accounts

E.	368	Lord Treasurer's Remembrancer, Memoranda Rolls
E.	401	Receipt Rolls
E.	403	Issue Rolls
E.	404	Warrants for Issue

COURT OF KING'S BENCH

| KB | 9 | Ancient Indictments |
| KB | 27 | Placita Coram Rege |

JUSTICES ITINERANT

| JUST | 1 | Assize Rolls |
| JUST | 3 | Gaol Delivery Rolls |

COURT OF COMMON PLEAS

| CP | 25 (1) | Feet of Fines |
| CP | 40 | Plea Rolls |

PALATINATE OF CHESTER

| CHES | 2 | Enrolments |
| CHES | 29 | Plea Rolls |

PALATINATE OF LANCASTER

PL	1	Patent Rolls
PL	3	Privy Seals and Warrants
PL	14	Chancery Miscellanea
PL	16	Docket Rolls

DUCHY OF LANCASTER

DL	25	Deeds, series L
DL	27	Deeds, series LS
DL	28	Accounts Various
DL	29	Ministers' Accounts
DL	30	Court Rolls
DL	36	Cartae Miscellanae
DL	37	Chancery Rolls
DL	40	Return of Knights' Fees
DL	41	Miscellanea
DL	42	Miscellaneous Books
DL	43	Rentals and Surveys

SPECIAL COLLECTIONS

SC	1	Ancient Correspondence
SC	2	Court Rolls
SC	6	Ministers' Accounts
SC	8	Ancient Petitions

GIFTS AND DEPOSITS

| PRO | 30 | |

PREROGATIVE COURT OF CANTERBURY

| PROB | 11 | Probate Registers |

(ii) British Library

Additional Charters	13910, 14665, 14713, 27313, 30744–5
Additional MSS	5845, 35115, 37494, 40859*A*
Additional Rolls	13972, 64320–2, 64803
Cotton Charters	XI. 70
Cotton MSS	Julius C IV
	Caligula D III
	Nero D VII
Egerton Rolls	8727, 8728, 8738, 8757, 8769, 8776
Harleian Charters	49 H 21
Harleian MSS	2119, 3988
Landsdowne MS	229
Sloane MS	248
Stowe Charters	64, 440
Wolley Charters	I.17, II.22

(iii) Cambridge University Library

MS Dd. III. 53

(iv) Derbyshire Record Office, Matlock

D	37	Turbutt and Revell
D	158	Beresford of Fenny Bentley
D	231	Okeover
D	1233	Pole of Wakebridge

(v) East Sussex Record Office, Lewes

GLY	Glynde Place MSS
AMS	Additional MSS

(vi) Kent Archives Office, Maidstone

PRC	32	Consistory Court of Canterbury, Register of Wills

(vii) Lancashire Record Office, Preston

Dd	B	Parker of Browsholme
Dd	Bl	Blundell of Little Crosby
Dd	Cl	Clifton of Lytham
Dd	F	Farington of Worden
Dd	Fi	Finch of Mawdesley

Dd	Fz		Brockholes
Dd	He		Hesketh of Rufford
Dd	In		Blundell of Ince Blundell
Dd	M		Molyneux of Sefton
Dd	Pt		Petre of Dunkenhalgh
Dd	Sc		Scarisbrick of Scarisbrick
Dd	To		Townely of Townely
Dd	Wh		Whittaker of Simonstown
Dd	X	293	Massy of Rixton

(viii)   Leeds Central Library

Grantley MSS

(ix)   Leicestershire Record Office, Leicester

26   D   53   Ferrers collection

(x)   Lincolnshire Archives Office, Lincoln

Anc.   Ancaster Manuscripts
D. and C.   Dean and Chapter
Reg. XII   Register of John Buckingham
FL   Foster Library

(xi)   London: College oif Arms

Arundel MS   49

(xii)   London: Guildhall Library

MS 9531/3   Register of Robert Braybrooke
St Paul's, Dean and Chapter MSS

(xiii)   London: Lambeth Palace Library

Reg. Whittesley   Register of William Whittesley
Reg. Sudbury   Register of Simon Sudbury
Reg. Arundel   Register of Thomas Arundel

(xiv)   Norfolk Record Office, Norwich

Le Strange   Le Strange MSS
NCC   Norwich Consistory Court, Register of Wills
NR   Gressenhall MSS
NRS   Norfolk Record Society MSS

(xv) Northamptonshire Record Office, Northampton

Fitzwilliam MSS

(xvi) Northumberland Record Office, Gosforth

ZSW   Swinburne of Capheaton

(xvii) Nottinghamshire Record Office, Nottingham

Dd   Fj   Foljambe of Osberton
Dd   4p   Portland of Welbeck
Dd   Sr   Saville of Rufford

(xviii) Nottingham University Library

Cl   D   Clifford of Clifford
Mi   F   Middleton MSS

(xix) Oxford, Bodleian Library

MS Corpus Christi College 495

MS Dodsworth 53, 87

MS Dugdale 18

MS Gough Yorks. 5

MS Rolls Norfolk 71

(xx) Oxford, Magdalen College

Benham MSS
King's Somborne MSS

(xxi) Sheffield City Library

Bagshawe Collection

(xxii) Somerset Record Office, Taunton

Dd   Wo   Trevelyan of Nettlecombe

(xxiii) Staffordshire Record Office, Stafford

D.   641   Lord Stafford's MSS

(xxiv) West Sussex Record Office, Chichester

Firle Place MSS

(xxv) Westminster Abbey

WAM Muniments 2177, 6039, 6040, 6045, 32777, 57067

(xxvi) York: Borthwick Institute

Bishops' Registers   XIV–XVI, XVIII
Probate Registers   2–3

(b) Abroad

(xxvii) Barcelona, Archivo de la Corona de Aragón

Cartas Reales y Diplomáticas (xerox)

(xxviii) San Marino, Huntington Library

HAD   Hastings Collection
HAP

(xxix) Washington, Folger Shakespeare Library

MS X. d. 91 (xerox)

II. Printed Sources

(a) Published and Calendared Documents

An Abstract of Feet of Fines Relating to the County of Sussex From 1 Edward II to 24 Henry VII, ed. L. F. Salzman (Sussex Record Soc., 23, 1916).
Abstracts of Inquisitions Post-Mortem, ed. W. Langton (Chetham Soc., os 95, 1875).
'Accompts of the Manor of the Savoy, temp. Richard II', *Archaeologia*, 24 (1832), 299–316.
Ancient Petitions Relating to Northumberland, ed. C. M. Fraser (Surtees Soc., 176, 1966).
'The Anglo-French Negotiations at Bruges, 1374–1377', ed. E. Perroy, *Camden Miscellany*, 19 (3rd series, 80, 1952).

Anglo-Norman Letters and Petitions, ed. M. D. Legge (Anglo-Norman Text Society, 3, 1941).

The Antient Kalendars and Inventories of the Treasury of His Majesty's Exchequer, ed. F. Palgrave, 3 vols. (London, 1836).

L'Apparicion Maistre Jehan de Meun et le Somnium Super Materia Scismatis d'Honoré Bonet, ed. I. Arnold (Publications de la Faculté des lettres de l'Université de Strasbourg, 28, 1926).

The Black Book of the Admiralty, ed. Sir T. Twiss (Rolls Series, London, 1871).

The Boke of Noblesse, ed. J. G. Nichols (Roxburghe Club, 77, 1860).

A Book of London English 1384–1425, ed. R. W. Chambers and N. Daunt (Oxford, 1931).

Calendar of Ancient Deeds.

Calendar of Charter Rolls, 1341–1417.

Calendar of Close Rolls.

A Calendar of the Deeds and Papers in the Possession of Sir James de Hoghton, Bart., ed. J. H. Lumby (Lancashire and Cheshire Record Soc., 88, 1936).

Calendar of Documents Relating to Scotland, ed. J. Bain, 4 vols. (Edinburgh, 1881–8).

Calendar of Fine Rolls.

Calendar of Inquisitions Miscellaneous.

Calendar of Inquisitions Post Mortem.

Calendar of Papal Registers, Papal Letters.

Calendar of Papal Registers, Petitions 1342–1419.

Calendar of Patent Rolls.

'Calendar of Recognizance Rolls of the Palatinate of Chester', *Deputy Keeper's Report*, 36 (1875).

'Calendar of Rolls of the Chancery of the Duchy of Lancaster', *Deputy Keeper's Report*, 32 (1871).

Calendar of Select Pleas and Memoranda of the City of London, 1381–1412, ed. A. H. Thomas (Cambridge, 1932).

A Calendar of the Register of Henry Wakefield, Bishop of Worcester 1375–1395, ed. W. P. Marrett (Worcestershire Historical Soc., NS 8, 1972).

The Cartulary of Burscough Priory, ed. A. N. Webb (Chetham Soc., 3rd series, 18, 1970).

The Cartulary of Tutbury Priory, ed. A. Saltman (HMC Joint Publications, 2, 1962).

The Charters of the Duchy of Lancaster, ed. W. Hardy (London, 1845).

The Chartulary of the High Church of Chichester, ed. W. D. Peckham (Sussex Record Soc., 46, 1946).

Chaucer Life—Records, ed. C. C. Olson and M. M. Crow (Oxford, 1966).

Collectanea Topographica et Genealogica, ed. J. G. Nichols, 8 vols. (London, 1834–43).

Collections for a History of Staffordshire, xiii–xvii, ed. G. Wrottesley (William Salt Archaeological Soc., 1892–6).

The Coucher Book of Furness Abbey, ed. J. C. Atkinson, 2 vols. (Chetham Soc., NS 9–14, 1886–7).

Dell, R. F., *The Glynde Place Archives, A Catalogue* (Lewes, 1964).

Derbyshire Feet of Fines, 1323–1546, ed. H. J. H. Garratt and C. Rawcliffe (Derbyshire Record Soc., 11, 1985).

'Duchy of Lancaster Records. Calendar of Patent Rolls', *Deputy Keeper's Report,* 40 (1879).

English Historical Documents, iv, 1327–1485, ed. A. R. Myers (London, 1969).

Expeditions to Prussia and the Holy Land Made by Henry earl of Derby, ed. L. T. Smith (Camden Soc., NS 52, 1894).

Fasciculi Zizaniorum, ed. W. W. Shirley (Rolls Series, 1858).

Feet of Fines for the County of York, 1347–1377, ed. W. P. Baildon (Yorkshire Arch. Soc., Record Ser., 52, 1915).

Final Concords of the County of Lancaster, 1307–1509, ed. W. Farrer, 2 vols. (Lancashire and Cheshire Record Soc., 46–50, 1903–5).

Fortescue, J., Sir, *The Governance of England,* ed. C. Plummer (Oxford, 1885).

Historical Manuscripts Commission, *Manuscripts of the Corporations of Southampton and King's Lynn* (London, 1887).

—— *Report on the Manuscripts of the Marquess of Lothian* (London, 1905).

—— *Report on the Manuscripts of Lord Middleton* (London, 1911).

—— *Report on the Manuscripts of the Late Reginald Rawdon Hastings,* 4 vols. (London, 1928–47).

—— *Report on Manuscripts in Various Collections,* i. (London, 1901); vii · (London, 1914).

Hoccleve, T., *The Regement of Princes,* ed. F. J. Furnivall (EETS, ES 72, 1897).

The Hylle Cartulary, ed. R. W. Dunning (Somerset Record Soc., 68, 1968).

'Indentures of Retinue with John of Gaunt, Duke of Lancaster, Enrolled in Chancery, 1367–1399', ed. N. B. Lewis, *Camden Miscellany,* 22 (Camden Soc., 4th series, 1, 1964), 77–112.

Inquisitions and Assessments Relating to Feudal Aids, 1284–1431, 6 vols. (1920–31).

Issue Roll of Thomas Brantingham, 1370, ed. F. Devon (London, 1835).

Issues of the Exchequer, Henry III–Henry VI, ed. F. Devon (London, 1837).

Itineraries. William of Worcester, ed. J. H. Harvey (Oxford, 1969).

James, M. R., *A Descriptive Catalogue of Manuscripts in the Library of Peterhouse* (Cambridge, 1899).

Jeayes, I. H., *A Descriptive Catalogue of Derbyshire Charters* (London, 1906).

John of Gaunt's Register 1372–76, ed. S. Armitage-Smith, 2 vols. (Camden Soc, 3rd series, 20–1, 1911).

John of Gaunt's Register 1379–83, ed. E. C. Lodge and R. Somerville, 2 vols. (Camden Soc., 3rd series, 56–7, 1937).

Lancashire Palatine Plea Rolls, ed. J. Parker (Chetham Soc., NS 87, 1928).

Leland, J., *Itineraries,* ed. L. T. Smith (London, 1906).

List of Escheators for England and Wales (PRO Lists and Indexes, 72, 1971).

List of Sheriffs for England and Wales (PRO Lists and Indexes, 9, 1898).

Madox, T., *Formulare Anglicanum* (London, 1702).

Manuscripts of St George's Chapel, Windsor Castle, ed. J. N. Dalton (Windsor, 1957).

Nicolai Uptoni de Studio Militari, ed Sir E. Bysshe (London, 1654).

'Norfolk Sessions of the Peace. Roll of Mainpernors and Pledges, 1394–1397', ed. L. J. Redstone, *Norfolk Record Society Publications*, 8 (1936), 3–14.

Northern Petitions, ed. C. M. Fraser (Surtees Soc., 194, 1981).

Œuvres de Georges Chastellain, ed. K. de Lettenhove, 8 vols. (Brussels, 1863–6).

Parliamentary Writs, ed. F. Palgrave, 2 vols. (London, 1827–34).

Paston Letters and Papers of the Fifteenth Century, ed. N. Davis, 2 vols. (Oxford, 1971–6).

Plumpton Correspondence, ed. T. Stapleton (Camden Soc., os 4, 1839).

Political Poems and Songs, ed. T. Wright, 2 vols. (Rolls Series, London, 1859–61).

Proceedings Before the Justices of the Peace in the Fourteenth and Fifteenth Centuries: Edward III to Richard III, ed. B. H. Putnam (London, 1938).

Recueil des actes de Jean IV, Duc de Bretagne, i, ed. M. Jones (Paris 1980).

'Recueil des documents concernant le Poitou contenus dans les registres de la chancellerie de France', ed. P. Guérin, *Archives Historiques du Poitou*, 19–21 (1888–90).

Records of the Borough of Leicester, ed. M. Bateson (Cambridge, 1901).

Records of the City of Norwich, ed. W. Hudson and J. C. Tingey, 2 vols. (Norwich, 1906–10).

Records of Some Sessions of the Peace in Lincolnshire, 1360–1375, ed. R. Sillem (Lincoln Record Soc., 30, 1936).

Records of Some Sessions of the Peace in Lincolnshire, 1381–1396, ed. E. G. Kimball, 2 vols. (Lincoln Record Soc., 49–56, 1955–62).

The Register of Bishop Philip Repingdon, 1405–19, ed. M. Archer, 3 vols. (Lincoln Record Soc., 57–8, 73, 1963–82).

Register of Edward the Black Prince, 4 vols. (London, 1930–43).

The Register of the Guild of the Holy Trinity, St Mary, St John the Baptist and St Katherine of Coventry, ed. M. D. Harris (Dugdale Soc., 13, 1935).

The Register of Henry Chichele, archbishop of Canterbury, 1414–1443, ed. E. F. Jacob, 4 vols. (Canterbury and York Soc., 1937–47).

Registrum Honoris de Richmond, ed. R. Gale (London, 1722).

Registrum Johannis Gilbert, episcopi Herefordensis, 1375–1389, ed. J. H. Parry (Canterbury and York Soc., 18, 1915).

Report from the Lords' Committees Touching the Dignity of a Peer of the Realm, 4 vols. (London, 1820–9).

'Rolls of the Collectors in the West Riding of the Lay Subsidy (Poll Tax) 2 Richard II', *Yorkshire Archaeological and Topographical Journal*, 5 (1879), 1–

51, 241–66, 417–32; 6 (1881), 1–45, 129–71, 287–342; 7 (1883), 6–31, 145–86.

Rolls of the Gloucestershire Sessions of the Peace, 1361–1398, ed. E. G. Kimball (Trans. Bristol and Gloucs. Arch. Soc., 62, 1940).

Rolls of the Warwickshire and Coventry Sessions of the Peace, 1377–1397, ed. E. G. Kimball (Dugdale Soc., 16, 1939).

Rotuli Parliamentorum, 6 vols. (London, 1783).

Rotuli Scotiae, 2 vols. (Record Comm., 1814–19).

Rymer, T., *Foedera, Conventiones, Litterae*, etc., 2nd edn., 20 vols. (London, 1727–35).

—— ed. A. G. Clarke and F. Holbrooke, i–iii (Record Comm., 1816–30).

The Scrope and Grosvenor Controversy: de controversia in curia militari inter Ricardum le Scrope et Robertum Grosvenor, 1385–90, ed. N. H. Nicolas, 2 vols. (London, 1832).

Select Cases Before the King's Council 1243–1482, ed. I. S. Leadam and J. F. Baldwin (Selden Soc., 35, 1918).

Select Cases in the Court of King's Bench, Edward III, ed. G. O. Sayles, vi (Selden Soc., 82, 1965).

Select Cases in the Court of King's Bench, Richard II, Henry IV, Henry V, ed. G. O. Sayles, vii (Selden Soc., 88, 1971).

Select Cases of Trespass from the King's Courts, 1307–99, ed. M. S. Arnold (Selden Soc., 100, 1984).

Sir Christopher Hatton's Book of Seals, ed. L. C. Lloyd and D. M. Stenton (Northants Record Soc., 15, 1950).

Some Sessions of the Peace in Cambridgeshire in the Fourteenth Century, ed. M. M. Taylor (Cambridge Antiquarian Soc., 55, 1942).

Sotheby's Sale Catalogue, 14/15 June 1971, 13 April 1981.

South Lancashire in the Reign of Edward II, ed. G. H. Tupling (Chetham Soc., 3rd series, 1, 1949).

'The Stanley Poem', *Palatine Anthology. A Collection of Ancient Poems and Ballads Relating to Lancashire and Cheshire*, ed. J. O. Halliwell (London, 1850), pp. 210–22.

Statutes of the Realm, 11 vols. (Record Comm., 1810–28).

The Stonor Letters and Papers, 1290–1483, ed. C. L. Kingsford, 2 vols. (Camden Soc., 3rd series, 29–30, 1919).

Testamenta Eboracensia, ed. J. Raine, i (Surtees Soc., 4, 1836).

Testamenta Vetusta, ed. N. H. Nicolas (London, 1826).

The Three Earliest Subsidy Returns for the County of Sussex in the Years 1296, 1327, 1332, ed. W. Hudson (Sussex Record Soc., 10, 1910).

Timbal, P.-C., *La Guerre de Cent Ans vue à travers les registres du Parlement* (Paris, 1961).

Treatises of Fistula in Ano, Haemorrhoids and Clysters by John Arderne, ed. D'Arcy Power (EETS, os 139, 1910).

The Vision of Piers Plowman, Text C, ed. W. W. Skeat (EETS, os 54, 1873).

The Visitacion of Norffolk, ed. W. Rye (Harleian Soc., 32, 1891).
The Visitation of the County of Nottingham, ed. G. W. Marshall (Harleian Soc., 4, 1871).
Wagner, A. R., *A Catalogue of English Medieval Rolls of Arms* (Oxford, 1950).
Wills and Inventories, ed. J. Raine (Surtees Soc., 2, 1835).
The Works of Sir John Clanvowe, ed. V. J. Scattergood (Cambridge, 1975).
Wyclif, J., *Opus Evangelicum*, ed. J. Loserth (Wyclif Soc., 1895).
Wykeham's Register, ed. T. F. Kirby, 2 vols. (Hampshire Record Soc., 11, 1896–9).
Year Books of Richard II, 13 Richard II, 1389–90, ed. T. F. T. Plucknett (London, 1929).
Yorkshire Deeds, i, ed. W. Brown (Yorkshire Arch. Soc., 39, 1909).
Yorkshire Sessions of the Peace, 1361–1364, ed. B. H. Putnam (Yorkshire Arch. Soc., 100, 1939).

(b) Chronicles

'Annales Ricardi Secundi et Henrici Quarti', J. de Trokelowe et anon., *Chronica et Annales*, ed. H. T. Riley (Rolls Series, London, 1866).
The Anonimalle Chronicle, 1333–1381, ed. V. H. Galbraith (Manchester, 1927).
The Brut, ed. F. W. D. Brie (EETS, os 126, 1908).
Chronica Johannis de Reading et Anonymi Cantuariensis 1346–1367, ed. J. Tait (Manchester, 1914).
Chronicon Adae de Usk, ed. E. M. Thompson (London, 1904).
Chronicon Angliae auctore monacho quodam Sancti Albani, ed. E. M. Thompson (Rolls Series, London, 1874).
Chronicon Henrici Knighton, ed. J. R. Lumby, 2 vols. (Rolls Series, London, 1889–95).
Chronique du Religieux de Saint-Denys, ed. M. Bellaguet (Paris, 1839).
Cochon, P., *Chronique Normande*, ed. C. de Robillard de Beaurepaire (Société de l'histoire de Normandie, Rouen, 1870).
Froissart, J., *Œuvres*, ed. Kervyn de Lettenhove, 27 vols. (Brussels, 1867–77).
Gesta Abbatum Monasterii Sancti Albani, ed. H. T. Riley, 3 vols. (Rolls Series, London, 1867–9).
'Historia sive Narracio de Moda et Forma Mirabilis Parliamenti apud Westmonasterium', ed. M. McKisack, *Camden Miscellany*, 14 (Camden Soc., 3rd series, 37, 1926), pp. 1–27.
Historia Vitae et Regni Ricardi Secundi, ed. G. B. Stow (Philadelphia, 1977).
'Historiae Croylandensis Continuatio', *Rerum Anglicarum Scriptores Veterum*, ed. W. Fulman (Oxford, 1684), pp. 449–592.
'The Kirkstall Abbey Chronicles', ed. J. Taylor, *Thoresby Society*, 42 (1952).
Life of the Black Prince, by the Herald of Sir John Chandos, ed. M. K. Pope and E. C. Lodge (Oxford, 1910).

Lopes, F., *Crónica de Dom Joao I: segunda parte*, ed. M. Lopes de Almeda and A. de Magalhaes Basto (Porto, 1949).

López de Ayala, P., *Crónica del rey Don Juan I*, ed. E. Llaguno y Amirola (Madrid, 1780).

Walsingham, T., *Historia Anglicana*, ed. H. T. Riley, 2 vols. (Rolls Series, London, 1863–4).

The Westminster Chronicle 1381–1394, ed. L. C. Hector and B. F. Harvey (Oxford, 1982).

William Thorne's Chronicle of St Augustine's, Canterbury, ed. A. H. Davis (Oxford, 1934).

(c) Secondary Sources

ARCHER, R. E., 'The Mowbrays: Earls of Nottingham and Dukes of Norfolk to 1432' (unpub. Oxford University D.Phil. thesis, 1984).

ARMITAGE-SMITH, S., *John of Gaunt* (London, 1904).

ASTILL, G. G., 'An Early Inventory of a Leicestershire Knight', *Midland History*, 2 (1973–4), 274–83.

—— 'The Medieval Gentry: A Study in Leicestershire Society 1350–1399' (unpub. Birmingham University Ph.D. thesis, 1977).

—— 'Social Advancement through Seignorial Service? The Case of Simon Pakeman', *Transactions of the Leicestershire Historical and Archaeological Society*, 54 (1978–9), 14–25.

ASTON, M. E., 'The Impeachment of Bishop Despenser', *BIHR* 38 (1965), 127–48.

—— *Thomas Arundel* (Oxford, 1967).

BAILDON, W. P., 'Notes on the Early Saville Pedigree', *Yorkshire Archaeological Journal*, 28 (1926), 380–427.

BAKER, J. H. (ed.), *The Order of Serjeants at Law* (Selden Soc., Suppl. Ser., 5, 1984).

BALDWIN, J. F., *The King's Council in England During the Middle Ages* (Oxford, 1913).

BARBER, M., 'John Norbury (*c*.1350–1414): An Esquire of Henry IV', *EHR* 68 (1953), 66–76.

BARRON, C. M., 'The Quarrel of Richard II with London', *The Reign of Richard II*, ed. F. R. H. du Boulay and C. M. Barron (London, 1971), pp. 173–201.

BEAMONT, W., *Annals of the Lords of Warrington* (Chetham Soc., OS 86 1872).

—— *An Account of the Rolls of the Honour of Halton* (Warrington, 1879).

BEAN, J. M. W., *The Estates of the Percy Family 1416–1537* (Oxford, 1958).

—— *The Decline of English Feudalism, 1215–1540* (Manchester, 1968).

—— ' "Bachelor" and Retainer', *Medievalia et Humanistica*, NS 3 (1972), 117–31.

BEANLANDS, CANON, 'The Swillingtons of Swillington', Thoresby Society, *Miscellanea*, 15 (1909), 185–211.

BELLAMY, J. G., 'The Parliamentary Representation of Nottinghamshire, Derbyshire and Staffordshire in the Reign of Richard II' (Nottingham University MA thesis, 1961).

—— 'The Coterel Gang: An Anatomy of a Band of Fourteenth-Century Criminals', *EHR* 89 (1964), 698–717.

—— 'The Northern Rebellions in the Later Years of Richard II', *BJRL* 47 (1965), 254–74.

—— *The Law of Treason in England in the Later Middle Ages* (Cambridge, 1970).

—— *Crime and Public Order in England in the Later Middle Ages* (London, 1973).

BELTZ, G. F., *Memorials of the Most Noble Order of the Garter* (London, 1841).

BENNETT, M. J., 'A County Community: Social Cohesion Amongst the Cheshire Gentry, 1400–1425', *Northern History*, 8 (1973), 24–44.

—— *Community, Class and Careerism. Cheshire and Lancashire Society in the Age of Sir Gawain and the Green Knight* (Cambridge, 1983).

BLOMEFIELD, F., *An Essay Towards a Topographical History of the County of Norfolk*, 2nd edn., 11 vols. (1805–10).

BOOTH, P. H. W., 'Farming for Profit in the Fourteenth Century: The Cheshire Estates of the Earldom of Chester', *Journal of the Chester Archaeological Society*, 62 (1979), 83–90.

—— *The Financial Administration of the Lordship and County of Chester 1272–1377* (Chetham Soc., 3rd series, 28, 1981).

BRIDGES, J., *The History and Antiquities of Northamptonshire*, 2 vols. (Oxford, 1791).

BROWN, A. L., 'The Authorization of Letters under the Great Seal', *BIHR* 37 (1964), 125–56.

—— 'The King's Councillors in Fifteenth-Century England', *TRHS* 5th series, 19 (1969), 95–118.

BUCKATZSCH, E. J., 'The Geographical Distribution of Wealth in England, 1086–1843', *EcHR*, 2nd series, 3 (1950), 180–201.

CARPENTER, C., 'The Beauchamp Affinity, A Study of Bastard Feudalism at Work', *EHR* 95 (1980), 514–32.

—— 'Fifteenth Century Biographies', *Historical Journal*, 25 (1982), 729–34.

—— 'Law, Justice and Landowners in Later Medieval England', *Law and History Review*, 1 (1983), 205–37.

—— 'The Fifteenth Century English Gentry and their Estates', *Gentry and Lesser Nobility in Later Medieval Europe*, ed. M. Jones (Gloucester 1986), pp. 36–60.

CATTO, J., 'Religion and the English Nobility in the Late Fourteenth Century', *History and the Imagination*, ed. H. Lloyd-Jones, V. Pearl, A. B. Worden (London, 1981), pp. 43–55.

CHERRY, M., 'The Courtenay Earls of Devon: Formation and Disintegration of a Late Medieval Aristocratic Affinity', *Southern History*, 1 (1979), 71–99.

CHETWYND-STAPYLTON, H. E., *The Chetwynds of Ingestre* (London, 1892).

CLANCHY, M., 'Law, Government and Society in Medieval England', *History*, 59 (1974), 73–8.

CLARKE, M. V., *Fourteenth Century Studies*, ed. M. McKisack and L. S. Sutherland (Oxford, 1937).

A Collection of Curious Discourses, ed. T. Hearne (London, 1771).

The Complete Peerage, ed. G. E. Cokayne, revised by Vicary Gibbs, H. A. Doubleday, and Lord Howard de Walden, 12 vols. (London, 1910–57).

CONTAMINE, P., *Guerre, état et société à la fin du moyen âge* (Paris, 1972).

—— 'Froissart: art militaire, pratique et conception de la guerre', *Froissart: Historian*, ed. J. J. N. Palmer (Woodbridge, 1981), pp. 132–44.

COPINGER, W. A., *The Manors of Suffolk*, 7 vols. (London, 1905–11).

COSS, P. R., *The Langley Family and its Cartulary: A Study in Late Medieval 'Gentry'* (Dugdale Soc., Occasional Papers, 22, 1974).

CROKE, SIR A., *The Genealogical History of the Croke Family*, 2 vols. (Oxford, 1823).

CROOK, D., 'Derbyshire and the English Rising of 1381', *BIHR* 60 (1987), 9–23.

CURZON OF KEDLESTON, THE MARQUIS, *Bodiam Castle, Sussex* (London, 1926).

DAVIES, R. R., 'The Bohun and Lancaster Lordships in Wales in the Fourteenth and Fifteenth Centuries' (unpub. Oxford University D.Phil. thesis, 1965).

—— 'Richard II and the Principality of Chester', *The Reign of Richard II*, ed. F. R. H. du Boulay and C. M. Barron (London, 1971), pp. 256–79.

—— *Lordship and Society in the March of Wales 1282–1400* (Oxford, 1978).

DELACHENAL, R., *Histoire de Charles V*, 5 vols. (Paris, 1909–31).

DRIVER, J. T., 'The Knights of the Shire for Worcestershire During the Reigns of Richard II, Henry IV and Henry V', *Transactions of the Worcestershire Archaeological Society*, NS 40 (1963), 42–64.

DU BOULAY, F. R. H., *The Lordship of Canterbury: An Essay on Medieval Society* (London, 1966).

DUBY, G., *La Société aux XIe et XIIe siècles dans la région mâconnaise* (Paris, 1953).

DUGDALE, W., *The Antiquities of Warwickshire* (London, 1656).

—— *The Baronage of England*, 2 vols. (London, 1675).

—— *Monasticon Anglicanum*, 6 vols. (London, 1846–9).

DUNHAM, W. H., *Lord Hastings' Indentured Retainers 1461–1483* (Transactions of the Connecticut Academy of Arts and Sciences, 39, 1955).

EMERY, A., *Dartington Hall* (Oxford, 1970).

FLEMING, P. W., 'Charity, Faith and the Gentry of Kent, 1422–1529', *Property and Politics in Later Medieval English History*, ed. A. J. Pollard (Gloucester, 1984), pp. 36–58.

FOWLER, K. A., 'Henry of Grosmont, First Duke of Lancaster, 1310–1361' (unpub. Leeds University Ph.D. thesis, 1961).

—— 'Les Finances et la discipline dans les armées anglaises en France au XIVe siècle', *Les Cahiers Vernonnais*, 4 (1964), 55–84.

—— *The King's Lieutenant* (London, 1969).

FOX, G., *History of Pontefract* (Pontefract, 1827).

FOX, L., 'The Honour and Earldom of Leicester: Origin and Descent, 1066–1399', *EHR* 54 (1939), 385–402.

FRYDE, N., 'A Medieval Robber Baron: Sir John Molyns of Stoke Poges, Buckinghamshire', *Medieval Legal Records*, ed. R. F. Hunnisett and J. B. Post (London, 1978), pp. 197–221.

GALBRAITH, V. H., 'A New Life of Richard II', *History*, NS 26 (1942), 223–39.

GANSHOF, F. L., *Qu'est-ce que la féodalité*, 3rd edn. (Brussels, 1957).

GILLESPIE, J. L., 'Thomas Mortimer and Thomas Molineux: Radcot Bridge and the Appeal of 1397', *Albion*, 7 (1975), 161–73.

—— 'Richard II's Cheshire Archers', *Transactions of the Historic Society of Lancashire and Cheshire*, 125 (1975), 1–39.

GIVEN-WILSON, C. J., *The Royal Household and the King's Affinity: Service, Politics and Finance in England, 1360–1413* (New Haven, 1986).

GOODMAN, A., *The Loyal Conspiracy* (London, 1971).

—— 'The Military Subcontracts of Sir Hugh Hastings, 1380', *EHR* 95 (1980), 114–20.

—— 'Responses to Requests in Yorkshire for Military Service under Henry V', *Northern History*, 17 (1981), 240–52.

—— 'John of Gaunt', *England in the Fourteenth Century*, ed. W. M. Ormrod (Woodbridge, 1986), pp. 67–87.

—— 'John of Gaunt: Paradigm of the Late Fourteenth-Century Crisis', *TRHS* 5th series, 37 (1987), 133–48.

GRAY, H. L., 'Incomes from Land in England in 1436', *EHR* 49 (1934), 607–39.

GRIFFITHS, R. A., *The Principality of Wales in the Later Middle Ages* (Cardiff, 1972).

—— 'Public and Private Bureaucracies in Fifteenth-Century England', *TRHS* 5th series, 30 (1980), 109–30.

—— *The Reign of Henry VI* (London, 1981).

GURNEY, D., *Records of the House of Gurney* (London, 1848).

GUTIERREZ DE VELASCO, A., *Los ingleses en España (Siglo XIV): Estudios de edad media de la corona de Aragón: sección de Zaragoza*, vol. iv (Saragossa, 1950).

HARDING, A., *The Law Courts of Medieval England* (London, 1973).

HARRISS, G. L., 'Preference at the Medieval Exchequer', *BIHR* 30 (1957), 17–40.

—— 'Cardinal Beaufort: Patriot or Usurer?', *TRHS* 5th series, 20 (1970), 129–48.

—— *King, Parliament and Public Finance in Medieval England to 1369* (Oxford, 1975).

—— 'Introduction', in K. B. McFarlane, *England in the Fifteenth Century: Collected Essays* (London, 1981), pp. ix–xxvii.

HARVEY, B. F., 'The Leasing of the Abbot of Westminster's Demesnes in the Later Middle Ages', *EcHR* 2nd series, 22 (1969), 17–27.

HARVEY, J. H., 'Side-Lights on Kenilworth Castle', *Archaeological Journal*, 101 (1944), 91–107.

HARVEY, J. H. AND OSWALD, A., *English Medieval Architects: A Biographical Dictionary Down to 1540* (London, 1954).

HASSELL SMITH, A., *County and Court* (Oxford, 1974).

HAY, D., 'The Division of the Spoils of War in Fourteenth-Century England', *TRHS* 4th series, 4 (1954), 91–109.

HICKS, M. A., 'Dynastic Change and Northern Society: The Career of the Fourth Earl of Northumberland 1470–1489', *Northern History*, 14 (1978), 78–107.

—— *False, Fleeting, Perjur'd Clarence* (Gloucester, 1980).

HILL, J. W. F., *Medieval Lincoln* (Cambridge, 1948).

HILTON, R. H., 'Lord and Peasant in Staffordshire in the Middle Ages', *North Staffordshire Journal of Field Studies*, 10 (1970), 1–20.

HODGSON, J., *A History of Northumberland* (Newcastle, 1858).

HOLMES, G. A., *The Estates of the Higher Nobility in Fourteenth-Century England* (Cambridge, 1957).

—— *The Later Middle Ages* (Edinburgh, 1962).

—— *The Good Parliament* (Oxford, 1975).

HOLT, J. C., *The Northerners* (Oxford, 1961).

HYAMS, P. R., *King, Lords and Peasants in Medieval England* (Oxford, 1980).

JACK, R. I., 'Entail and Descent: The Hastings Inheritance, 1370–1436', *BIHR* 38 (1965), 1–19.

JAMES, M., *Family, Lineage and Civil Society* (Oxford, 1974).

JOHN, E. L., 'The Parliamentary Representation of Norfolk and Suffolk, 1377–1422' (unpub. Nottingham University MA thesis, 1959).

JONES, M. C. E., *Ducal Brittany, 1364–1399* (Oxford, 1970).

JONES, R. H., *The Royal Policy of Richard II* (Oxford, 1968).

KAEUPER, R. W., 'Law and Order in Fourteenth-Century England: The Evidence of Special Commissions of Oyer and Terminer', *Speculum*, 54 (1979), 734–84.

KEEN, M. H., 'Brotherhood in Arms', *History*, 47 (1962), 1–17.

—— *The Laws of War in the Late Middle Ages* (London, 1965).

—— *Chivalry* (New Haven, 1984).

KERR, W. J. B., *Higham Ferrers* (Northampton, 1925).

KNOWLES, D. and HADDOCK, R. N., *Medieval Religious Houses: England and Wales*, 2nd edn. (London, 1971).

LANCASTER, W. T., *The Early History of Ripley and the Ingleby Family* (Leeds, 1918).

LANDER, J. R., *Crown and Nobility 1450–1509* (London, 1976).

LEGG, L. G. W., *English Coronation Records* (London, 1901).

LEHOUX, F., *Jean de France, Duc de Berri*, 4 vols. (Paris, 1966–8).

LEWIS, N. B., 'Re-election to Parliament in the Reign of Richard II', *EHR* 48 (1933), 364–94.

—— 'The Organization of Indentured Retinues in Fourteenth-Century England', *TRHS* 4th series, 27 (1945), 29–39.

—— 'The Last Medieval Summons of the English Feudal Levy, 13 June 1385', *EHR* 73 (1958), 1–26.

LEWIS, P. S., 'Decayed and Non–Feudalism in Later Medieval France', *BIHR* 37 (1964), 157–84.

LONGFORD, W. W., 'Some Notes on the Family History of Nicholas Longford, Sheriff of Lancashire in 1413', *Transactions of the Historic Society of Lancashire and Cheshire*, 76 (1934), 47–71.

MADAN, F., *The Gresleys of Drakelowe* (Oxford, 1899).

MADDICOTT, J. R., *Thomas of Lancaster* (Oxford, 1970).

—— 'Thomas of Lancaster and Sir Robert Holland', *EHR* 86 (1971), 449–72.

—— 'The County Community and the Making of Public Opinion in Fourteenth-Century England', *TRHS* 5th series, 28 (1978), 27–43.

—— *Law and Lordship: Royal Justices as Retainers in Thirteenth and Fourteenth Century England* (Past and Present Supplement, 4, 1978).

—— 'Parliament and the Constituencies, 1272–1377', *The English Parliament in the Middle Ages*, ed. R. G. Davies and J. H. Denton (Manchester, 1981), pp. 61–87.

MATHEW, G., 'Ideals of Knighthood in Late Fourteenth-Century England', *Studies in Medieval History Presented to F. M. Powicke* (Oxford, 1948), pp. 354–62.

MCFARLANE, K. B., 'Parliament and "Bastard Feudalism" ', *TRHS* 4th series, 26 (1944), 53–79.

—— 'Bastard Feudalism', *BIHR* 20 (1945), 161–80.

—— *The Nobility of Later Medieval England* (Oxford, 1973).

—— *England in the Fifteenth Century: Collected Essays* (London, 1981).

'Members of Parliament for Northumberland, 1327–1399', *Archaeologia Aeliana*, 4th series, 11 (1934), 21–82.

MILNER, J. D., 'Sir Simon Felbrigg, KG: The Lancastrian Revolution and Personal Fortune', *Norfolk Archaeology*, 37 (1978), 84–91.

MOOR, C., *Knights of Edward I* (Harleian Soc., 83, 1931), iv.

MORGAN, P. J., *War and Society in Medieval Cheshire 1272–1403* (Chetham Soc., 3rd series, 34, 1987).

NAMIER, L. B., *The Structure of Politics at the Accession of George III* (London, 1929).

NAPIER, H. A., HON., *Historical Notices of Swyncombe and Ewelme* (Oxford, 1858).

NAUGHTON, K. S., *The Gentry of Bedfordshire in the Thirteenth and Fourteenth Centuries* (Leicester, 1976).

NEILSON, G., *Trial by Combat* (Glasgow, 1890).

Northumberland County History, 12 (Newcastle, 1926).

OMAN, C. W., *The Great Revolt of 1381* (Oxford, 1906).

OWST, G. R., *Literature and Pulpit in Medieval England* (Cambridge, 1933).

PALMER, J. J. N., *England, France and Christendom 1377–1399* (London, 1972).

—— 'Froissart et le Héraut Chandos', *Le Moyen Âge*, 88 (1982), 271–92.

PAPE, T., *Medieval Newcastle-under-Lyme* (Manchester, 1928).

PAYLING, S. J., 'Inheritance and Local Politics in the Later Middle Ages: The Case of Ralph, Lord Cromwell and the Heriz Inheritance', *Nottingham Medieval Studies*, 30 (1986), 67–95.

PERROY, E., *L'Angleterre et le grand schisme d'occident. Étude sur la politique religieuse de l'Angleterre sous Richard II* (Paris, 1933).

PHILLIPS, J. R. S., *Aymer de Valence, earl of Pembroke 1307–1324* (Oxford, 1972).

PIAGET, A., *Otho de Grandson, sa vie et ses poésies* (Lausanne, 1941).

PLATTS, G., *Land and People in Medieval Lincolnshire* (Lincoln, 1985).

PLUCKNETT, T. F. T., *The Legislation of Edward I* (Oxford, 1949).

POLLARD, A. J., 'The Family of Talbot, Lords Talbot and Earls of Shrewsbury in the Fifteenth Century' (unpub. Bristol University Ph.D. thesis, 1968).

—— 'The Northern Retainers of Richard Neville, Earl of Salisbury', *Northern History*, 11 (1976), 52–69.

—— 'The Richmondshire Community of Gentry During the Wars of the Roses', *Patronage, Pedigree and Power in Later Medieval England*, ed. C. D. Ross (Gloucester, 1979), pp. 37–59.

POLLOCK, F. and MAITLAND, F. W., *The History of English Law Before the Time of Edward I*, 2 vols. (Cambridge, 1898, repr. 1968).

POST, J. B., 'King's Bench Clerks in the Reign of Richard II', *BIHR* 47 (1974), 150–63.

—— 'Courts, Councils and Arbitrators in the Ladbroke Manor Dispute, 1382–1400', *Medieval Legal Records*, ed. R. F. Hunnisett and J. B. Post (London, 1978), pp. 289–339.

—— 'Sir Thomas West and the Statute of Rapes, 1382', *BIHR* 53 (1980), 24–30.

—— 'The Obsequies of John of Gaunt', *Guildhall Studies in London History*, 5 (1981), 1–12.

POSTAN, M. M., 'The Costs of the Hundred Years War', *Past and Present*, 27 (1964), 34–53.

POWELL, E., *The Rising in East Anglia in 1381* (Cambridge, 1896).

POWELL, E., 'Public Order and Law Enforcement in Shropshire and Staffordshire in the Early Fifteenth Century' (unpub. Oxford University D.Phil. thesis, 1979).

—— 'Arbitration and Law in the Late Middle Ages', *TRHS* 5th series, 33 (1983), 49–67.

POWICKE, M. R., *Military Obligation in Medieval England* (Oxford, 1962).

POWICKE, M. R., 'Lancastrian Captains', *Essays in Medieval History Presented to Bertie Wilkinson*, ed. T. A. Sandquist and M. R. Powicke (Toronto, 1969), pp. 371–82.

PRESTWICH, J. O., 'The Military Household of the Norman Kings', *EHR* 96 (1981), 1–35.

PRESTWICH, M., *War, Politics and Finance under Edward I* (London, 1972).

PRINCE, A. E., 'The Indenture System under Edward III', *Historical Essays in Honour of James Tait*, ed. J. G. Edwards, V. H. Galbraith, and E. F. Jacob (Manchester, 1933), pp. 283–99.

PUGH, T. B., 'The Magnates, Knights and Gentry', in S. B. Chrimes, C. D. Ross, and R. A. Griffiths (eds.), *Fifteenth-Century England* (Manchester, 1972), pp. 86–128.

PUTNAM, B. H., 'The Transformation of the Keepers of the Peace into the Justices of the Peace 1327–1380', *TRHS* 4th series, 12 (1929), 19–48.

RAIMES, A. L., 'Reymes of Overstrand', *Norfolk Archaeology*, 30 (1952), 15–64.

RAINE, J., *The History and Antiquities of Hemingborough* (York, 1888).

RAMSAY, N., 'Retained Legal Counsel, *c*.1275–*c*.1475', *TRHS* 5th series, 34 (1985), 95–112.

RAWCLIFFE, C., *The Staffords, Earls of Stafford and Dukes of Buckingham, 1394–1521* (Cambridge, 1978).

—— 'The Great Lord as Peacekeeper', *Law and Social Change in British History*, ed. J. A. Guy and H. G. Beale (London, 1984), pp. 34–53.

RAYNER, D., 'The Forms and Machinery of the Commune Petition in the Fourteenth Century', *EHR* 56 (1941), 198–233, 549–70.

Return of Members of Parliament, Part I: Parliaments of England, 1213–1702 (London, 1878).

REVILLE, A., *Le Soulèvement des travailleurs d'Angleterre en 1381* (Paris, 1898).

RICHARDSON, H. G., 'John of Gaunt and the Parliamentary Representation of Lancashire', *BJRL* 22 (1938), 175–222.

RICHARDSON, H. G. and SAYLES, G. O., *The Administration of Ireland, 1172–1377* (Dublin, 1963).

RICHMOND, C., *John Hopton. A Fifteenth Century Suffolk Gentleman* (Cambridge, 1981).

ROSENTHAL, J. T., *The Purchase of Paradise. Gift Giving and the Aristocracy, 1370–1485* (London, 1972).

ROSKELL, J. S., *The Knights of the Shire of the County Palatine of Lancaster, 1377–1460* (Chetham Soc., NS 96, 1937).

—— 'Sir Richard Waldegrave of Bures St Mary', *Proceedings of the Suffolk Institute of Archaeology*, 27 (1957), 154–75.

—— 'The Parliamentary Representation of Lincolnshire During the Reigns of Richard II, Henry IV and Henry V', *Nottingham Medieval Studies*, 3 (1959), 53–77.

—— *Parliament and Politics in Late Medieval England*, 3 vols. (London, 1981–3).

Ross, C. D., 'The Yorkshire Baronage, 1399–1435' (unpub. Oxford University D.Phil. thesis, 1951).

—— *The Estates and Finances of Richard Beauchamp, Earl of Warwick* (Dugdale Soc., Occasional Papers, 12, 1956).

—— *Edward IV* (London, 1974).

Rowling, M. A., 'William de Parr: King's Knight to Henry IV', *Transactions of the Cumberland and Westmorland Antiquarian and Arch. Soc.*, NS 56 (1957), 87–103.

Rowney, I., 'Government and Patronage in the Fifteenth Century: Staffordshire 1439–1459', *Midland History*, 8 (1983), 49–69.

—— 'The Hastings Affinity in Staffordshire and the Honour of Tutbury', *BIHR* 57 (1984), 35–45.

—— 'Resources and Retaining in Yorkist England: William, Lord Hastings and the Honour of Tutbury', *Property and Politics: Essays in Later Medieval English History*, ed. A. J. Pollard (Gloucester, 1984), pp. 139–55.

Russell, P. E., 'Joao Fernandes Andeiro at the Court of John of Lancaster', *Revista da universidade de Coimbra*, 14 (1938).

—— *The English Intervention in Spain and Portugal in the Time of Edward III and Richard II* (Oxford, 1955).

Rye, W., *Norfolk Families* (Norwich, 1913).

Rylands, J. P., 'Two Lancashire Rolls of Arms', *Transactions of the Historic Society of Lancashire and Cheshire*, 37 (1888), 149–60.

Salzman, L. F., *Building in England, Down to 1540* (Oxford, 1967).

Saul, A. R., 'Local Politics and the Good Parliament', *Property and Politics: Essays in Later Medieval English History*, ed. A. J. Pollard (Gloucester, 1984), pp. 156–71.

Saul, N., 'The Religious Sympathies of the Gentry in Gloucestershire, 1200–1500', *Transactions of the Bristol and Gloucestershire Arch. Soc.*, 98 (1980), 98–112.

—— *Knights and Esquires: The Gloucestershire Gentry in the Fourteenth Century* (Oxford, 1981).

—— 'The Despensers and the Downfall of Edward II', *EHR* 99 (1984), 1–33.

—— *Scenes from Provincial Life: Knightly Families in Sussex 1280–1400* (Oxford, 1986).

Sharp, M., 'A Fragmentary Household Account of John of Gaunt', *BIHR* 13 (1935/6), 154–60.

Sherborne, J. W., 'Indentured Retinues and English Expeditions to France, 1369–1380', *EHR* 79 (1964), 718–46.

Shirley, E. P., *Stemmata Shirleiana* (London, 1873).

Smith, A., 'Litigation and Politics: Sir John Fastolf's Defence of his English Property', *Property and Politics in Later Medieval English History*, ed. A. J. Pollard (Gloucester, 1984), pp. 59–75.

Somerville, R., *History of the Duchy of Lancaster*, i (London, 1953).

Starkey, D., 'The Age of the Household', *The Later Middle Ages*, ed. S. Medcalf (London, 1981), pp. 225–90.

STATHAM, S. P. H., 'Later Descendants of Domesday Holders of Land in Derbyshire', *Journal of the Derbyshire Archaeological and Natural History Society*, 49 (1927), 51–106, 233–328.

STEEL, A. B., *Richard II* (Cambridge, 1941).

—— *The Receipt of the Exchequer 1377–1485* (Cambridge, 1954).

STONES, E. L. G., 'The Folvilles of Ashby Folville, Leicestershire and their Associates in Crime, 1326–41', *TRHS* 5th series, 7 (1957), 117–36.

STOREY, R. L., *Thomas Langley and the Bishopric of Durham, 1406–1437* (London, 1961).

—— 'Liveries and Commissions of the Peace, 1388–90', *The Reign of Richard II*, ed. F. R. H. du Boulay and C. M. Barron (London, 1971), pp. 131–52.

—— 'The North of England', *Fifteenth-Century England*, ed. S. B. Chrimes, C. D. Ross, and R. A. Griffiths (Manchester, 1972), pp. 129–44.

SUTHERLAND, D. W., *Quo Warranto Proceedings under Edward I* (Oxford, 1963).

SWINTON, G. S. C., 'John of Swinton', *Scottish Historical Review*, 16 (1918–19), 261–79.

SYME, R., *The Roman Revolution* (Oxford, 1939).

TEMPLE-LEADER, J. and MARCOTTI, G., *Sir John Hawkwood* (London, 1889).

THOMPSON, A. H., *The History of the Hospital and the New College of the Annunciation of St Mary in the Newarke, Leicester* (Leicester, 1937).

THOROTON, R., *The Antiquities of Nottinghamshire* (London, 1677).

TOUT, T. F., 'The Earldoms under Edward I', *TRHS* NS 8 (1894), 129–55.

—— *Chapters in the Administrative History of Medieval England*, 6 vols. (Manchester, 1920–33).

TUCK, J. A., 'Richard II and the Border Magnates', *Northern History*, 3 (1968), 27–52.

—— 'Richard II's System of Patronage', *The Reign of Richard II*, ed. F. R. H. du Boulay and C. M. Barron (London, 1971), pp. 1–21.

—— *Richard II and the English Nobility* (London, 1973).

TUCOO-CHALA, P., *Gaston Fébus et la vicomté de Béarn* (Bordeaux, 1959).

VALE, M. G. A., *Piety, Charity and Literacy Among the Yorkshire Gentry, 1370–1485* (Borthwick Papers, 50, 1976).

VALOIS, N., *La France et le grand schisme d'occident*, iii (Paris, 1901).

VAUGHAN, R., *Philip the Bold. The Formation of the Burgundian State* (London, 1979).

Victoria History of the Counties of England: Cambridgeshire, iv (London, 1953); *Gloucestershire*, viii (London, 1968); *Lancashire*, iii–viii (London, 1907–14); *Oxfordshire*, v (London, 1957); *Shropshire*, ii (London, 1973); *Staffordshire*, i (London, 1908); *Suffolk*, ii (London, 1907); *Warwickshire*, vi (London, 1951); *Yorkshire*, iii (London, 1925); *Yorkshire, North Riding*, i–ii (London, 1914–23).

VIRGOE, R., 'The Crown and Local Government: East Anglia under Richard

II', *The Reign of Richard II*, ed. F. R. H. du Boulay and C. M. Barron (London, 1971), pp. 218–41.

—— 'The Murder of Edmund Clippesby', *Norfolk Archaeology*, 35 (2) (1972), 302–7.

—— 'The Crown, Magnates and Local Government in Fifteenth-Century East Anglia', *The Crown and Local Communities*, ed. J. R. L. Highfield and R. Jeffs (Gloucester, 1981), pp. 72–87.

WALKER, S., 'Lancaster v. Dallingridge: A Franchisal Dispute in Fourteenth-Century Sussex', *Sussex Archaeological Collections*, 121 (1983), 87–94.

—— 'Profit and Loss in the Hundred Years War: The Subcontract of Sir John Strother, 1374', *BIHR* 58 (1985), 100–6.

—— 'John of Gaunt and his "Affinity": A Prosopographical Approach to Bastard Feudalism', *Prosopographie et genèse de l'État moderne*, ed. F. Autrand (Paris, 1986), pp. 209–22.

—— 'John of Gaunt and his Retainers, 1361–1399' (unpub. Oxford University D.Phil. thesis, 1986).

WEDGWOOD, J. C., 'John of Gaunt and the Packing of Parliament', *EHR* 45 (1930), 623–5.

WOLFFE, B., *Henry VI* (London, 1981).

WRIGHT, S. M., *The Derbyshire Gentry in the Fifteenth Century* (Derbyshire Record Soc., 8, 1983).

WROTTESLEY, G., 'An Account of the Family of Okeover of Okeover', *Collections for a History of Staffordshire*, NS 7 (1904), 4–187.

—— 'A History of the Bagot Family', *Collections for a History of Staffordshire*, NS 11 (1908), 1–224.

INDEX